To Garlette —
All good things on
your birth day.

From your friend
Gail 2005

Beethoven:
Man of His Word

This book is dedicated to those people
who believe that Truth
should prevail over that
which is simply accepted—
and that Honor
deserves never to be tarnished
without irrefutable proof.

❊

"Truth is within the reach of the wise man."
—Beethoven, quoting Schiller's *Don Carlos,*
Act IV, Scene 21
written in Lorenz von Breuning's album,
October 1, 1797.

Beethoven:
Man of His Word

❈

Undisclosed Evidence for His Immortal Beloved

Gail S. Altman

Anubian
Press

Tallahassee, Florida

ACKNOWLEDGEMENTS

Excerpts from *Beethoven Remembered* by Franz Wegeler and Ferdinand Ries, Fredereick Noonan, translator, reprinted by permission of Great Ocean Publishers © 1987.
Excerpts by Alexander Wheelock Thayer taken from *Thayer's Life of Beethoven*, Elliot Forbes, editor, Princeton University Press © 1967.
Excerpts from Beethoven's letters taken from *The Letters of Beethoven*, Emily Anderson, editor and translator, St. Martin's Press/MacMillian & Co. © 1961.

The author also would like to extend sincerest thanks to the following people for their assistance in this endeavor: to my extraordinary editor, Melanie Warren, for her valuable advice and suggestions; to my husband, archivist Burt Altman, for his support and expertise in conducting electronic research over the InterNet and securing valuable documents; and to Florida State University's Music Library, for the use of their extensive holdings.

Publisher's Cataloging in Publication Data
(Prepared by Quality Books Inc.)
Altman, Gail S.
    Beethoven—a man of his word: undisclosed evidence for his Immortal Beloved/ Gail S. Altman. — 1st ed.
    p. cm.
    Includes bibliographical references and index.
    LCCN: 95-079183
    ISBN: 1-888071-01-X (hardbound)
    ISBN: 1-888071-00-1 (softbound)

1. Beethoven, Ludwig van, 1770-1827—Relations with women. 2. Composers—Austria—Biography.   I. Title

ML410.B4A58   1996   780'.92
                                      QBI95-20791

❖ Table of Contents ❖

List of Illustrations:

❖ Preface ❖

A Presumption of Innocence

On March 27, 1827, one day after 56-year-old Ludwig van Beethoven's death, his sole surviving brother, Johann, and his friends, Stephan Breuning, Karl Holz, and Anton Schindler, began searching through the composer's personal effects looking for bank shares that the composer had willed to his nephew, Karl. After a long search, Holz found them at last, in a secret drawer in a cabinet. With them were two miniature portraits, the *Heiligenstadt Testament*—a will written in 1802—and a three-part letter: the letter to the famous unidentified woman known to the world only as the Immortal Beloved.

In the many years that have passed from that day, Beethoven's numerous biographers have championed a variety of women as being the composer's mysterious Beloved. Guilietta Guicciardi was proposed by Schindler. Therese Malfatti, Therese Brunswick, Amalie Sebald and others have been brought forth in turn. Many biographers have supported Josephine Brunswick, to whom the composer wrote several love letters in 1805, and whom, at the time, he unquestionably loved.

In the wake of Bernard Rose's 1994 film, *Immortal Beloved*, reviewers and other journalists have scurried to their encyclopedias in search of information about Beethoven and his mysterious love. Their research led them to the discovery that the film was, historically speaking, greatly flawed. What they did not know was that very often the sources they had used to weigh the accuracy of the film were in themselves not as factual as one would hope. The sorrowful fact is that in trying to point out the inaccuracies in the film, more fuel has been added to the mythical fire of Beethoven's life.

One of the things the movie-reviewing journalists found and reported was that American musicologist Maynard Solomon had successfully ended the quest for Beethoven's secret Beloved. In 1977, Dr. Solomon proclaimed the mystery of the Immortal Beloved solved at last, putting forth a married woman named Antonie Brentano as the most likely candidate, and supposedly providing irrefutable evidence on her behalf. Solomon claimed that

> The weight of the evidence in her favor is so powerful
> that it is not presumptuous to assert that the riddle of
> Beethoven's Immortal Beloved has now been solved.[1]

Was he right? Was his evidence really so weighty? Many scholars thought so. His *Beethoven* was a prize-winning book. Antonie Brentano's name was listed in encyclopedias as the Immortal Beloved. Respected universities adopted Dr. Solomon's text for their music courses. Many scholars and laymen alike nodded their heads in affirmation: Yes, Frau Brentano was indeed the composer's mystery love.

No, she was not.

But was it not proven beyond a reasonable doubt?

No, it was not.

Then was Solomon presumptuous in his assertion?

Most definitely, yes.

Presumption in itself is not necessarily a bad thing, but it must be accompanied by accurate evidence, and, as we have discovered, this theory does not alwsays follow that criterion.

This widely accepted theory implies that Beethoven had coveted another man's wife, for Antonie Brentano was married to Beethoven's friend, Franz Brentano, a successful Frankfurt merchant. Yet such behavior would have been contrary to what friends closest to the composer knew about him: that despite his

---

[1]Solomon, p. 170.

faults and flaws, his standards for honesty and morality were of the highest degree and beyond reproach. They were not affectation which he donned at whim like a suit of clothes. He strived always to maintain the high standards he set for himself. Under those circumstances, it is inconceivable that a man like Beethoven could or would covet another man's wife. As in a court of law, however, simple belief in a defendant is not enough for acquital. "He could not have done it," is hardly an acceptable argument. It does little good to *presume* innocence without *proving* it. This book began as an attempt to find that proof. It ends with what I believe is enough evidence to find Beethoven not guilty.

How did such a theory come about in the first place? That question, fueled by a belief in the man's innocence, prompted an investigation into the alleged evidence against him. What was found was shocking—not in terms of Beethoven himself, but in the distortions and misconceptions which have wormed their way into the realm of fact.

It was astonishing to learn how unquestioningly people accept the well-written word, and embrace books whose authors have impressive credentials, works that appear thoroughly researched, and information that seems factual because of the lucid and convincing way in which it is presented. It also was surprising to find that once several eminent scholars proclaim an issue closed, their pronouncement often is accepted, at times ending further discussion and research. For example, in 1977, the eminent Beethoven scholar, Robert Winter, asserted that "the sole possible verdict, beyond any reasonable doubt, is that Beethoven was completely innocent of having done any more than thought about the Tenth Symphony." For many, that settled the issue of the elusive work. Fortunately, Dr. Barry Cooper did not allow the lack of reasonable doubt to prevent his search. By 1988, he had found enough sketches for the Tenth Symphony to have the first movement performed. Had he not continued the quest despite scholarly pronouncements to the contrary, we would not now have this music to enjoy. So it is also with the quest for Beethoven's Immortal Beloved. I feel the case is far from closed.

A LOVE OF TRUTH

In the last weeks of his life, Beethoven related to Breuning and Schindler his feelings about biographies that might come to be written about him after his death, acknowledging that there would be numerous stories circulated which would be devoid of truth. He therefore said to his two friends that

> It was his sincere wish that whatever might be said about him in the future should in every respect adhere strictly to the truth, even though it might bear hard upon this or that person, or even upon himself.[2]

On July 6, 1827, a few months after Beethoven's death, his friend and personal secretary, Anton Schindler, wrote a letter to Beethoven's boyhood friend, Franz Wegeler. In it, Schindler wrote:

> Beethoven in the last weeks of his illness, often spoke to Breuning and myself of the vexatious talk there would be about his moral character if he died of this malady ...It grieved him exceedingly, all the more because these calumnies were spread abroad by men whom he had received at his table. He implored us to preserve for him after his death the love and friendship we had shown him during his life, and to see that at any rate his moral life was not besmirched.[3]

Beethoven had been afraid that his fatal illness, cirrhosis of the liver, usually but not accurately associated with alcoholism, would cause others to spread the story that he was addicted to heavy drink, which was not true. The idea that his memory would be so tarnished "grieved him exceedingly." It surely never occurred to him that his morality would be brought into far more serious question by his biographers than merely excessive use of alcohol.

Beethoven claimed that it was "one of my first principles never to stand in other than friendly relationship with the wife of another man." Truth and virtue were the two qualities he valued most highly, both in himself and in others. Friends claimed he was "a man of his word." How grieved would Beethoven be now to learn that his ideals of morality have been called into question,

---

[2]Schindler, p. 31.
[3]Scherman & Biancolli, p. 383.

that he has been accused of living under pretense and self-deception, that both his honesty and his honor have been found lacking?

In February 1815, Beethoven lamented to his attorney, Johann Kanka: "Whenever the truth can injure me they accept it; then why not accept it too where it might benefit me?" Beethoven's plaintive question must be answered. The current theory of the Immortal Beloved and the psychoanalysis which accompanies it have distorted the truth, and placed an undeserved blot upon Beethoven's character. It is time to take up the gauntlet that death forced Schindler and Breuning to lay down, and fulfill the wish of a dying Beethoven that his moral life no longer be unfairly besmirched.

A DISTORTION OF FACT

Solomon's assertion that Frau Brentano was the Immortal Beloved was based primarily on a few key items:

• that she was closely associated with Beethoven during the period preceding the writing of the letter (1811-1812);

• that she was in Prague between July 1-4 of 1812, the same time as Beethoven;

• that she was in Karlsbad, Czechoslovakia—the place long assumed to have been where the Beloved letter was destined—the first week of July; and

• that she had reencountered Beethoven shortly after the letter had been written, fulfilling the promise the composer had made to his Beloved in the letter that he would see her soon.

Other evidence was then produced to further prove that Antonie Brentano must have been the famous mystery woman. A closer look at this proof than most scholars evidently have been willing to give it, shows that much of it is erroneous, misleading, distorted, or unsubstantiated. On that basis, there is still very much a reasonable doubt as to the Beloved's identity. Moreover, the entire romantic aspect of Beethoven's life, outside the context of the Immortal Beloved, has been presented in such a way that a false impression of the great composer has been created. Over and over, in one biography after another, it has been stressed that Beethoven was constantly in love, and that his many affairs involved both single and married women. This impression has been formulated through the use of quotes taken out of context or truncated, from the use of questionable authorities, and from the faulty opinions of earlier writers being taken for fact and passed along by subsequent biographers.

What we have been told is that Beethoven constantly made poor choices in the women with whom he involved himself, that his fear of responsibility led him to subconsciously sabotage his desires for marriage and family, and that numerous love affairs followed by as many rejections even caused him to doubt his manhood.

This is pure nonsense.

When the quotes are put back into context and presented in their entirety and within their historical frameworks, when the reliability of the "authorities" is closely examined, when the theories and their proponents are carefully questioned, and when documents disproving these assertions are at last disclosed, the truth becomes clear: Beethoven was neither a womanizer nor a woman-hater. He was not filled with doubts about his masculinity. He was not afraid of responsibility. He was most definitely not the emotional cripple he has been made out to be. And, above all, Antonie Bretano, the wife of the composer's friend, was not Beethoven's Immortal Beloved.

OF PRIMARY CONCERN

Certainly the main thrust of this book is to give the reader a more accurate understanding of Beethoven's infamous love life, give him back his claim to morality, and restore him as a "man of his word." In addition, it will

- ask pertinent questions about the current theory of the Immortal Beloved which at present do not have satisfactory answers;

- present evidence which not only conflicts with this theory, but presents a case for another lady; and

• point out the flaws in Solomon's psychoanalysis of Beethoven, and prove that the composer had not lived with pretense, self-deception, and self-doubts as a man.

These tasks will be accomplished in several ways:

• by examining the sources biographers have used in drawing their conclusions, the reliability of the purported authorities, and the time, place, and context in which their opinions were rendered.

• by placing quotes back into context, and giving in their entirety those that have been foreshortened so that a truer understanding of their meaning can be achieved; and,

• by drawing upon the notes, letters, and opinions of contemporaries, and, most importantly, the primary sources left to us by Beethoven himself, taking a fresh look at this important information rather than relying heavily upon the interpretations and opinions of previous biographers. To do otherwise would serve only to perpetuate the myths I am attempting to dispel.

A SECONDARY MOTIVE

In conducting research for this book, I have discovered that it is not enough simply to be concerned with Beethoven and his eternal love, despite the desire to "set the record straight" on behalf of this great, but much-maligned composer. We must recall that he was a man to whom honesty was one of the most important virtues to which a person might aspire. I feel he would approve of a secondary motive in writing this book, one which explores the nature of historical research and reporting, which discloses how easy it is to manipulate the facts in order to support a theory, and how simple it is to mislead the unsuspecting reader.

Having found so many quotes in previous biographies to be altered, truncated or taken out of context, I expressed my surprise to several Napoleonic scholars at Florida State University. Their replies shocked and dismayed me all the more: "We find that sort of thing all the time." When the reader has come to the end of this book, I do not believe he or she will take the convincing argument for granted, nor look at scholarly works in quite the same way, ever again.

Thus I have provided extensive footnoting in this book. There is a purpose for that. I do not want my readers to take what I say for granted. Most of the primary sources, such as Beethoven's letters, are available in public or university libraries.

Find them.

Read them.

I invite scrutiny, because that is the only way one may reach the truth. I further urge the reader to adhere to the following precepts:

- Accept nothing.
- Question everything.
- Apply a healthy dose of common sense to anything.
- And, above all, always use the content of a man's heart as a measure of the truth.

ADDITIONAL NOTE TO THE READER

I am compelled to interject into this Preface a personal note to my readers. I realize that there may be some —perhaps even many—who will find the writing and publishing of this book to be highly presumptuous on my part. I am, after all, challenging what has been accepted for many years by scholars whose credentials probably are far superior to mine. Believe me or not, I have agonized over whether I had the "right" to question what has been established. Yet after careful study and consideration, what I found in the primary sources simply did not support many accepted theories. Was I to ignore or suppress evidence that I believe supports other ideas? Withholding one's new discoveries instead of placing them in the public view where they may be examined and discussed surely must be worse than being presumptuous. Without ordinary men and women "presuming," how far would mankind have come? Not very far, I think.

Another thing I realized as I wrote this book was that my motives for writing it would be questioned. No doubt some may suspect that the lure of fame, if not fortune, was my primary motivation. As I will do many times in this book, I will ask you to look at the common sense behind that assumption. One must note that in many cases I am questioning what has been accepted as fact by eminent scholars all over the world for many years. It is hardly likely that such a move will lead to accolades. I am leaving myself open to criticism, attack, abuse, and ridicule by professional academicians who often will not accept ideas proposed by those outside their exclusive community. Despite that, I am willing to endure whatever comes, because I believe strongly in what I have written. I shall and must remain unwavering in my convictions. Yet, I assure you I have no masochistic tendencies. As Dr. Ben Weider noted in his 1995 book on Napoleon, *Assassination at St. Helena Revisited*, "Of what purpose is research that lacks the courage to interpret its findings?" Again, whether I am believed or not, my motive in writing this book was to arrive at a better understanding of the truth, perhaps to share a new insight, and to exonerate a man I believe to have been judged unfairly. Too altruistic to be believed? I hope not, but I know that the world has become a cynical place. I even have found that some Beethoven scholars will use the argument that Beethoven himself was fabricating the truth if what he wrote in his letters conflicts with their theories, a convenient but unfair excuse. The fact is, I have come to believe that my discoveries will be important in helping define the truth—at least as far as we are able to know it. I also believe that a man's honor deserves to be defended, no matter how long he has been parted from us, if he did nothing in life for which he should be shamed. If I did not believe these things, I would not have given up a great deal of time—nights, weekends, holidays, and hours after work—in researching and preparing this manuscript. I hope that, by writing this book, I have in some way validated the right of everyone—regardless of how insignificant one might feel in comparison to academic giants—to question and to voice a new opinion, particularly when the reputation of another depends upon that action being taken.

Gail S. Altman
December 16, 1995

❧ Part I ❧

The Myth of Beethoven's Love Affairs

INTRODUCTION

The misconceptions surrounding Beethoven's love life echo through his biographies like a shout in the hills, that not only perpetuates itself, but also distorts the truth, until reality fades into the background, obscured by the noise of misunderstanding and innuendo. Among the myths that have been maintained by biographers are the following premises:

- **Myth: The state of "being in love" was a perpetual one for Beethoven.** Biographers have used dubious authorities and their opinions, innuendoes, and a general misinterpretation of Beethoven's letters to prove this assertion, which is not true. There is also a misconception of what "being in love" is, as opposed to innocent and meaningless flirtations which have been taken far more seriously by his biographers than they ever were by Beethoven himself.

- **Myth: Beethoven consistently made poor choices in his relations with women resulting in numerous rejections.** Actually, he suffered rejection only twice in his life, and one of those times was by a woman who truly loved him—albeit, perhaps not sensuously but whose family circumstances prevented her from accepting him as her husband.

• **Myth: Beethoven had numerous, all-consuming, but transient affairs.** Rather than having had many fleeting attractions, Beethoven actually had only three genuine loves in his entire life, which were anything but transient. There were no brief "all-consuming affairs," and the "list" of women Beethoven had loved was generated only by the imaginations of his biographers.

• **Myth: The composer feared the responsibility that marriage demanded**, and therefore subconsciously sabotaged his efforts to form a permanent relationship. In fact, the composer readily took on responsibilities for his family—his brothers and nephew. Notes, letters, and statements written at various times during his life show that he very much wanted to be married, and that this desire remained constant throughout the years.

• **Myth: Constant rejection caused Beethoven to doubt his manhood.** This is untrue, and only the use of quotes taken out of context or severely truncated support this erroneous statement. When seen in their entirety and within their correct context, it becomes clear that Beethoven had had no such doubts about his masculinity, nor had he had any *reason* to have them.

Admittedly, one must approach the recollections of Beethoven's personal secretary in later years, Anton Schindler, with caution, for his account of Beethoven's life is filled with many inaccuracies, both deliberate and accidental. Further, his first-hand knowledge stems from no earlier than 1814. Occasionally, however, he makes a statement which is not dependent upon hard fact, but which offers an opinion worthy of being repeated, simply because he had known the composer for twelve years. In other cases, he makes an observation about the time period itself—about which he certainly had knowledge—which, if relevant to the discussion, will also be included. Schindler's observations about Beethoven's love life, for example, are so compatible with this author's research that there is no reluctance to share it:

I felt that the composer's love life was worthy of no greater emphasis than other equally interesting chapters of his life. The literary world disagreed. What I had written was too short and prosaic for them, and so they distorted the facts, turning the sober musician into a romantic hero crazed with love. For to them any composer whose work is often so wildly passionate must be himself a prodigious and passionate lover, certainly no ordinary man with normal emotions! They depict his personal idiosyncrasies as signs of madness, arising from unnatural excesses; they clothe him with totally false attributes; they put into his mouth words and critical judgments that are at complete variance with his true feelings and ideas. His passions and affairs have been elaborated upon and shamelessly exploited by both French and German writers.[1]

And by numerous other nationalities as well! In the following chapters, one will find that Schindler's assessment was far more astute than perhaps even he imagined.

---

[1]Schindler, p 56.

❖ 1 ❖
Beethoven: "Always in Love"

Maynard Solomon's opening paragraph of his chapter on Beethoven's Immortal Beloved reads: "Ries was the first to observe that although Beethoven was 'very often in love' his 'attachments were mostly of very brief duration.'" Solomon then noted that: "Thayer also noticed this pattern." One item of information missing here is Thayer's opinion of Ries as a competent authority on the subject of Beethoven. Thayer wrote:

> Howsoever strong were Beethoven's gratitude to Franz Ries and affection for Ferdinand, fourteen years was too great a disparity in age to allow that trustful and familiar intercourse between master and pupil which could enable the latter to speak with full knowledge; nor does a man of Beethoven's age and position turn from old and valued friends... to make a youth ... a new-comer and previously a stranger, even though a favorite pupil, his confidential adviser.[1]

What is interesting is that Thayer made this statement to refute the idea that Ries was a competent authority when it came to offering an opinion about the relationship that existed between Beethoven and his two brothers, Caspar Carl and Johann. Although Thayer did not think Ries possibly could have spoken with "full knowledge" about this issue, he readily accepted Ries's opinion about Beethoven's love life, although why Ries could be a "confidential adviser" in this matter and not in the dealings with the two brothers certainly is not clear.

---

[1]Thayer/Forbes, p. 315.

Thayer then went on to form his own opinion, quoted by Solomon, namely, that Beethoven repeatedly had

> One all-absorbing but temporary passion, lasting until its object is married to a more favorable lover... forgotten in another destined to end in like manner, until, at length, all faith in the possibility of a permanent, constant attachment to one person is lost.[2]

Thayer formed this opinion based on the testimony of Wegeler, Breuning, Romberg, and the very same Ries whose credibility he later questioned in regard to the issue of Beethoven's brothers. Since these four men were all contemporaries of Beethoven, it would be prudent to check exactly when these testimonies were given to see how valid they truly are.

Looking at the time frame when these opinions were formed, one finds that these gentlemen's conclusions that "Beethoven was never out of love" came from the 1790s, when Beethoven was in his twenties. Following is a brief look at these men and their conceptions of Beethoven's love life.

Franz Wegeler was a boyhood friend of Beethoven's, and naturally, it was to him that many biographers turned when seeking information on Beethoven's amorous adventures. They were not disappointed, for Wegeler unwittingly gave them fodder for their romantic mill when he wrote:

> In Vienna, at all events so long as I lived there, Beethoven was always in love and occasionally made a conquest which would have been very difficult if not impossible for many an Adonis.[3]

What biographers focused on was the statement that "Beethoven was always in love," and ignored the most important part, which was, "so long as I lived there." Wegeler lived in Vienna from October 1794 to 1796, a period of 18 months. It should be remembered that at this time, Beethoven was a very young man, and it would have been far more unusual had he *not* been frequently in love. As another Beethoven biographer, Dana Steichen, wisely reminded us, "to be young is to be in love with love, constantly searching for *the* one above all others."[4] Are not most

[2]Thayer/Forbes, p. 293.
[3]Wegeler & Ries, p. 43.
[4]Steichen, p. 40.

25-year-old men frequently in and out of love? It is hardly fair to judge a mature man's true romantic attachments by the meaningless flirtations in which he had indulged in his twenties! We cannot know what Wegeler meant by "conquests," but if a young man flirts with a woman and she responds to his charm by flirting back, is that any reason to claim that the man was "always in love?" Can such frivolous behavior even be deemed *love*?

The next authority on Beethoven's love life is Stephan Breuning, also a boyhood friend. From him biographers got the statement, "Beethoven always attracted women. He fascinated women, and more than one offered herself to him." Note that Breuning did not say Beethoven always *pursued* women, only that women were naturally drawn to him. Breuning found this odd since he, like most men, did not think Beethoven particularly handsome, ugly even. Beethoven's biographers—notably, almost all male—also echo this sentiment. Although his portraits may have concealed some of his physical flaws, the life mask and resulting bust by Klein is as objective a picture of Beethoven as any photograph would have been. In this author's feminine opinion, Klein's mask-based sculpture is not that of an ugly man.

"HE WAS UGLY, AND HALF MAD!"

Was Beethoven really so ugly? Can it be said that he was uglier than a sharp-featured Mozart, or an overweight Bach, or a bushy-bearded Brahms? Of course not, but while those men conformed to the styles and fashions of their day, Beethoven often did not. Biographers write, "Beethoven was short." Beethoven was approximately five feet, five inches tall, certainly short for a twentieth century man, but average for his time when a man was between six and seven inches over five feet, and a woman less. One hundred and forty years after his death, the average height for 18-year-old males had risen only to five feet, eight and a half inches. Both Wegeler and Breuning, Beethoven's contemporaries who certainly should know, described the composer as being "of average height." This assessment was echoed by other contemporaries who probably were not much taller.

Biographers write, "Beethoven was very dark." Health permitting, Beethoven spent every day out walking, sometimes for hours. Often he was hatless, or wore his hat on the back of his head so that it rubbed against the collar of his coat. Regularly

exposed to the sun, he became tanned, ruddy, unlike his contemporaries. The societies of the eighteenth and early nineteenth
centuries prized porcelain skin; men and women were powdered
and pale. No wonder they found Beethoven with his more natural
complexion an oddity. The nonsense of his being "African" came
about only because he contrasted so strikingly with his far fairer
peers, causing some to describe him as "dark" or "black." It certainly would have been a surprise to his Dutch ancestors if he had
had African roots!

Biographers write, "Beethoven was pock-marked." There
is no evidence that Beethoven ever had smallpox, but the telltale
marks of this and other disfiguring diseases were common among
Beethoven's peers, men and women, and would not have been
cause to label a person ugly. Even Rousseau's beloved Elizabeth
d'Houdetot was so marked, and it did not stop him from being
transformed by a mere glance at her face. Gerhard von Breuning,
Stephan's son, wrote that the description of Beethoven's "un-
sightly red pockmarked round face" called for correction in that
it was only spotted here and there with brown smallpox depres-
sions, and that his face when he smiled had "the charm of
childlike innocence."

These physical characteristics, in later years coupled with
Beethoven's uncoiffed, uncut—sometimes uncombed—hair, his
misshapen coat with pockets bulging with papers, and the men-
acing look he had when he did not bother to shave his heavy beard,
contributed to the myth of his ugliness. In his younger days, when
he was more inclined to follow the fashion, his "ugliness" was less
apparent. Most women had an entirely different opinion of the
composer's looks than the men, writing adoringly of "that angel,
Beethoven." This led Müller to observe that

> ...hardly has he begun to speak or smile when all of [the
> ladies], the frivolous and the serious, the romantic and
> the quizzical, are at his feet. They notice then that he
> has a fine mouth, dazzling teeth, and beautiful speaking
> eyes that mirror the changing expression of the mo-
> ment. They are delighted to find ridiculous things in
> him; these indeed are their defense, for without them he
> would be dangerous; in this little duel of hearts they
> assure their advantage over him.[5]

---

[5]Sherman & Biancolli, p. 396.

One is compelled to add that Beethoven's strict adherence to regular bathing also must have appealed to the ladies whose male companions may have had less stringent ideals of cleanliness. Thayer added that "...far from being the melancholy and gloomy character of popular belief, he shows himself here [in his letters]—as he was by nature—of a gay and lively temperament, fond of a jest, an inveterate though not always happy punster, a great lover of wit and humor." There was only one woman, Magdalena Willmann, who had the opinion that Beethoven was ugly. No doubt his dynamic, fun-loving and witty personality coupled with his striking dark hair and eyes led every other woman who met him to consider him otherwise. Even when he was 45, a love-struck young woman 20 years his junior wrote, "I never thought him ugly, and now I even like his looks." No, Beethoven was not handsome, but he was charming enough to give him physical appeal. And being attractive to the ladies made him fodder for gossip-mongers on whose opinions so many biographical sketches rely.

MORE AUTHORITIES TESTIFY

The next authority on the list, Bernhard Romberg, met Beethoven in 1788 when the latter was only 17. They were both part of the Court Orchestra organized by the Elector of Bonn, Maximillian Franz. Romberg played the violoncello and Beethoven the viola. Nikolaus Simrock and Franz Ries, Ferdinand's father, were also part of this group. Simrock—later a music publisher who would publish some of Beethoven's work—played the horn, and Ries the violin. We have no direct quotes from Romberg. What we do have is mention of his opinion by Wegeler, apparently in concert with Wegeler and Breuning, that Beethoven was "never out of love." Romberg also passed on some anecdotes about Beethoven's "passion" for two young ladies, Jeanette d'Honrath and Maria Anna Westerholt, to Anton Schindler some four decades after the fact. Wegeler reminds us in a comment often ignored that "These affairs... were passions of his adolescence and left no more profound impression than they had aroused in the pretty young ladies."[6] Romberg did not associate with Beethoven after the latter left Bonn for Vienna in 1792—at age 21. They did not see one another again until some thirty years later

---

[6]Wegeler & Ries, p. 43.

when Romberg gave a concert in Vienna. As Wegeler said, since Romberg could only relate information about the love life of a very young Beethoven, we may be assured that the applicability to the mature Beethoven of anything he might have said is highly questionable.

As noted earlier, Ferdinand Ries was not a peer, but the son of Franz Ries, a boyhood friend and fellow musician of Beethoven's. When Ries the younger met the 30-year-old Beethoven he was all of 16 and Beethoven's pupil. Further, Ries was only in Vienna until 1805 and left when he was just barely out of his teens. Friends of Beethoven's who knew him twenty or thirty years were not privy to information about Beethoven's love life; they claimed he was always extremely reticent about deeply felt emotions. Why should Ries have had the confidante status they did not?

> Beethoven to Josephine Brunswick, Spring 1805:
>
> Quite by chance L[ichnowsky] had seen the song "An die Hoffnung" (To the Hope) lying about my place, although I had not noticed this. But he gathered from this that I must surely have some affection for you. And then when Zmeskall went to him about the affair in which you and Tante Gu[Susanna Guicciardi, Josephine's aunt and mother of Guilietta] were involved, he asked him if he knew whether I went to see you fairly often. Zmeskall said neither yes nor no. After all, there was nothing he could say, for I had dodged his vigilance as much as possible—[7]

This note shows Beethoven's discretion in matters of the heart. Even with his close friend, Zmeskall, whom he knew many years, he "dodged his vigilance as much as possible."

Had any one of Beethoven's male friends been his confidante in these matters, the mystery of the Immortal Beloved never would have been a mystery at all. Keeping that in mind, it becomes ludicrous to use a young man 14 years Beethoven's junior, who lived in the same town with him four or five years at most, as a reliable source on the composer's romantic escapades.

Ries confessed to once teasing Beethoven about the "conquest of a beautiful young lady" seemingly without the slightest inkling that Beethoven was teasing him back when the composer

---

[7]Anderson, pp. 131-132.

claimed that he had liked her longer than most others—a full seven months. Such candor with a pupil of his, when feelings of love were not shared with truly close friends, points only to the fact that Beethoven was having some sport with young Ries for his impudent remark. Ries also wrote that

> Beethoven very much enjoyed looking at women[8]; lovely, youthful faces particularly pleased him. If we passed a girl who could boast her share of charms, he would turn around, look at her sharply again through his glasses, then laugh or grin when he realized I was watching him.[9]

Unfortunately Ries, like most biographers, took Beethoven's actions and remarks far too seriously. Nineteenth century decorum did not approve of such blatant appreciation of a woman's charms, and it was naturally by those standards that Ries judged Beethoven's behavior. Some contemporaries have written—with an almost visible blush—of Beethoven's habit of removing his coat in hot weather and baring his arms in public! Had Ries (and others reporting on his habits) understood the composer better, he would have realized that Beethoven was no more inclined to censor his actions than he was his speech. As he was free and open about things he said, likewise he freely expressed his appreciation of a beautiful, hot day by rolling up his sleeves, and of a beautiful woman by turning around and looking at her. No doubt Ries—who certainly was not unaware of the "lovely, youthful face" that could "boast her share of charms"— was more discreet in his appreciation, more in keeping with the socially acceptable standards of the times. That Beethoven would "laugh or grin" at Ries's perhaps disapproving observation of his behavior shows that there was nothing very serious about it.

Ries cited another occasion that occurred when both he and the composer were in Baden. One evening he found Beethoven sitting with a woman on a sofa. Ries immediately jumped to the conclusion that she was yet another lady Beethoven sought to "conquer." Yet did the amorous Herr Beethoven shoo away his intruding young pupil? No, he did not. In fact, he asked his pupil to stay and play the piano for them! Had Beethoven had any romantic intentions toward the lady, he hardly would have done

---

[8]Ries says this as if most men do not.
[9]Wegeler & Ries, p. 104.

so. Yet, incredibly, this harmless little story is used as another example of Beethoven's many amorous adventures.

Other acquaintances, too, had noted that Beethoven was "fond of pretty women," and this lead biographers to assume that an enjoyment of looking at attractive women meant he also was inclined to fall passionately in love with them. Before making such an assumption we must ask, what heterosexual man is *not* fond of looking at pretty women? Although Grillparzer tells the tale of Beethoven's enjoyment of watching a farmer's daughter at her work, it is certainly innocent enough:

> During one of the summers which followed I made frequent visits to my grandmother who had a country house in the adjacent village of Döbling. Beethoven too was living at Döbling at the time. Opposite my grandmother's windows stood the dilapidated house of a peasant named Flohberger [who] possessed a pretty daughter, Lise, who had none too good a reputation. Beethoven seemed to take a great interest in this girl. I can still see him, striding up the Hirschgasse, his white handkerchief dragging along the ground in his right hand, stopping at Flohberger's courtyard gate, within which the giddy fair, standing on a hay cart, would lustily wield her fork amid incessant laughter. I never noticed that Beethoven spoke to her. He would merely stand there in silence, looking in, until at last the girl, whose taste ran more to peasant lads, roused his wrath either with some scornful word or by obstinately ignoring him.[10]

Grillparzer related that this interest in Lise Flohberger had taken place in 1807, although Beethoven was not living in Döbling or vicinity at the time. If true, it probably took place in 1804, when Grillparzer, born in 1791, was twelve or thirteen.

We must ask again, is it so odd for a man to find interesting a lusty, laughing girl who was brazenly flirting with him? Grillparzer himself seemed to have been quite taken with her, if he remembered her—and even her name—so clearly after so many years! Should this place a blot on Beethoven's moral character? We would defy any man to stroll onto any college campus in the spring or summer and not take enjoyment from the sight of the

---

[10]Scherman & Biancolli, p. 850

coeds there, even without them laughing and lustily wielding any pitchforks. Should we also consider—as Solomon suggested— that Lise's preference for peasant boys had in any way negatively affected Beethoven's conception of his own masculinity? The idea is ludicrous.

Solomon faulted Beethoven for his youthful escapades, claiming that no serious relationships could possibly have resulted from his infatuations because the ladies did not have any real feelings for him. In reality, Beethoven did not have any real feelings for the young ladies with whom he innocently flirted, either. Suggesting that it was Beethoven's own fault that he never married would come as a painful shock to other unmarried people who have similar difficulty finding their own "significant others."

CONTRASTING TESTIMONY

Such is the nature of the "abundant testimony" which supposedly proved that "Beethoven was constantly in love." Gerhard von Breuning wrote that

> The period in Beethoven's life extending from the time when he began to be famous...produced an enormous number of reports, anecdotes and incidents, often untrue and at best distorted. The stories in *Jungend-Album* intended as romantic, are not only false, but vulgar. Also entirely fictitious is everything written, in a popular over-wrought style, in connection with the much-quoted saying 'Beethoven was never out of love.'[11]

Let us now contrast the observations of the preceding four men with that of Johann Dolezalek. Beethoven met Dolezalek in 1800. Dolezalek was a capable musician who played the pianoforte and violoncello, was a popular composer of Bohemian songs, and an exceptional music teacher. He was 20 at the time the two men met, nine years Beethoven's junior. Thayer tells us that he was a lifelong admirer of Beethoven's and enjoyed the composer's friendship until the latter's death. Their relationship spanned over 25 years, and because of that, he is qualified as an authority on Beethoven's character, although most biographers tend to mention him only in passing, if at all. It was Dolezalek who

---

[11]Breuning, p. 44.

observed, "You never knew when he [Beethoven] was in love." If a long-term, personal acquaintance of Beethoven's was unaware of his amorous proclivities, how is it that biographers, writing many years after the fact, came to a totally different conclusion? The main reason stems from rampant, repeated misinterpretation of Beethoven's letters and notes which, over the years, has come to be accepted as the truth. And perhaps because only rare people like Dolezalek really understood what the word *love* means.

A case in point is provided by biographer Ludwig Schiedermair who in 1925 wrote that Beethoven's "first deep love was Eleanor von Breuning," a childhood friend. And how did Schiedermair come to that conclusion? Because Beethoven 1) had been pleased with a waistcoat she had made for him, 2) because he had preserved until his death an ornately decorated birthday greeting she had once sent him, and 3) because he underscored "my dear friend" in a letter to her. First, why would it be unusual for a person to keep a particularly beautiful hand-made note from a woman he had known since childhood? Second, would he *not* be pleased with the gift of a piece of clothing that she had made for him? Third, anyone who has read even one authentic Beethoven letter would know that underscoring runs rampant in his letters, along with emphatic dashes and exclamation points. Finally, Eleanor's brother, Stephan, maintained that there had never been more than a friendship between Beethoven and his sister, an essential testimony which is often ignored completely.

Building on assertions such as Schiedermair's, and using criteria as flimsy as his, various beloveds were added to Beethoven's collection of romantic conquests. In 1948, previous biographers caused another writer, Peter Latham, to write that "in Vienna the list of ladies he had loved and lost soon grew really imposing." What list is that? And who, we wonder, is on it? As we shall see, it included virtually any Viennese female who happened to have come in contact with Beethoven during his lifetime. When one reviews this lengthy list, it becomes clear that it was generated and added to by Beethoven's many biographers, rather than through any efforts by Beethoven himself. Had he actually had as many affairs as have been attributed to him, it is doubtful that he would have had time to compose any music at all!

Thayer wrote that

A few notes upon certain young women to whom Beethoven dedicated compositions at this period of his life [1790s] may be appropriate here. It was much the custom then for teachers of music to dedicate their works to pupils especially to those who belonged to the higher social ranks—such dedications being at the same time compliments to the pupils and advertisements for the instructors, with the further advantage often of being sources of pecuniary profit. Beethoven also followed the custom; and the young ladies, subjects of the following notices, are all known to have taken lessons from him: Anna Louisa Barbara 'La Comtesse Babette' Odescalchi, Countess Henriette Lichnowsky, Countess Guilietta Guicciardi, Josepha Sophia Princess von Liechtenstein, Baroness Braun, and Countesses Therese and Josephine Brunswick.[12]

It does not seem as if biographers keep this fact in mind, since most, if not all, of these women have come to be included on The List.

A LIBERAL TONGUE

Beethoven's liberal nature advertently may have contributed to the myth of his romantic escapades. He once wrote to Herr Bigot "...with the deepest regret am I forced to perceive that the purest, most innocent feelings can often be misconstrued..." He did not consider that this would someday apply to his own biographers, but it is unfortunately true that it does.

The exuberance of his letters suggests that he may have been a little too open in expressing his affections, and that on occasion his behavior offended his more genteel contemporaries. Yet we cannot believe that Beethoven ever meant to be offensive. His contriteness at such times shows that it hurt him greatly when his expressions of friendship were misunderstood, as can be seen in the following letter to Frau Marie Bigot:

Judging by the way you welcomed me, dear M[arie], I never dreamed of reading anything more into your behavior than the gift of friendship—You must think me very vain and petty if you assume that the friendliness of so excellent a person as yourself might lead to my believing that—I had immediately won your affection...

[12]Thayer/Forbes, pp. 233-234.

I myself told you that sometimes I am very naughty—
I am extremely natural with all my friends and I hate
any kind of constraint... Visions of all of you pursued me
everywhere and the whole time I was being reminded
that 'the Bigots are so good and are suffering perhaps
through your fault'—so in a fit of depression I hurried
away [from the Redoute tavern].[13]

Keeping in mind that it was his habit to be rather loose in
expressing love and admiration to his friends, imagine a researcher coming across the letter Beethoven sent to his new
friend, Christoph Tiedge, in which he wrote "Press the hands of
the Countess in a thoroughly tender and yet respectful manner,
to Amalie [Sebald] a right fiery kiss, when no one sees us..." The
immediate assumption was that Beethoven must have been
passionately involved with Fraulein Sebald, else he would not
have sent her a "fiery kiss." Yet this was just typical Beethoven—
what he wrote was not insincere, but it was certainly not as
meaningful as the readers who came across this statement
thought. It was even to his attorney, Dr. Kanka, that Beethoven
wrote "I kiss and press you to my heart." Yet we can be sure
Beethoven had no amorous feelings for him! Again, it was simply
typical, expressive Beethoven. He himself admitted that he was
"very free in speech—perfectly natural with all my friends."
What regret would he feel now, knowing how deeply those same
pure, innocent feelings expressed in his free speech have affected
his honor and contributed to his undeserved reputation as being
a "ladies' man?"

We now will consider each of the women on the infamous
List who are purported to have been Beethoven's passions. We
will look at whatever evidence exists that he had been in love with
any or all of these women. After doing so we must keep in mind
Charles Carpenter's amusingly pertinent statement about the
nature of proof such as this:

"I would not hang my mother-in-law's cat
on the weight of such evidence."

[13]Anderson, p. 163.

❧ 2 ❧
The Ladies of the List

MAGDALENA WILLMANN (1795-1799)[1]

    This woman rightfully belongs on the list of Beethoven's loves. The composer met renown singer Magdalena Willmann when he was 24, and between 1797 and 1799 he wrote quite a few songs for her, including his famous *Adelaide*. Although biographers make much of Beethoven's "fleeting passions," his attraction to Magdalena lasted nearly four years until she broke off their relationship in order to marry someone else. Solomon wrote that she "exhibited little or no feeling for him," but obviously this cannot be true or Beethoven would not have invested several years of his life in their relationship. However "ugly and half mad" as she may have considered him, he never knew her true feelings about him. Somehow she managed to deceive him into believing that she had an interest in him so that he would use his talent on her behalf. It must have been a blow for him to learn, either personally or through public announcement, of Magdalena's intentions to marry another man. One can only imagine how shocked and crushed Beethoven had been to find that he had invested not only his time and his genius but his very heart in this woman for nothing. Although he has been held accountable for not realizing that she did not love him, Beethoven can hardly be blamed for not seeing through her deception. He was neither the first nor last person to have been so deceived. Was he wrong to place his trust in a woman he loved? Should he have been more guarded, more suspicious?

    Shortly after she left his life, Beethoven wrote to his friend, Karl Amenda:

---

[1]Dates in parentheses note the approximate time period with which the woman was associated with Beethoven.

Summer 1799:

> The invitation [to Mödling] was all the more welcome to
> me, as my heart which was already bruised would have
> been suffering even more. Although the main tempest
> has spent itself, I am not yet quite sure how my plan of
> resistance will turn out.[2]

Magdalena died in 1801 and it was 60 years after the fact
that Magdalena's niece told Thayer that her aunt's real reason for
rejecting Beethoven had been because "he was so ugly, and half
mad." Not so ugly or mad, however, that she had been adverse to
using him to advance her career.

GUILIETTA GUICCIARDI (1801-1803)

More has been made of Beethoven's "affair" with the
young Julie than actually occurred. In November 1852, Otto
Jahn interviewed her, asking her about her relationship with
Beethoven. Because 50 years had passed, it would have been
strange for her to have been reticent about discussing this topic,
even though it may have been somewhat delicate. Jahn's notes
show no hint at all that a "great passion" had existed between
them, and she did not so much as admit that she had loved him,
which she easily could have done without going into any detail. In
her recollections, Julie noted only that

> Beethoven was her teacher. He allowed her to play his
> compositions but was exceedingly severe with her until
> the interpretation was correct to the very last tiny
> detail. He insisted on a light touch. He himself was
> often violent, throwing the music around and tearing it
> up.[3]

That certainly is an interesting way for a man to treat a
woman with whom he supposedly was ardently in love. We may
compare Beethoven's teaching technique with Julie to that which
he used with Therese and Josephine von Brunswick during the
same time period. Therese noted that "he never tired of lowering
and bending my fingers which I had been taught to keep flat."
Josephine added, "Beethoven is charming. He has told me that

---

[2]Anderson, p. 34.

[3]Thayer/Forbes, p. 307.

he will come every third day and give me lessons..." This is quite a contrast in behavior: Julie recalled him as violent and severe; the Brunswicks as gentle and patient.

While the assumption generally has been made that the romantic "Moonlight" Sonata *(Sonata una quasi fantasia in C-sharp minor*, Op. 27 #2) had been written for Guilietta, this is not true. Not only was this sonata not written for Julie—it was sketched two months before Beethoven met her—but it was not even a particular favorite of his. Thayer noted that "The notes of [Otto] Jahn's conversation with the Countess in 1852 make it clear that Beethoven did not have her in mind at the time of composition."[4] In fact, the "Moonlight" Sonata was given to Julie as a substitute for the *Rondo in G* which Beethoven had decided to give to Princess Josepha von Liechtenstein instead. Forbes noted that "As Beethoven's relationship to the Countess was exaggerated, so also more significance was attached to this sonata than is justified from a sober point of view."[5] About the sonata Beethoven complained, "Everybody is always talking about the C-sharp minor sonata! Surely I have written better things. There is the *Sonata in F-sharp minor*— That is something very different."[6] So much for the romantic dedication of the "Moonlight" Sonata to Julie Guicciardi.

Although in a letter to his friend, Wegeler, Beethoven referred to Julie as an "enchanting girl who loves me and who I love," the remark is curiously light for a such "great passion." In that same letter, Beethoven also said that he once again believed marriage for him might be possible, yet he did not mean marriage to *her*. He then also noted that—again, rather off-handedly—that she was not of his class, something that mattered to him far more as a young man than it would later. Although some biographers felt that his *Heiligenstadt Testament* (his Will) had been written in response to the broken heart he had suffered as a result of Julie's marriage to Count Robert Gallenberg, Beethoven's own words in the *Testament* tell us that was not so, that the cause of his despondency was solely the prospect of becoming deaf. He tells us himself that his torment stemmed from the fact that

---

[4]Thayer/Forbes, p. 297.
[5]Forbes, p. 297.
[6]Quoted in Carl Czerny's memorandum to Otto Jahn, Kerst, Vol. 1, p. 48.

for the last six years I have been in a wretched condition, aggravated by senseless physicians, cheated year after year in the hope of improvement... compelled early to isolate myself, to lead a lonely life... oh how harshly was I repulsed by the doubly sad experience of my bad hearing, and yet it was not possible for me to say to people: speak louder, shout, for I am deaf...[7]

At the time of the Testament's writing he had not known Julie for six years, and if his "wretched condition" had stemmed from losing her, it certainly had not been aggravated by senseless physicians. It also should be noted that Beethoven maintained his relationship with the Guicciardi family after the announcement of Julie's engagement to Gallenberg, therefore, his heart could not have been too badly damaged by her loss. And since he had never intended to marry her, how can her marriage to someone else be considered rejection?

MARIE BIGOT DE MOROGUES (1807-1809)

Marie Bigot was a great pianist; even Haydn embraced her as such. Beethoven, too, much admired her piano playing. He once invited Frau Bigot, along with her child, Caroline, to accompany him for a ride in the country. That he was so open about the invitation—even putting it in writing where it easily could be seen by her husband—indicates that he meant nothing improper, otherwise he surely would have been more discreet, even clandestine. Nevertheless, Herr Bigot took a dim view of Beethoven's invitation, and in innocence and indignation, Beethoven replied:

> March 5, 1807[8]: I cannot deny it, I felt very much hurt; I still cannot understand why it would have been improper if Marie and Caroline had come out driving with me. Am I to withdraw myself timidly, and with a feeling of regret that I should have failed to win the confidence of people who are so dear to me and so precious to me, and in whose company, ever since I have made their acquaintance, I have constantly felt a desire to be treated by them no longer as a stranger? Am I do to that?[9]

[7]Anderson, pp. 1351-1354.
[8]There has been disagreement as to whether this was written in 1807, 1808, or 1809.
[9]Anderson, p. 162.

Beethoven's original letter to Marie Bigot indicated that he certainly would have invited her husband to accompany him, as well:

> The weather is so divinely beautiful—I therefore propose to come and fetch you today about 12 noon for a drive—as Bigot is probably already out, we cannot of course take him with us—but to give it up entirely on that account, even Bigot himself would not make such a demand.[10]

That constituted the entire extent of his "love affair" with Marie Bigot. Herr Bigot reacted quite jealously over the incident, requiring Beethoven to write a long letter of apology. (However, having been offended by Bigot's mistrust, Beethoven also insisted that Bigot apologize to him, as well, for thinking so ill of him: "The matter really deserves careful reflection on your part, how you can make amends for having spoiled this day so bright for me.") There is a difference of opinion as to whether this incident occurred in 1807, 1808, or 1809. In the earlier year, it would have come on the heels of Beethoven's final separation from Josephine; in the latter year, after his quarrel and separation from Anna Marie Erdödy. Gossip in town about the either the Beethoven-Brunswick or the Beethoven-Erdödy relationship certainly could have colored Herr Bigot's view of Beethoven's invitation to his wife and daughter, whereas otherwise, unless he was a man prone to jealousy, he might have thought nothing or very little of Beethoven's gesture.

BARONESS DOROTHEA VON ERTMANN (1803-)

"Beethoven was never anything but polite to her," composer Felix Mendelssohn noted. Baroness von Ertmann was an exceptionally gifted pianist, one of the finest in Vienna. She often helped Beethoven with his concerts, particularly after his deafness became so profound that he could no longer perform in public himself. A letter written by Mendelssohn described the Ertmanns as "the most agreeable, cultured people conceivable, both in love as if they were a bridal couple, and yet married 34 years." This does not describe a woman who would have considered Beethoven

---

[10]Anderson, p. 161.

as more than a friend, nor would Beethoven have been oblivious to the love that Dorothea had for her husband. This did not deter biographers from proposing her as the Immortal Beloved. Certainly the composer respected her greatly and had a deep affection for her, but the most loving gesture Beethoven ever made toward her simply had been in showing her kindness in a time of great sorrow. Mendelssohn wrote:

> She related that when she lost her child, Beethoven at first did not want to come into the house; at length he invited her to visit him, and when she came he sat himself down at the pianoforte and said simply: "We will now talk to each other in tones," and for over an hour played without stopping, and, as she remarked: "he told me everything, and at last brought me comfort."

AMALIE SEBALD (1811, 1812)

The singer Amalie Sebald has been deemed as both the Immortal Beloved and the Distant Beloved. Beethoven met her in 1811, a crucial date for many biographers as we shall later see. She was in and out of his life within a month, and he did not see her again until he encountered her briefly in 1812. While his notes to her were friendly, seeing her was far from urgent to him, for they were filled with excuses. That he should write a song "To the Distant Beloved" for her in 1816 when he had not seen her for four years, and when, in fact, she had married in 1815, is neither a logical, nor supported, assumption. He sent Amalie a "fiery kiss" by way of a letter to his acquaintance, Christoph Tiedge, written only a few weeks after he met her. Thayer claimed that Amalie "powerfully attracted" Beethoven and that he had been "taken an unresisting captive by her charms." He based this opinion primarily on this "fiery kiss." Had it truly been as ardent and fiery as Thayer believed it was, Beethoven hardly would have sent it to her using a go-between whom he barely knew. Besides, such "ardent"kisses sent off in letters was a habit of Beethoven's —as we saw, he even sent them to his lawyer. Earlier in that same letter, Beethoven wrote, "Concerning Amalie, I know at least that she is alive," showing that he had very little if any interaction with her, yet this part of the letter receives no attention from biographers who are easily diverted by the "fiery (but essentially meaningless) kiss."

In 1811, the Teplitz guest list also included a Frau Wilhelmine Sebald of Berlin, who had arrived August 9 with her sister, a Madame Sommer, at the same time as Amalie. We know this to have been Amalie's mother, since Beethoven mentioned the woman's health in one of his notes to Amalie. Beethoven hardly would have engaged in a love affair with the singer with her mother and aunt present!

In 1812, Beethoven wrote Amalie a series of notes that biographer Max Unger called "charming billets." In nearly every one of these "charming billets" Beethoven tells Amalie only how ill he is (certainly a romantic subject) and that he is unable to see her. The most charm he exuded was in thanking her for the chicken she sent him for soup! Supposedly, dead fowl are the things on which powerful attractions are based. Unfortunately, these brief, uneventful summer encounters with Amalie Sebald were all that were necessary for biographers to add her to the list of Beethoven's loves. One writer of liner notes for the Seventh Symphony, James Lyons, claimed that she had inspired this work, "completed after a particularly pleasant spring vacation at Teplitz during which the composer had been charmed by the lovely Amalie Sebald." Not only had Beethoven not been in Teplitz in the spring, it had never been a "pleasant vacation"for the sick man, and we also know that he completed the symphony in May 1812, four months before he even reencountered Amalie at the spa. Perhaps Mr. Lyons thought that spicy liner notes would sell more recordings.

THERESE MALFATTI (1809-1811)

Beethoven was introduced by his friend Gleichenstein to the Malfatti family in 1809. The introduction, which came soon after Beethoven's separation from the woman with whom he had been living, Countess Erdödy, no doubt had been the result of Gleichenstein recognizing Beethoven's need for a pleasant diversion at this unhappy time. Therese's uncle had become Beethoven's physician in 1808 upon the death of Dr. Schimdt in February of that year, but letters to Therese and the Malfatti family do not appear until 1809, thus an earlier friendship with the family is unlikely. Therese has been deemed the object of Beethoven's unsuccessful plan to marry in 1810. Yet her uncle was still Beethoven's doctor in 1811 and most likely even as late as 1817.[12] If there had been a failed "marriage project" in 1810 involving Therese, Beethoven's relationship with the family would have been awkwardly strained.

Beethoven was nearly 40 when he met Therese, and she was a teenager. In a letter to her he wrote "Who would ascribe anything of the kind [a deeply serious musing] to the lively T who takes life so easily?—" Beethoven recognized the differences between them, not only in age and temperament, but more importantly, in their values and interests. He could not have believed that a union with her would have made either of them very happy. Most of his letters were addressed to the Malfatti family as a whole, rather than to Therese alone. The one written directly to her shows his friendly feelings for her, but there is disappointment evident, too, in her lack of depth, and the letter is far from passionate. A more indepth discussion on Therese Malfatti and Beethoven's relationship with her appears in Chapter 6: *The Marriage Project.*

ELIZABETH "BETTINA" VON BRENTANO (1810)

Bettina was the half-sister of Beethoven's friend, Franz Brentano. When the Brentanos told Bettina that the composer was "morose and unsociable" they were unwittingly issuing a challenge to her charms. She enjoyed the company of great men and her flirtatious behavior shows that she had been determined to capitivate the composer. Beethoven was in her company a mere four weeks, from May 1810 until she left for the Bohemian spas in mid-June, and despite her attentions and some mild flirting, he showed no extraordinary interest in her. Although there had been barely time to kindle a friendship, let alone a romance, she, too, has been labeled one of his passions. A brief look at the lady herself shows that their relationship was passionate only within the confines of her imagination.

Of the letters she claimed to have received from Beethoven, only one has ever been substantiated as authentic by virtue of the existence of the original autograph. Clearly this letter was not

---

[12]Anderson, p. 683. In an 1817 letter to Anna Marie Erdödy, Beethoven referred to his "wily Italian doctor" whom Emily Anderson understood to be Malfatti.

written to a beloved. It reflects only typical, exuberant Beethoven, using his characteristically excitable language, being warm and witty, but showing no romantic passion. The most romantic line in the letter is the following:

> I carried your first letter about with me the whole summer, and it was often the source of happiness.

But not so much happiness that he was in any special hurry to answer it. He did not write to her until February of the next year. He added:

> If I do not write to you frequently, still I write to you 1000,1000 times a thousand letters in my thoughts—

Of course, some 999,999 of them were never committed to paper. After a brief discourse on Berlin society and superficial art, Beethoven continued:

> You are going to be or are already married, and I have not been able to see you once beforehand. May all good wishes wherewith marriage blesses married folk attend you and your husband—[13]

In the rest of the letter, he spoke reverently about Goethe, described a party (a "bacchanal") he had enjoyed until four o'clock that morning, and closed with "I kiss you on your forehead." Well, that was certainly a passionate gesture!

When asked to show the other letters she claimed to have received from Beethoven, Bettina refused to do so, casting suspicion on the intimacy she said she had with the composer. Biographer Max Unger wrote that letters by Bettina "must be included in the circle of those poetic inventions of which she was so fond." Another biographer, Edouard Herriot, added that "the most well-wishing critics have not been able to protect [Bettina] from suspicions of untruth. Goethe's mother reproached her for her excessive faculty of fabrication, for her freedom with falsehoods." And a contemporary of Bettina's, Varnhagen von Ense, wrote that she "throws herself with a sort of mania on men noted for their power of intellect; she wishes to gnaw at all of them and finally to throw their bones to the dogs." Her half-brother, Franz, admonished her for spreading tales of her relationships with

---

[13]Anderson, pp. 312-313.

celebrated men, probably out of embarrassment. As for her relationship with Beethoven (and other great men, such as Johann Goethe), Thayer reminded us that Bettina "could not resist weaving herself into all she described so that... she made it seem that in their lives she played a much greater role than was actually the case." When on one occasion she shared with Beethoven a letter she had written to Goethe about him, Beethoven exclaimed, "Did I say that? Well, then, I had a raptus!" It appears that her imagination left even the composer himself incredulous. Bettina also wrote, "[Beethoven] begged me to write him at least once a month, since he had no other friend save myself." Beethoven had many friends, and hardly would have told such an outrageous lie, not even to induce a pretty woman to write to him.

The little stories about their brief "romance" are merely the fabrication of a prolific and perhaps gifted fiction writer. She cannot be considered a Beloved, immortal or otherwise.

THE OTHERS

THERESE BRUNSWICK (1799-)

Therese was the sister of Josephine, who over the years, maintained a sincere, affectionate friendship with Beethoven...but little else. Therese recognized her sister's love for the composer, and never attempted to interpose herself between them. Therese *was* deeply in love with a "Louis," which led some biographers to connect her romantically with Beethoven who was sometimes referred to as Louis or Luigi. But Therese's romantic interest had been in Louis Migazzi, not Louis van Beethoven.

Despite the fact that Josephine loved Beethoven—at least spiritually—Therese, her other sister, Charlotte, and their mother, convinced Josephine to separate from the composer. The Brunswick family did not consider him a suitable new husband for the young widowed Josephine, not because they had anything personal against Beethoven—in fact, they liked him very much—but because they considered his financial situation too precarious to take on responsibility for Josephine and her children. Unfortunately, Josephine was persuaded to agree with them. Beethoven's relationship with Josephine, because of its special nature, will be discussed further in this chapter under *"The True Loves"* and in subsequent chapters.

RAHEL LEVIN (A.K.A. RAHEL ROBERTS) (1811)

Rahel was suggested as a love affair of Beethoven's because of a minor event involving herself and her fiance, Karl August Varnhagen von Ense. When she and Varnhagen—a writer, diplomat, and aide to Prince (General) Bentheim—were in Prague in 1811, it was coincidentally at the same time as the Beethoven. Solomon suggested that a quarrel had ensued between Varnhagen and Rahel, because of the mutual attraction between Rahel and the composer. Letters between Varnhagen and Rahel, as well as Varnhagen's recollections of Beethoven's interactions with his fiancee (as reported in his memoirs) do not support this claim. Varnhagen wrote,

> Near the middle of September, Rahel traveled to Dresden where Marwitz [Alexander von der Marwitz, a young and close friend of Rahel's] was expecting her and thereupon back to Berlin. I accompanied her as far as Mariaschein. The parting broke my heart, only the confident hope that this was all leading to a lasting reunion gave me the courage to endure the separation. The sympathy of good Oliva and the honest Beethoven helped me over the next days.

Varnhagen received a letter from Rahel on September 16 which contained no hint of a quarrel between them. At this time, Varnhagen wrote back to Rahel that "Only Oliva could I endure about me for any length of time; he was sympathetic, but deeply depressed because of violent altercations which he had had with Beethoven." Varnhagen's letter does not show that even a simple lover's quarrel had parted them, let alone interference on Beethoven's part. All the same, the mere presence of that infamous Lothario Beethoven made it clear to biographers that Rahel's abrupt departure surely had been the composer's fault.

In addition, Varnhagen wrote in his book about what had constituted Beethoven's attraction to Rahel:

> At that time [1811] the Master was already hard of hearing and not easy to approach. On his lonely strolls in Cläri's garden, Beethoven had seen Rahel [Levin] many times. The unusual expression of her face im-

pressed him, reminding him of somebody close to his heart.

It was clear to Varnhagen, as it is not to most biographers, that Beethoven's interest in Rahel stemmed only from her resemblance to one he loved. That, in itself, would not have caused Beethoven to fall in love with her. In truth, the composer barely knew the woman, and it is obvious from his remark to Varnhagen regarding what it was about Rahel that interested him, that his romantic inclinations lay elsewhere.

MARIE KOSCHAK-PACHLER (1817)

This lady met Beethoven in 1817 when she was a 23-year-old bride. Beethoven greatly admired her ability to play the piano, especially his compositions, and called her the "foster mother of the children of my intellect." That is as far as his "love" for her went. Marie herself said only that she and Beethoven had "often been in one another's company" when she played the piano for him. This innocent remark caused Thayer to go to great lengths to prove an intense passion between them. However, years later, Marie's own son thoroughly quashed the idea of his mother having been one of Beethoven's loves. She had been suggested as being the mysterious "M" whose glance opened a terrible wound in Beethoven's heart in Baden, however it is now known that the note had been written at least 10 years before Beethoven met her.

JULIE VON VERING (1800-1809)

Julie was the daughter of Beethoven's doctor, and the composer occasionally played duets with her. Julie has been added to Beethoven's List because of an ambiguous statement he made many years later to the Giannatasio sisters. Beethoven told them about one of his friends who had loved the same girl he did. Although her preference had been for Beethoven, the composer said he had withdrawn, knowing that his friend loved her greatly. The girl, Beethoven added, did not live very long, and died soon after marrying his friend. As Julie von Vering had married Beethoven's boyhood friend, Stephan von Breuning, in 1808 and died in 1809, it has been assumed that it had been Julie about whom

Beethoven spoke. But was it? We must look at this remark in its historical context.

Beethoven had chosen her father, Dr. Gerhard von Vering, as his physician in 1800 upon Wegeler's recommendation. Thus at the the time he met Julie, she was only nine years old! Stephan married her eight years later when she was 17, and had courted her about a year. When, then had Beethoven "withdrawn"from the scene? Certainly not in 1804, 1805 or 1807, when his romantic intentions were focused on Josephine Brunswick. Perhaps in 1806, although 15 seems a bit young for a 35-year-old man even in those days.

It is possible that Beethoven had been referring not to Julie von Vering, but to Magdalena Willmann. Although he had not been in competition with a friend for her attentions, she had died shortly after her marriage. Beethoven's gallant story about withdrawing from the scene in order to allow his friend to have the woman he loved, could have been a slight stretch of the truth to save his pride, and avoid telling the Giannatasio sisters that he had been a rejected suitor. The very fact that Beethoven made this "confession" to the Giannatasios—people who were not close friends of his—leads one to believe that this love story was neither terribly serious nor completely accurate.

Except for Beethoven's dedication of a violin concerto to Julie von Vering—which was not unusual given that she was married to his friend Breuning—there is no other evidence of an infatuation for her. In fact, Beethoven was not particularly happy with Dr.Vering. To Wegeler, who had recommended Vering to him, Beethoven complained, "I should never see him unless I went to his house, which is very inconvenient for me. On the whole I am not at all satisfied with him." Had he truly had an infatuation for Julie, surely he would have welcomed an excuse to visit with her at her father's house, no matter how "inconvenient."

ELIZABETH RÖCKEL (1806)

Elizabeth was the sister of the tenor who sang the part of Florestan in *Fidelio* in 1806. There is no evidence of an infatuation for her, and Beethoven wrote not one letter to her. Elizabeth married pianist Johann Hummel in 1813. Beethoven was friends with Hummel, and both he and Elizabeth were at Beethoven's bedside during his last illness. Schindler believed that there was animosity between Hummel and Beethoven, presumably because years before, they both had been interested in the same girl— Elizabeth—yet there is no indication that this was true. Schindler claimed that Beethoven had loved Elizabeth and that Hummel had "snatched her away from him." But Elizabeth and Johann Hummel were married before Schindler even met Beethoven. Further, Hummel's tears at his dying friend's bedside in 1827 makes the presence of hard feelings difficult to believe.

ELISE VON DER RECKE (1811)

Beethoven only associated with Elise in October 1811 while they were both in Teplitz, she with her fiance, Christoph Tiedge. Tiedge was a summer acquaintance and poet whose work Beethoven found interesting. Her inclusion on The List is puzzling as she was 14 years older than the composer and at the time of the Beloved letter, she was 55 years of age. Beethoven thought Elise was a very fine pianist and called her a "noble friend." His interest in her musical ability was enough for biographers to ignore the disparity in their ages and note her as one of Beethoven's many passions. Thayer said that "No hint anywhere appears that Beethoven renewed his intercourse with Tiedge and the Countess von der Recke (in 1812)—they may have departed (from Teplitz) before his arrival." Elise and Beethoven had only the briefest interaction, and there is no indication that she meant anything special to him. Elise and Christoph lived in Dresden and did not see Beethoven again after that summer.

COUNTESS BABETTE KELEVICS ODESKALKY (1799-1801)

Carl Czerny added this Countess to The List because Beethoven dedicated to her the *Sonata in E-flat Op. 7*, also called *Die Verliebte* ("The Maiden in Love"). Not that this "maiden in love" was in love with Beethoven or he with her, nevertheless, she also became one of Beethoven's infamous passions. Originally, Babette was a pupil of Beethoven's, and as we already have noted, it was customary at the time for teachers to dedicate pieces of music to their students. She married Prince Odeskalky in 1800 or 1801 and it was after their marriage that Beethoven dedicated his first piano concerto, Op. 15, to her. Notes to his friend,

Zmeskall, show that Beethoven was on good terms with Babette's husband and entertained at the Odeskalkys' house on several occasions.

CHRISTINE GERHARDI VON FRANK (1801)

Dr. Andreas Bertolini, Beethoven's physician from 1806 to 1815, claimed that "Beethoven generally had a flame," though we must note that the word "flame" denotes frivolity and does not suggest a serious relationship. Among these "flames" he listed Guilietta Guicciardi (whose relationship with Beethoven ended before Bertolini even knew the composer), Bettina Brentano (who we know raised their relationship to new fictional heights), and Madame von Frank. Obviously Dr. Bertolini never read Beethoven's correspondence to her, or he never would have added this lady to The List.

The Madame von Frank regarded as one of Beethoven's flames by Bertolini was Christine Gerhardi von Frank, an amateur singer who, early in 1801 (again, before Dr. Bertolini knew Beethoven), gave a concert as a benefit for those wounded in the battle of Hohenlinden which occurred December 3, 1800. The first public announcement of this concert listed no other artist except herself—"the famous amateur singer Frau von Frank nee Gerhardi." Beethoven immediately sent her the following letter of protest, on behalf of himself and his fellow artists:

> I think it my duty, dear lady, to remind you that in the second announcement of our concert you do not allow your husband to forget again that those who contribute their talents to the same should also be made known to the public.— This is the custom... Punto is not a little wrought up about the matter, and he is right.... Look after this, dear lady, since if it is not done you will be faced with real ill humor.— Because I have been convinced by others as well as myself that I am not a useless factor in this concert, I know that not only I but Punto, Simoni, and Galvani will ask that the public be informed also of our zeal for the philanthropic purposes of this concert; otherwise we must all conclude that we are useless.—[14]

---

[14]Anderson, p. 49. Herr Punto was a French horn player who accompanied Beethoven in the performance. Madame Galvani and Herr Simoni were singers who performed with Madame von Frank.

Beethoven's sharp remonstration notwithstanding, the
public announcement appeared two more times—verbatim.
Beethoven could not have had any romantic interest in this vain
and thoughtless woman, and why Bertolini thought she was a
"flame" is beyond imagination. One guesses that because she was
female and within Beethoven's proximity, she naturally should
be added to the infamous List.

* * *

In these latter cases, and others whom we will not bother
to list, there is no evidence to link Beethoven romantically with
any of them: no letters; no information from a named, reliable
contemporary; in many cases, not even gossip. In a word: nothing.
Their female sex and their proximity to the composer are the only
two qualifications necessary to become one of Beethoven's "ardent passions," and an entry on The List. We should perhaps be
grateful that biographers limited their list of the composer's
lovers to women.[15] Goodness knows that list is long enough.

JOHANNA VAN BEETHOVEN (1806-)

Johanna was Beethoven's sister-in-law and the mother of
his nephew, Karl. Although it is absurd to consider Johanna as
one of Beethoven's loves, she is included here for two reasons: 1)
at the time of Beethoven's lawsuit over the guardianship of Karl,
Johanna spread the rumor that Beethoven was in love with her,
and 2) it was Johanna who was Bernard Rose's choice for the
Immortal Beloved in his 1994 film of the same name. It is important, therefore, to dispense with her.

Even though Johanna and Caspar Carl had had sexual relations prior to marriage, as evidenced by the birth of their son
just six months after their wedding, this did not cause Ludwig to
think her immoral or to especially dislike her. After all, he himself
had wanted Josephine to become his lover outside of marriage.
Instead, his opinion of Johanna deteriorated during Carl's final
illness. Her lack of concern for her husband rankled Beethoven,
and he became aware that she had not been faithful to his brother.
She was with her lover, a man named Hofbauer, while Carl was

---

[15]We discount here the ludicrous theories of Editha and Richard Sterba who
concocted an elaborate psychosexual biography of Beethoven and who, no doubt,
would have gladly added another gender to The List.

dying, even if Hofbauer had not been actually living in the house she shared with her husband, as has been thought. She later had a child by Hofbauer, and Beethoven mentions him with contempt in several letters. On two occasions during her marriage to Carl she had been in the hands of the police; once ever her own husband had had her arrested, albeit for petty crimes. Beethoven became aware of her less-than-exemplary wifely behavior when he began tending to his brother's affairs during Carl's illness. Beethoven's letters about her prove that there was not even a brotherly-sisterly affection between them, let alone any feelings of love. Beethoven managed to tolerate her on occasion solely for his nephew's sake. His low opinion of her is evident in this letter to an unknown recipient written in 1820:

> ... neither housekeeper nor wife, excessively addicted to finery, so lazy and slatternly that when my poor brother happened to be in constant pain from his disease even I had to admonish her to work. Well, shortly before his death she drew 200 gulden without his knowing anything about it. Although I could never defend, still less approve, her actions, yet I warded off my brother's anger from her. Any vexation endangered the life of that poor fellow.[16]

Beethoven also complained about her behavior to Giannatasio del Rio, owner of Karl's boarding school, in February 1816:

> Last night that Queen of the Night was at the Artists' Ball until three a.m. exposing not only her mental but also her bodily nakedness — it was whispered that she —was willing to hire herself— for 20 gulden! Oh horrible! And to such hands are we to entrust our precious treasure even for one moment? No, certainly not.[17]

Although Beethoven has been accused of treating her more harshly than she deserved, his peers held an equally low opinion of her. A second letter from Beethoven to Giannatasio on February 22, 1816, shows that the schoolmaster was not very fond of Johanna, either:

---

[16]Anderson, p. 878.
[17]Anderson, pp. 561-562.
[18]Anderson, p. 563.

> In regard to Karl's mother I have now decided to comply
> fully with your desire that she should not see him at all
> at your school.[18]

In Beethoven's conversation book, Oliva noted that "The mother
[Johanna] is a mean-spirited whore," and then asked: "Is it not so
that Karl knows that she slept with her lover?"[19]

Mr. Rose may have gotten his idea about portraying
Johanna as the Immortal Beloved from these two Memoranda
written by Beethoven:

> H[err] Refer[ent] P[iuk] again retained the well-known
> complaints of F[rau] B[Beethoven] about me, even add-
> ing 'that I was supposed to be in love with her etc.' and
> more rubbish of that kind.[20]

> To Joseph Bernard, attorney, February 1820: Frau
> B[eethoven] has accused me, and on a former occasion
> the statements that I was supposed to be in love with
> Frau B[eethoven] and so forth. Is that kind of talk
> suitable for an Obervormundschaft, or, to put it more
> plainly, do those people indulge in that kind of tittle-
> tattle?[21]

Mr. Rose defied anyone to refute his theory that Beethoven's
Queen of the Night had actually been his Immortal Beloved. The
composer's own letters do that quite well.

ANTONIE BRENTANO (1809-1823)

Although we have listed their relationship as spanning
the years 1809 to 1823, Beethoven did not see her after 1812. The
composer maintained a sporadic correspondence with her and
her husband, Franz, through the latter year.

Although Antonie will be dealt with in detail later because
at present she appears to be the leading contender for the title of
the Immortal Beloved, it should be noted that in his theory,
Solomon suggested that her love affair with Beethoven began late
in the fall of 1811, culminating in the famous letter at the beginning of July 1812. Geographic distance and illness made their

---

[19]*Konversationshefte*, Vol. 2, p. 149.
[20]Anderson, p. 1400.
[21]Anderson, p. 875 .

interactions sporatic, and there was little time or opportunity for them to have developed an intimate relationship such as Beethoven had had with the true Beloved.

According to Schindler, Beethoven had met Antonie's father, Johann von Birkenstock, in 1792, a statement which Solomon claims is untrue by virtue of there being no mention of these people in Beethoven's correspondence for that time, although surviving letters from those years are spotty, and may not give a true picture of his interactions. At the time, twelve-year-old Antonie had been away at a convent receiving a religious and secular education. She did not return to her father's house until 1795. While it is possible that Beethoven saw her at Birkenstock's house between 1795 and her marriage to Franz Brentano, and subsequent move to Frankfurt, in July 1798, Beethoven had been involved with giving concerts outside Vienna between 1796 and 1798, and perhaps recuperating from a bout with typhus—hardly a time for indulging in a romance. If he had known Birkenstock at that time, he had had little opportunity to get to know Antonie. It is not surprising then that he made no note of her in any correspondence or journal entries. And if Antonie had met Beethoven at that time, he had not yet become quite the celebrity he would someday be, and she would have had little cause to notice him. Besides, from Solomon we learn that she had had four suitors, and that her "true love" had wept outside the church as she married Franz. Whoever this love was it certainly had not been Beethoven, who had been giving a concert in Prague at the time, and who, upon returning to Vienna, had begun his relationship with the Brunswicks, and grown closer to Anna Marie Erdödy.

THE TRUE LOVES

Of all the women Beethoven knew strictly as friends, there were very few who truly captured his heart. This is the only valid "list" that should exist, and on this list should be the names of three women: Magdalena Willmann, Josephine Brunswick von Deym Stackelberg, and Anna Marie Erdödy. Magdalena already has been discussed, and we shall spend no further time with her. She was the love of his callow youth, and though she broke his heart, her effect on him was not lasting. Of these three ladies, only the latter two reciprocated Beethoven's love, and only Anna Marie loved Beethoven as a woman does a man. They are the only women who have a rightful place on any list, for they were the only ones who had found their way into Beethoven's heart, and he into theirs.

Unfortunately, Josephine not only had strong feelings for Beethoven, she also had a strong family who, although they cared deeply about the composer, thought he was an unsuitable husband for their daughter and sister, a frail, financially needy young widowed mother. They firmly discouraged a union between Josephine and Beethoven, a stance they many years later regretted, for unwittingly they had robbed Josephine of her happiness. In her July 12, 1817, diary Therese wrote: "Josephine must suffer remorse on account of Luigi's (Ludwig's) sorrow—his wife! What could she not have made of this Hero!" Twenty years after Beethoven's death, Therese made another entry into her diary:

> ....Beethoven! It seems like a dream that he was the friend, the intimate of our house—a stupendous spirit! Why did not my sister J., as the widow Deym, accept him as her husband? She would have been happier than she was with St(ackelberg). Maternal love caused her to forego her own happiness.[22]

Only Anna Marie Erdödy remained a constant in Beethoven's life for twenty years. Abandoned by her husband at an early age, she was never attached to any other man, and she had the strength of character to resist whatever family pressures may have been placed on her to terminate her serious relationship with Beethoven. Her importance in his life has been underrated by most of Beethoven's biographers, and her candidacy as his Beloved has been scoffed at and ridiculed. With new evidence at hand, however, this author feels that another look at Anna Marie is warranted. Countess Erdödy's relationship to Beethoven will be fully covered in Part IV.

MODERN VS. CONTEMPORARY OPINION

Why are the opinions of Beethoven's contemporaries — relating to his affairs of the heart—so radically different from those of his biographers? Nearly all of the latter, with a few exceptions, adhere to the notion that Beethoven had regularly en-

---

[22]Landon, p. 102.

gaged in passionate affairs with married and unmarried women. Although we have seen that this concept has no validity, it has not deterred some from suggesting that he had sexual relations with with the wives of male friends (sometimes secretly, other times at his friends' invitation!) and had been a regular customer at houses of ill repute. These accusations are unfounded, and came about by distorting or misinterpreting the meanings of Beethoven's letters and notes. As we will later show by example, it is simple enough to "prove" a point by changing the nuance of what was written or said.

It would be interesting to hear a Beethoven biographer define the term *passion*, for they seem to have no clear concept of what the word means. The most common definition notes that it is an "emotion of burning intensity and an overpowering desire." Do they honestly see that sort of emotion inherent in Beethoven's relationships with the Ladies of the List?

Surely, if Beethoven had had such a bad reputation with women, his male acquaintances would not have trusted him so completely in the company of their wives and daughters. The worst he is accused of is merely having "flames." We cannot attribute Beethoven's avoidance of a bad reputation to the fact that Viennese men were ignorant, stupid, or indifferent to their wives' extramaritial activities, nor to the fact that the composer and his alleged paramours were exceptionally adept at sneaking about. No man with such a bad character could ever have been so discreet. Such behavior would have formed the basis of juicy gossip and been widely bantered about. Knowing Beethoven's personality, with his childlike openness of expression and earthy humor, most of the people acquainted with him were able to shrug off as innocent and meaningless any flirtatious behavior in which he might have indulged, something modern biographers have been unable or unwilling to do.

In the more than twenty-five years that Beethoven lived in Vienna—most of those years in the public eye, with his life, his character, and his reputation under scrutiny—the only man who, as far as is known, ever objected to Beethoven spending time with his wife was Herr Bigot, who was either by nature a jealous man, or whose view of the situation had been colored by other events of that year. In other households, Beethoven came and went as a valued and trusted friend, whether or not husbands or fathers were present at the time to guard the virtues of their families' female members. Contemporary opinion regarded him as honorable, although cynical twentieth century writers seem to find such an appraisal difficult to accept. It is a sad commentary on our modern society that we cannot believe that great genius and a sense of morality can coexist in one person.

Numerous letters written by Beethoven to male and female friends alike are filled with great warmth and expressions of deep friendship, yet the "ardor" that he exudes has been misunderstood only by his biographers. The recipients of those letters—and their families, who surely were privy to at least most of them—generally were not offended by Beethoven's exuberant means of expressing himself. They were able to accept Beethoven simply being Beethoven. They understood what his biographers do not seem to understand at all, that he was being "perfectly natural with his friends." Perhaps that is because they knew him *personally*, knew that it was part of his innate and rather childlike nature to say exactly whatever was on his mind—both good and ill—whenever and wherever the mood struck him, and to whomever he pleased. Those of us far removed from him by the passing of time can judge him only by the inanimate words we read in his letters, notes, and journals. Many modern biographers have gone to great lengths to disprove Beethoven's adherance to a moral code, and have done everything short of calling him a liar. If unwilling to do so outrightly, they couch their disbelief in terms such as "self-deception," intimating that he was not by nature a moral man, but had deluded himself into believing that he was. Unfortunately, Beethoven must remain a psychoanalyst's easy target, for he himself can offer no defense.

Beethoven once wrote to his friend, Gleichenstein, in a bitter jest:

> Now you can help me look out for a wife—but she must be beautiful, for I cannot love anything that is not beautiful—otherwise I should have to love myself.[23]

Many biographers must lack a sense of humor, otherwise they would not take Beethoven's sometimes earthy jokes so seriously. Yet we must not take Beethoven's attempt to make a joking remark to a friend as evidence that he was ever so shallow and superficial. Beethoven's letter to Josephine Brunswick which

---

[23]Anderson, p. 219.

follows tells us that a pretty face—however much he may have enjoyed looking at one—was far from what he considered important in a lasting relationship:

> Oh beloved J. it is not a desire for the opposite sex which draws me to you. No, you, your whole self with all your characteristics, have fettered all my feelings, my entire sensitivity to you. . . [Our love] is noble—based so much on mutual respect and friendship—indeed the very similarities in so many things—in thinking and feeling.[24]

The important qualities Beethoven listed—mutual respect, friendship, similarities in values and interests—are not aspects of a personality that become evident with only sporadic encounters, or in the course of indulging in harmless flirtations. Such conclusions are drawn only after a long and intimate relationship such as he enjoyed with a few—and only a few— special women. The trivialities he exchanged with the Ladies of the List are less than nothing compared to the feelings he had for his True Loves which he kept deep within in his heart.

Beethoven's criteria for a life's partner will be important to keep in mind when we later consider the letter to the Immortal Beloved. We will see that it could have been written only to someone with whom he shared a special intimacy. It was not born out of the brief blaze of an intense but transient passion, nor out of a frivolous infatuation, but out of a long-term, loving association, out of shared thoughts, emotions, and values, which had been nurtured by mutual respect, and out of deep feelings of friendship on which Beethoven placed so high a premium.

---

[24]Anderson, p. 131.

❖ 3 ❖

Always Poor Choices

Beethoven has been accused of sabotaging his desire for marriage by consistently seeking out women who were beyond his reach, either because they were already attached to other men, or were members of an upper social class that excluded him. However, we already have seen that Beethoven did not seek out nearly as many women as has been claimed, and of those that he did, their social status was not a factor in the relationship. Magdalena had never been above his station. With Josephine, money and the potential loss of her children, not social position, had been the main issue. Anna Marie cared nothing for the differences in their social and financial status though, like Josephine, her children had been a factor. Only Guilietta had Beethoven, in his youth, considered socially superior to himself—although he had had no inclination to marry her. Nor were any of these women attached to other men. At the time he approached them, both Guilietta and Magdalena were single. Josephine was a widow. Anna Marie was irrevocably separated from her husband. And if one also wishes to include Therese Malfatti or Amalie Sebald, neither had been attached to anyone, nor superior to Beethoven socially.

BEETHOVEN AND THE ARISTOCRACY

With his fierce democratic ideals, Beethoven never would have considered female members of the aristocracy unattainable.

Beethoven was perhaps as liberal as any nineteenth century man could have been in treating men and women as equals.[1] He expressed his affections for both with little difference, giving no more than cursory thought to whether he was acting or speaking appropriately. Yet while no psychological importance is given to his calling a male friend "dear Beloved Amenda," or to pressing his male attorney to his heart, all sorts of deep meanings are attached to similar expressions made to women. Let Beethoven, in all innocence, utter a simple word of loving kindness to a female friend and she is deemed one of his love affairs and ardent passions, and relegated permanent status on The List.

Gender made no difference to Beethoven in choosing his friends, and their numbers were well balanced between men and women. The primary criterion for becoming one of his intimates was a passion for music which equaled his own. Of secondary importance was an interest in literature, philosophy, history, and politics. His friends were intelligent, well-versed conversationalists. Although Beethoven has been criticized for choosing companions from among those occupying social stations above his, where else would he have found such ardent lovers of the fine arts and sciences? Few working class women—or men, for that matter—would have had the leisure time to cultivate an interest in and talent for music and other intellectual pursuits. But such things were very much an integral part of an upper-class education. Schindler noted that

> As for the music-lovers of that time, we know that they were found almost exclusively among the educated classes, who by inclination and breeding assigned to music its place among the disciplines.[2]

---

[1] As far as is known, the only documentation that exists of a less-than-liberal attitude toward women came in his letter to the Landrechte in 1815: "It must be borne in mind that a woman, even though she be equipped with moral and intellectual qualities...can never be capable of supervising adequately the education of a boy as soon as he has passed the age of nine years." Perhaps he can be forgiven this sexist attitude in light of his other, more enlightened opinions of women's rights and abilities before his bitter fight with Johanna van Beethoven colored his view. On the other hand, it may also be said that, in a sense, he was right in his observation, for he recognized the importance of a strong, positive male role model in a boy's life.
[2] Schindler, p. 65.

Could Beethoven have been happy with a wife who was like the women chosen by his brothers—a housekeeper or the daughter of an upholsterer? Doubtful, for such a woman likely would not have been his intellectual equal, nor shared his sophisticated interests.

Although not formally educated, Beethoven was very well read, particularly in classical literature. He had an interest in history and politics, and in the world both within and beyond Austria. Thayer tells us that "Beethoven had become to some considerable degree a self-taught man; he had read and studied much and had acquired a knowledge of the ordinary literary topics of the time." He enjoyed Persian and Egyptian philosophy and literature, and "exhibited a keen perception and taste for the lofty and sublime, far beyond the grasp of any common or uncultivated mind."[3] Could a working class woman have provided him with the intellectual and musical companionship he required? Why then should he be faulted for seeking a woman who shared his interests, and ignoring the narrow view that one did not marry outside one's class?

Beethoven perhaps was somewhat naive in not considering that members of the nobility did not always share his liberal views. No doubt he misconstrued the aristocracy's acceptance of him into their social circle, and failed to see that many of them would have drawn the line when it came to him marrying into it. But the members of the nobility with which he interacted were not entirely blameless. Every time they acquiesced to his complaints and demands, every time they had a servant tend to Beethoven before themselves, every time they issued a warning to their lackeys that Beethoven was not to be disturbed, and lightheartedly accepted his abuse, they led him to believe that he was one of them, standing on their level, as if he were a noble himself with all the privileges that they enjoyed—including marriage to one of their women. Beethoven paid attention to class distinctions only when he was a very young man and unproven in his career—as he noted when thoughts turned to marrying someone of Guilietta's station—but that opinion changed when he came to see himself as having true worth as a composer. Because he saw himself as a man of value—and rightly so—he felt

---

[3]Thayer/Forbes, p. 480.

his personal worth elevated him to the level of the nobility with which he interacted, even though the circumstances of his birth otherwise excluded him from it. The aristocracy did not do much to make him think otherwise. There were few instances in which a nobleman ever "put him in his place." The Archduke Rudolph once chastised an unrepentant Beethoven when the latter corrected his faulty piano playing with a sharp rap on the hand, but such incidents were rare, and in the end, the Archduke relented to "the master." It was only a myth concocted by Schindler that Beethoven once pointed to his head and his heart and declared that it was there that his nobility lay, but it is not difficult to imagine that Beethoven may have felt that way. As for being a commoner wishing to marry into their ranks, even that did not find much opposition from Beethoven's aristocratic friends. In a spring 1805 letter to Josephine, Beethoven wrote, "There was nothing which he [Lichnowsky] desired more than the formation of such an association between you and me, if it were possible."[4] This indicates that Lichnowsky, a prince, not only had no qualms about a commoner such as Beethoven marrying into the nobility, he encouraged it. It is also fair to assume that, had Beethoven's financial situation been more secure, many a noblewoman would gladly have become his wife—had he asked—regardless of the disparity in their social stations.

Another fault that Solomon—reiterating the pronouncements of his predecessors—assigned to Beethoven was that in his "other infatuations, there was little possibility of their evolving into serious relationships. Either the woman was firmly attached to another man... or she exhibited little or no feelings for him..."[5] This claim that Beethoven had attachments solely to "unattainable" women in terms of their marital status is also unfair; as we have seen, at the time of his interest in them, the women were quite attainable.

THE "STRONGLY ATTACHED"

As examples of women firmly attached to others, Solomon listed the following. Since we have already covered these women in depth, we will revisit them here only briefly:

---

[4]Anderson, pp. 131-132.
[5]Solomon, p. 158

- **Guilietta Guicciardi's** engagement to Count Gallenberg came after her friendship with Beethoven had already taken hold, and it came as a surprise to the composer. Was she "firmly attached to another man?" No, when Beethoven met her she was very much available.
- **Julie von Vering** did not become "firmly attached" to Stephan von Breuning until 1808, eight years after Beethoven met her. Of course, except for Beethoven dedicating a violin concerto to her, there is little evidence that he had anything more than a passing interest in her.
- Beethoven's "infatuation" for **Bettina Brentano** was only in her own mind. Solomon himself unwittingly eliminated her from this category by writing that she had "aroused [Beethoven's] expectations without revealing that she was then deeply in love with and about to marry Achim von Arnim."[6] Was Beethoven supposed to have been able to read her mind? Regardless, there is no evidence of any "expectations" on Beethoven's part.
- Beethoven's "infatuation" in the case of **Frau Marie Bigot** took the form of asking her and her daughter to take a ride in the country, and he also admired her piano playing. Obviously a major affair on Beethoven's part.
- **Elizabeth Röckel,** whose brother sang the part of Florestan in *Fidelio*, was a single woman when Beethoven met her; she married Johann Hummel in 1813, seven years after meeting Beethoven. **Antonie Adamberger** was a Viennese actress, and acquaintance of Baroness von Ertmann. She was likewise single when she met Beethoven, but later married Joseph von Arneth. She played the part of Klarchen in Goethe's *Egmont* for which Beethoven composed the music. She herself stated that she had had no personal relationship with Beethoven. There is absolutely no evidence—other than one statement of dubious validity offered by Schindler that Beethoven had loved Elizabeth—that Beethoven had been infatuated with either one of these women.

THOSE OF "LITTLE FEELING"

Of the second type, women who exhibited little or no feelings for Beethoven, Solomon cited the following ladies:

---

[6]Solomon, pp. 183-184.

• **Magdalena Willmann**. We already know that her lack of feeling came as a supreme shock to Beethoven who had known her for four years. In this case, Beethoven had been cruelly misled. It had not been his fault that she had been clever enough to conceal her lack of feelings for him. Surely in this case he deserves sympathy rather than condemnation for being gullible enough to believe she cared for him. We also know that she had not been beyond Beethoven's station and, therefore, his reach.

• **Therese Malfatti**. Beethoven certainly liked her, but, despite the rumors of a "marriage project" involving Fraulein Malfatti, he had little beyond a fondness for her. She shared none of his interests, and was careless with her music, something Beethoven would not have tolerated for long. Thayer wrote "A relative of the Baroness [Drosdick, a.k.a. Therese Malfatti] who knew her intimately, knew also that she and Beethoven had formed a lasting friendship, but as to any warmer feeling on either side he knew nothing, nor anything to the contrary.' When conversation turned on Beethoven, she spoke of him reverentially, but with a certain reserve.'"[7] We cannot imagine that Beethoven would have cared terribly if she had "exhibited little feeling for him," for his sole letter to her, while friendly, was hardly written by a man in love.

Each of the women cited above provides a flimsy example of Beethoven's poor choices in romance. None of these women may have loved Beethoven, but then Beethoven had not loved them either! The two women for whom he did have strong emotional attachments also had reciprocal feelings for him. Josephine perhaps had been compelled to deny her true feelings, but it is certain that she loved Beethoven at least on some level. We know from her sister's letters that when Beethoven had proclaimed to Josephine, "I have won your heart," he may not have been entirely wrong in his assumption. Anna Marie Erdödy on the other hand, reciprocated his loving feelings in all ways for many years and never denied them, even when circumstances threatened to drive them apart.

LOVE LETTERS

Solomon called Beethoven's letter to the Immortal Beloved "the only unalloyed love letter of his bachelor existence."

---

[7]Thayer/Forbes, p. 459.

Earlier, Oscar Sonneck also claimed that this letter had been the only love letter Beethoven had ever written. Had neither of these gentlemen ever read Beethoven's letters to Josephine? At least it is plain to see where Solomon heard this false echo which was repeated in his own book, but how did Sonneck come to this conclusion? One would be hard-pressed to categorize Beethoven's 1805 letters to Josephine Brunswick if they are not love letters! Beethoven poured out his heart in them, and it is little wonder that some biographers were and are convinced that she was also the intended recipient of the Beloved letter. To Josephine he wrote:

> Oh, if only you would be willing to establish my happiness through your love—to increase it. Oh Heavens, what more could I not tell you—how I think of you— what I feel for you—but how poor in spirit is this language. For a long time may our love last. Oh let me hope that your heart will long beat for me. Mine can only cease beating for you when it no longer beats at all—beloved J.[8]

This is not a love letter? Of course it is. Despite Solomon's qualifier that the Beloved letter was the only "unalloyed" love letter of Beethoven's bachelor existence, there is nothing weak or unclear about the Josephine love letters. The main difference between the Josephine letters and the one to the Beloved is the level of intimacy, which is greater in the latter. The man who wrote the Josephine letters was seeking to win a lady's heart; the man who wrote the Beloved letter had already won it. What these letters— to the Beloved and to Josephine—show us is what a genuine Beethoven love letter looks like. We also learn that Beethoven was capable of expressing deeply felt emotions to a woman in private correspondence although he was reluctant to admit having such feelings to his male friends. Letters to most other women not only pale by comparison with these letters, but fade to nothing. That alone should tell us that he was not in love with most of the women with whom he corresponded. The only exceptions to this were letters written to Countess Erdödy to whom he repeatedly referred as "cherished" and "adored." She and Josephine were the only women he ever addressed in that way.

---

[8]Anderson, p. 132.

In January 1805, Therese wrote her sister, Charlotte:

> But tell me, Pepi (Josephine) and Beethoven, what shall
> become of it? She should be on her guard! I believe you
> were referring to her when you underlined the specific
> words: 'Her heart must have the strength to say No,' a
> sad duty, if not the saddest of all!!... May the grace of God
> aid Pepi so that she is not tormented with care...[9]

From her sister's letter, we might infer that it was primarily the interference and objections of her sisters and mother and
their persuasiveness that the composer would not be a suitable
husband and father, that prevented Josephine from accepting
Beethoven as her spouse. But we suspect Josephine may have
had reasons of her own as well.

In her 1805 response to Beethoven's ardent note, the
widowed Josephine wrote, in part:

> The closer association with you, my dear Beethoven,
> during these winter months left impressions in my
> innermost self which neither time—nor any other cir-
> cumstances—will ever destroy... A feeling which lies
> deep within my heart and is not capable of expression,
> made me love you.... the pleasure of being with you,
> could have been the greatest jewel of my life if you loved
> me less sensually. Because I cannot satisfy this sensual
> love you are angry with me—I would have to break holy
> vows were I to listen to your desire. Believe me—it is I
> through the fulfillment of my duty who suffers the
> most—and my actions have been surely dictated by
> noble motives.[10]

Had the lady felt anguish at having to hurt the man she
claimed to hold so deeply in her heart? Likely she felt some pang
of guilt at having unintentionally misled him. When a woman
writes to a man of feelings deep within her heart that made her
love him, he would have to be a psychic wonder to realize she was
speaking only a spiritual love. After having known one another
six years, Beethoven quite naturally was ready to move their
relationship beyond spiritual love to physical expression. After
she had expressed her feelings for him so ardently, he must have
been shocked when she said no. Perhaps she had vowed chastity

---

[9]Thayer/Forbes, p. 377.
[10]Ibid.

outside of marriage, but more likely, she was not sexually attracted to him. In any case, they were never lovers, not in 1805, not in 1807, and, unless her inclinations changed radically, not in 1812.

Josephine, then, joins Magdalena Willmann as one woman Beethoven had loved who had rejected him. Yet Josephine is also in a class by herself. She certainly never "exhibited little feeling" for Beethoven; in fact, it was her exhibition of feeling that had led the poor man to an entirely wrong conclusion about their relationship. Josephine must take some of the blame here. She did not make it clear to Beethoven from the outset that her guidelines for their relationship did not include the possibility of them becoming lovers. It is little wonder that he might have assumed more and been hurt when she told him, "I cannot satisfy this sensual love." Was Josephine one of Beethoven's "poor choices" in women? Perhaps. But by her behavior, and also Lichnowsky's encouragement, there is no reason why he should have believed her to be.

Now what of Anna Marie Erdödy? Can she also be considered another one of Beethoven's "poor choices?" No, she cannot. Countess Erdödy had been separated from her indifferent husband for seven years by the time she and Beethoven made the decision to live together in 1808. She never "exhibited little feeling for him" and she certainly was not "firmly attached" to another man. In fact, her attachment to her husband and his to her was so tenuous that we feel their situation had led Beethoven to believe that the marriage might someday be dissolved completely. Despite her noble background, she did not feel she was beyond Beethoven's station or she would not have invited him to live with her, nor, as we shall see later, would she have addressed him in highly intimate terms. And as for Anna Marie's feelings for him, they were both deeply rooted in her heart and openly expressed to him. As such, it is little wonder that she remained an integral and faithful part of Beethoven's life for more than twenty years.

❧ 4 ❧
Fear and Avoidance

MUSIC AS AN ESCAPE

In a 1967 revised edition of Thayer's *Life of Beethoven*, editor Elliot Forbes commented that Beethoven frequently made the "decision to plunge into work when faced with the possibility of a permanent attachment with a woman."[1] Solomon used this statement to paint a picture of Beethoven as an emotionally immature man who lived in fear of responsibility and commitment. Actually, Forbes's comment was attached to his assessment of Beethoven's relationship with Guilietta Guicciardi, and, in fact, stemmed from a comment the composer made in a letter written to his friend, Wegeler, on November 16, 1800:

> This change [that he was once again among people] has been brought about by a dear enchanting girl, who loves me, and whom I love;...for the first time I feel that marriage can bring happiness; alas she is not of my station—and now—I certainly could not marry;—I must hustle and bustle about— If it were not for my hearing, I should already long ago have traveled half over the world, and that I must do. ...My youth, yes I feel it, is only now beginning...[2]

---

[1]Thayer/Forbes, p. 289.
[2]Anderson, p. 66.

To use Beethoven's letter in order to make a sweeping statement that Beethoven used his work as his escape from women, without putting the letter in its proper context, is wrong. At the time Beethoven wrote Wegeler of his need to work and travel rather than to marry, he was 29 years old, believed he was only 27, and felt that his "youth [was] only now beginning." The enjoyment he felt in Guilietta's company made Beethoven realize that, despite his deafness, he could still take pleasure from the company of others, and it had convinced him that he need not be condemned to a life of loneliness—that marriage still could be possible for him someday, although not necessarily to her. At this point in his life, and so early in his career, there was nothing "escapist" about Beethoven feeling the need to "hustle and bustle about" and to travel, that is, to establish himself as a composer of merit. In fact, his future livelihood and his ability to one day support a wife and family depended on his doing just that. He said, after all, "—And *now*—I certainly could not marry," not that he could not *ever* marry. His professional life was just beginning, having been interupted by serious illness only a few years before. It was not then, nor is it now, uncommon for any person to suppress their immediate desires for marriage and a family in order to launch a budding career. To apply this feeling of Beethoven's youth to the entire rest of his life is not valid.

In later years, Beethoven continued to "plunge" into his music at those times when he was involved with a woman. Yet these "plunges" were not his means to escape from his relationship with her, but to express those deeply felt emotions of love and joy which he found difficult to share verbally with even his closest friends, but which readily found expression in his music. "What more could I not tell you—," he wrote to Josephine, "but how poor in spirit is this language." When the Baroness Dorothea von Ertmann lost her child, Beethoven, words failing him, at first avoided his grief-stricken friend, but was at last able to comfort her with his music and offer her his sympathy and consolation. Every note that Beethoven wrote—with the possible exception of those pieces he called his "breadworks," which he composed to keep food on the table—came straight from his heart, and when his heart was filled with joy, it was all he could do to keep up with the music that poured from it. Anyone who knows Beethoven's life and his music readily can see the connection. It is thus surprising when one finds a serious biographer like Peter Latham (c.1920s) oblivious to this, and arriving at this surprising conclusion:

> From Heiligenstadt [the place where in a state of despondency Beethoven wrote his Will] he returned with the sunny second symphony, the most lighthearted of them all!—a warning to those who insist on reading a composer's life into his work.[3]

In 1956, Paul Nettl, professor of musicology at Indiana University, reiterated Latham's statement in his own observations:

> The peaceful mood of the Second Symphony is unruffled throughout, this in spite of the fact that it was conceived during one of the most trying periods of the master's life. The famed Heiligenstadt Testament was written during the same summer of the year 1802, but at no place in the symphony does this cry of anguish disturb the confidence and contentment of the music.[4]

Of course it doesn't. Both Latham and Nettl dated these two events incorrectly. Nottebohm found sketches for the Second Symphony in Beethoven's 1801 sketchbook. As Forbes said, "For nearly all the works completed in 1802, studies are to be found in the Kessler sketchbook, described in full by Nottebohm, which covers the period from the fall of 1801 to the spring of 1802. The sketches for the Second Symphony are happily plentiful."[5] Forbes also added that this symphony was the "grand labor of this summer," that is the summer of 1802. The Testament was not written until October of that year. In an addendum to the Testament itself which Beethoven wrote on October 10, several days after the main portion, he reveals that throughout the summer, he still was hopeful of a cure for his deafness:

> Thus I take leave of you — and, what is more, rather sadly— yes, the hope I cherished— the hope I brought with me here of being cured to a certain extent at any rate— that hope I must now abandon completely. As the autumn leaves fall and wither, likewise— that hope

---

[3]Sherman & Biancolli, p. 379.
[4]Nettl, p. 257.
[5]Thayer/Forbes, p. 317.

has faded for me. I am leaving here, almost in the same
condition as I arrived. Even that high courage—which
has often inspired me on fine summer days—has van-
ished.[6]

Beethoven went to Heiligenstadt on the advice of his doct-
or, with the hope that the quiet of the countryside would restore
his impaired hearing. Thus, he spent the summer with the hope
of being cured, and that hope is reflected in his second symphony,
completed at that time. Yet, with the coming of fall, it became
clear to him that his doctor's prescription had failed. That realization caused his "high courage" to vanish, and spawned the despondency in the Testament.

This biographical echo, as so many others which repeat
through work after work even though untrue, had not yet had its
final reverberation. Another respected biographer, H. C. Robbins
Landon, also agreed with Latham's and Nettl's observations,
repeating Nettl's almost verbatim.

Had Landon not taken his predecessors' word as fact, this
erroneous statement would not have appeared in his 1974 Beethoven biography. How Latham came to his conclusion, and why
both Nettl and Landon thought he was correct, is unknown, but
it is obvious that not only did the Second Symphony have no
connection at all to the *Heiligenstadt Testament* and the despondency found therein, it was completed when Beethoven was in the
vicinity of Jedlersee and Anna Marie Erdödy, his "movingly gay"
Countess and intimate confidante.

Contrary to these gentlemen's assertions, if any composer's
life was written in his music, it was Beethoven's, and if his life was
there, his love was there also. A study of the chronology of Beethoven's music, when it was sketched and when completed (see
Appendix B), shows an interesting pattern: it was precisely when
he had someone special in his life that his music was most prolific.
Far from being an escape from a relationship, the relationship
became his inspiration. Beethoven himself told us this is true in
his 1805 love letter to Josephine Brunswick:

I have won your heart. Oh, I know for certain what this
will mean to me; my activity will increase once again —
and this I promise you by all I hold highest and most

---

[6]Anderson, p. 1354.

precious, in a short time I will be there, worthier of myself and of yourself.[7]

And again, Beethoven himself tells us: "I never thought of writing for reputation and honors! What is in my heart must out, and so I write it down." Franz Wegeler, Beethoven's lifelong friend, eloquently expressed how deeply the composer's life was reflected in his music:

> Beethoven's entire soul lives on in his works; all his joys and sorrows have been consigned to his art. His music is his real biography, the true and imperishable story of what he strove for and what he accomplished, written for all people and all times.[8]

FEAR OF RESPONSIBILITY

Beethoven has been labelled as a man afraid of the responsibility of marriage. This is another unfair and untrue accusation, made without valid corroboration. The only "evidence" which exists is in the form of opinions and interpretations of biographers which we do not find convincing. In a moment we will look at the solitary note of Beethoven's—a single, somewhat ambiguous scrap—which was used to support this assertion. First, a brief look at Beethoven's history is important to accurately assess the validity of this claim.

A man who fears responsibility does not take on the enormous task of being head of a household and of caring for his younger brothers when he is still very young himself. Through Beethoven's letters we know that at the age of 18 he had petitioned for one-half of his father's salary so that he could take care of his two brothers and his alcoholic parent. He constantly was placed in the position of rescuing his inebriated father from the police, as well as looking out for Carl and Johann—and this while still a teenager himself. Ludwig was not legally required to take on responsibility for the Beethoven family; he chose to do so. After he moved to Vienna and his father died, Ludwig brought Carl and Johann to live with him, supporting them until they could find employment and become self-sufficient. At this point, one might

---

[7]Anderson, p.131.
[8]Wegeler & Ries, pp. 164-165.

argue that this enormous responsibility which he had under-taken as a teenager had soured him toward any future involve-ment. Yet we find that his sense of responsibility and commit-ment to family did not change over the years. Sixteen years later he took on responsibility for his brother's child, fully cognizant of the commitment that that entailed.

Anyone who is a parent will attest to the tremendous demands of a child, yet Beethoven willingly and eagerly took on the raising of his nephew. This he was not required to do, for the child was not an orphan. Beethoven easily could have left the boy in the hands of his mother. Yet when Caspar Carl's ambiguous will entrusted to his brother Ludwig the care of young Karl, and the elder brother chose to take on the difficult role of parent when he was under no obligation to do so, we must assume that he did not fear the responsibility he surely knew came with such an undertaking. Beethoven tells us that it was his sense of familial responsibility which prompted his actions and urged him to adopt his nephew:

> To The Imperial and Royal Landrechte of Lower Aus-tria, November 28, 1815: I hereby declare that I intend to undertake this guardianship without delay, because I cherished a deep affection for my brother, because his last charge is sacred to me, and because he committed the welfare of his son to me several times by word of mouth. Thus in many respects I consider myself bound to discharge the duties of this guardianship in the most conscientious manner.[9]

Many have scoffed at Beethoven's show of altruism, claim-ing that his acquisition of his nephew had been done *purely* for selfish reasons. Of course, an indepth study of Beethoven's rela-tionship with his nephew is beyond the scope of this book. We do concede that it had not been solely Karl's welfare which had motivated Beethoven, but that unrelenting loneliness and a desperate need to love someone who could not leave him surely had been contributing factors. However, whatever his motives, the very fact that he *did* adopt Karl as his son negates the argu-ment that he feared responsibility, whether as a husband or as a father. Karl took an enormous commitment on Beethoven's part, as the composer surely knew he would, yet Beethoven upheld it

---

[9]Anderson, p. 1360.

as best as he could—financially, educationally, and emotionally. If he was far from being an exemplary parent, can he be blamed for that? He was nearly 45 when nine-year-old Karl came into his bachelor life, and he had had little experience with raising youngsters other than with his own brothers, who had not been small children when he took over their care. His interactions with the children of friends—the Brentanos, the Erdödys, the Spohrs— show us that he was fond of them, and could elicit affection from them. We cannot deny that he made many mistakes with Karl— as most parents do—being too harsh one moment, too lenient the next. Still, he put his whole heart into parenting, such as seeking out the best schools and the latest books on child development and education. He wrote to Haslinger, "I should very much like you to get me the article on education. It is a matter of moment to me to be able to compare my ideas on the subject with other people's and still more, to improve on them." It is clear that, at least in his own mind, he did the best he could.

Beethoven did not place Karl in boarding schools to be rid of the responsibility of raising him, but to provide the boy with the stable environment he knew he could not give him within his own home. Beethoven's philosophical musings on a manuscript show us that he would have preferred to keep Karl nearer to him: "A thousand lovely moments are lost when children are placed in wooden institutions, when good parents could give them the most soulful impressions that last until extreme old age." Concern for Karl's welfare caused Beethoven to place his nephew in housing other than his own home: his hours were not suitable for a boy, his health was often poor, his lifestyle was erratic, his deafness made interaction difficult. He placed the boy in a live-in school, such as the Giannatasio's Institute for Learning, which provided a family-like atmosphere. Even though Karl lived apart from his uncle much of the time, Beethoven managed to live nearby and maintained a close relationship with Karl's teachers. He wrote to Czerny, Karl's music instructor, "I beg you to exercise as much patience as possible with Karl... treat him with as much love as possible, yet serious." And to Giannatasio, "I beg you to take into greater consideration his feelings and disposition, as the latter is especially the lever to all that is good..." Biographer Dana Steichen noted that

Over a period of two or three years, Beethoven wrote some sixty letters to Frau Streicher, over thirty to Giannatasio, and dozens of notes to Zmeskall, all on the subject of his nephew Karl and of his efforts to find suitable servants and set up a home for the boy.[10]

Did Beethoven fear marriage and the responsibility that went with being head of a household? Of course not. To him, the benefits of companionship, security, and stability that marriage would have given him far outweighed any restrictions being married would have placed on him. His touching bewilderment and subsequent pleas for assistance from his old friend Frau Streicher in accomplishing the most simply and ordinary household chores, show how a wife with a tolerant and patient personality would have benefited him. He was not oblivious to the fact that a spouse would have alleviated, rather than added to, his responsibilities. A loving wife and family was something Beethoven wanted desperately all of his adult life. He showed this in his letters and notes, and the sentiments expressed in them did not change throughout the years:

> (1794, to Simrock) "If your daughters are already grown up, train one to be my bride, for if I have to stay in Bonn unmarried I shall certainly not stay there for long..."

> (1810, note to himself) " Let me at last find the one who will make me happy in virtue—*who will lawfully be mine*." (emphasis is his)

> (1810, note to himself) "Without the society of some loved person, it would not be possible to live even in the country."

> (1813, note to himself) "O fearful conditions which do not suppress my feeling for domesticity..."

> (1813, to Zmeskall) "I should like to have one [a servant] who is married; for greater orderliness though perhaps not greater honesty, can be expected from a married servant."

---

[10]Steichen, p 343.

(1816, to Ries) "Kindest regards to your wife; unfortunately I have none; I found only one who will probably will never be mine."

(1817, note to himself) "Sensual enjoyment without the union of souls is and remains beastial, after same one has no trace of an exalted feeling, rather remorse."

(1825, to Joseph Bernard) "That awful fourth floor, O God, without a wife, and what an existence; one is prey to every stranger."

(1827, to Hummel) "You are a lucky man... You have a wife who takes care of you, who is in love with you... (sighed) poor me..."

Gerhard Breuning's sister, Marie, related that Beethoven had often spoken to her mother about his desire for domesticity, and that "he regretted never to have married."[11]

Beethoven had a habit of underlining passages in favorite books which he found to be relevant to himself. It is significant therefore that in his copy of *The Odyssey* Beethoven underlined this passage:

> There is no better, no more blessed state
> Than when the wife and husband in accord
> Order their household lovingly. Then those
> Repine who hate them, those who wish them well
> Rejoice, and they themselves the most of all.[12]

And is it any surprise that his opera, *Fidelio*, had originally been titled *Conjugal Love,* and that it had love and marital commitment as one of its major themes?

Let us now consider the quote which Solomon felt proved Beethoven's fear of responsibility. On May 13, 1813, Beethoven wrote the following note to himself:

> To forego a great act which might have been and remains so—O what a difference compared with an unstudied life which often rose in my fancy—O fearful

---

[11]Marek, p. 238.
[12]*The Odyssey*, Vol. VI, pp. 230-234.

conditions which do not suppress my feeling for domesticity, but whose execution O God, God look down upon the unhappy B, do not permit it to last thus much longer...

About this quote, Solomon wrote: "His union with Antonie [Brentano, Solomon's choice for the Immortal Beloved] was barred... by unspecified terrors which overwhelmed the possibilities of a fruitful outcome." Solomon used this quote and Beethoven's use of the word *fearful* to show that Beethoven was afraid of domesticity, but is that true? Used in this context, *fearful* is a common nineteenth century term which meant *terrible*, not *frightening*, as in "He had fearful manners." Ries once commented that Beethoven had a "frightful beard." Did this mean that Ries found Beethoven's beard *terrifying*? Of course not, no more so than Beethoven found the conditions of his life terrifying. Terrible? Certainly. But frightening to the point that they did not allow him to give and accept love? Never.

No matter what deplorable situations befell Beethoven, nothing—not his deafness, nor poor health, nor dire financial straits, nor his Beloved's unchanging marital status—could make him cease wishing for a family of his own that he could establish with her. What kept him from realizing his desires were hardly "unspecified terrors." They were all real and difficult problems with which Beethoven had to contend: again, not *frightening*, but *terrible*. The ability for him to marry under these dreadfully adverse conditions was almost nil. He acknowledged that. Yet he still could not suppress his desire for marriage. He also was unwilling to simply settle for any wife, preferring no one rather than trying to replace the one he truly loved with an inferior substitute.

We must note that the quote did not end where Solomon ended it, and the rest of it, a reprimand Beethoven wrote to himself, is an interesting addendum:

> Learn to keep silent, O friend! Speech is like silver. But to hold one's peace at the right moment is pure gold.

With this last portion reinserted, the part quoted by Solomon takes on a new meaning. This journal entry shows no fear of marriage. Rather, Beethoven was lamenting the fact that terrible conditions *should* have extinguished his conjugal desires, but *they did not*. Unchecked even by the reality of his situation,

Beethoven had expressed these desires when he should not have done so—probably to his Beloved. He did not "keep silent" nor "hold his peace." Other circumstances explored in later chapters led this author to believe that Beethoven may have pressed the issue of marriage with his Beloved, and caused a brief rift in his relationship with her.

DOWN THE GARDEN PATH

As we have seen, it is unfortunately all too easy to "prove" the composer's lifelong inhibition against responsibility if quotes in Beethoven's letters are presented out of context. For example, consider what impression the following line might give if this author were to present it as evidence of Beethoven's fears in regard to Karl:

> I am, however, filled with anxiety, for I am the actual corporeal father of my dead brother's child...

It would be easy to point to Beethoven's statement that he was "filled with anxiety" about being Karl's father, and present the conclusion that this proved Beethoven feared the responsibility of raising Karl. Under these circumstances, the reader might be inclined to agree—it is, after all, a primary source, a direct quote from Beethoven, and therefore confirms the author's contention.

Except it does not.

Beethoven's meaning becomes clear only if the author is willing to reveal the circumstances under which this comment was written. In truth, this line was taken from a letter to an attorney, Johann Kanka of Prague, in which Beethoven was seeking his assistance to obtain money for some music he had written, which he needed for Karl's support. In this letter, Beethoven also expressed his frustration in dealing with his sister-in-law. The letter reads, in part:

> I sent to you, as desired, the receipt, and I beg you kindly to see to it for me, so that I may really receive the money before the 1st October, and indeed without deduction, which hitherto has always happened.... The said terzet soon appears in print, which is always to be preferred to all written music. You will therefore receive a printed copy, together with some other ill-bred children of mine.

I beg you meanwhile only to look at the really good in them, and to overlook chance weakness in these poor innocent ones.—I am, however, filled with anxiety, for I am the actual corporeal father of my dead brother's child, and in this I, also, could have brought the 2nd part of the Magic Flute into the world, just now I, likewise, have to do with a Queen of the Night.[13]

Now it is clear that it was money—or the lack of it—and the distress of dealing with his sister-in-law Johanna, rather than a fear of personal responsibility, which was the true source of Beethoven's anxiety in regard to Karl. It was his constant wish that he be able to adequately support and provide for his nephew, and his equally constant worry that he might not be able to do so. In addition, he worried about the control Johanna had over Karl, and whether he would be able to counteract her bad influence on the boy.

ANOTHER "PATH"

Beethoven diligently put away bank shares[14] for Karl—frequently putting himself into financial difficulties by doing so —and his pursuit of money was not for himself, but for his nephew. Personal greed was never his motive. But what if an author wanted to "prove" that Beethoven was avaricious (which is, unfortunately, another label which has been placed on the composer). Again, it would be easy for an author to point to several letters in which Beethoven demanded money in order to support a contention that Beethoven was greedy. At the same time, he or she might *suppress* other evidence (rather than only truncating it, as was done, above), such as Beethoven's simple lifestyle, and the inexpensive entertainments he pursued (reading, walking), which would *disprove* the author's contention. For example, Schindler accused Beethoven of being extravagant with money because the latter tended to take his meals in taverns rather than at home. Again, this might seem a logical assessment to a reader who had not been given Beethoven's reasons for his dining habits. Yet in the days before refrigeration, Beethoven's actions were prefectly reasonable. Unfortunately, Beethoven's explanation to

---

[13]Anderson, pp. 596-597.
[14]Beethoven managed to save an equivalent of $24,000 for his nephew.

Frau Streicher in January 1818 never appeared in Schindler's book:

> I never dine at home now unless I have a guest, for I don't want to buy so much for one person that three or four people can have their meals out of it too. I shall soon have my dear son Karl living with me, so it will be all the more necessary for me to be economical.[14]

Many erroneous statements—that Beethoven feared responsibility, that he used music as an escape from his relationships, that he was avaricious—have been made and perpetuated about Beethoven. How did these come about in the first place? We believe that the biographers who made these contentions were overreacting to an earlier tendency to portray Beethoven as a "heroic genius," a man without flaws. They wanted to "humanize" him. But goodness knows Beethoven had enough genuine faults without burdening his personality with ones he did *not* have!

How have these contentions been sustained? Unfortunately, too many biographers have accepted and built upon the observations of predecessors without ascertaining for themselves whether those statements were true. Although readers do this also, they cannot be held accountable, for they are at the mercy of the writer. Most do not have the time, and in many instances the ability, to check sources for validity, and thus must by necessity trust the writer's reports and observations. However, a reader should not assume that wide acceptance is synonymous with truth.

Sometimes, *caveat emptor* can apply as appropriately to a reader (a "buyer" of information) as it can to a buyer of merchandize. That said, the next chapter, dealing with Beethoven's doubts about his masculinity, has been aptly placed. Another trip down the garden path is at hand.

---

[14]Anderson, pp. 748-749.

❖ 5 ❖
Manhood in Doubt

"No one," Solomon asserted, "can be rejected so consistently without having in some way contributed to the process, without having actually assisted in bringing about an unconsciously desired result."[1] Because Solomon assumed that Beethoven had had numerous love affairs, he naturally concluded that there had followed an equal number of rejections, since none of those involvements had led to marriage. Yet as we have shown, both the affairs and the rejections, with very few exceptions, never happened at all. The vast majority of Beethoven's relationships were merely close friendships which never resulted in love affairs. It cannot be said that the women with whom he enjoyed these friendships ever rejected him, for most maintained relations with him to the end of his life. Therese Brunswick, Dorothea Ertmann, Antonie Brentano, and, of course, Anna Marie Erdödy, remained in his circle always. Others, such as Marie Bigot, Guilietta Guicciardi, Therese Malfatti, Bettina Brentano, and Amalie Sebald, simply faded away; but their departure from his life could not be considered rejection, and Beethoven suffered no trauma from their loss. Still others, such as Rahel Levin, Elizabeth Röckel, Elise von der Recke, and Julie von Vering, were never intimates , and when they were no longer a part of Beethoven's life, he did not even miss them. They were simply here and gone, without consequence.

---

[1]Solomon, p. 184.

As we also saw, only two women can be said to have rejected him: Magdalena Willmann, who did so cruelly; and Josephine Brunswick, who tried to do so as kindly as possible, given
that it was not her heart's desire to do so. Guilietta Guicciardi is
not included here because Beethoven never intended to marry
her; she could not reject what she was never offered. Some might
wish to include Therese Malfatti here, because it has long been
assumed that Beethoven had proposed marriage to her. In Chapter 6, we will explore the plausibility of that assumption and find
it lacking. Since there were no "consistent rejections"—only these
two—it follows that it was not his manhood Beethoven questioned, for he had no reason to do so. In fact, his ever-constant
relationship with Anna Marie who "despite this and that devilish
human-thing... remained always with [him]," surely convinced
Beethoven of his worth as a man.

Solomon added "The unbroken series of rejections must
have had a devastating cumulative effect on his pride, causing
painful doubts and self-questioning concerning the quality of his
manhood."[2] Once again we will find a severely truncated quote
raise its ugly and misleading head, once again see a quote ripped
from its context and twisted to fit an erroneous supposition. Once
again we are asked to take a trip down the garden path.

Solomon used this small portion of a line from Beethov-
en's 1812 *Tagebuch* (Journal) as evidence for his claim:

> You may no longer be a man, not for yourself, only for
> others.

It is important that the reader be able to examine the
entire quote, both what precedes Solomon's solitary line and what
follows it. The entry begins:

> Submission, absolute submission to your fate! Only this
> can give you the sacrifice—for the service business—Oh
> hard struggles!—

Here it is obvious that Beethoven was not writing about his
manhood, but about his work, his art, and the effect that the
"service business"—such as having to give lessons on demand—
had upon his music and himself.

---

[2]Solomon, p. 170.

The quote from the *Tagebuch* continues:

> Do everything, that still is to do—in order to prepare for
> the distant journey—you must yourself find all that
> your most blessed wish can offer, you must force it to
> your will—keep always of the same mind. You may no
> longer be a man, not for yourself, only for others—for
> you there is no longer happiness except in yourself, in
> your art—O God! give me the strength, to conquer
> myself, nothing must chain me to life—

There is admittedly a despairing tone to this entry, but it
also is filled with frustration and anger. Does it at any point refer
to feelings of doubt about his masculinity? It does not, not only
because Beethoven had not suffered from constant rejection
which could have led to such doubts, but also because there were
other issues from which Beethoven *did* suffer which gave him
reason enough to feel frustrated and angry. These included the
unconscionable negligence of patrons and publishers in paying
the composer for his work and their failure to follow-through on
promises of financial support, the Viennese people's inability to
consistently appreciate his musical efforts, and, most critically,
the demands made on him and his time—such as for lessons—
which he felt interfered with what was more important: composition. In relation to having to deal with the "service business," he
often had unflattering things to say about Vienna, referring to it
as the "Austrian Barbary" a place where the uncultured, crude,
coarse, and demanding abounded.

Of course, we have no way of knowing exactly when in
1812 this entry was written, although his reference to preparation for the "distant journey" was probably to the Bohemian spa
at Teplitz, Czechoslovakia, and thus the entry was made before
the summer. We also can surmise the circumstances under which
it was written—and *why* it was written— using what we know of
events in Beethoven's life that year. Now that we may consider
the quote in its entirety, we find that it is markedly similar in tone
to several notes and letters he wrote to his friend, Zmeskall, early
that year:

February 2, 1812:

> Life here in this Austrian Barbary is a cursed thing—I
> now go mostly to the Swan as I cannot get away from
> importunate folk at other inns.

> If, dear Z, it were only a matter of creating a product, all
> would be well, but in addition to implant in bad soil—
> This morning I am the slave of A(rchduke)—[3]

His complaints to Zmeskall about constantly having to
deal with annoying, demanding people, as well as contending
with being the "slave" of Archduke Rudolph who wanted lessons
from him, clearly show us the circumstances under which the line
Solomon quoted: "You may no longer be a man, not for yourself,
only for others," as well as the rest of the entry, came to be written.
Beethoven felt his life was not his own. He was the "slave" of the
Archduke and all the other people he found so importunate, thus
not a man for himself, but only for others. His frustration, echoed
in the *Tagebuch* entry, is evident in the next letter to Zmeskall,
written only a short time later:

> February 19, 1812:
> Dear Z,
>
> Only yesterday did I receive a written notice that the
> Archduke will pay his share in notes of redemption— I
> beg of you now to note down for me approximately what
> you said on Sunday so that I may send it to the other
> two— It is felt that I should be given a certificate that
> the Archduke pays in redemption bonds, but I think this
> unnecessary, the more since these courtiers in spite of
> their apparent friendship for me say that my demands
> are not just!!!!! Oh heaven help me to bear this; I am no
> Hercules who can help Atlas bear up the world or do it
> in his stead.— It was only yesterday that I heard in
> detail how beautifully Herr Baron Krupt had spoken
> about me at Zizius's, had judged me— Never mind, dear
> Z, it will not be for much longer that I shall continue the
> shameful manner in which I am living here. Art, the
> persecuted one, finds everywhere an asylum. Did not
> Daedalus, shut up in the labyrinth, invent the wings
> which carried him upwards into the air; and I, too, will
> find them, these wings—
>
> Always your
> Beethoven[4]

---

[3]Anderson, p. 356.
[4]Anderson, p. 358.

The "shameful manner" in which he was living referred not only to the fact that his music was sometimes misunderstood and received with little warmth, but that he was often denied the financial support promised him. His art was therefore "the persecuted one."

From the timing, tone, and content of these letters we may infer that the entry in his journal was written at the same time. It is little wonder that he felt he was "chained to this life." He was, by the *needs* of life—that is, for food, shelter, clothing. Certainly he wished not to be. He wanted to live only for his art. But as a human being with physical needs, this was not possible. Thus he could not be a man "for himself," only for others, because he was dependent upon them for his livelihood, as he said, their "slave." Therefore he exhorted himself to "submit to his fate" in order to deal with the "service business," a necessary evil in terms of his survival.

MONEY WORRIES

The war had devalued Austrian currency to a third or fourth of its original value, and Beethoven's patrons—with the exception of Archduke Rudolph—usually did not pay the composer with redemption bonds which were worth their full amount in silver. On top of that, Beethoven often was placed in the position of having to fight for payment of his contracted annuity, although under the terms of the agreement he should have been able to expect prompt, full payment. The *Tagebuch* entry also reflected a *recurring* problem, one not confined to early 1812. Another incident in Beethoven's financial life, briefly touched on earlier, was the unexpected death of Prince Kinsky, one of the suppliers of the annuity.

When Beethoven arrived in Prague in July 1812, Prince Kinsky gave him sixty ducats as payment on what was due him, and planned to direct his treasurer in Vienna to pay Beethoven the remainder when the composer returned to the city. Unfortunately, Kinsky was thrown from his horse shortly thereafter and died, and the order was never delivered. Initially, Beethoven appealed to the Prince's widow to fulfill her late husband's contract and pay the amount due him. She referred the matter to the trustees of her late husband's estate. They wanted to keep to the provisions of the current devaluation act, which would have reduced the sum to one-fifth of its original amount. Beethoven felt this was unfair, and after writing several unprofitable letters to the Princess, brought suit against Kinsky's estate through his attorney and long-time acquaintance, Johann Kanka of Prague. Beethoven wrote numerous letters between 1812 and 1815 in regard to this problem, and it caused him great frustration. To the Archduke Rudolph he wrote, December 1812:

> Since Sunday I have been ailing, although mentally, it is true more than physically.[5]

He followed that with another letter less than a month later:

> January 1813: As for my health, it is pretty much the same, the more so as moral factors are affecting it and these apparently are not very speedily removed; the more so as I must now look to myself alone for help.[6]

Lest there be any misunderstanding, the "moral factors" to which Beethoven was referring had nothing to do with Antonie Brentano but rather with the Kinsky lawsuit. Other letters of his show this clearly. To Franz Brunswick he wrote in the summer, 1813:

> I am sorry to have to tell you that this untidiness still haunts me everywhere and that nothing has been decided in my affairs. Presumably this disastrous war will hold up the finally settlement or render my affairs even worse. — Oh fatal decree, as seductive as a siren! To resist it I should have had ... my arms bound fast... to prevent me from signing.[7]

The Kinsky lawsuit dragged on nearly three years. The sentiments first voiced in the *Tagebuch* entry were reflected in the following letters. The first he wrote to Johann Kanka, September 19, 1814:

> Indeed you may easily conceive how I am sighing and longing to see the Kinsky affair brought to an early and satisfactory conclusion— I beg you — I entreat you — I throw myself at your feet, into your arms, I throw my arms around your neck — I really don't know what I

---

[5]Anderson, p. 395.
[6]Anderson, p. 401
[7]Anderson, p. 421.

shall do or not do, whether I shall be struck dumb or
again overflow in a rush of talking, etc., etc., etc. Do
conclude this affair, begin and finish it again — at last
— completely — so that we may say Finis — End — the
End—[8]

In another letter to Johann Kanka, Beethoven even para-
phrased the *Tagebuch* entry he had written earlier. The connection between them is evident:

> You yourself know that a man's spirit, *the active creative
> spirit, must not be tied down to the wretched necessities
> of life. All this business robs me of many other things
> conducive to a happy existence.* ... How ready people are
> to rob the poor artist of what they owe him in other ways.
> Lend wings, dear friend, to the slow feet of justice.[9]
> (emphasis ours)

The Kinsky affair was finally settled in Beethoven's favor
April 19, 1815. Because Beethoven always hated the business
aspect of his art, we can imagine the anguish that the Kinsky
affair caused him. Clearly the *Tagebuch* entry reflected serious
money issues, and the annoying demands of day-to-day living,
and did not relate in any way to doubts about his manhood.

A MUSICAL DISAPPOINTMENT

It must be added that the despair Beethoven felt—and
noted in his *Tagebuch*—over money matters and demands on his
time, was coupled at this time by the failure of his *Piano Concerto
#5 Op. 73* which was (unbelievably!) coldly received at its pre-
mier, just eight days before Beethoven wrote his February 19,
1812 letter to Zmeskall. It should be little wonder that the miserable reception of this magnificent work at this time had contributed to his frustration and his overall despondent tone in the
journal entry. Beethoven did not dash off his compositions over a
weekend. Most of his pieces—and this *Emperor* concerto was no
exception—took years of rewriting before he was satisfied with
them.Thus, knowing how much of himself Beethoven put into his
music, it should be no surprise that when it was misunderstood
or ill-received by the public, it angered and dismayed him—as

---

[8]Anderson, p. 469.
[9]Anderson, pp. 473-474.

such a reception would any artist who believed strongly in his work. That he was able to withstand these occasional crushing blows to his ego shows us how very resilient his self-esteem was, for he kept on producing music to please himself as an artist, having absolute faith that someday his work—as dear to his heart as any person ever was—would be appreciated for the remarkably unique music that it was.

DEAFNESS: A SOURCE OF DOUBT?

In this 1987 book, *Beethoven Essays*, Solomon attempted to further his argument that Beethoven doubted his masculinity by linking these anxieties to his deafness. He first suggested that the ear, because it protrudes from the body, has been viewed in psychosexual literature as a phallic symbol. In his argument, it would follow, then, that a man such as Beethoven who had become deaf—that is, lost the use of his ears—would subconsciously see himself as having suffered a form of castration. If this psychoanalysis is correct, one cannot help but wonder how a hearing-impaired *woman* would consider herself. Certainly hearing loss can have a profoundly detrimental impact on one's sense of self in a social setting. In Beethoven's day, it would have been an even far more isolating a handicap than it is today in our technologically superior society. Yet we see no need, nor any valid reason, to give this trauma a sexual bent.

FEW REJECTIONS, MANY DOUBTS?

One would be hard-pressed to find many men—or women, for that matter—who, in the course of their lifetimes, had not suffered several rejections from members of the opposite sex. Yet very few of them come to question their manhood—or womanhood—as a result. Since Beethoven had not engaged in many romances, there were consequently no "unbroken series of rejections" with which he was forced to deal. And since the quote used as "evidence" to show that he doubted his manhood referred to nothing of the sort, it confidently can be concluded that at this particular time it was not romantic heartbreak that plagued Beethoven. It is an insult to him to suggest that his masculinity was ever in question, by himself or anyone else.

Certainly Beethoven often felt lonely isolation as a result of his deafness. Anyone who has known a person with hearing impairment unrelieved by modern technology, knows the devastating effects such a loss can have. In Beethoven's time, there were no schools to teach lip-reading, or sign language, no way for him to restore his connections to the world at large other than his cumbersome conversation books. Regardless, no physical affliction ever made Beethoven doubt himself or his masculinity. Nor had his experiences with Magdalena and Josephine plagued him with anxieties about his worth as a man. The proof for these doubts simply is not there. In fact, it was his constant belief in himself, his lack of self-doubt, not only as an artist with great ability, but as a man who could overcome any hardship that upheld him through trying times. He may have faltered on occasion, but he never fell. In the Kinsky affair, as later in his battle over his nephew's guardianship, Beethoven proved his strength of will, never abandoning his course, never doubting his convictions, no matter how many years of struggle he had to endure in order to achieve what he believed in his heart was just and right. No man who doubted his maculinity, the very core of his being, could have persevered with such tenacity. It was precisely this strength of character that sustained him through all the dark disappointments others inflicted upon him, financially and emotionally in terms of his art... and, sometimes—but not as often as we have been led to believe—his heart.

❀ 6 ❀

The Marriage Project

Stephan von Breuning assumed that when Beethoven asked their mutual friend, Franz Wegeler, to find his baptismal certificate, it indicated that the composer had a "marriage project" at hand. The sole mention of such a plan was in a letter from Breuning to Wegeler, written in July or August 1810, which said

> Beethoven tells me at least once a week that he intends to write to you; but personally I believe his marriage project has fallen through and for this reason he no longer feels the lively desire to thank you for your trouble in getting him the baptismal certificate.[1]

We see from this letter that Beethoven had not *told* Breuning that there was, indeed, such a project in the works. We know only that Breuning *believed* there had been such a plan and that, for some reason, it had not come to fruition. We do not know what caused Breuning to come to this conclusion, but we can make an educated guess. We do know from the letter presented below that Beethoven had mentioned to Breuning his interest in obtaining a copy of his baptismal certificate via Wegeler, because Breuning had a "running account" with him, and Breuning would be instrumental in getting Wegeler reimbursed for incurred expenses. Beethoven may have told Breuning only that he wanted the certificate without telling him why. Breuning then simply

---

[1]Wegeler & Ries, p. 152.

assumed it was because Beethoven was planning to get married. To Breuning, this would seem a logical assumption, because obtaining a marriage license would be the reason most adults would need their baptismal certificates. Beethoven, however, had another reason for wanting it which he did not deem important enough to share with Breuning.

Beethoven's letter to Wegeler, written May 2, 1810, does not bear out any "marriage project" as the reason he was requesting the certificate. He wrote:

> I am sure you will not refuse me a friendly request, if I beg you to see to my certificate of baptism.—Whatever expenses you incur, as Steffen Breuning has a running account with you, you can at once pay yourself, and I can settle everything here with Steffan,—If you yourself think it worth the trouble to hunt up the matter, and care to make the journey from Coblenz to Bonn, put everything down to my account.—But there is one thing that you must bear in mind, namely that a brother was born before me who was also called Ludwig, only with the additional name Maria, but he died. In order to fix my age beyond doubt, this brother must first be found, inasmuch as I already know that in this respect a mistake has been made by others and I have been said to be older than I am—I have lived for a long time without, unfortunately, knowing myself how old I am.— I had a family register but it has been lost—heaven knows how— So do not be angry if I commend this matter very warmly to you, viz., to find out about the Ludwig Maria and the present Ludwig who came after him.—The sooner you send the certificate the greater will be my obligation.—[2]

Wegeler was one of Beethoven's closest friends. If the latter had been contemplating marriage, surely he would have told Wegeler his news. Are we to assume that Beethoven confided in Breuning and not in Wegeler? No. From Beethoven's letter, it is clear that his reason—which he stated twice—for asking Wegeler to find his baptismal certificate was simply to learn his correct age. He had long assumed that he had been born in 1772. Early arguments attributed this to either a clerical error to his father, claiming that the elder van Beethoven had deliberately

[2]Anderson, p. 270.

misrepresented his son's age when he was a boy, decreasing it by two years to make him seem more a child prodigy. Some writers contend that there had been an error of only one year, with his December birthday and an older deceased brother also named Ludwig, contributing to the confusion. To Maximilian Friedrich, Elector of Cologne, Beethoven had written on his dedication to the Elector of *Drei Sonaten für Klavier (Three Sonatas for Piano)*, October 14, 1783, "I have now reached my eleventh year..." He was actually almost twelve, but it was customary at that time to describe one's age in respect to the year to come. Thus "eleventh year" meant he thought he was ten, and would be eleven in December. He remained convinced that his birth year had been 1772 for many years, at least until he was in his forties, and he may never have known or admitted otherwise. The actual cause for this confusion is unclear, although some have suggested that all his life Beethoven wished to appear younger than he actually was. If so, why would he deduct a mere two years, which is so insignificant.

As he said, if Beethoven had his family register, he would have known his actual birth date and would not have felt the need to ask Wegeler to find his correct baptismal certificate. What had prompted his interest is unknown, but had he wanted to marry, it was not necessary for him to ask Wegeler to send him another copy of his certificate. He simply could have used the baptismal certificate *he already owned* which Ferdinand Ries had sent him *just four years before*. Ries wrote

> Some friends of Beethoven wished to know exactly the day of his birth. I gave myself much trouble when I was at Bonn in 1806 to find his certificate of baptism; I was at last successful and sent it to Vienna. He would never speak about his age.[3]

The certificate which Ries had sent him had been dated correctly, listing his date of birth as 1770. Although Beethoven did not believe the date was correct, this was irrelevant to the issue of marriage for *any* certificate would have allowed Beethoven to procure a marriage license without having Wegeler go through the trouble of locating another copy. Beethoven's explicit instructions to Wegeler about locating the "right" Ludwig was, in his mind, simply to avoid another mistake being made. Beethoven

---

[3]Wegeler & Ries, p. 120-121.

continued to believe that the 1770 date belonged to his older brother, Ludwig Maria, who was born and died in 1769. Naturally, all sorts of deep psychological causes, including a morbid attachment to his deceased sibling, have been given as reasons for this behavior. To this author, Beethoven's search for a 1772 birthdate seems only an indication of his inherent stubbornness and unwillingness to admit that, in this instance, he could be wrong.

If the "present Ludwig" had been contemplating marriage, locating the correct certificate would not have been at all important; he could have married regardless whether he was 38 or 40 or 42. Who would have known otherwise, or cared? Clearly, his purpose for making this request of Wegeler was to find out, once and for all, *as he said*, his correct age, believing that there *had* to be a certificate with his name on it that read 1772. Wegeler did send it to him, as Ries had, with the correct date, 1770, on it. Frustrated in his attempt to get a "correct" certificate, Beethoven wrote "1772" on the back and did not pursue the issue again. It was probably his view that Wegeler had ignored his instructions and failed to separate him from Ludwig Maria,thereby sending him what Beethoven thought was yet another incorrect certificate. If Beethoven had been annoyed that Wegeler had not heeded his instructions, it is little wonder that Beethoven had no "lively desire" to thank Wegeler for his trouble in finding the certificate.

AN URGENT REQUEST

Wegeler remarked on the "urgency" of Beethoven's request, and Beethoven's willingness to underwrite the cost of Wegeler's trip from Koblenz (a.k.a. Coblenz) to Bonn. It is difficult to see any true "urgency" in the letter, other than Beethoven writing "The sooner you send the certificate the greater will be my obligation." That does not sound terribly urgent.

There are several points of which the reader should be aware. First, the trip from Bonn to Koblenz was only approximately 30 miles. According to *Dutens Journal of Travel* published in 1782, it was a trip that took about nine hours. The Beethoven family had made excursions to the town of Coblenz several times during Beethoven's youth. Such a trip would not have cost an exorbitant amount. If one is not made aware of this, Wegeler's remark makes it sound as if the trip were an exceedingly long and arduous one. Naturally Beethoven would not ask his friend to do him a favor without offering to pay any expenses incurred as a result of it: Beethoven knew from his family's experience, for example, that the road from Bonn to Koblenz was a toll road.

In asking Wegeler to do him the favor, Beethoven said "If you should yourself think it worth while to investigate the matter for me and make the trip from Koblenz to Bonn, charge everything to me." Obviously the matter was not so urgent that Beethoven did not give his friend the opportunity to gracefully refuse.

THE (PRESUMED) OBJECT OF HIS AFFECTIONS

Biographers who knew of Beethoven's friendly association with the Malfatti family at this time, immediately—like Breuning—made some assumptions of their own: that the object of Beethoven's affections and marriage project was the young Therese Malfatti, niece of Beethoven's doctor, who was some twenty years younger than Beethoven. In 1956, Paul Nettl wrote "It may be worthwhile mentioning that the beautiful third *Sonata, Op. 69*, reveals, according to tradition, the master's love affair to Therese Malfatti." The Opus 69 *Sonata in A major* was written in 1807, a year before he made the acquaintance of Dr. Malfatti, and two years before he became friendly with the Malfatti family and Therese. Once again we see the erroneous path down which such traditions lead us.

While Beethoven certainly enjoyed the company of both Therese and the entire Malfatti family it is unlikely that he would have formed such a close attachment to young Therese alone. She "took life so easily," was spoiled, coquettish, and hardly an intellectual or emotional match for such a man. Almost all of Beethoven's correspondence was with the Malfatti family, rather than with Therese, or else was in the form of a note to Gleichenstein, who at the time was serving as Beethoven's secretary, directing him to convey a message to Therese or the Malfattis.

A letter written to Therese only a few days before the one to Wegeler—at the very end of April or beginning of May, 1810—does not, as even Thayer admits, sound like the letter of man about to propose marriage. Surprisingly, biographer Richard Specht writing in 1933, said of this letter that in it Beethoven reveals his trembling heart, his quivering hopes, his fears, his inner solitude, and his touching efforts to lay bare his world to the fickle, fascinating creature.[4]

He *does*? Where Specht got that interpretation of the following letter is anyone's guess. There certainly is no evidence of any trembling or quivering. More than anything else, this was a letter that began to close the door on a relationship which was neither intense nor satisfying. Both letters, the one to Therese and the other to Wegeler, were written at virtually the same time. Why would Beethoven have requested a baptismal certificate for the purpose of marrying on almost the same day as he was saying goodbye to the object of his matrimonial plans? If there had been any "marriage project," it could not have involved Therese. Following is the text of Beethoven's only letter to Fraulein Malfatti. Despite Specht's interpretation, it is not at all heart-wrenching:

> You received herewith, honored Therese, what I promised, [some music] and had it not been for urgent hindrances, you would have received more, in order to show you that I always offer more to my friends than I actually promise—I hope and have every reason to believe that you are nicely occupied and as pleasingly entertained—but I hope not too much, so that you may also think of us.—It would probably be expecting too much of you, or overrating my own value, if I ascribed to you "people are not only together when they are in each other's company, also the Distant One, the Absent One lives in us." Who would ascribe anything of the kind to the lively T. who takes life so easily?—[5]

If anything, Beethoven here sounds exasperated, for the immature Therese took life a little bit too "easily" for his taste. This tone continues in the next part of the letter.

> Do not forget the pianoforte among your occupations, or, indeed, music generally, you have such fine talent for it, why not cultivate it? You who have such feeling for all that is beautiful and good, why will you not make use of it in order to learn the more perfect things in so beautiful an art, which always reflects its light upon us—

---

[4]Specht, pp. 160-161.
[5]Anderson, pp. 272-274.

As Beethoven noted later to the Giannatasio sisters, he "would not be able to love a woman who did not appreciate his art."[6] How, then, could he be in love with Therese who did not share Beethoven's love for music, and took it—and her own talent for it—as lightly as she did life in general? Beethoven reveals his disappointment in her lack of interest for those things which held so much meaning for him, and knew already that he was "expecting too much of [her]" for her to behave otherwise. Perhaps he once thought he might be able to elevate her to his level, but soon realized he had little hope of accomplishing it.

> I live very solitarily and quietly, although now and then lights might awaken me; but since you all went away from here, I feel in me a void, which cannot be filled; my art, even, otherwise so faithful to me, has not been able to gain any triumph—

His use of the word "all"—"since you all went away from here"—is noteworthy, since he was not referring just to missing Therese, but her family in whom he found comfort and happiness at a time when his life was devoid of joy. He then shifted to more mundane topics. An earlier note to Gleichenstein indicated he had offered to help the family select and order a piano. In it, Beethoven wrote: "As Frau von M[alfatti] told me yesterday that she wanted after all to choose another piano at Schanz's today, I would like her to give me full liberty to choose one."[7] We see from this note that the request had come from Frau Malfatti and not from Therese. His letter to Therese continued:

> Your piano is ordered and you will soon receive it— What a difference you will have found between the treatment of the theme I improvised one evening, and the way in which I recently wrote it down for you. explain that for yourself, but don't take too much punch to help you—

Typical Beethoven then moved to more philosophical issues, probably more important to himself than to Therese:

> How lucky you are, to be able to go so soon to the country, I cannot enjoy that happiness until the 8th. I am happy

---

[6]From the diary of Fanny Giannatasio, June 15, 1817.
[7]Anderson, p. 269.

as a child at the thought of wandering among clusters of bushes, in the woods, among trees, herbs, rocks, nobody can love the country as I do—for do not forests, trees, rocks re-echo that for which mankind longs—

Therese obviously had complained about Beethoven giving her music which she found too difficult to play, prompting him to write:

> Soon you will receive other compositions of mine, in which you will not have to complain much about difficulties—

It is likely that the simple melody *Für Elise*, practiced by many beginning piano students even today, had been composed for her in response to her complaint. The score, written in 1810, had been found among Therese's personal effects.

Again, in an vain attempt to stimulate her appreciation for the arts on a higher plane than she did—and on par with his own enjoyment—he offered her some reading material for her sojourn in the country:

> Have you read Goethe's *Wilhelm Meister*, the Schlegel translation of Shakespeare, one has much leisure in the country, and it will perhaps please you if I send you these works.—I happen to have an acquaintance in your neighborhood, so perhaps I shall come early one morning and spend half an hour at your house, and be off again, notice that I wish to bore you as little as possible.— Commend me to the good wishes of your father, your mother, although I can claim no right yet for doing so,— and the same, likewise, to cousin M[athilde]. Farewell, honored T. I wish you all that is good and beautiful in life. Remember me and willingly—forget the nonsense— be convinced that no one more than myself can desire to know that your life is joyous, happy even though you take no interest in
>
> your most devoted servant and friend
Beethoven
>
> NB It would be really nice on your part to send me a few lines to say in what way I can be of service to you here—

How on earth can such sentiments be viewed as indicative of a man and woman in love with each other? Would a man want to take as his bride a woman who felt that he bored her, or took no interest in him, or hardly ever thought of him? Would a woman in love with a man have to be coaxed into writing to him? Why on earth would a man consider marrying a woman who gave him no joy? Not even a man who wanted to be married as much as Beethoven could be that desperate.

It is also interesting to note that elsewhere in Beethoven's letter to Wegeler regarding his baptismal certificate, the composer had written

> If I had not read somewhere that a man should not voluntarily quit this life...I would have left this earth long ago. Oh, life is so beautiful, but to me it is forever poisoned.

Beethoven was obviously so deliriously happy about getting married that his thoughts turned to suicide. This is hardly the attitude of a man in love and hoping to marry!

In May 1810, the same month in which he wrote his letter to Wegeler and Therese, Beethoven also wrote a revealing little note to his friend, Zmeskall:

> Don't be vexed with me for sending you this little sheet of paper — Are you not aware of the kind of situation in which I am placed, just as Hercules was formerly with Queen Omphale???[8]

According to legend, Hercules was placed in bondage to Omphale, Queen of Lydia, by the Delphic oracle as punishment for sacking the kingdom of Pylos. Queen Omphale treated Hercules shamefully, forcing him to dress in women's clothing and take on women's chores, and ordering him to do menial and degrading tasks. Is this how Beethoven felt about his association with Therese Malfatti? If so, this is a very negative view of their relationship. Whoever Beethoven had in mind for the role of Omphale, it was a woman whose treatment of him he did not enjoy, and wished to escape. He certainly would not have placed himself in even greater bondage to her by actually marrying the woman!

Beethoven possibly wrote a final letter to Therese about three months later, July or August 1810, although there is some question as to whether this letter had actually been addressed to

---

[8]Anderson, p. 274.

her.[9] If it had, she may have asked him why he was behaving odd-
ly toward her, perhaps coolly, and he wanted to assure her that
it was no fault of hers.

There were no other letters found addressed solely to
Therese. With this letter Beethoven was able to make a clean
break with her. Although her uncle remained his doctor, letters
about the Malfattis written to Gleichenstein (who had married
Therese's older sister, Anna) indicate he had no further personal
interaction with the immediate family.

Perhaps Therese had cared for Beethoven in some way,
but it is obvious from his letters that Beethoven cared much less
for her than most biographers are willing to admit. While it is possible that he may have briefly entertained an idea that she might
be more to him than just a friend—an idea borne out of the devastating quarrel with an important woman in his life the year before—that notion seems not to have been very serious nor lasted
very long. They had a vast disparity in their interests and outlook
on life. She appears to have had a demanding nature which would
have suffocated him. It quickly became obvious to Beethoven that
Therese would not make a very satisfactory wife for him, and
prompted him to extricate himself from the relationship as gently
as possible. All biographical contentions and scholarly sputterings
to the contrary, the truth is that Therese had never rejected Beethoven; *he* had rejected *her*. In light of the fact that Beethoven's
interest in Therese was never anything more than cursory, there
is something tragically comic in Specht's conclusion that

> the real tragedy is in the fact that such loves and the con-
> stantly recurring cycle of irresistible ardor and weary
> renunciation were typical of him.

Is what Specht said a fact? No, it is not, but other biographers have echoed this sentiment time and again. We have
already seen, by taking a close look at the women supposedly on
Beethoven's "list" of loves, that no such recurring cycle ever existed. Unfortunately, many statements such as this one worm
their way into the realm of fact—where they really have no business—purely because they have had a number of repetitions in
scholarly works.

---

[9]Unger believed that the letter usually thought to have been written to Therese
had, in fact, been addressed to Countess Erdödy. This author agrees that his
conjecture makes sense based on the tone and content of the letter. Its text can
be found in Chapter 27, *The Quarrel... and Forgiveness.*

Although Therese's niece once remarked, many years later, that Beethoven had loved her aunt and had wished to marry her, this was purely wishful thinking on Therese's part. Perhaps *she* had wanted to marry *him*, but he did not have the same inclination. Certainly Beethoven's closest friends were unaware of any strong feelings he had for her, and as we have read, his letter to her was far from passionate and certainly showed none of the "irresistable ardor" so evident to Specht. Unfortunately, this did not prevent biographers from assuming otherwise, and magnifying the episode out of proportion. In fact, several went so far as to indicate that this alleged affair caused Beethoven to sink into a severe depression, and precipitated an estrangement with the entire Malfatti family. This statement ignores several facts: that Beethoven's depression lasted only through early 1810 as a reaction to his devasting quarrel with Anna Marie Erdödy the year before, that his mood brightened considerably by the spring when he once again became Anna Marie's neighbor and despite the fact that he had ended whatever tepid relationship he had had with Therese Malfatti. One other fact to consider is that Dr. Malfatti remained Beethoven's physician until at least the summer of 1812—two years after the alleged affair had ended—and most likely all the way into 1817. Yet Specht went on to say that Malfatti was

> so embittered against the Master presumably by this love affair

(once again we find the distortions inherent in too much presumption)

> that he at first refused to come to [Beethoven's] deathbed

(sixteen years is a long time to hold a grudge)

> and finally obeyed his importunate call so late that even his vaunted skill could no longer delay the end. It is said that otherwise he might have been able to save his threatened life or at least have extended it for a considerable time. Thus the purest of all artists died, perhaps prematurely, owing to the coquetry of a heartless woman.

This would be an appropriate ending for a Gothic romance, but hardly belongs in a scholarly biography. While it is true that a rift had occurred between Malfatti and Beethoven, it had nothing to do with Therese.

When on his deathbed, Beethoven sent for Dr. Malfatti, Malfatti's reply was "Say to Beethoven that he, as a master of harmony, must know that I must also live in harmony with my colleagues." We note that Malfatti said "colleagues" and not "family." Beethoven's letters show that his relationship with this physician actually was strained by his animosity toward Malfatti professionally, rather than personally.

To say that Beethoven was not fond of doctors in general is an understatement. So many of them had given him false hope about the recovery of his hearing that understandably, he did not trust them. He was a man who always spoke his mind, and he was not ususually very diplomatic when he did so. He frequently expressed his low opinion about these "charlatans and quacks," those "senseless physicians" who "cheated him year after year"— as he wrote in his *Heiligenstadt Testament*. This attitude did not endear him to the physicians who attended him. To Anna Marie Erdödy he wrote, in June 1817: "I changed doctors, because my own doctor, a wily Italian (Johann Malfatti), had powerful secondary motives where I was concerned and lacked both honesty and intelligence." The doctor replacing Malfatti suited Beethoven no better. In September 1817, he wrote to Zmeskall: "Today I must pay another visit to the doctor, of whose stupidity I am now getting thoroughly tired."[10] Even Thayer wrote that Beethoven had "quarreled with and insulted Malfatti," making no mention of Therese as being at the core of the insult or quarrel. Notes from various other doctors who came into Beethoven's life through the years confirm that Beethoven had been disgrunted with them on occasion, as well.[11]

At any rate, we can be sure that Therese Malfatti, regardless of how much of a "heartless coquette" she was, was not responsible for Beethoven's premature death, and certainly not the object of Beethoven's alleged—and in all likelihood, nonexistent—"marriage project."

---

[10]Anderson, pp. 709-710.

[11]Medical care in the 19th century was certainly poor, and the treatments sound outrageous and barbaric to us today. But, to be fair, the doctors were as skilled as the limited medical knowledge of the time permitted. Beethoven was no model patient. He frequently changed his prescriptions to suit himself. The medicines were so ineffective, however, that he probably did not do himself significant harm in doing so.

❧ PART II ❧

PRIMARY EVIDENCE FOR
THE IMMORTAL BELOVED

INTRODUCTION

To make it easier for the reader to refer to portions of the famous letter to the "Immortal Beloved," it is presented here in its entirely. Sieghard Brandenburg and the Beethovenhaus in Bonn provided the letter's facsimile and transcription, and the document was translated by Virginia Beahrs in 1990 with the assistance of Lori Dormer. The translation appeared in the Journal of the American Beethoven Society in that year. This translation is a literal one, which preserves Beethoven's characteristic punctuation, orthography, and nuances of language—even if archaic —which is as close as possible to the original meaning. This is not meant in any way to denigrate the work of Emily Anderson who did an extensive study of Beethoven's handwriting in order to do her translations, and to whom the English-speaking world owes gratitude for her formidable accomplishment.

Many translations attempted to "clean up" Beethoven's capitalization, punctuation, spelling, and, most critically, actual language which, in some cases, inadvertently distorted the original meaning. In some versions, different words and word orders were used—perhaps to make Beethoven seem more "literate." We will note any significant differences between this translation and others, if pertinent to our discussion of the Immortal Beloved.

July 6 in the morning—

My angel, my all, myself.—only a few words today and indeed with pencil (with yours)—only tomorrow will my lodging be positively fixed—what a worthless on such —why this deep grief where necessity speaks—can our love exist except by sacrifices,by not demanding every- thing, can you change it that you are not completely mine, I am not completely yours—O God look upon beautiful Nature and calm your soul over what must be—Love demands everything and completely with good reason, so it is for me with you, for you with me— only you forget so easily, that I must live for myself and for you, were we wholly united, you would feel this pain- fulness just as little as I—My trip was frightful. I arrived here only at 4 o'clock yesterday morning, because they lacked horses the postal service chose another route, but what a horrible way, at the next to last sta- tion they warned me about traveling at night, made me afraid of a forest, but that only provoked me and I was mistaken; the coach had to break down on the terrible route a mere bottomless country road—without two such postillions as I had, I would have been stranded on the way. Esterhazy on the other customary route here, had the same fate with 8 horses as I with four.—still I had some pleasure again, as always, whenever I fortunately survive something—Now quickly to interior from exterior—we will probably see each other soon; even today I cannot convey to you observations I made during these few days about my life—were our hearts always close together I would of course make none of the sort. My heart is full of much to tell you—Ah—there are still moments when I find that speech is nothing at all— cheer up—remain my faithful only treasure, my all, as I for you, the rest the gods must send, what must and should be—

> Your faithful
> Ludwig—

Evening Monday the 6th July—

You are suffering you my dearest creature—just now I notice[1] that letters must be posted very early in the morning, Mondays—Thursdays—the only days on which the mail-coach goes from here to K. —You are suffering— Ah, wherever I am, you are with me, I say to myself and to you arrange so that I can live with you, what a life!!!! as it is!!!! without you—persecuted by the kindness of people here and there, which I think I want to deserve just as little as I deserve it—Humility of man to man— it pains me—and when I regard myself in the framework of the universe, what am I and what is he whom one calls the Greatest—and yet—herein is again is the divine spark of man—I weep when I think that you will probably not receive the first news of me until Satur- day—as much as you love me—I love you even more deeply—never hide yourself from me—good night—as one bathing[two long words crossed out] I must go to sleep. O God—so near! so far! is not our love a true heavenly edifice—but also firm, like the firmament.

Good morning on July 7—

While still in bed thoughts thrust themselves toward you my eternally beloved, now and then happy, then again sad, awaiting Fate if it will grant us a favorable hearing—I can only live wholly with you or not at all, yes I have resolved to stray about in the distance until I can fly into your arms and can call myself entirely at home, can send my soul embraced by you into the realm of spirits—yes unfortunately it must be—you will compose yourself all the more since you know my faithfulness to you, never can another own my heart, never—never—O God why have to separate oneself from what one loves so, and yet my life in V.[ienna] as it is now a miserable life—your love makes me the most happy and the most unhappy at once —at my age I would need some comformity, regularity of life—can this exist in our relations? —Angel, I have just been told that the mail-coach goes every day—therefore I must

---

[1]We must note here that all other translations have here "learned," a significant discrepancy that will be considered in Chapter 8.

close at once so that you may receive the l.[etter] at once—Be calm, only by calm contemplation of our existence can we reach our goal to live together—be calm—love me—today—yesterday—what yearning with tears for you—you—my life—my all—farewell Oh love me on and on—never misjudge the most faithful heart of your beloved

L.

forever yours

forever mine

forever us

THE THEORY AND THE CRITERIA

Solomon theorized that Antonie Brentano, a married woman and the mother of several children, was Beethoven's Immortal Beloved. It is this author's opinion that this conclusion is wrong, despite the numerous nods it has received from the academic community. In examining this prevailing theory of the mystery woman's identity, it will be important to consider not only the independent pieces of proof, but also to view them in the context of the entire scenario and the players within it in order to see whether Antonie Brentano could indeed have been the Beloved. A combination of both actual, substantiated facts and a measure of common sense and logic must be used in making this determination.

Solomon established several criteria which he felt a woman had to meet in order to be the Beloved. The first of these was that she had to have been a woman closely acquainted with Beethoven between 1811 and 1812, otherwise a love affair which culminated in the love letter could not have ensued. We have no argument with this criterion, for the Beloved certainly was with Beethoven during that time. However, the intimacy of the letter indicates a relationship which had begun far earlier.

Second, Solomon believed she must have been someone that Beethoven had seen in Prague—although possibly in Vienna—immediately prior to July 6-7, the dates that the letter had been written. This premise is acceptable only because Solomon added the possibility of Beethoven and the Beloved having seen each other in Vienna. The Beloved need not have been, and actually was not, in Prague that summer, and the reason for this will be shown later.

Finally, Solomon stated that she *must* have been a woman who was in Karlsbad, Czechoslovakia, during the week of July 6, 1812, and that she "must have arrived in Karlsbad very recently, en route from Vienna and/or Prague, otherwise she and Beethoven could not have had the meeting which necessarily preceded the letter." Solomon believed also that she would be a woman whom Beethoven anticipated he would re-encounter sometime after writing the letter. Solomon said that "the expected or actual place of the reunion is not significant," however the place of reunion is important to the extent that the Beloved *must* have been some-where which coincided with the place *where Beethoven himself had expected to be at the time he wrote his letter*. Otherwise he could not have stated that "We probably will see one another soon." Conversely, if Beethoven had *not* planned to go where he knew the Beloved to be, he could not and would not have made such a statement. One other obvious point is that Beethoven must have known where his Beloved was, or he could not have sent a letter to her.

The crux of the solution rests on discovering where Beethoven had *expected* to be, for it is there that we can expect to find his Beloved. Any woman who *fails* to meet this criterion, and who was not in the expected place, *cannot* have been the Immortal Beloved.

In the following chapters, we will offer evidence—which in most cases will be Beethoven's own letters—showing that:

1. It was not necessary for Beethoven and his Beloved to have been in Prague together, and, in fact, had *not* been, having seen each other in Vienna prior to his trip.

2. Karlsbad was not the letter's intended destination, de-spite its wide-spread acceptance.

3. Although Antonie Brentano had been in Karlsbad and *did* see Beethoven there at the time he wrote the Beloved letter, Beethoven had not planned to go there, and she was not the person he had in mind when he wrote that he would see her soon.

4. Beethoven planned to see his Beloved in the vicinity of Vienna where in fact he *did* go and *did* see her after leav-ing Teplitz in September, fulfilling the supposition in his letter that they would "see one another soon."

7

The Karlsbad Connection

Solomon purported that "the *sine qua non* [essential condition] for identification of the Immortal Beloved is that she must be a woman who was in Karlsbad [a Bohemian spa] during the week of July 6, 1812." On the surface, this would appear to be a reasonable criterion, because most researchers have concurred that Karlsbad was both the intended destination of the Immortal Beloved's letter (designated only as "K") and the place where Beethoven planned to meet his Beloved that summer. This conclusion was reached on the basis of three main pieces of evidence: 1) the location of a postal schedule listing Karlsbad on a mail route which seemed to conform to a delivery schedule Beethoven alluded to in his letter; 2) the time Beethoven indicated it would take for a letter mailed from Teplitz to reach his Beloved, and 3) the fact that Beethoven had gone to Karlsbad that summer. Have researchers examined this evidence closely enough to say that this conclusion is true beyond a reasonable doubt? No, in fact they have accepted it on face value. For this author, there are still too many unanswered questions.

Viewed on their own, these three pieces of information appear convincing, yet in previous chapters we have already established the importance of considering evidence in the total context under which it came to be, rather than in isolation. Even primary source evidence, if it conflicts either with its context or with other data, must be reevaluated before its validity may be confirmed. In cases where conflicts cannot be resolved, the evidence must be deemed invalid, or at least suspect.

In this chapter the contention that Karlsbad had been the letter's destination and the place where the Immortal Beloved was will be addressed. The issues of the postal schedule and the time-distance factor noted in the Beloved letter have their own complex problems and will be dealt with separately in the next chapter.

Important statements made by Beethoven not only in the Beloved letter, but in other letters he wrote while still in Teplitz some days later, seem to have been overlooked, yet these letters give reason to believe that Karlsbad had not been the intended destination of the letter. They indicate that, at the time the Beloved letter had been written, Beethoven had no intention of going to Karlsbad nor to any other spa except Teplitz that summer, and therefore he could not have planned to see his Beloved in any of those places. If this is true, then a woman who *was* in Karlsbad or another Bohemian spa in the summer of 1812 cannot have been the Immortal Beloved.

CONCLUSION: KARLSBAD?

Beethoven wrote: "We probably will see one another soon." He clearly anticipated a reunion with her. But the question still remains: see one another *where*?

Sonneck felt that Beethoven's use of the letter "K" as an abbreviation for Karlsbad in an August 9, 1812, letter to Breitkopf & Härtel was a significant clue. However, Beethoven's use of abbreviations was extensive in all his letters, and in that particular instance he did not use the abbreviation "K" in the letter until he had already written out the word "Karlsbad" twice in the previous sentence.

Other biographers assumed the letter's destination and the lovers' meeting place had been Karlsbad because of a postal schedule uncovered by Max Unger in 1928. Solomon concluded that the Beloved was Antonie Brentano because she and Beethoven were both there at the same time that summer, and he believed she also fit other important criteria. But what if, at the time Beethoven wrote the letter and made the promise to see his Beloved soon, he himself had not planned to go to Karlsbad? If he had not, then Solomon's conclusion that the Beloved must be a woman who Beethoven knew to be in Karlsbad because he would soon see her *there*, can no longer be true.

Solomon's first premise was that "We may safely assume that the main purpose of [Beethoven's] journey [to Karlsbad] was a reunion with Antonie and her family..."[1] We may assume nothing of the sort. There were several letters written by Beethoven which prove that this was not the case.

First, his August 9 letter written in Franzensbrunn, to his publishers Breitkopf & Härtel, said that it was his physician, Dr. Staudenheim, who urged him to go to the other Bohemian spas. He wrote: "My doctor drives me from one place to another in search of health, from Teplitz to Karlsbad, from there back here."[2] In a second letter written just three days later on August 12, Beethoven made the same complaint to the Archduke Rudolph, saying that

> From T[eplitz], however, my physician, Staudenheim, commanded me to go to Karlsbad and from there to here [Franzensbrunn]— What excursions! and yet but little certainty touching an improvement in my condition![3]

Beethoven reiterated this to Breitkopf & Härtel on September 17 when he wrote "My Aesculapius [Dr. Jakob Staudenheim] has led me round and round in a circle, seeing that after all the best cure is to be found at Teplitz."[4]

This is hardly the tone of a man who had planned a carefree "summer vacation" with his Beloved and her husband. Rather it was one of a man who was tired of being ordered to travel all over Czechoslovakia in search of better health. These three letters clearly show that Beethoven did not go to the other spas because of a prearrangement with the Brentanos, and if we carefully read four other letters Beethoven wrote that summer— which will be presented in a moment—we will see that, initially, Beethoven had not planned to go to either Karlsbad or Franz-

---

[1]Solomon, p. 172.

[2]Anderson, p. 384. One recent writer, Susan Lund, contends that Beethoven was lying in these letters, and that Staudenheim would have had to have travelled with Beethoven in order to give him this prescription. More likely the doctor advised Beethoven to try both spas before the composer left Teplitz.

[3]Anderson, p. 387

[4]Anderson, p. 387. Aesculapius was a legendary Greek physician who had learned the secret of raising the dead.

ensbrunn at all. Of course, he wrote no formal itinerary before his trip, nevertheless letters he wrote while he was on his trip do give an itinerary of sorts. These indicate that his original plan had been to return to Vienna after his sojourn in Teplitz, as he had done in 1811, without going on to any other spa. Thus he *would* see his Beloved soon. . . only not in Karlsbad, but in or around Vienna.

EVIDENCE: EXHIBIT A

On July 17, 1812, Beethoven wrote a letter to Emilie M., a little girl of eight to ten years of age, an admirer of his, who had sent him a hand-made wallet as a token of her esteem. On that day, Beethoven—still in Teplitz—acknowledged her gift with a kind letter that said, in closing: "If you wish, dear Emilie, to write to me, only address me directly here where I shall be still for the next four weeks, or to Vienna; it is all one."[5]

We see from this that his original plan had been to go from Vienna to Prague on brief business, then to go on to Teplitz and stay there for six weeks (from early July to mid-August), and then return home. This plan is almost identical to his 1811 trip when he was in Teplitz from the beginning of August to mid-September—again, about six weeks, by his doctor's order. He wrote to Franz von Brunswick in June 1811, "I am bound to tell you that by order of my physician I must spend two full months at T[eplitz], and therefore could not leave with you in the middle of August... the physician is already grumbling at my remaining here [in Vienna]so long..." He did as his doctor prescribed, stayed in Teplitz a month and a half, then returned to Vienna via Lichnowsky's estate in Silesia. That he planned to follow a similar pattern in 1812 is logical from the standpoint of his doctor's orders. In 1811, Malfatti had instructed Beethoven to stay at the spa for two months. Why then, a year later, would Malfatti have had his patient remain at the spa barely three weeks? He probably would not. Recall that it was another physician entirely, Staudenheim, who had sent Beethoven on to Karlsbad and Franzensbrunn.

---

[5]Anderson, p. 382.

EVIDENCE: EXHIBIT B

There were several other letters Beethoven wrote that summer which are similar to the one addressed to Emilie. A postscript in a letter to Joseph von Varena in Graz on July 19, 1812, reads: "I am staying here for a few weeks more. Write to me if necessary."[6] Varena was one of the founding members of the Graz Music Society and Beethoven corresponded with him regularly in regard to charitable concerts with which he was involved. Thus, Beethoven issued an invitation to Varena to correspond with him which was similar to the one he had sent to Emilie, with the same time frame, and with no mention of being anywhere except Teplitz.

EVIDENCE: EXHIBIT C

Another letter was written to Breitkopf & Härtel on the same day as the one to Emilie, July 17. In it Beethoven said "My rooms are not exactly what I should like, but I hope soon to get better ones.—"[7] If it had been in his plans to leave Teplitz within the next ten days or less, it is unlikely that he still would have been searching around for better rooms than he already had, particularly since he had no idea how long it would take him to find more suitable lodgings. Why would he go through the trouble of moving if he was leaving town in just a few days? If, however, he had planned to remain another month as he indicated in his letter to Emilie, then acquiring better lodgings to make the remaining four weeks more pleasant for him would have made sense.

In this same letter, Beethoven requested that his publishers, who were in Leipzig, Germany, some 75 miles away, mail him some music: "You can also send me here [i.e. to Teplitz] some copies of the last of the works." The earliest this letter could have been posted was July 18. The actual traveling time from Teplitz to Leipzig is unknown, but given the distance, the trip probably took about one day, slightly longer if the coach had had a layover in Dresden. Thus the *earliest* the letter could have arrived in Leipzig would have been July 19 which was a Sunday. Breitkopf

---

[6]Anderson, p. 382.
[7]Anderson, p. 378.

& Härtel could not have received Beethoven's request any sooner than Monday, July 20, and probably not even by then. If they had complied with his request immediately, the earliest they could have placed the music in the post was July 21, and it would have gotten to Teplitz around July 22, at best. This, of course, assumes optimal traveling time, and does not take into account stops along the way, road conditions, or the weather, all of which could have lengthened the turn-around time. It also is unlikely that a busy publishing firm would have answered mail so rapidly, even if it came from a Beethoven. They might have "dropped everything" to comply with a request from so illustrious a client, but even so, the best possible arrival date for the music still would have been extremely close to the date that Beethoven left Teplitz (between July 27 and 30). Beethoven's request for the music to be sent to him at Teplitz makes sense only if he had planned to remain in Teplitz the rest of the summer. Otherwise why did he not ask his publishers to forward the music on to Karlsbad to await his imminent arrival there, so as to avoid any unnecessary delay a stop in Teplitz would have created?

EVIDENCE: EXHIBIT D

Goethe's diary indicated that Beethoven left Teplitz on July 24 or 25. This is not correct because on July 24, Beethoven was still in Teplitz writing to his publishers:

> Send me by letter post my six songs, one of which is Goethe's 'Kennst du das Land...' Have an offprint made on the thinnest and finest paper as quickly, as speedily, in the quickest way, with the greatest expedition and so quickly that one cannot express it in words, and send it to me here on the wings of thought...[8]

Here once again, Beethoven asked his publishers to send him a reprint of some music, still advising them to send it to Teplitz, despite the fact that he wanted it quickly, speedily, and sent "on the wings of thought." By now, it was July 24, and his departure supposedly was imminent. Why then would he ask for music to be sent to Teplitz if, by the time it arrived, he knew he was going to be in Karlsbad?

---

[8]Anderson, p. 383.

Likely Beethoven left for Karlsbad around July 30 because he was registered on July 31. (He may have left earlier and simply failed to register immediately which is possible given how quickly he had changed his plans. Under the circumstances, he may have found only temporary quarters upon arrival.) He stayed in Karlsbad about two weeks, and then went to Franzens-brunn for several more weeks. If he had known anytime during the latter part of July that he would be going on to the other spas, or be anywhere else besides in Teplitz that summer, surely he would have mentioned that to Emilie, and Varena, and his pub-lishers rather than advising all of them to send letters and packages only to Teplitz (or, in the case of Emilie, to Vienna). In an earlier part of his letter to Emilie, Beethoven wrote "If you should want something at any time, my dear Emilie, write to me trustingly." He would not have issued *two* invitations in the same letter for her to correspond with him "trustingly" and then not have given her the proper place(s) where she might address her letters. At the very least, he would have told all of them that he planned to travel that entire summer, and that he would not be able to receive mail from them until the end of the year after he had returned to Vienna. Beethoven's letters characteristically show that he took care to note his addresses, locations, or other places mail could be sent to.[9] It was not his habit to allow mail for him to accumulate at the Vienna post office. Following are examples, only a few of many:

> To Joseph von Varena: "Should you write to me, please enclose your letter in a cover with the following address in V[ienna], i.e. to Herr Oliva, to be delivered to Gebrüder Offenheimer in the Bauernmarkt." (May 27, 1813 from Baden)

> To Franz Brunswick: "In the future write the following address on the covers of letters to me 'To J.B. von Pasqualati'..." (Summer 1813)

> To Zmeskall: "To Herr LvB at Baden, to be delivered at the Sauerbad (an inn in Baden)"— (September 1814)

---

[9]Until the 1820s, Beethoven regularly told his correspondents where to write to him. Only when fame was clearly his did he begin to tell them that it was enough to "write simply Ludwig van Beethoven, Vienna," for letters to reach him.

To Kanka: "For the time being please address letters to
me in the following way — to be delivered at the house
of Herr Johann Wolfmayer..." (August 22, 1814)

Also, why should he have tried to hide his itinerary from
anyone, or pretend he was staying in Teplitz? None of his correspondents knew or cared that the Brentanos were in Karlsbad.
And as it was a popular resort, it would not have seemed odd to
them for Beethoven to go there.

A CHANCE REUNION

Another minor point involves timing. The Brentanos left
Karlsbad for Franzensbrunn around August 8. Was this a spur-
of-the-moment decision brought about by their unexpected reunion with Beethoven, or the result of preplanning? We do not
know for certain, but most likely they had had some sort of travel
itinerary in place before leaving Vienna, and at least would have
made reservations for lodgings since they had a child traveling
with them. Most likely they would have left Karlsbad at the end
of the first week of August regardless of Beethoven's presence
there. Beethoven's letter to Emilie indicated that he was planning to stay in Teplitz until four weeks after July 17, or roughly
until August 17. Under his initial itinerary, even if he had gone
on to Karlsbad on his own volition after staying in Teplitz, he
would have missed the Brentanos by a week and a half. Thus
their reunion there was simply fortuitous.

As we now know, Beethoven's plans changed radically at
the end of July: he not only went to Karlsbad and Franzensbrunn,
but also visited his brother, Johann, in Linz, with a brief stop back
in Vienna in between. In fact, rather than being gone from Vienna
only six weeks as he had originally planned, he was gone a total
of six months! Something must have happened between July 24
and July 30 to have brought about this change in plans. While
something extraordinary might have caused this alteration, far
more likely it was his chance meeting with the eminent Dr. Jakob
Staudenheim that brought about this sudden change.

Dr. Staudenheim[10] was a famous physician, and was, in
fact, the personal physician of the Emperor Franz. In 1812 he

---

[10]Staudenheim kept in touch with Beethoven until April 1824, but both he and
Dr. Braunhofer refused to keep the composer as a patient because of Beethoven's
unkind treatment of them.

happened to accompany the Imperial family to the Bohemian resorts where he met Beethoven. He advised the composer, who suffered from chronic digestive ailments, to leave Teplitz and try the waters in Karlsbad and in Franzensbrunn, spas which specialized in such disorders. The doctor's esteemed position within the royal family no doubt was a factor in Beethoven agreeing to take his advice. It also is probable that Beethoven, who had found that he felt no better after spending nearly a month in Teplitz, was eager for this "second opinion."

Having established that at the time he wrote the Beloved letter on July 6-7 it was not his plan to go to Karlsbad, we must ask: would Beethoven have sent a letter to a woman whom he knew to be in Karlsbad, telling her that he would see her soon, if he was not planning to go there himself? Of course not. This makes no sense, not unless she also had anticipated a quick return to Vienna. The Brentanos did not journey home until late September or early October, just shortly before their return to Frankfurt, having spent—and having planned to spend—their entire summer at the resorts. Therefore it was not Antonie—who we know was in Karlsbad, and who Beethoven knew was there as well—whom Beethoven expected to re-encounter "soon." It was some*one* else, some*where* else, in all likelihood, near or in Vienna. We shall soon see that that was *exactly* where she was, that she was there when the Beloved letter was written, and that Beethoven, indeed, saw her there "soon," albeit not quite as soon as he originally had hoped.

We also now know that at the end of July Beethoven's newfound doctor ordered him to take the waters at Karlsbad and Franzensbrunn, and that he chose to take Staudenheim's advice —with the hope of getting well—rather than returning immediately to Vienna. Since he knew the Brentanos were at the spa, he looked them up in the guest register, and as they were friends of his, he decided to find lodgings near them. Solomon contended that Beethoven and the Brentanos

> discussed their respective summer vacation plans,[11] and perhaps arranged to meet in Prague. Second, and decisively, they undoubtedly discussed a possible meet-

---

[11]A misnomer. All three of them were ill at the time; this hardly could have been considered a "summer vacation" by any of them.

ing later in the summer, for a reunion actually took place that was possible only through prearrangement.[12]

This conclusion is faulty. As we know, Beethoven had not originally planned to go anywhere else except Teplitz. His later reunion with the Brentanos was *not* through prearrangement, nor was such a prearrangement necessary. Most likely the Brentanos had told Beethoven their plans before leaving Vienna. When Beethoven arrived in Karlsbad, it would not have been difficult for him to find his friends since the city's police register told him not only that they had arrived on July 5, but also that they were staying at 311 Aug' Gottes auf der Wiese—a guest house where Beethoven also was able to find lodgings, at least by July 31 when he offficially registered there.

At this point, the reader usually is led to believe that Beethoven, after spending several weeks in Karlsbad and Franzensbrunn, had returned to Teplitz for a while, and then had left Teplitz in October and *gone on to Linz*. This constitutes a critical omission of information. Beethoven did *not* go directly to Linz. He went back to Vienna, and saw his Beloved at her summer residence in a village outside the city, just as he said he would in his letter to her. Solomon wrote that "Beethoven was visibly elated at this time [while in Karlsbad]." Of course he was. He had sent his love letter to his Beloved, and was anticipating "flying to her arms." She either had sent him an invitation to come to her which had been forwarded to him from Teplitz, or they had prearranged their meeting at her estate. Therefore it is no wonder that he expressed annoyance at his doctor for keeping him at the spas for so long a time. The prescription kept him away from his Beloved far long than he had wanted. His "flight" was postponed until September. Another of Beethoven's letters written on December 30 to Princess Kinsky complaining of being detained at the spas, shows that this was so.

Beethoven wrote his last note to Amalie Sebald around September 17. His next letter was written shortly thereafter, *from Vienna*, addressed to Gleichenstein. It was a short letter, and its brevity no doubt lent to its being overlooked by researchers. Its length notwithstanding, the note contains critical information:

[12]Solomon, p. 171.

How can one get to Linz most quickly and most cheaply?—Please answer this question exhaustively — Have you then no prospect whatever of getting another apartment? — *On Saturday or Saturday [Sunday] I shall perhaps invite you to Hernals* — (emphasis is the present author's)[13]

Countess Erdödy had a summer residence in Hernals, a village just to the west of Vienna. She was summering there in 1812; thus Beethoven invited their mutual friend, Gleichenstein, to join them there briefly at her summer house before taking his trip to Linz. This quick trip to Hernals outside Vienna fulfilled the supposition in the Beloved letter which said "We will probably see one another soon." It also points to Klosterneuberg and *not* Karlsbad, as being the mysterious "K" in the letter. Klosterneuberg, an important market town at the time, would have been the postal stop where Anna Marie normally would have received her mail while she was at her estate in Jedlersee. Jedlersee is about three miles—about half an hour—from Klosterneuberg. While she was at Hernals—just under six miles and roughly an hour from Klosterneuberg—in the interest of expediency, she still would have continued to have her mail sent to her there.

When this evidence against Karlsbad is later tied into additional problems with this city being the letter's intended destination—problems of a logical, mathematical nature—there should be little doubt that Karlsbad had *not* been the place where Beethoven anticipated seeing, and in fact saw, his Beloved that summer of 1812.

---

[13]Anderson, p. 391, also notes 2 and 4. It is interesting that in his excitement, Beethoven wrote "Saturday or Saturday."

❖ *8* ❖

Karlsbad and the Postal Schedule

At this point, can Karlsbad still be considered the letter's intended destination, *beyond a reasonable doubt*? Perhaps many still might answer *yes*. However,the assumption that Karlsbad was the destination still has other problems, in addition to those already discussed

We already know that since Beethoven himself had not planned to go to Karlsbad, there was no reason for him to send his letter to a woman there. A second problem with Karlsbad revolves around a postal schedule which has been used as primary evidence.

Biographers at first puzzled over to what city Beethoven was referring when he wrote "K." Then, in 1928, Max Unger uncovered what Solomon termed a "contemporary postal schedule." It reads as follows:

Outgoing Mail:
Monday. Early, about 8:00 o'clock, the Reichspost goes to Saaz, Karlsbad, and Eger. After midday, about 4:00 o'clock, to Prague, Vienna, Silesia, Moravia, Italy, Hungary, Bavaria, France, etc.
Tuesday. After midday, about 3:00 o'clock, to Dresden, Leipzig, Prussia, and the other northern countries.
Thursday. Early, about 8:00 o'clock, same as early Monday.
Friday. After midday, about 4:00 o'clock, same as Monday afternoon.
Saturday. Same as Tuesday.

From May 15 until September 15, the mail...leaves daily for all Austian dominions...about 11:00 o'clock....

Researchers were very excited about this discovery because it seemed to prove that Karlsbad was the city in question. Did anyone take more than a cursory look at this schedule? Look at it in a historical context? Compare it to Beethoven's letter? Examine it in the light of logic and common sense? Question it at all? Like Emilie's letter which, on the surface, appeared insignificant but which took on enormous importance when carefully evaluated, there are aspects of the schedule which diminish its value as evidence when one begins asking pertinent questions about it.

It must be noted at the outset that the label "contemporary" is misleading. Unger's postal schedule was not for 1812 when the letter was written, but 1815. One might be tempted to believe that the difference of three years is inconsequential. Even Unger claimed that postal schedules did not change significantly from year to year, and that we may presume that the one in effect for 1815 was valid for 1812 as well. We cannot presume anything of the sort. These were not simply *any* three years, and there are several important factors which make the 1815 postal schedule inapplicable to 1812, issues which will show that this document cannot be used as irrefutable proof that the letter's destination had been Karlsbad.

First, Unger claimed that his research had shown that the roads between Prague and Teplitz were exceedingly bad until new ones were constructed around 1815. Interestingly, we find —and likely not coincidentally—that the postal schedule also was from that year. A significant improvement in the roads certainly could have contributed to a change in the mail schedule.

Second, we believe that there has been a mistake in determining how Beethoven learned about the mail schedule. Unger found a printed postal schedule, and presumed that Beethoven had seen one like it as well. He wrote:

> ...especially convincing however is the verification which the author was able to make, how, namely, the master of tone came to fall into the error with regard to the times of departure of the post for Karlsbad. The writer was able to refer to a postal route schedule of the year 1815...

Later, picking up on Unger's observation, Solomon wrote,

> Beethoven presumably saw this notice [the postal schedule] and concluded that he could not mail his letter until

> Thursday. . . Evidently, however, he later learned that
> he had overlooked the following in small type at the
> bottom of the postal notice: "From May 15 until Septem-
> ber 15, the mail... leaves daily for all Austrian domin-
> ions... about 11:00 o'clock . . ."[1]

Once again we find that infamous word "presumably." But in this
instance we simply cannotpresume that Beethoven saw this
notice, nor that he overlooked the small print. In the third portion
of his letter, in which the wording in all translations has been
consistent, he indicates that *he had not seen an actual postal
schedule at all*. With the two issues of Karlsbad and the postal
schedule so closely related, we shall work on them together,
beginning with the premise that Beethoven misread the postal
schedule. Let us work backwards from the second day, July 7, and
the last portion of the letter which contains an important bit of
information, and ask some questions to see why the assumption
that Beethoven saw the schedule cannot be true. We also will
address why it is significant that Beethoven did not see the
schedule himself.

      In the second (July 6, evening) portion of his letter, Beet-
hoven wrote, according to only one translation,[2] "just now I *notice*
that letters must be posted..." All other translations, however
(notably Kalischer/Shedlock, Anderson, Thayer/Forbes, Solomon,
et.al) contain the word "learned." As we shall see, this word is
debatable because of what Beethoven wrote later on.

      **Where was Beethoven when he finished writing his
letter?** Beethoven himself said that he was still in bed. He wrote
to his Beloved: "Good morning on July 7. *While still in bed*, my
thoughts thrust themselves toward you..." No doubt he wrote
this entire portion of the letter all at once since it is not very long,
and there are no abrupt breaks in his chain of thought except
when he writes that: "Angel, right now I *hear* that the mail goes
every day—" All other translations confirm this in their versions:
"Angel, I have just been *told* that the mail coach goes every
day—" This is an important remark: unquestionably he *heard* or
was told about the different mail schedule while in bed writing his
letter. We can be sure he did not have a sudden urge to confirm
the mail schedule, jumped out of bed, dressed, went to the lobby

[1]Solomon, p. 166.
[2]Beahrs, *Journal of the American Beethoven Society*, 1990.

of the inn—or, worse, to the post office—reread the mail schedule, realized his error, and then went back and finished his letter. Not only does that scenario not make sense, that is not what *Beethoven* said happened. If you "hear" or are "told" something you do not "read" it.

The next logical question should be, **Who told Beethoven about the mail coach leaving every day?** It must have been someone who had access to his room early in the morning while he was still in bed. Therefore, it was probably not a fellow guest, but a worker there—a maid, a servant, or the proprietor of the inn. Also, no maid, innkeeper or servant would have come to Beethoven's room early in the morning with the express purpose of announcing a change or error in the postal schedule unless that person had been *aware* that Beethoven had been given incorrect information previously and felt obligated to correct it. Here is the discrepancy between "noticed" and "learned." If Beethoven had read the postal schedule himself, no one possibly could have known that he had *mis*read it. Already we see that there is something wrong with the presumption that Beethoven read the schedule and later noticed the fine print.

Since we now know that Beethoven was told about the postal schedule and did not read it, one might be tempted to inquire about the state of his hearing at this time, and wonder whether he simply had not heard correctly. However, the question is irrelevant. Yes, Beethoven was hard of hearing, but regardless, he could not have been told correct information which he simply had heard incorrectly. The situation is the same as if he had been given the printed schedule, or someone had written down the information for him. Just as no one would have been able to know whether he had *misread* the information, so they also would not have been able to know that he had *misheard* it. The information, whether verbal or written, must have come directly, and incorrectly, from some person.

Logically, the person who gave Beethoven the correct schedule on the morning of July 7 was either the person he had asked on July 6 who originally had given him the wrong information, or a representative of that person—the innkeeper, or a maid, or servant. No one else would have had access to his room, and with his poor hearing, we cannot even imagine that while in bed, Beethoven had overheard people discussing the postal schedule in the hall!

Now that we can presume that some person had supplied the wrong information, we must ask, **what caused this person to be wrong?** We cannot assume that the person Beethoven had asked about the schedule simply had gotten it wrong because Beethoven had inquired upon arrival at 4:00 a.m., and the person giving the information had been in a stupor from just having been roused from bed. We know from his letter that Beethoven had gotten the initial information about the schedule between the time when he wrote the first part of his letter and when he wrote the second part. His note about the incorrect postal information is in the portion of his letter written on the *evening* of July 6. He wrote "...*just now* I notice (or have learned) that letters must be posted very early in the morning on Mondays-Thursdays..."

Biographer George Marek noted that the Teplitz post office was on the same street as Beethoven's inn, "The Oak," but this, too, is irrelevant. Beethoven could not have seen the postal schedule there, nor could he have inquired of the schedule of anyone who worked there. If he had, then we would have to assume that a person who worked at the post office did not know the mail schedule, and that is an absurd assumption. Second, why would a postal worker visit Beethoven early in the morning at the inn, while the composer was still in bed, to give him the correct information? Again, another silly conclusion. Thus, it makes no difference where the post office was located because at most, Beethoven went there simply to post his letter, not to inquire or to read about the schedule. Its location only made posting the Beloved letter convenient for him.

It is reasonable to believe that Beethoven had asked about the mail schedule from someone who worked at the inn, as most of us would inquire at the front desk of a hotel if we were planning to mail a letter in a strange city. We would not assume that a fellow guest would be as knowledgeable as a resident or worker there. Again, question must be, **how could a person who lived and worked in Teplitz—particularly at an inn where the question must have been asked with some regularity so that the person would be reasonably familiar with such a schedule—have made this mistake?**

There are several possibilities.

One, the person Beethoven asked had consulted the printed schedule and misread the information himself before relaying it verbally to Beethoven. Some time later, perhaps when having to consult the schedule again for some other guest, the innkeeper noticed (or remembered) the small print. Realizing his mistake, he took steps to rectify his error with Beethoven by sending a servant to the composer's room early the next morning, guessing that Beethoven had a letter to mail or else he would not have inquired.

In a second situation, which this author feels the more likely of the two, the person asked had been *unsure* about the postal schedule and had given Beethoven faulty information. We believe that the reason Unger only could find a mail schedule for 1815 was because there had been no printed schedules issued in that unstable year of 1812. Thus the person Beethoven asked had had to rely on his own memory for the answer. In this event, Unger's premise about unchanging postal schedules would be in error. Otherwise it would be extremely odd that this person would not know that the mail went out daily when we can see by the printed information that the summer schedule—at least in 1815—had been in effect since May 15, *nearly two months*. Logically, switching to a summer schedule also should have been a regular occurrence, if Unger was right and the city followed the same schedule year after year. Further, the summer schedule was simple: the mail went to all destinations every day at the same time, 11 o'clock in the morning. Anyone who could not have remembered that after two months must have suffered from serious memory loss!

The fact is, we cannot ignore the very real probability that the imminent Napoleonic invasion had caused the postal schedule to be erratic during that entire three-year period (i.e. 1812-1815), and probably even for years *before that*, at least from the time of the French invasion and bombing of Vienna in 1809. This is evident from a series of letters Beethoven wrote during this time period:[3]

> To Breitkopf & Härtel, May 26, 1809: "For the moment the uncertainty of the postal arrangements prevents me from despatching any manuscripts to you —"

> To Dr. Ignaz Troxler, September, 1809: "The post from Baden is the most wretched of all; it resembles the whole Austrian state. I received your letter only today."

---

[3]All excerpts taken from Anderson, pp. 230, 242, 293, and 466, respectively.

To Breitkopf &Härtel, September 23, 1810: "As our post is just as uncertain as everything else, please enclose the letter you address to me in another cover directed to Herr von Oliva... As I am seldom in Vienna during the summer and the autumn, that is the safest way—"

To Breitkopf & Härtel, April 12, 1811: "Yesterday I received your parcel; our post, like everything else, has become still dearer..."

The problem with the postal system continued for several years thereafter:

To Archduke Rudolph, September 1814 : "I don't care to entrust to the post my letters for the Burg, for several times already I have found that they have never been delivered..."

To Simrock, Bonn, 1820: "....since our letter posts are known to be not of the most reliable kind, or perhaps the revolutionary upheavals in your part of the world may be causing tiresome delays in the delivery of letters in Vienna as well..."

From Beethoven's complaints we must conclude that the postal schedule for over a decade had been erratic and unreliable, and that problems with it stemmed primarily from the unstable political situation in Europe. Even years later, Dr. Gerhard von Breuning would write about "the pressure of military events, during which delivery of mail by post-chaise, limping along even in peace time, was sometimes completely interrupted."[4] One of the greatest "military events" of the period, the Napoleonic invasion, would have required a flexible postal schedule to facilitate rapid exchange of information. Thayer wrote of Napoleon's 1812 campaign that

Teplitz (that neutral ground, but central point of plot and agitation against the parvenu Emperor) became the scene of a virtual congress of imperial personages, or their representatives, accompanied by families, ministers, and retinues. Ostensibly they met for health,

---

[4]Dr. Gerhard Breuning, *Aus dem Schwartzspanierhause*, p. 31.

recreation, social diversion; but views and opinions were exchanged and arrangements made for such concerted action as the result in Russia might render politic.[5]

Herr August Hiekel, Magisterial Adjunct in Teplitz, provided Thayer with a list of arrivals in the resort that summer. Among them were such people as:

> Emperor Franz and attendants: Wrbna, Althaer, Kinsky, Zichy, etc.
> Empress Marie Louise of France and attendants
> Grand Duke of Wurzburg and attendants
> Empress of Austria and household
> Duke Anton of Saxony, wife, and household
> King of Saxony, wife, and attendants
> Prince Maximilian of Saxony, wife, and attendants
> Prince Wittgenstein, Baron von Humboldt, and the Prince of Curland in the Prussian service
> Prince Carl von Lichnowsky
> Grand Ducal Privy Councillor of Weimar

This list shows that an inordinate number of nobility and statesmen were at the resort that summer. If the resorts accommodated the regular summer crowd by altering the mail schedule between May and September, it is very likely that they also would have altered it to accommodate the need for more efficient mail service for these important heads of state at this time, particularly if these people were considering possible actions in the event of an invasion.

The postal schedule informs us that, besides Karlsbad, the Monday-Thursday mail went in the morning to Saaz and Eger (the Franzensbrunn resort) and in the afternoon to Prague, Vienna, Silesia, Moravia, Italy, Hungary, Bavaria, France, etc. But this is only according to the *1815 schedule* which may not have been the one in effect in 1812, when the threat of imminent invasion may have caused capital cities (e.g. Prague and Vienna) to be included in the morning mail runs in order to expedite the exchange of information with areas within the Austrian Dominion. There is little reason to believe that the postal schedules for 1812 and 1815 were identical or even as stable as Unger would have us believe. In fact, as we have noted, the reason Unger had

---

[5]Thayer/Forbes, p. 532.

located a schedule for 1815 rather than 1812 may have been because no schedules had been printed during those unstable years. It was not until better roads (built in 1815) and improved political conditions stablized the mail system that printers' ink and paper were committed to printing a schedule to which a mail coach might adhere with a reasonable amount of reliability over an extended period of time. The 1815 schedule may have been similar to the one used in 1812—as noted by Beethoven's letter—with the only significant difference being that in 1815 the stabilized system and decrease in urgency for mail delivery had allowed the postal system to add an afternoon run to which Vienna, Prague, and other cities had been moved.

It must be pointed out that even though Karlsbad is the only town listed on the 1815 postal schedule whose name begins with a "K," it still does not make Karlsbad the only possibility. Karlsbad was only 50 miles from Teplitz and a substantially large and important resort. It naturally would have been included on a Teplitz mail schedule. Most of the large cities included on the schedule have small "K" towns or villages nearby, en route, or as suburbs: e.g., Prague has Karolinenthal, Vienna has Klosterneuberg, Korneuburg, and Krems. However, their distance from the resort would have precluded them from being individually listed on the Teplitz postal schedule. If for example, Beethoven had wanted to send his letter to Klosterneuberg or Karolinenthal, these would have been included on the Vienna and Prague routes, respectively, but would not have been listed separately.

AN INTERESTING MATHEMATICAL PROBLEM

Another problem with Karlsbad being the letter's destination has to do with a puzzling time-distance factor between the towns involved.

The first interesting piece is that Unger wrote, "Without any further circumlocution, Karlsbad may be accepted as the letter's place of destination. It took two days to send a letter from Teplitz to Karlsbad—as is mentioned in one place in the letter." In other words, Unger used Beethoven's letter as corroborating evidence on the length of time it took for a letter to go from Teplitz to Karlsbad when Beethoven *had never before made the trip*! Despite that fact, Solomon also stated that *"Beethoven knew 'K'* to be two days or less distance from Teplitz, because he assumed that a letter mailed early Thursday would not arrive until Saturday." Beethoven could not *know* or *assume* anything of the sort.

To begin, let us address some minor points: First, early Thursday to Saturday is not, as Solomon said, two days or *less*, it is two days and *more*, with Thursday and Friday counting as two full days, and Saturday as a portion of day. Second, we cannot know for certain that Beethoven was referring to the Beloved letter when he wrote the time factor. What he said was: "I weep when I think that you will probably not receive *the first news* of me until Saturday," not "*this* letter" and not "*this* first news." What if there had been another letter mailed from Prague that had been the "first message?" If there had been some other "first message," it would also explain why he did not relate details of his stay in Prague in the Beloved letter. Third and most important: how would *Beethoven* know what the traveling time was between Teplitz and Karlsbad if he had never made the trip before? The only possibility is that he had *asked*, but if he had asked, why would a person in Teplitz believe that it would take more than two days to reach Karlsbad? Further, he made the point twice in his letter that he "learned/noticed" and then "heard/was told" about the postal schedule without saying anything about asking or being told how long the letter would take to get to its destination, *as if he already knew the answer*. However, Beethoven's first and only trip to Karlsbad was late in July 1812. Without having made an inquiry, Beethoven himself could have known only the traveling time between cities he had just visited—Vienna, Prague, and Teplitz—or where he previously had been or had sent correspondence. That, too, would eliminate Karlsbad.

The next question logically should be, **what was the actual traveling time from Teplitz to Karlsbad?** Solomon said that Johann Goethe, who had made the trip many times, wrote in his journal that it took one and a half days.[6] First, we do not know whether Goethe took the mail coach or hired his own carriage in order to make for a more leisurely trip, or whether he made unrecorded stopovers anywhere which added to his travel time. We also do not know whether Goethe recorded the time

---

[6]We also are told that Goethe kept track of when mail was received by him from Karlsbad, but unless the party writing him noted the exact time he or she actually mailed the letters, how could Goethe accurately judge the mail delivery time? One can certainly write and date a letter and then not post it until some time later.

factor *every* time he made the trip (which seems terribly obsessive) or whether he noted it only when it took more or less time than it should have. Most importantly, we do not know what Goethe meant by "a day and a half." Did he mean, literally, *36 hours*, or did he mean a "day" to be *sunrise to sunset* (about eight hours) plus *part of the evening* (about four hours) which would have been a reasonable assessment of 12 hours. [We must interject here that most of us who travel assess our time this way. If we leave home at seven in the morning and arrive at our destination that evening, we complain that we had been "traveling all day." If we truly had traveled "all day" we would not have arrived until the following morning.] With a more rational interpretation of Goethe's estimate, a mail coach leaving at 8:00 in the morning on Thursday would arrive in the evening that same day.

Given everyone's estimations—Goethe said a day-and-a-half, Unger said two days, Solomon said two days or less, Beethoven wrote two-and-a-half days—it almost seems as if no one really knows! However, if one accepts Goethe's "day and a half" as being 36 hours rather than the more reasonable 12, and as the traveling time between Teplitz and Karlsbad, then one also must accept that it took a mail coach with at least four horses roughly 36 hours to travel 50 miles, an inordinately slow pace (less than one-and-a-half miles per hour!) for a vehicle that needed to deliver mail and passengers quickly. This speed factor is not supported when one checks the traveling times between other cities, for example:

- Prague to Teplitz, 50 miles, less than one day
- Vienna to Krems, 45 miles, less than one day.
- Vienna to Prague, 150 miles [three times the distance from Teplitz to Karlsbad], just over two days.

Louis Schlosser once noted that his trip from Darnstadt to Vienna was taken via a "hurrying mail coach." *Hurrying* implies speed. Yet both Solomon and Unger proposed that a trip of just 50 miles took two days which would have slowed the carriage to just over one mile per hour, an unlikely speed for a "hurrying" coach. And by Beethoven's estimation of two and a half days, the coach would have been at a virtual standstill—8/10 of a mile per hour. Maybe the horses were pushing the coach!

Another question one might ask at this point is, **how fast did the average mail coach travel**? Various letters and notes give us an estimation. Although there are numerous examples, in the interest of brevity, only four will be given here:

• In 1811, Oliva asked Beethoven to stop and visit him in Reichenberg while en route to Teplitz. In a letter to Offenheimer & Herz, Beethoven said that "according to his [Oliva's] letter, [Reichenberg] is a half day's journey from Teplitz." Teplitz is 50 miles northwest of Prague; Reichenberg is 50 miles north-north-east of Prague. They are approximately 50-60 miles apart. If it took a half-day (12 hours) to travel 60 miles, then the coach would have to travel at a speed of five MPH. (And again we have a distance similar to Teplitz-Karlsbad which we see that a coach can navigate in less than one day.)

• Sir George Smart reported that: "We went in a hired carriage from Mödling to Baden. This distance is about six miles south of Mödling and sixteen miles southwest of Vienna. The journey [Mödling to Baden] cost five florins in paper money and took us about an hour." Coach speed: about six MPH.

• Solomon stated that the Brentanos left Prague either on the 4th or 5th of July and arrived in Karlsbad on the 5th. They could not have *left* on the 5th and *arrived* on the 5th if the trip were longer than 24 hours. Logically it had been a lot less. At approximately five miles per hour, a coach going from Prague to Karlsbad would arrive in about 14-15 hours—a reasonable estimate.

• *Dutens Journal of Travel* published in 1782 noted that the 30-mile trip from Bonn to Koblenz took about nine hours, giving the coach an average speed of almost 3.5 mph. Here we have Bonn to Koblenz, 30 miles, 9 hours; but Teplitz-Karlsbad, 50 miles, 48 (or more) hours?

What these mathematical excursions tell us is that the typical mail coach travelled at an average speed of four to five miles per hour.[7] Thus a trip of 50 miles—such as between Teplitz and Karlsbad—could not have taken much more than a half day (12 hours), and any letter mailed at 11 o'clock Thursday morning would have arrived *late that same day* (just before midnight), with delivery on Friday morning, *not* Saturday.

---

[7]The coach may have traveled at a faster rate of speed, but the average takes stopovers into account.

SAME DISTANCE, LONGER TIME[8]

Let us look at this problem from a slightly different point of view. Considering the relative traveling times and distances between various cities involved, and taking into consideration the average speed of a mail coach being five miles per hour, another puzzling mathematical situation arises:

First, the distances from Prague to Teplitz and from Teplitz to Karlsbad are both approximately 50 miles—*approximately* because one must take into account the circumlocutions of the roads which connected them.

Second, Unger stated that the usual traveling time from Prague to Teplitz was from forenoon to evening. Although Unger's definitions of "forenoon" and "evening" are not known, we will estimate the former at 11 o'clock and the latter at 7 o'clock— giving a traveling time of eight hours (conservatively ten to twelve). Beethoven's actual time, 17 hours, included a carriage breakdown, and there is no indication how long he was delayed. Therefore, for now we will accept that Unger was right. (As a mathematical double-check, that would mean that the coach traveled about four to five miles per hour, which is reasonable according to previous estimates.)

Here, then, is the problem: If the distances between Teplitz-Karlsbad and Teplitz-Prague are virtually the same, then the traveling time between each pair cannot be significantly different. Yet we are expected to believe that it took no more than twelve *hours* to go the 50 miles from Prague to Teplitz—on bad roads—but more than two *days* to go the same distance from Teplitz to Karlsbad! This implies that the mail coach going from Prague to Teplitz was able to travel over bad roads at an average speed of five miles per hour, but the one going from Teplitz to Karlsbad went just one and a half miles per hour. Again we have a situation where a coach with at least four horses traveled slower than the speed the average person is able to *walk*! Under these circumstances, a seasoned pedestrian like Beethoven could have hand-delivered his letter in less time than it took the mail coach to do so!

---

[8]Another example: it is about 70 miles from Prague to Karlsbad, 20 miles *longer* than from Prague to Teplitz. Why, then, would it take at least twice as long to travel a distance which is 20 miles *shorter*? (Prague to Karlsbad, 70 miles, about 18 hours; Teplitz to Karlsbad, 50 miles, 36 hours).

This situation defies all logic, particularly when there were no inordinate obstacles (e.g. mountains) along one route as opposed to the other, and when, amazingly, the road which provided the better speed actually was worse than the one on which the coach traveled unusually slowly. We must note that Karlsbad had been a popular spa since 1370, and was one of the best known health resorts in Europe. It is impossible to believe that in 400 years Europeans had not managed to build an adequate road to a place regularly frequented not only by ordinary citizens, but by royalty. Surely the road between Teplitz and Karlsbad had not been still worse than the one between Prague and Teplitz! Thus even though the roads were not straight and some variations in time could be accounted for by the circumlocution of the roads, there still is an inordinate discrepancy in the time-distance factor between these cities.

The only other possibility is that there were four times as many stops between Teplitz and Karlsbad as there were between Prague and Teplitz, or that the coach paused at the stops longer on the former run than it did on the latter—long enough to add at least an extra full day to the trip. There were three stops between Prague and Teplitz; does this mean there were twelve between Teplitz and Karlsbad, and that the coach stopped every four miles? These explanations are very unlikely.

We know that Beethoven had made the Prague-Teplitz trip in less than a day, and, despite the fact that he was no mathematical giant, surely he would have had the sense to know it would have been a lot less than that had his carriage not broken down. Why, then, would he have assumed that it would take almost *two and half days* (or even one and a half days, for that matter) for a letter to go from Teplitz to Karlsbad if he had any idea that the distance was roughly the same as the distance from Prague to Teplitz? It is hard to believe that he would have made such an illogical assumption. More likely he would have assumed that if one mailed a letter to Karlsbad early Thursday morning it would arrive sometime that evening, and be delivered no later than Friday morning, and possibly that same day.

Aha. But if Beethoven had never been to Karlsbad before, **how could he possibly have made any estimation at all about the delivery time to that resort town**? Answer: he *could* not, and he *did* not. His estimation for the delivery time must have been *within the realm of his experience*.   Since Beethoven had not yet made Goethe's acquaintance at the time the letter was written, he certainly did not have Goethe's estimation of the time factor. How, then, would Beethoven have determined how long the traveling time would be? Logically, he would have used what most people use: experience and estimation. Arithmetic was not his forte. He would not have done complicated mathematical equations in order to determine when his letter would arrive at its destination. He would have done what most of us do: roughly estimate by counting days. Yet there is still a problem with assuming that Beethoven estimated if he had never been to Karlsbad before. Thus, his letter could *not* have been destined for Karlsbad, but to the place from where he had just come a short time before: Vienna.

Now, can one really assume that Beethoven meant to send his letter to Karlsbad *beyond a shadow of a doubt*? No, one cannot, because there are too many unresolved questions. And if the letter was *not* intended for Karlsbad, then Antonie Brentano was *not* the intended recipient.

IF NOT KARLSBAD, THEN WHERE?

The only traveling time that Beethoven knew for certain was Vienna-Prague-Teplitz. Those were the only cities that were within his immediate experience. His letter to Emilie indicated an initial plan to return to Vienna, and if he also expected to see his Beloved "soon," then he must have believed her to be in, near, or returning to Vienna, as well. Further, we know from Beethoven's departure and arrival times that the Vienna-Prague-Teplitz trip was about two and a half days. If Beethoven had considered the Vienna-Prague trip he had just made (slightly more than two days) and the Prague-Teplitz trip (one-quarter day), he would have concluded that a letter mailed toward Vienna (such as to Klosterneuberg, which is just slightly closer to Prague than Vienna) would take about two and a half days: that is, Thursday (all day), Friday (all day), and part of Saturday. The reader should recall that Vienna was one of the cities on the original Monday-Thursday mail run, even though in 1815, the coach did not leave for Vienna until midday. Again, that is not to say that in 1812, the mail coach to Vienna did not leave in the morning out of the necessity to exchange mail quickly with that important city (and others, such as Prague) due to the unusual political climate, and that in 1815 the time of day is the *only* difference between the Karlsbad and Vienna runs.

There are several possibilities for the identity of "K," which must be some place that is about two and a half days from Teplitz. The most logical are near Vienna: Klosterneuberg or Korneuberg. Two women who were special to Beethoven were in Vienna at the time: Anna Marie Erdödy and Josephine Brunswick. Advocates of Josephine Brunswick as the Beloved point out that:

• the Beloved letter is similar in intensity and language, such as referring to her as "angel" as he had done in his 1805 letters to her.

• They note that although Beethoven had not been in direct contact with Josephine since 1807, he had maintained a correspondence with her sister, Therese, and a close friendship with her brother, Franz.

• Josephine's marriage to Stackelberg was shaky at this time. She and her husband separated sometime in 1814. However, while Beethoven may have inquired after Josephine, there is no way to know if either Therese or Franz had advised Beethoven of Josephine's marital situation in particular or hinted at a possible break. This author thinks not, if only to keep from rekindling the hope in their dear friend that he and their sister might someday marry; after all, Josephine was still a countess with children and Beethoven was still a commoner

• Letters indicate that Josephine was in Vienna in 1812, but where she would have received her mail is unknown. However, she was living within the city limits, not in a suburb that would necessitate her receiving her mail anywhere other than Vienna, unless by prearrangement.

• Josephine's husband apparently was there with her part of the time, for on June 14, he wrote a letter to his mother which indicated he and his family hoped to visit Reval. A

letter regarding an ongoing problem with a shipment of
wine written by Franz Brunswick to Josephine on July 25,
says "I haven't heard a syllable from Stak[elberg]..." Another letter written on August 13 was one of confirmation
regarding a social visit which says in part "we...also hope
to find Monsieur de Stackelberg there." Solomon feels that
these last two letters indicate that the Stackelbergs were
in Vienna together. What they tell this author is that Josephine was in Vienna, but whether Stackelberg was there
with her after June 14 is questionable.

Unfortunately, however romantic the scenario may be,
that Beethoven's love for Josephine still could have burned so
brightly after the passing of seven years, there are also arguments against Josephine:

• From all indications, Beethoven's break with Josephine
in 1807 had been permanent. As far as is known, Beethoven
did not see or correspond with Josephine directly ever
again. Since she had rejected him twice before—however
gently—it is difficult to believe that he would risk being
wounded a third time. Further, she had had six years
between her marriages to reunite with him, but had not
done so. Although a bad marriage to Stackelberg could
have made a union with Beethoven seem more attractive,
this seems a selfish motive for a woman so highly regarded
by others. By comparison, the Beloved was a woman with
whom he had associated before the letter was written, and
from whom he had assurance of love. Josephine had led
Beet-hoven to believe just the opposite.

• Beethoven would have had no reason to believe that he
and Josephine would "see one another soon" since they
had not seen one another before he left Vienna, and not for
five years before that. After her February 1810 marriage
to Christoph von Stackelberg and from that time the
Brunswick family rarely revisited Vienna. There is no
evidence that connects them between 1807 and 1812.

• Beethoven would not assume that he and Josephine had
a "goal to live together." In the Beloved letter, Beethoven

spoke of the woman's love for him, and that the goal to be together was *theirs*, not simply *his*.

• Beethoven had never used the *Du*-form of address with Josephine in other love letters he had sent her, and none of her letters used it with him. That is not to say that they did not do so verbally.

• As for Minona, the often-presumed illegitimate daughter of Beethoven and Josephine: her conception had occurred around July 3, when Beethoven was already in Prague. We know from various letters that summer, that Josephine was in Vienna at least until mid-August. Whoever had fathered Minona, it most definitely had not been Beethoven. Further, Josephine had not found Beethoven sexually attractive in either 1805 or 1807. Was her marriage to Stackelberg so bad that Beethoven started looking good to her by 1812?

Anna Marie Erdödy has several arguments in her favor as being the recipient of the letter, the main one being that she was in the right place at the right time.

• By the time the Beloved letter was written, she and Beethoven already had established a long-term (at least 12-year) intimate relationship. Intimacy is evident in the Beloved letter, and the mixture of philosophy and mundane news in the letter is similar to other letters he wrote to her, though admittedly not in terms of passion (although some letters to her have been lost or destroyed). Josephine is the only woman we know for certain had received a love letter from Beethoven; even Antonie Brentano cannot make that claim

• They had seen each other prior to his trip to Prague-Teplitz. They had been close neighbors, as they usually were, throughout 1811 and the first part of 1812, and notes indicate that they saw one another regularly during this time period (i.e. Beethoven remarked to Zmeskall that he was "enjoying Erdödyian feasts").

• As we shall see in a moment, they did use the *Du*-form of address with one another.

• Most importantly, Anna Marie spent the summer of 1812 at her home in Hernals, a small town just west of Vienna. Klosterneuberg (a "K" town also west of Vienna) was an important market town of the day and would have been the point of the nearest post-delivery to both Jedlersee (Anna Marie's estate just north of the city) and Hernals. Beethoven visited Hernals in September 1812, and therefore saw his Beloved as he had indicated he would in his letter to her. This fulfills our main criteria that wherever Beethoven expected to be at the time he wrote his letter, that was where the Beloved would have been also, both to receive the letter and to have a reunion with him.

A RESPONSE TO THE BELOVED

It has been assumed that the Beloved letter had been written in response to a letter Beethoven had just received from his Beloved. This was presumed because in the first part of his letter, Beethoven wrote "Why this deep sorrow when necessity speaks?" as if he were answering a sorrowful letter he had just received. Solomon suggested that Antonie Brentano—Beethoven's alleged Beloved—had mailed a letter on July 5 from Prague and that it had arrived on the morning of July 6. Note that there is absolutely no evidence of any such letter, from Prague or anywhere else—only what *appears* to be Beethoven's question or response to someone. Had Beethoven received any letter at all, there is no reason to believe that it had to have come from Prague—that is simply where Antonie was, and since Solomon theorized her to be the Beloved, it was a natural progression of thought to assume that the letter had come from there. Since it is more likely that the Beloved was still in Vienna, if there had been any letter at all, it would have come from there instead. It is even possible that a letter had been received by him while he was in Prague and that he took it on to Teplitz with him before answering it. If, for argument's sake, we assume that there had been a letter from the Beloved, even though there is no evidence for it, the question is, could Beethoven have received the letter in

Teplitz from Prague in time to reply to it when he dated the portion of the letter containing this question as "July 6 *in the morning*?" No, because the two events would have coincided.

Beethoven had arrived in Teplitz in the middle of the night and had been housed in *temporary* quarters until his regular room was ready. The sender, mailing a letter to Teplitz, could not have known exactly where to address the letter, so no letter could have gone *immediately* from the mail coach to his hands. Beethoven was not registered on the *Kurliste*—aka *Kurgaste*,the Teplitz police guest list—as guest #806 until July 7—the day he *finished* his letter. It was only then, when he had taken a room at the "Eiche" that his exact location would have been known and the letter could have been delivered to him. Under these circumstances, no letter could have reached him in time for him to make a reply on the morning of July 6. Only a letter sent to him while he was in Prague could have been received in time for him to reply at the time that he did. There was no time for Antonie to have mailed a letter to Beethoven in Prague because the Brentanos did not arrive until July 3 and Beethoven left the morning of July 4. Of course, she could have mailed it before leaving Vienna, but how could she have known to where the letter should be addressed? Did Beethoven tell her where he would be staying in Prague?

Another possibility is that Beethoven was not answering a letter at all, and that his comment on the "deep sorrow" was simply his own philosophical question to himself. His notes and journals show that it was a habit of his to pose quite similar thoughts and questions, and he often referred to himself as "B" or "Beethoven" rather than as "me." In 1813, for example, he wrote a note that read: "God look down upon the unhappy B" not "down upon me." There is no reason why Beethoven could not have been asking of himself why *he*—or they—felt such sorrow when "necessity speaks."

One other possibility is that he was continuing a conversation he had had with her prior to leaving Vienna. Although it is conceivable that such an encounter had taken place in Vienna with either Josephine or Antonie, both of those ladies had husbands and families at home, which would have afforded little privacy for what appears to have been an emotional conversation. As there were legal changes pending in Anna Marie's relationship with her husband, such a private conversation with her in Vienna was entirely possible, and would have generated Beethoven's musing about their relationship and the verdict of "the Fates" which he expressed in his letter.

In any event, the existence of such a letter is pure speculation, and actually, not terribly important.

POSTED OR NOT POSTED?

One other question remains: did Beethoven post the letter to his Beloved? This cannot be known for certain, however, the situation certainly makes it seem as if he did. First, he took two days to write his letter, long enough to consider whether or not to send it. If he did *not* post it, then we must imagine that he hurried to finish writing it, ran down to mail it at the nearby post office it, and *at the last moment*, changed his mind. That is not impossible, but it does not seem likely. Second, he finished the third part of the letter quickly in order to make the midmorning mail, that is, he was in a hurry to post it. If the letter was his "first news" to his Beloved, he had already lamented in the letter itself that she would not receive it quickly enough to suit him. From his tone, he was quite anxious to mail it. Someone that eager to mail a letter does not usually change his mind.

If he did not send it, but reconsidered at the last moment, which admittedly is entirely possible, perhaps he considered it too personal a message to entrust to the written word. He may have felt that he would be compromising the lady were it to be found in her possession and read by eyes other than hers. Yet, as already noted, the urgency with which he acted does not make this scenario likely, either.

On the other hand, if he *did* post it, how did his letter get back to him? In the event that the letter had been sent to Josephine, this author feels she would have returned it immediately. It is doubtful that she would have kept it for very long, for to do so would have weakened her resolve, and would have made a painful situation even more agonizing. Although her mother knew of her daughter's unhappiness with Stackelberg and encouraged her to divorce him, Josephine did not do so. She had already resigned herself to honoring her marriage vows and protecting the financial interests of her children whom Stackelberg supported. To encourage Beethoven surely would have seemed cruel to her, for marriage to him still was out of the question.

Returning his letter might have seemed to her the kindest response. What other could she have offered him?

If sent to Antonie, one must wonder when she had the opportunity to return it to him, considering that she was with her husband and child? Surely its return would have been accompanied by a highly emotional interchange between the two of them, something Franz Brentano certainly would have noticed.

Now what of Anna Marie? We know that Beethoven saw her in Hernals prior to his trip to Linz. There are two possibilities: she returned it to him or he asked for its return, either then, or sometime later. She kept all his other letters, why would she have returned this one? From his letters to her, we know that when he made her angry, she was capable of "paying him back sixfold." She had no qualms about expressing anger and she was as capable of inflicting wounds as Beethoven himself. (See Chapter 26: *The Quarrel... and Forgiveness*). So the question becomes, when was it returned to him (or retrieved by him)?

This author thinks it unlikely that Beethoven and Anna Marie had quarreled in Hernals during his visit(s) in 1812, because Beethoven displayed no dispondency either while he was in Linz, or after his return to Vienna late that year. In fact, his attendance at various soirees in Linz, and his completion of his exuberant Eighth Symphony and the second movement of the magnificent and joyful *G major Violin Sonata*, point to his light-heartedness. If he had only just lost his Beloved, why did he not grieve over her loss immediately rather than delaying his reaction until many months later? The answer is simple: Beethoven had *not* lost his Beloved; he was very much with her, as his musical output and demeanor shows.

Because there was a sudden cessation of correspondence between Beethoven and Anna Marie the following year, coupled at that time by a change in Beethoven's mood and creativity, another quarrel seems likely, although the actual time of its occurence is not known. We think most likely it had taken place sometime after their return to Vienna, probably in the early spring. We believe that Beethoven, encouraged by her warm reception in Hernals, and by the 1812 property transfer to her, once again had pressed the issue of marriage with her. We note from a letter to Josephine that Beethoven could be "pushy" on issues of importance to him: "Don't break [my heart] by pressing a wider course on me," she wrote in 1807. One item among others (which will be discussed later) pointing to a quarrel is Beethoven's admonishment to himself in the following note written May 13, 1813:

> Oh fearful conditions which do not suppress my feeling
> for domesticity...Learn to keep silent, O friend! Speech
> is like silver, But to hold one's peace at the right moment
> is pure gold.

Knowing that hardly anything could have hurt him as deeply as having his heartfelt letter given back to him, an angry Anna Marie paid him back "sixfold" by returning it to him. Likewise, nothing could have wounded her as much as Beethoven demanding his letter's return, which he may have done in retaliation for her continued refusal to marry him. We cannot know which occurred, but surely one or the other. (We note that this argument also could be applied to Josephine.)

Because the letter was one of the deepest expressions of emotion he had ever committed to paper, Beethoven chose to keep it rather than destroy it. He had not written the Beloved's name in it, therefore if it were ever found, it would not compromise her. Keeping it in a secret compartment ensured that it would not come to light until after his death. In that way, it was much like the *Heiligenstadt Testament:* he did not go through with any suicidal plans he may have had, and there was little likelihood of his dying immediately (given that he was only 31 at the time), yet it was so expressive of his inner self that he did not destroy that document either, but preserved it all of his life. In that light, it is not surprising that he also kept the Beloved letter.

Although the Josephine love letters expressed similarly deep feelings, the lady kept them herself, and Beethoven was in no position to decide whether they should be maintained or destroyed. With his inclination to preserve such things, he perhaps might have kept them as well,hidden away, as most people are inclined to keep old love letters among their personal momentos of happy times with those who were once dear to them.

The Beloved letter was the greatest personal treasure Beethoven ever owned, a testament to the height of his undying passion and devotion. Such an item would not have been simply tossed into the trash.

9
The Proximity of the Beloved

There has been general agreement among biographers that Beethoven had been in proximity to the Beloved during 1811 and 1812 since the passion in the letter could not have been generated through correspondence alone. Unger stated that "Thayer... takes for granted the probability that [Beethoven] had enjoyed a conversation with his Immortal Beloved prior to his setting out on his journey." Although it is unwise to "take things for granted," because Thayer noted that the conversation took place sometime *prior* to Beethoven's journey and not while he was *on* his journey, his statement may be accepted. If however, as we believe, Beethoven had enjoyed a long-term relationship with his Beloved, spanning years, such an immediate conversation might not have been necessary. From 1810 to the time he left for Prague in 1812, Beethoven resided at the Pasqualati House where he was a close neighbor of Anna Marie Erdödy. The house where Beethoven lived was only three or four doors removed, about a block away, from the Countess's. By contrast, the Birkenstock-Brentano house was situated in a remote suburb of Vienna, the Landstrasse. While Beethoven was virtually next door to the Countess, he was across town from the Brentano family. Beethoven lived on the Landstrasse only twice: once in 1817 when Karl's boarding school belonging to the Giannatasio del Rio family moved there, and again in 1820 when Countess Erdödy took up residence there. When Beethoven did live there, he noted that it was far away from the hub of Vienna. To Rudolph, who lived in the "Inner City" he wrote, on December 31, 1817: "Unfortunately I am obliged to live at a great distance from Y.I.H." None of this needs to be taken for granted as the residences of everyone involved are firmly documented. Further, through Beethoven's notes to Anna Marie, we know that she was very much a part of his life at this time. They had reconciled following their 1809 quarrel, and this reconciliation had come prior to March 1811, with their relationship continuing throughout 1812. Corroborating letters will be presented in Part IV: *The Beethoven-Erdödy Relationship.*

Although Beethoven was surely in proximity to his Beloved prior to his trip, Solomon asserted that Beethoven and his Beloved *must* have been in contact with one another *on or around July 4* of 1812, while he was *on* his trip. This was so, Solomon said, because in the Beloved letter Beethoven wrote "Today—yesterday—what tearful longings for you." "This last," Solomon wrote, "implies that they parted on July 4." It implies nothing of the sort. Here is yet another example of what happens when only a portion of a quote is presented: truth again becomes distorted. The *actual* quote is "Love me—today—yesterday—what longing with tears for you—you—my love—my all—farewell—O continue to love me—." This indicates a past (yesterday), a present (today), and a future (continue), not strictly a measure of specific days. A person's memory is hardly restricted to the events of one or two past days, and Beethoven was not necessarily referring to July 3 and 4. *Yesterday* can as easily refer to a "time past"—days, weeks, months—as it can to "the day before today."

Solomon claimed that Beethoven only alluded to events which occurred between July 4 and 7, although there was one important event to which he did not allude at all, and that was of seeing his Beloved. Beethoven made no mention of Prague at all, nor of anything they might have shared there. It is unusual for a person to see someone, particularly someone dear, and then, in a follow-up letter to say absolutely nothing about their meeting.

Solomon believed that Beethoven had not mentioned Prague because he had not had a need to do so, because his Beloved had been there, yet if she *had* been there, surely Beethoven would have said something about it: that he had been glad to see her, or sorry that they had had to part. He spoke instead of Vienna and how her presence there made him the "happiest and unhappiest of men."

Beethoven had been traveling, and during those "last few days"—between July 4 and 5—he had been in transit or stuck en route. It was not a requisite that his thoughts had to be connected with events in Prague prior to his departure. Over the course of a long carriage ride and a period of time waiting for a repair, he had begun thinking about his life. That is not unusual. How many of us have spent time thinking similar thoughts about our lives while similarly engaged? While in Prague, he had been in close contact with both a married couple (the Brentanos) and with a man engaged to be married (Varnhagen von Ense). It was only natural that such interactions had brought to mind his own lonely singleness, his own Beloved, and his desires to be married to her. It does not follow that he had to have been in contact with his Beloved or with any significant person during that particular time period in order to have such reflections, since our thoughts are hardly restricted to such a narrow view. Unless Beethoven was suffering from some sort of memory problem, there is no "existing evidence" that he had to be thinking solely of a woman he had seen in Prague during the few days preceding the writing of his letter. It also is not significant that Beethoven did not mention his Vienna-to-Prague trip in the Beloved letter since there are at least three explanations as to why he did not:

- he could have written about that portion of his travels to the lady in question in a separate letter while he was still in Prague, the "first news" he had mentioned in the Beloved letter, or

- since his visit to Prague was strictly business, he did not think it important enough to mention, or, most likely,

- while he was alone in Teplitz his thoughts turned to more pressing inner concerns. Having already covered other mundane details of his trip to Teplitz such as his carriage and room problems, he had not wanted to burden his letter further with details of a short and uneventful business trip. It was, after all, a passionate letter to his lover, not a memorandum to his publisher.

Because Solomon believed the Beloved had been in Prague prior to the letter being written, and since Antonie and her husband had indeed been there, this provided him with "evidence" toward her being the Beloved. It was his contention—completely unsubstantiated—that it was in Prague (or shortly before) that she had declared to Beethoven her intention to leave her husband and children in order to be his wife. While there may be reason to suspect that Antonie, in a desperate move to remain in Vienna, may have told Beethoven of her love for him while they were in Franzensbrunn, and that Beethoven had gently but firmly rebuffed her advances, there is no evidence that she did so in Prague.

At this point, it is important to interject an important fact relative to the issue. Antonie Brentano's last child was born March 8, 1813. This means the child was conceived—based on a normal 280-day gestational period—around June 2, *before* the time that Solomon claimed she had declared her love for Beethoven in Prague. It is a wonder (and a thankful one, at that) that paternity for this child was not summarily assigned to Beethoven!Only Susan Lund, a novelist, has given this serious thought, an issue with which we will deal in the next chapter. Perhaps it was only the fact that he was dreadfully ill, and thus ill-disposed both mentally and physically toward having any sexual relations at the time of the child's conception that protected him from other biographers giving credence to Lund's speculation and, as Beethoven called it, "tittle-tattle."

Antonie had already borne three children,and was not a first-time mother who might not have recognized the early signs of pregnancy. The June 2 conception date means that she must have known she was pregnant a fourth time by the time she and her husband reached Prague, if not before. Although William Kinderman stated that this child had been born "approximately nine months after the letter had been written," this is a slight stretch of the truth. The child had been born *eight* months after the letter, and she would have been four weeks pregnant, and two weeks overdue on her monthly cycle, at the time Solomon suggested that she had declared her love for Beethoven. At any rate, she surely discovered she was pregnant long before the summer's end. Why, then, did she not discourage Beethoven from joining them in Karlsbad and accompanying them to Franzensbrunn?

Probably for the logical reason that she did not know Beethoven was coming to Karlsbad, as that had not been his intention when they parted in Prague.When he unexpectedly came to Karlsbad, she may have seen his arrival as an answer to her prayer. She wanted desperately to stay in Vienna, and suddenly Frankfurt was looming on her horizon. Under the circumstances she might have considered leaving her husband for another man even though she was carrying her husband's child. Normally she would have known that Beethoven would not want her as soon as he found out she was pregnant by Franz, but her desperation may have clouded her rationality. In the best of times, she had a fragile hold on mental stability, and the realization that her time in Vienna was coming to an end easily could easily have been too much for her to handle.

Although in his essays, Solomon noted quite frankly that he knew of Antonie's pregnancy, for some reason it did not deter him from claiming that she was the Immortal Beloved. Solomon's suggestion that Antonie had declared her intention to leave her family for Beethoven in Prague was based on the following note that Beethoven wrote to his friend Varnhagen von Ense:

> I was sorry, dear Varnhagen, not to be able to spend the last evening with you in Prague, I myself felt that it was not the right thing, but a circumstance which I could not foresee prevented me from doing so—therefore do not think badly of me for it—by word of mouth more about it.—[1]

It was from this that Solomon came to the conclusion that the Beloved's sudden and unexpected presence in Prague, and the declaration of her love and her intentions, had been the "unforeseen circumstance" to which Beethoven referred. If Antonie had been Beethoven's Beloved, and if she had declared anything to him in Prague, it would have been the fact of her pregnancy, necessitating the termination of their relationship. Such news would have killed all hope of their being together, and there would have been no optimism whatsoever in the Beloved letter—and likely no letter at all! Under these circumstances, they would have made a clean break of it, and avoided one another—or, at least, Beethoven would have avoided her to spare her emotional

---

[1]Anderson, pp. 377-378.

turmoil—rather than spending an extended period of time with her and her husband that summer.

We will explore Antonie's alleged declaration more fully in Chapter 15. For the moment, let us return to Beethoven's note to Varnhagen von Ense. In order to let logic and common sense guide us, we must consider Beethoven's relationship with Varnhagen. Beethoven met him in 1811 in Teplitz through Franz Oliva—Beethoven's sometime secretary and assistant since 1810. Varnhagen was a playwright and novelist. The two men took a liking to one another—they were both anti-French and pro-German—and Beethoven hoped that Varnhagen could write opera librettos for him. An interesting fact about Varnhagen is that he was acquainted with Bettina Brentano—and probably the rest of the family, as well—well enough to comment to Leopold Schefer that Bettina "throws herself with a sort of mania on men noted for their power of intellect; she wishes to gnaw at all of them and finally to throw their bones to the dogs."[2] Beethoven and Varnhagen knew each other about six weeks before they parted company. They met again, briefly, in Prague, the following year. On June 3, 1812, Oliva asked Varnhagen, on Beethoven's behalf, to persuade Prince Kinsky to pay the composer the full amount of the annuity contract due Beethoven in notes of redemption. Varnhagen was successful, and wrote Oliva on June 9 that Beethoven could collect the notes due him when he passed through Prague on his way to Teplitz in July. An earlier letter written in March from Oliva to Varnhagen shows that it was Oliva who kept Varnhagen abreast of what was happening with Beethoven. There exists only one letter addressed directly from Beethoven to Varnhagen. Although there may have been other letters, now lost, it cannot be assumed that Beethoven and Varnhagen were particularly close, even though they had similar political views and certainly liked and respected one another. In terms of their relationship it is unimaginable that Beethoven would even *think* of confiding something as delicate as Antonie's confession of love, or a love relationship he had with her, to Varnhagen. Since the man knew the Brentanos, Beethoven never would have gossiped about one of them to von Ense—revealing something embarrassing to everyone concerned, particularly when it concerned a love affair in which Beethoven himself was a principal player. Beet-

---

[2]Herriot, pp. 193-194.

hoven did not confide such things to men he had known twenty years. He certainly would not have done so with someone he knew only a few months, at best. Thayer noted that "With Varnhagen... the meetings during the sojourn at Teplitz this year (1812) seem to have been few and fleeting."[3]

Solomon presumed that Beethoven did not end up telling Varnhagen what the "unforeseen circumstance" had been, and wrote that "Varnhagen's memoirs are silent on this matter; apparently he never received the promised explanation."[4] In his letter, Beethoven had been under no obligation to provide Varnhagen with details for cancelling their plans. He simply could have told Varnhagen that something had come up to prevent their seeing each other that last day in Prague without going into detail. Yet Beethoven *chose* to add "more about it by word of mouth," leaving himself open to being questioned about it by Varnhagen later on. Clearly Beethoven *intended* to tell Varnhagen about the "unforeseen circumstance," and had no compunction about doing so. And after this tantalizing bit of potential gossip had been dangled before Varnhagen, could one imagine that Varnhagen *would not have asked about it*?

There is another explanation for Beethoven's unexpectedly cancelling his meeting with Varnhagen which is far more likely than Solomon's dramatic, but improbable, little rendezvous scenario. For argument's sake, we might assume that the "circumstance" *had* involved the Brentanos (though just as easily, not). What occurred was probably this: July 3 was the composer's last night in Prague, and the Brentanos' first. From there, Beethoven was going on to Teplitz, and the Brentanos to Karlsbad. The latter were not planning to return to Vienna until October, and then only briefly. Upon returning, they planned to pack up their household and move back permanently to Frankfurt. Thus July 3 was the only night the three friends could be sure of seeing each other, for—with the task of packing to leave before them—there was no guarantee that the Brentanos would have time to visit with their friend Beethoven one last time once they were all back in Vienna. (And, of course, Beethoven might have considered that he also would be too busy—in the welcoming arms of his Beloved—to spend time with the Brentanos.) Thus the

[3]Thayer/Forbes, pp. 536.
[4]Solomon, pp. 164.

Brentanos arrived in town and prevailed upon Beethoven to have a farewell dinner with them. Although he felt it was "not the right thing" to do in that he had already made plans with Varnhagen, under the circumstances he agreed to dine with them. It was not a situation important enough for him to go into detail with Varnhagen in his short note to him, thus Beethoven promised to explain his sudden cancellation in person later. There is no reason to believe that Beethoven did not do exactly that. It is not "apparent" at all, as Solomon asserted, that Varnhagen had never been told what the circumstance had been. Its sheer lack of importance and interest more likely was the reason that Varnhagen excluded it from his memoirs, either on purpose, or simply because he had forgotten about it.

Here, common sense must prevail: The trio was in Prague together less than a day, and Antonie was in the company of her husband and child. There was no opportunity for any such dramatic scene, as Solomon proposed, to have taken place between Antonie and Beethoven at that time. Further, the trio had no reaction to it: Antonie and Franz continued on to Karlsbad and Beethoven went on to Teplitz. True, Beethoven did then pen his letter, but it was not one of goodbye as it should have been under those circumstances. And, logically, Beethoven would not later have gone on to Karlsbad as if nothing had happened and confronted her yet *again*. Prague would have been the setting for the end of their relationship, for the final chapter in their love affair. Thus no "declaration of love" in Prague on Antonie Brentano's part could have been Beethoven's "unforeseen circumstance" in Prague, at least, not as it related to his Beloved.

⚜ *10* ⚜
Matters of Paternity

In 1988, the *Journal of the American Beethoven Society* printed an essay by Susan Lund which took Solomon's theory of the Immortal Beloved a giant step further. Lund, a novelist, demonstrated in this article how truly fine a one she is. It was her contention, using distorted and misplaced quotes and innuendo—and in one instance, an outright fabrication—to prove her point: that Beethoven had fathered Antonie Brentano's last child, a son named Karl Josef. Because there inevitably will be some who will give credence to this outrageous assumption, it is important to hold up Lund's major points for examination and thus dispense with them.

We should recall that Beethoven was quite ill in 1812, which prompted his trip to the Bohemian spas in the first place. This fact did not deter Lund—as it did not Kaznelson[1]—from asserting that he had fathered children that summer. It is difficult to imagine a man too sick even to write letters having so much sexual energy. In Antonie's case, we also recall that during his visits, she was in her bedroom while Beethoven remained in her anteroom, playing the piano. If he was able to impregnate her under those conditions, he surely was a greater man than any of us previously suspected!

---

[1]Kaznelson put forth the theory that Beethoven had fathered Josephine Brunswick von Stackelberg's last child, Minona.

GUILT AND ATONEMENT

It was Lund's supposition (following Solomon's idea) that Beethoven had "appropriated" his nephew as "atonement" for having fathered Karl Josef Brentano, a child he was unable to raise himself. To suggest that Beethoven "appropriated" Karl for reasons of guilt is ludicrous as he had no reason to feel guilty. However, the issue of Beethoven and his nephew is so complex, that it cannot be addressed here except in the most cursory fashion. Lund wrote, "...writing of the adoption by Beethoven of his nephew Karl in 1816, Solomon shows that Beethoven believed he had become a father." It was her contention that Beethoven often became "confused" when speaking of Karl van Beethoven and Karl Josef Brentano, and, unable to keep their relationships to him straight, tended to call his nephew, "my son," and referred to himself as Karl van Beethoven's father. But why shouldn't he? The very act of adoption confers genuine fatherhood upon a man, and any man who cannot regard himself as a "true father" to his adopted child has no business raising that child. Lund's statement implies that there is something psychologically amiss with adoptive parents seeing themselves as their child's "true parents."

THE SEDUCTIVE INVALID

"If Antonie Brentano did pursue Beethoven," Lund asserted, "it would seem impossible for the relationship not to have been of a sexual nature." Why is that impossible? Lund assumed here that an obsessive love for Beethoven on Antonie's part was —must have been—reciprocal, which was not the case.This implies that men are creatures driven by uncontrollable lust and therefore are incapable of avoiding sex with obsessed "groupies." Yet common sense should tell us that a woman's fantasy does not mean that the man who is the object of her delusions—particularly one with moral standards—necessarily has had, or even wanted to have, sex with her. Why must we assume that Beethoven had been ensnared by Antonie's ardor and found her irresistable, when he already had at this time a satisfying relationship with another woman? We also must remember two things: one, Beethoven felt that man's baser instincts could be controlled with reason, so that even if he had been inclined to take advantage of Antonie's misplaced passion, he would not have done so; two, to give credence to this idea is to say that an emotionally and physically ailing Antonie was capable of seducing him.

EASILY RELINQUISHED MOTHERHOOD

"Given the fact that she had been orphaned of her own mother at age 7," Lund said, "it might have been easier for Antonie Brentano to envisage leaving her children than for Beethoven to face taking her from them." This is nonsense. No mother who loved her children as much as Antonie did hers would find it easy to leave them. Mothers invariably feel great responsibility for their children's welfare, sometimes even more than they should. In addition, a mother who, as a child, had endured the trauma of losing her parent would find it extremely difficult to inflict that same pain upon her own offspring, and she would do anything to avoid having them live through her anguish. Antonie's diary indicates how much the love of her mother had meant to her, how deeply she missed her, and how she believed in the importance of children growing up close to their parents, especially their mother. She also wrote to her father that, "These dear and lively children mean everything to me, and my striving to having them develop good qualities is the highest tendency of my life." To accuse Antonie Brentano of being able to easily leave her children for Beethoven does her a grave injustice as a mother. Only in a time of extreme emotional stress—which did not become a factor in her life until late in the summer of 1812 when her move back to Frankfurt became imminent—might she have been tempted to abandon them as a means to save herself and her sanity.

SHOCKING DEVELOPMENTS

Lund claimed, as did Solomon, that in Prague, Beethoven had been "shocked" by developments in that city when the Brentanos arrived. Solomon attributed the composer's shock to Antonie's declaration of love for him; Lund to Antonie advising him of her pregnancy and his impending fatherhood. Lund made this claim by distorting Beethoven's letter to Varnhagen in which he wrote: "I was sorry, dear V, not to have been able to spend the last evening in Prague with you, and I found that shocking..."[2] The "that" refers very clearly to the breaking of Beethoven's promise to see Varnhagen, not to anything which he might have heard.

Beethoven did make one reference to being "startled" during his stay in Franzensbrunn. In his letter to Breitkopf & Härtel, he wrote: "I have too much of several things, of bathing, idling, and so forth; and I am weary of many other unavoidable incidents and startling events—" From this, we feel that if there had been any declaration by Antonie of her passionate devotion to Beethoven, it only could have been in Franzensbrunn. With time running out and her return to Frankfurt at hand, this would have been one desperate and unplanned attempt on her part to remain in Vienna with the one man who was not only firmly rooted there, but for whom she had an almost religiously fervent attachment. While still in Prague, Antonie would not have felt so intensely the reality of her situation: that she would soon be leaving her beloved Vienna forever. But in Franzensbrunn, that reality was suddenly thrust upon her. She was not a woman who coped well with change, and it was this inability which, we believe, may have caused her to momentarily forget her children's welfare, and her "good man Franz," and grasp at Beethoven as her savior. Naturally, any such overture on her part would have shocked Beethoven, for he had given her no reason—at least knowingly—to assume that he loved her. We believe she may have mistaken his kindnesses toward her for love, and, in her own mind, built a fantasy around him which alleviated her unhappiness. Beethoven's letter to his publishers indicates that he quickly wearied of her desperate devotion, yet it would have been difficult for him to extricate himself immediately from the situation. His arrival in Karlsbad had been unexpected. Thus he must have told the Brentanos why he had come—on the advice of his physician—and it would have seemed odd to Franz if he had absented himself so soon after his arrival against his doctor's order. Not wanting to hurt Franz by telling him the truth about his wife's delusions, he was trapped there for a time, and it is no wonder he found the situation wearying. Finally he was able to leave them in early September, returning to Karlsbad alone. We note that his first letter to the Brentanos after 1812 was not written until November 1815—three years later. Why did he put

---

[2]Other translations do not use the word "shocking" but read instead: "I felt that was not right."

such distance between himself and his "best friends in the world" if not to discourage Antonie's unrequited feelings? If he had known, as Lund contends, that Antonie had been carrying his child, would he not have written sooner, if only to inquire how she was? We believe he had decided to prudently let time and distance have a chance to temper her feelings, perhaps recognizing her declaration of love for what it truly was: the desperate act of an emotionally fragile woman.

As Lund also believed that Beethoven had learned while in Prague that Antonie was carrying his child, Lund thus concluded: "What more likely than that Beethoven would flee to his Beloved at this stage in their relationship?" Flee? The word denotes hurried movement. Beethoven had hardly "flown" to Antonie's side, for first he went on to Teplitz, and he did not go to Karlsbad until a month later. Such a delay can hardly be called a "flight" by any stretch of the imagination.

LIES AND DECEIT

"He moved with the Brentanos to Franzensbrunn allegedly on his doctor's orders, hardly credible unless Staudenheim was traveling round with his patient." Lund thus openly accuses Beethoven of lying to several different people about why he had gone to Karlsbad and Franzensbrunn. But why should he have felt the need to do so? He was not obligated to explain his movements to them, nor were they aware that the Brentanos were at the spas. Visiting several spas over the course of a summer was not uncommon. What never occurred to Lund was that Staudenheim probably either had prescribed visits to both spas before Beethoven had left Teplitz, or kept in touch with Beethoven via mail. Lund claimed that Beethoven had "left Teplitz in a hurry." Of course he had. He already had been in Teplitz a month with no alleviation of his physical ailments. He was anxious to be cured and eager to go back to Vienna. As soon as Staudenheim gave him his prescription to visit the other Bohemian spas—both of which dealt with digestive ailments—Beethoven left in the hope of quickly being restored to health. Does Lund believe he would have solicited advice from Staudenheim and then ignored it for several weeks until his originally planned stay in Teplitz had ended in mid-August? That only would have prolonged his absence from Vienna. When Staudenheim said "go," he went; why would he do otherwise?

Franz Brentano wrote to his half-brother in October, "Our journey depends on Toni's recovery." Lund found it odd that Franz did not mention Antonie's pregnancy to Clemens, when she was already in her fourth month. She therefore jumped to the unfounded conclusion that Franz was keeping Antonie's condition a secret, never considering that Clemens, a brother, already knew. Antonie had been sick a long time prior to becoming pregnant, and her illness was not related to it, nor was her recovery.

TO FRANKFURT...OR BONN?

In December 1816 Beethoven spoke of leaving the country. In his notes he wrote:

> Something must be done—either a journey and to this end the writing of the necessary works or an opera—if you are again to remain here during the coming summer, an opera would be preferable in case of circumstances that are only tolerable—if the summer sojourn is to be here, a decision must be made, where, how?

He also added

> In my opinion first the saline baths like those of Wiesbaden, etc. then the sulphur baths like Aix-la-Chapell [aka Aachen] (warm) Nenndorf (cold)...

Beethoven, ill, had consulted a copy of Hufeland's book on various spas and the medicinal treatments each offered. (Hufeland's book was in his personal library.) Lund, however, attempted to make the case that Beethoven had considered spas "close to Frankfurt" so that he could visit Antonie and his son. To the contrary, several of these spas are on the Rhine and fairly close to Bonn—a place where Beethoven had long wished to return. In fact Aix-la-Chapell (Aachen) is not at all near Frankfurt. It is in Westphalia near Belgium and Holland, and likewise far closer to Bonn than Frankfurt.

Lund does not make note of the fact that part of Beethoven's intention that summer had been to travel to Italy—where Anna Marie Erdödy happened to be—nor that he had written a note to himself which said "Be of good cheer for the sake of C..."

KARL JOSEF'S 1817 ILLNESS

Lund wrote, "As I reconstruct the story, Beethoven learned of Karl Josef's illness in April 1817." Lund was certainly right about one thing: it definitely is a story. The boy suffered from seizures, severe mental retardation, and violent behavior which manifested itself when he was about four. Lund attempted to connect his faulty genetics with Beethoven's alleged venereal disease, without noting that Antonie's eldest son, Georg, exhibited similar symptoms in his twenties. Both boys certainly could have traced their mental instability to their mother.

Lund claimed that the news of Karl Josef's illness caused Beethoven suddenly to become violent, yet his behavior in 1817 is little different from the way he characteristically was. For many reasons other than the Brentanos he was quite depressed that year, yet at no time could he have been characterized as "violent." Lund came to this conclusion based on a remembrance of Carl Hirsch who, from November 1816 to May 1817, took lessons from Beethoven. Beethoven, who hated having pupils, nevertheless took on Hirsch briefly out of respect for the deceased Albrechsberger. Hirsch's recollection, here noted, was given to Frimmel 63 years after the fact:

> Beethoven watched his student's hands closely, and when a mistake was made he would get very angry, become red in the face, and the vein in his temples and forehead would become swollen; he would also give his pupil a severe pinch through indignation or impatience; and once even bit him on the shoulder.[3]

Although Lund said that this violent reaction came as a result of Beethoven learning of Karl Josef's illness in April, there is no indication that the "bite"—if indeed there had been such a thing—had occurred in April or May. Beethoven had displayed anger with other pupils: in 1801 with Guilietta by shouting and tearing up music; with the Archduke by rapping him on the knuckles. This was not the isolated incident Lund tried to make it appear.

Lund also concluded that a letter from Beethoven's publisher, Simrock, written on October 23—which Beethoven said he never saw—contained news of Karl Josef. But why should it? At

---

[3]Thayer/Forbes, pp. 664-665.

the time, Simrock had known the Brentanos only a month! Why should the Brentanos discuss their deeply personal family life with a stranger?

Lund also "supposed" that Beethoven, having learned about Karl Josef's illness, had discussed this with his doctor, Malfatti, yet there is no basis for this supposition. She concluded this from a letter Beethoven wrote to Anna Marie in which he said:

> I changed doctors, because my own doctor, a wily Italian,
> had powerful secondary motives where I was concerned
> and lacked both honesty and intelligence.

Why should this refer to Karl Josef when it is well known how suspicious Beethoven was in general about physicians? And what secondary motives could Malfatti have had? Was he planning to blackmail Beethoven in regard to his "illegimate son?" There is no logical or sensible connection there.

UBIQUITOUS VIEWS

Lund claimed that the Sterbas' view of Beethoven's sexuality has become "ubiquitous" and as proof, cited four authors who have quoted the Sterbas in their work. Four people hardly constitute a wide-spread consensus. For those unfamiliar with the work of Richard and Editha Sterba, we will say in brief that they presented Beethoven as a psychologically abnormal man suffering from severe emotional and sexual problems bordering on the perverse, and that they used ambiguous statements and distorted quotes in order to support their contentions. Why Beethoven has stimulated so much Freudian analysis is anyone's guess, but from some of the things written about him, it appears that the psychoanalysts have far more serious sexual problems then the composer ever did.

DEATH WISH

In one of her more convoluted theories, Lund attempted to tie several diverse pieces of information into proof that Beethoven actually had wished Franz Brentano dead. In 1817, Beethoven had written Franz what Lund believed was an insincere letter prompted by his guilt:

All the members of the Brentano family have ever been dear to me; and you especially, my esteemed friend, I shall always remember with sincere regard. I myself would like you to believe that frequently I have prayed to Heaven for long preservation of your life so that for many years you may be usefully active for your family as its esteemed head.[4]

Lund was amazed by this letter, written as it was from one man to another, but it is little different from most of Beethoven's other letters, either in tone or content. To this letter, Lund tied a comment Beethoven made in his 1823 conversation book about Robert Gallenberg, Guilietta Guicciardi's husband. Beethoven wrote, "He was always my enemy, that was exactly why I did him all the good I could." What Lund wished to do here was to tie Beethoven's animosity toward Gallenberg expressed in 1823, to a letter of admiration he wrote to Franz Brentano six years earlier in order to prove that Beethoven wished Franz Brentano dead and therefore, out of guilt, wished him well instead, just as he had Gallenberg! Lund wrote, "It takes no stretch of the imagination to assume that Beethoven was filled with guilt at wishing this particular 'head of the family' dead." No? Well, she certainly stretched this author's imagination!

A PAINTING

Lund claimed that Franz Brentano had commissioned the artist Stieler to paint Beethoven's portrait for Antonie, and further noted that this was done with great secrecy. Now let us use some common sense: according to Lund's theory, Beethoven fathered a child with Antonie; why then would Franz want to have Beethoven's portrait painted as a gift for his unfaithful wife? Not only is this incomprehensible, it also is not true. According to Thayer, Stieler was given a letter of introduction to Beethoven by Franz Brentano. Stieler had done a painting of Antonie Brentano , and in the course of his work, no doubt had expressed his desire to paint Beethoven. Franz accommodated him by giving the artist a recommendation. Beethoven took a liking to Stieler and gave him three sittings, but afterwards grew tired of posing and refused to sit further. The portrait Stieler painted did not go

---

[4]Anderson, pp. 667-668.

to the Brentanos, as it would have had they commissioned it. Franz Brentano was, after all, an astute businessman; he hardly would have paid for a painting and then never asked for it! The portrait remained with the artist and his family for years until it was sold to Countess Sauerma in Berlin. The Brentanos later received a miniature copy of this painting. Also, none of this was done in secret as Lund suggested. Beethoven's conversation books have many references to the portrait, where comments were written by Bernard, Peters, and Oliva, along with a discussion of its merits in comparison to other portraits which had been painted.

FRANTIC LETTERS

The *Tagebuch* for 1817 has the following entries which Lund described as "frantic letters" to the Brentanos:

> a few days ago posted an unregistered letter, to Frankfurt
> On 22 April another unregistered letter to Frankfurt
> sent by post The same on the 26th. The same on the
> 29th, with a song.

Without seeing the letters, it is impossible to corroborate any of Lund's contentions: that they were frantic simply because they were sent within a few days of one another, that they had been sent to the Brentanos,[5] or that they concerned Karl Josef. On April 19, Beethoven had sent a lengthy (and also rather "frantic") letter to Sir Charles Neate[6] regarding his piano sonatas and other compositions. These, Beethoven said, he would send to Simrock in Germany if London decided not to publish them, and he wanted a decision immediately. His letter ends excitedly: "I swear you have done nothing for me, nothing, nothing!!" As Franz Brentano was Beethoven's intermediary with Simrock, there is every indication that the Frankfurt letters dealt with this issue of the sonatas. If the letters had dealt with Karl Josef instead, why would there have been a flurry of correspondence for one month—with one letter serving as a cover letter for a piece of music—followed by nothing more until December 6? Would Beethoven not have

---

[5]At this precise time, Beethoven was also in correspondence with Ferdinand Kessler who likewise lived in Frankfurt. One cannot be certain that at least some of the missing letters had not been intended for him. See Anderson, pp. 675-676.

[6]Anderson, pp. 669-681. A portion of the text is on page 287 of this book.

been at all concerned with the boy's health between May and December? At that time, there was another month of letters and then, again, nothing more. These letters, noted in the *Tagebuch* as having been dated December 27, 1817, and January 3 and 10, 1818, most likely dealt with his nephew Karl and Beethoven's urgency at having him relocated in a school in Bavaria. A January 6 letter to Giannatasio, Karl's schoolmaster, indicates that Beethoven was anxious to withdraw Karl from Giannatasio's school and put distance between the boy and his mother, who Beethoven felt had a negative influence on him.

Why are these letters missing? Lund assumed because they were of a delicate nature, but it is just as likely that Beethoven had written them with the same impatient or "pushy" tone he had used with Neate, and as such the Brentanos had not wanted to save them. And as we have noted before, the other possibility is that they were Beethoven's attempt to reject Antonie's desperate efforts to involve him in a love affair, and thus had been destroyed by her.

STRIKING CONCERNS?

In August 1823, Beethoven wrote a letter to Franz Brentano (the first since March of that year) regarding the composer's Mass. In the letter Beethoven added:

> You said in your letter that your little boy's health is improving. I am extremely glad about this. I hope that your wife too is well and also all your children and brothers and sisters.[7]

Lund commented that, "The specific exclusion of the 'little boy' from the other Brentano children is striking." She thought it odd that Beethoven should have "singled out" a child he had never met. Why is this odd? The "little boy" was the only one that Franz had also "singled out" in his letter to Beethoven by indicating that he had been ailing, so it was natural for Beethoven to make such a comment. And Beethoven hardly had excluded the other children, and not even Franz's siblings. Besides that, in that same letter, Beethoven also singled out Franz's older son who was by then living in London, hoping that this son might serve as an intermediary for him in England.

---

[7]Anderson, pp. 1077-1078.

A QUARREL

Lund wrote that Beethoven had had a "quarrel with the Brentano woman" in 1820, an assumption she made from an entry in Beethoven's conversation book made between January and February of that year.[8] Her translation of the note was "Are you reconciled with the Brentano woman?" From this she postulated that Beethoven had quarreled with Antonie Brentano over his failure to visit his son. Let us look at the German version of this note in Beethoven's conversation book:

Sind sie ausgesöhnt mit der Brentano?

Two things need to be pointed out: one, Lund's translation is "Are *you* reconciled..." when it should read "Are *they* reconciled..." A capital letter in *Sie* indicates a formal *you*, but a lower case *S* reads *they*. Two, the reference is to *der Brentano*, not *die Brentano*. *Der* is a masculine reference, not feminine.

From this, we know that Lund's suggestion that Antonie was angry because Beethoven did not make an effort to see Karl Josef is wrong. Whoever had needed to be reconciled with Franz Brentano, it had not been Beethoven. (We note, too, that "reconcile" also can mean "bring into agreement with.") To compound her error even further, in an earlier part of her essay, Lund claimed that Franz Brentano "probably" had forbidden Beethoven to visit the boy. Lund does not resolve this contradiction and, in fact, stated in still another part of her essay that Franz had wished to discuss authorizations for medical treatments for the boy with Beethoven. Even Lund was confused about whether Beethoven was to be included in making decisions about "his son," or be totally excluded from the boy's life.

THE DEATH REPORT

Lund attempted to connect Antonie with Beethoven's family by claiming that "of all the people Johann van Beethoven might have sent word about Beethoven's death, it had been to Antonie Brentano." This is untrue. Johann never sent Antonie any word of his brother's death. It had been a Viennese friend of Frau Brentano's, Moritz Trenck von Tonder, who had told her of the composer's passing. Solomon's note that Lund misread is:

---

[8]*Konversationshefte*, Vol. 1, p. 253.

"Trenck also sent to [Antonie] a report about Beethoven's last days written by his brother, Nicholas Johann."

THE CONVERSATION BOOKS...AGAIN[9]

Lund wrote that, "In a conversation book of late 1819, a striking entry in the hand of Beethoven's friend, Oliva, reads 'Because you always talk about the woman, the husband will recognize as your child among his children the one who possesses musical talent.'" This by itself seems an odd statement, because the book page on which this comment is written contains a four-way conversation involving Franz Oliva, Carl Peters, Joseph Bernard, and Beethoven. The conversation ranged from Chinese physionomy, to a tragic play by Weissenback, to an actor in Leipzig, to the Obervormundschaft (Board of Guardians), to a request from Beethoven to Bernard to help him draft a petition to the Magistrat regarding his nephew, Karl. As such, this was a strange interjection by Oliva, and difficult to explain. However, it in no way could have referred to Karl Josef Brentano who, now six years old, was both mentally and physically handicapped, and had been since he was four, and to whom no musical talent has ever been ascribed. The only woman who had musically-inclined children, (in particular, her daughter, Mimi) and who we know from both Beethoven's notes and a canon he wrote for her, was in Vienna and in Beethoven's life at the time this entry was written, late 1819, was Anna Marie Erdödy. She the only woman he would have had reason to talk about repeatedly. While this author is loath to throw yet another child into the paternity fray, one must note that what *was* reality and what Peter Erdödy *thought* was reality may have been two different things. A later chapter will show that Count Erdödy may have suspected Anna Marie of infidelity. Oliva's caution may have been a gentle reminder to Beethoven that being too open about his continuing relationship with Anna Marie might cause her family to make life even more difficult for her than they had already.

Lund wrote further: "An entry in Beethoven's hand a month later [early 1820], in the context of taking a child from its father, says 'And that I was and am.'" Lund's attempt to connect this statement to the Brentanos was not very clever, for its context shows that the line not only does not refer to the Brentanos,

---

[9]*Konversationshefte*, vol. 1, p. 149 and 193, respectively

it immediately follows a notation by Peters which reads "Countess Erdödy Kärthnerstrasse 1138, 2st." This author contends that Beethoven was expressing his feeling that he had been more of a father to the Erdödy children, than had their biological parent, Peter, who had abandoned them. As indeed he had.

FRANZ BRENTANO

In various speculations about the relationship between Beethoven and Antonie Brentano, Franz Brentano is the most neglected character. He was a brilliant businessman, and yet by inference, he must have been either the most exceptionally liberal or exceedingly stupid man ever born. Briefly, let us review Franz's involvement in this alleged relationship concocted by Lund:

Franz's best friend falls in love with Franz's wife.

Does this bother him? No, even when they are together for months at a time, he either never notices or does not care.

His best friend gets his wife pregnant. According to Lund, Franz's wife even tells him that he is not the father.

Does this bother him? No, in fact, he is willing to continue doing his "friend" favors. He even loans him large sums of money. After the child is born, he is discovered to have medical and emotional problems. On one hand, Franz wants advice from the boy's father on how to handle the boy's treatment. On the other hand, Franz forbids his friend, the father, to see the boy. Franz obviously is a very confused man.

Franz's wife decides she wants a portrait of her lover.

Does this bother him? No, he is even willing to pay for it.

Does no one find any of this behavior the least bit strange?

As we noted, Susan Lund is a novelist by trade, and from these speculations about Beethoven and the Brentanos, an imaginative one. She has written a two-volume novel about Beethoven which she claims was based on source material—very loosely, if this essay is any indication. As fiction obviously is her forte, we are at a loss to explain her inclusion in a scholarly journal. Because she *was* given that exposure as a legitimate scholar, however, we felt it necessary to address her ludricous hypothesis. As we have shown, her theory has no basis in fact at all, and Beethoven was not, as she claimed, the biological father of Antonie Brentano's son.

❖ 11 ❖
Elements in the
Letter to the Beloved

What clues might there be in the text of the Beloved letter itself that might lead us to the recipient's identity? George Marek, author of *Beethoven: Biography of a Genius*, said of the Beloved letter that it had been written to

> a woman he has known and loved a long time. The letter breathes familiarity and intimacy which is almost conjugal. The letter is by a man who has consummated his relationship with a woman. He addresses her as 'Du.' A man did not do so unless he knew the woman intimately. 'Du' among adults not members of the same family was used only by lovers.[1]

Thus the first most important element to examine in the letter to the Immortal Beloved is its use of the intimate *Du*-form of address, always reserved for family members and extremely close friends, and rarely used without permission except in a master-servant or superior-subordinate situation. Biographers have noted correctly that this was the only letter—at least, that we know of—Beethoven wrote to a woman in which he addressed her using the *Du*-form throughout the entire letter.[2] What they

---

[1]Marek, p. 304. *Du* means *you*, as does *Sie* which is formal usage. Beethoven consistently used the *Sie* form of address, except with very special friends. Even most men Beethoven addressed only as *Sie*, and not as *Du*.
[2]Writer Alessandra Comini noted that Beethoven used *Dich* (informal) toward the end of his letter to Bettina Brentano, although the rest of his lengthy letter

have not noted was that one woman used the *Du*-form in writing to *him*. Although his surviving letters to this special woman do not use that form,[3] that is not surprising because Beethoven did not always trust that the words he put into writing would be seen only by the addressee. Many of his letters avoid speaking of issues by saying "more about this by word of mouth," and he frequently wrote his postscripts in French so that his servants—who usually delivered his notes—could not read them. Perhaps he feared that someone noting the *Du*-form in his letters to her might have tarnished her reputation or caused "tittle tattle," which he despised. Beethoven, ever the gentleman who never said an inappropriate word in front of a refined member of the opposite sex,[4] would not have wanted to compromise her. The lady obviously did not feel the same, or did not believe her letters to Beethoven were in danger of falling into others' hands, since she did not refrain from using the *Du*-form in writing to him. This may be why no other letters from her to him have survived. This one that did survive he had left behind at her home by mistake. The others he himself may well have destroyed in order to protect her. One also notes that, overall, he was not in the habit of saving letters.

Because the lady felt comfortable in using the *Du*-form with Beethoven, and the fact that its use between peers is mutual, it is safe to assume that he likewise used the *Du*-form, even if only verbally, with her. Not only the depth of emotion in the Beloved letter, but the level of his intimacy with her surely had prompted him to use the *Du*-form in this letter. It is interesting that his letters to Josephine, while passionate, are formal, indicating that although he loved her, they had not enjoyed physical intimacy. We also note that Beethoven had been careful not to put his Beloved's name, nor any initial referring to her, anywhere in his letter, although he customarily addressed his other correspon-

---

had used only the formal Sie. This was evidently not a "slip of the pen," as Beethoven had made corrections in his letter. It may have been his way of inviting her to use *Du* with him, as he had done in letters to another writer, Christopf Tiedge. But more likely he was only being playfully naughty, as he said he sometimes was, and perhaps curious whether this rather earthy and somewhat bawdy woman would notice his unorthodox familiarity, his "naughtiness."

[3]There are indications that some letters from him to her have been partially or completely destroyed or otherwise lost. See Chapter 31, *The Countess's Letters.*
[4]He was decidedly less decorous with lower class women and female servants who sometimes had items thrown at them or suffered verbal abuse.

dents, male and female, by name or initial, within the texts of his letters.

Who was this woman on such intimate terms with Beethoven? We have already encountered her, for at the time of the Beloved letter's writing, she already had been a part of Beethoven's life for more than a dozen years. Her name was Anna Marie Erdödy, and in 1815 she sent Beethoven a rhymed invitation asking him to come and stay with her at Jedlersee, in which she used the *Du*-form of address and other informal verbs which imply the *Du*-form. It follows that if she used the *Du*-form with him, he had done likewise with her. The invitation, in its original German and its translation, reads as follows:

Apollons erster Sohn!	Apollo's foremost son!
Du grösster grosser Geister,	You greatest of great spirits,
Der Tonkunst erster Meister	Music's first master,
Den jetzt Europa kennt	Now known to Europe,
Dem selbst Apollo frohnt,	To whom Apollo himself yields,
Und von demn Musenthrone	And from the Muses' throne
Belohnt mit seiner Krone:	Rewards with his crown:
Erhöre unsere Bitte,	Hear and grant our entreaty,
Bleib heut in unsere Mitte—	Remain today in our midst—
Der grosse Mann Beethoven	Great man Beethoven
Gibt Fiat unserm Hoffen	Give fiat to our hopes.
* * *	* * *
Marie die Alte	The old Marie,
Marie die Junge	The young Marie,
Fritzi die Einzige	The unique Fritzi
August detto	August ditto
Magister ipse	Magister ipse
Violoncello das verfluchte	The Accursed Violoncello[5]
Alter Reichs Baron	Old Baron of the Empire[6]
Ober-Mann-Amt	Chief Bailiff
* * *	* * *
An die	To the
die lorbeerbekrönte Majestät	laurel-crowned Majesty
der erhabenen Tonkunst	of the noble art of music

---

[5]Beethoven always referred to his longtime friend, Joseph Linke, this way.
[6]Probably Joseph Brauchle, the Erdödy children's tutor and another old friend of Beethoven's.

Ludwig v. Beethoven	Ludwig v. Beethoven
sehnlichste Bitte	a most ardent entreaty
der Jedlersee Musen	from the Jedlersee muses
dass ihr geliebter Apollo	that their beloved Apollo
noch den heutigen Tag	may pass this day
in ihrer Mitte zubringen	in their
möge	midst.[7]

In addition to the pronoun *Du* (you), other words such as *erhöre* (hear), *bleib* (remain/stay), and *gibt* (give) are all informal (familiar) uses of the verbs one would use in a *Du*-form letter.

Surviving letters to Beethoven from other women, most notably Josephine with whom he was clearly in love and certainly intimate on an emotional basis, did not use the *Du*-form, but rather the formal *Sie*. It is unthinkable that he would have used the *Du*-form with Antonie Brentano, not only because he had known her for only such a short time, but also because of her sensitivity to such matters. We note that she had found it awkward to use the *Du*-form with her own husband after their wedding, even though she had known him for two years before their marriage.

TONE AND CONTENT

Supporters of Josephine as the Beloved point to Beethoven's 1805-07 love letters to her as being similar to the Beloved letter. But are they? Both speak of eternal love, true, but his letters to Josephine, while certainly sincere, sound rather contrived. It is as if, his own words failing him, he borrowed language from Romantic writers in order to express his feelings for her. In these letters, he was eager to impress her, to win her heart. The tone and language of the Beloved letter are far different.

With his Beloved, he had no need to be other than himself. He had never had difficulty in opening his heart to this woman, and expressing his feelings to her in words rather than simply in music. In this case, unlike the letters to Josephine, his words are truly his own, heartfelt if clumsy, endearing in their lack of rhythm and grace, powerful in their sincerity. There is a truth here which rings deeper than any other letter he ever wrote. His Beloved's heart was won already. In his letter to her there was the

---

[7]Text taken from *Brief von Beethoven an Marie Gräfin Erdödy geb. Gräfin Niszky*, edited by Alfred Schöne, pp. 26-27 (Leipzig: Breitkopf & Härtel, 1867). Also reprinted in Steichen, p. 278

need to reassure, but not to impress. The impact of the Beloved letter overwhelms the Josephine letters, and we get a sense that this was not a letter he could have written to her.

OTHER REFERENCES, OTHER CONNECTIONS

Are there any other elements in the Beloved letter which possibly could refer to Antonie Brentano? Or could these elements, like the *Du*-form, refer more appropriately to someone else? The reader once again is referred to the Introduction to Part II for the full text of the letter.

"My Angel, my all, my self..."
Beethoven used the term "angel" several times in letters he wrote to Josephine. Again, this had convinced some that she had been the Beloved. As an example, we cite the following:

> You were so very sad yesterday, dear J[osephine] — am I really unable to influence you? — although you have so great an influence on me — and make me so happy — Do not give in so much to your tendency to be sad, for indeed it hurts me to see you thus — All good wishes, angel of my heart.[8]

In another 1805 letter to her he closed with "All good wishes, angel—of my heart—of my life—" However, it is possible, and even probable, that calling a loved one "angel" was simply the endearment he preferred using with a woman close to his heart, as some men are inclined to call their wives, or other women they know and love, "darling" or "sweetheart."[9]

The most telling portion of this line is "my self." There was only one woman who was Beethoven's "other self," his feminine counterpart in terms of her strength of will, her courage, her independence, her love of music which sustained her through physical pain, and most of all in terms of her outspokenness, her fiery personality, and her passion: Anna Marie Erdödy. Beethoven even referred to himself and Anna Marie as two "mortals with immortal minds." An "other self" indeed.

---

[8]Anderson, pp. 135-136.

[9]In one of the letters Bettina Brentano fabricated and alleged that Beethoven had sent her, she used "angel" as an endearment several times. Either she had heard him use it, or it was simply a common expression of affection at the time.

"Can our love exist but by sacrifices? ...by not demanding everything?"

Sacrifice would have been inherent in any of Beethoven's relationships. In the case of Anna Marie, she would have had to sacrifice her title were she to marry a commoner, but worse, her children. Even though Peter Erdödy had demonstrated indifference to his family, undoubtedly she would have lost her children to other members of his family. In addition, the children might have lost their right of inheritance, another factor which might have made her reluctant to remarry. There was also the matter of sacrificing her independence and the life she had painstakingly built for herself over the course of more than 10 years. In the case of "not demanding everything," she would not be able expect Beethoven, in his early forties, to change significantly so that he would be easier person with whom to live. Their personalities and lifestyles were firmly set, their legal complications were many, and only mutual compromise and great sacrifice—"not demanding everything," would allow them to achieve a satisfying conjugal relationship. Beethoven may have begun to realize that he was asking a great deal of her, but still hoped they might overcome the obstacles that stood in their way.

The situation was similar for Josephine, who, like Anna Marie, would have had to relinguish her title, financial security, and probably her children as well, for Stackelberg would not have allowed them to be raised by a commoner . However, as we have seen, these were not sacrifices she was willing to make or even consider, despite her love for Beethoven.

Antonie would have had to abandon her small children, as well as a good and decent husband, so great a sacrifice, in fact, that we do not believe she, like Josephine, would have made it. We do not believe it was a sacrifice that Beethoven ever would have asked of her, and because her husband, Franz, was Beethoven's friend, we also do not believe Beethoven would have considered sacrificing Franz's heart in the bargain.

"Esterhazy, traveling the usual road hitherward, had the same fate with 8 horses as I had with four..."

Beethoven's mention of Esterhazy is interesting because both Countesses—Erdödy and Brunswick—were well acquainted with him. The Erdödy, Brunswick, and Esterhazy families all represented old Hungarian ruling class nobility. In addition, the Erdödys had attended the same musical parties as the Esterhazys, hosted by van Swieten in the 1790s, and these two families were, in fact, related by marriage since 1763.[10] In addition, Beethoven had composed part of his *Mass in C* for Paul Anton's father, Nicholas, at Anna Marie's estate. News about Esterhazy—a fellow Hungarian nobleman and a person both Josephine and Anna Marie knew quite well—would have had far more meaning and interest for the Countesses than for Antonie who had lived in Frankfurt, Germany for many years, and who likely had little knowledge of the Esterhazys beyond the common knowledge that he was ambassador to Dresden. It is also interesting that Beethoven did not tell his Beloved *which* Esterhazy, although the family was quite large. Antonie had been in Prague, so it could be argued that she would have known from the newspapers which Esterhazy had been in the city and was able to guess which one of them had had the mishap. The Countesses likewise could have read of Esterhazy's departure for Prague in their Vienna newspapers. It also could be argued that Beethoven, in his "first news" had told Anna Marie or Josephine that Paul Anton was there in Prague with him because such news would have been of interest to either of them.

"My heart is full of much to tell you."

With others, such as Antonie Brentano and Dorothea Ertmann, close as he may have been to them, he could bring himself to speak only "in tones." Only with Anna Marie, and a few male friends, could he give voice to his feelings and emotions, and express himself in words. Even with Josephine he lamented that

> there are so many more things I should love to tell you—how much I think of you—what I feel for you—but how weak and poor are those words—at any rate, my words.[11]

It was seven years before he could confess his deafness to this woman, Josephine, the one he professed to love so much. Only to Anna Marie, his *Beichtvater*, his "father confessor," could he always say the words that filled his heart.

---

[10]Gates-Coon, p. 66.
[11]Anderson, p. 132.

"You are suffering you my dearest creature..."

Twice Beethoven mentioned his Beloved's suffering, but Antonie Brentano was certainly not the only person in his life who suffered from illness, infirmities, and personal anguish. Letters to both Josephine Brunswick and Anna Marie Erdödy remarked on their suffering, and on his wish to alleviate their pain. In one letter to Anna Marie, he mentioned her suffering three times:

> October 19, 1815, sent to Schloss (Castle)
> Paukowitz, Croatia:
>
> I see that my anxiety about you in connection with your journey must have been reflected in your intermittent sufferings during your travels. But — you really seem to be able to achieve your object. Hence I console myself with this thought and am now trying to console you. We mortals with immortal minds are born to suffer both joy and pain; and one might almost say that the best of us obtain joy through suffering —[12]

Anna Marie's physical ailments were far from her only source of suffering. She endured great personal loss as well. The Countess's only son, August (Gusti), a boy of 15 or 16, was killed in 1816. Beethoven wrote to her when he heard the news from Linke. "I weep here with you, grief seizes me for you and also for me, for I loved your son."

Dorothea Ertmann likewise suffered the loss of a child. While Beethoven was accustomed to sharing his deepest feelings with Anna Marie, and had been able to express his grief to her in a letter, he was unable to so with Dorothea. He offered her his condolences by way of his music, as he did with Antonie Brentano during her times of illness. And though Antonie Brentano later had a seriously ill child and Beethoven was aware of it, there were no letters of comfort written by Beethoven to her.

Josephine Brunswick, too, was often ill—another fellow sufferer. Letters to her as well remark on his desire to see her restored to health. His sympathies were not reserved for women; his letters to men, such as Archduke Rudolph, often expressed his concern over illnesses they suffered. This is not to say that Beethoven was not empathetic toward Antonie, only that he sympathized with all those who suffered emotionally and physically. It

---

[12]Anderson, p. 527.

cannot be said that Antonie was the only woman toward whom he had these feelings, nor that she was the only "sufferer" in his life, thus his references in the Beloved letter to suffering cetainly do not prove he had written these sentiments to her.

On the subject of fellow sufferers, it is important to interject a note here with regard to Beethoven's choice of women. Among other accusations made against him is the one that he usually chose to associate himself with frail and delicate women, invalids whose infirmities precluded them from becoming his sexual partners. Yet this is hardly true of Anna Marie. There is a firm distinction between being *handicapped* and being *challenged*. As such, Countess Erdödy does not deserve the label "invalid." While true that she suffered from a delibilating illness, she hardly was infirm. No woman can be called frail who raises three small children alone, builds a fortune by her own handiwork,[13] manages several estates and a summer residence, and actively participates in social and political activities. There was nothing in her physical or emotional makeup which would have prevented her from being romantically intimate with Beethoven, if she had wished to be.

"I say to myself and to you, arrange that I can live with you."

In no way could Beethoven have arranged Antonie's divorce from Franz Brentano, nor Josephine's from Stackelberg. The only thing *he* possibly could "arrange" was a change in himself, making it possible for a woman to live with him on a day-to-day basis: to control his easily wounded sensitivities and pride, his jealousy, his tendency to imagine slights, his irritability.

Antonie worshipped Beethoven, and was oblivious to those flaws in his personality that would have made living with him difficult. He had no need to convince her of his desire to change for she saw nothing in him that needed changing.

On the other hand, neitherAnna Marie nor Josephine had any such delusions. In Anna Marie's case, she knew all too well what he was like to live with, and she would have required such a pledge if she were to be convinced to try living with him again. Further, both of these women had various "arrangements" that needed to be made if they were to be able to live with Beethoven

---

[13]Countess Erdödy was a wealthy woman, not simply by inheritance, but by her own ingenuity and perserverence.

legally. Both had legal matters pending: Anna Marie, her changing financial status with her husband; Josephine, her contemplation of divorce from Stackelberg.

"Never hide yourself from me."

Various Viennese police reports from 1811 through 1820 indicate that there had been much in Anna Marie's life that she may have kept hidden from Beethoven over the years: domestic problems, scandals, family hatred, financial hardships, and political mishaps. Anna Marie indicated that at one point in her life, she had become so destitute that she had been forced to make and sell handcrafts in order to support herself and her small children. Not telling Beethoven of her situation was not deceptive on her part. We cannot imagine her wanting to burden him with her own problems when he had so many of his own. Like Anna Marie, Josephine, too, had serious financial problems—ones she was never able to overcome, partly because of her own extravagance but mostly due to her rather shiftless husband. Josephine may have tried to conceal her impoverished situation from Beethoven as well. But Beethoven always wanted to know when his friends were in need, particularly in money matters, and was genuinely hurt when no appeal was made to him for help. We see that he made a remark similar to the one in the Beloved letter to his friend, Ferdinand Ries, upon learning that he was in desperate need of money:

> Why do you hide your need from me? None of my friends
> go in want as long as I have anything.[14]

Helping others was an ardent desire of his, and Beethoven's friends consistently remarked on his generosity. Even those he did not particularly like could expect aid from him, although he himself might have had little to spare. Naturally he would have urged both Josephine and Anna Marie to confide their problems and needs to him. Would Josephine have been too proud to ask for Beethoven's help? Perhaps. We know that Anna Marie certainly was, and that she was inclined to make decisions and take actions without Beethoven's input, which bothered him. While he certainly admired her ability to function so well in a male-dominated society, his letters make it clear that at times he would

---

[14]Wegeler & Ries, p.114.

have liked her to consult with him before making a decision, particularly if it had some effect on him.

> October 19, 1815: My anxiety for you is aroused for what
> may happen to you in regard to your journey and your
> occasional sufferings when traveling, as I see—the aim
> appears really to have been reached by you alone, and so
> I console myself...[15]

Josephine had once physically "hidden herself" from Beethoven when she had her servant turn him away from her door. However, Beethoven's note to Ries indicates that to Beethoven "hiding" meant not confiding in him.

What did Antonie have to hide from Beethoven? Nothing. She had no financial difficulties, and she had a supportive and loving family in her husband and children. Solomon suggested that this line sprang from Beethoven's suspicions that his Beloved would betray him as he had been deceived by lovers before. This is nonsense. As we know he had not suffered repeated deceptions by lovers, there is no reason to believe that Beethoven's loving invitation to his Beloved for her to confide in him and lean on him was actually a veiled warning to her not to betray him. This author finds it odd that such negativism and suspicion is attached even to Beethoven's most loving words.

"...my eternally[16] beloved..."

> Beat, though in silence, poor heart — that is all you can
> do, nothing more — for you — always for you — only you
> — eternally you — only you until I sink into the grave.
> My refreshment — my all. Even if you had not fettered
> me again to life, yet you would have meant everything
> to me —[17]

Beethoven wrote this great expression of love in a letter to Josephine Brunswick in 1805. It is easy to see from the depth of his adoration why so many biographers have felt that she was his "eternally beloved." It would be nice to be able to believe that such a spiritual love had survived. However, his history with her does

---

[15]Anderson, p. 527-528. Written as she was leaving Vienna for an extended time.
[16]"Immortal" has come into standard expression, although the words "Unsterbliche Geliebte" in Beethoven's letter more correctly translate as "eternally beloved."
[17]Anderson, p. 134.

not make her a likely candidate for an *eternally* beloved. Beethoven had approached Josephine with romantic intentions in 1804-05, and she had refused his advances. He had approached her again in 1807, and, again, she had refused him. Under these circumstances, why would he have tried a third time in 1812 when she had denied him twice before? Such persistence in the face of unequivocal rejection would have been stupid. If she *was* the Beloved, how, after twice turning him away, did Josephine convince Beethoven that she had loved him all along, that this time was somehow different? Because it was *not* different. Nothing had changed. She was married and unwilling to divorce Stackelberg. She still had children to consider. And she was still not physically attracted to him. After repeatedly breaking Beethoven's heart, and having felt so much pain herself for doing so, why would she beckon him to her, knowing she once again would only be offering him a friendship, or, at most, one night of passion, neither of which he wanted? Did she not imagine that she would hurt him yet *again*? Josephine was not a deliberately cruel woman, and we cannot imagine her toying with Beethoven's emotions in that way. As the drafts of her letters to him are undeniably cool, it would seem she did her best to discourage his romantic feelings. Further, she had been unmarried for six years after von Deym's death. Why had she not approached Beethoven then, during this time when she was free? We note also that Beethoven did not approach her either before her marriage to Stackelberg, even though she was available. We can only conclude that by 1807— or at least 1810, when she remarried— he had finally "gotten the message," and would not have continued what was a hopeless pursuit. "I was mistaken in you," he told her. He would not make that mistake again.

For Beethoven, the emotions of true love ran deeply. Thus it should be no surprise to find him using sentiments with the Beloved which are similar to those he had used to convey his feelings of love to Josephine. We easily see that he loved this woman, this Beloved, more ardently than he had Countess Brunswick. Such a letter, such sentiments, could hardly have been written to Antonie, a woman with whom he had no history, no intimacy. But certainly a woman who, for twelve years, had held a special place in his life and heart—one that no one else ever occupied— would qualify as an "eternally beloved." A woman, such as his Countess Erdödy.

"...awaiting fate, if it will grant us a favorable hearing."

What plea could Beethoven and Antonie have issued to fate? That Franz would meet with an untimely death? One might laugh, but that is the only way that a pregnant Antonie would have been freed from her marriage bonds. More logically, Beethoven had been referring to the severance of ties between Anna Marie and her husband, Peter Erdödy. In 1812, Peter turned over his property to Anna Marie. A legal notice in the *Wiener Zeitung* read that he was "entrusting the management of his fortune to his wife." No reasons were given for this move, and its effect upon her marital status is unknown. However, it could have led Beethoven to wonder what effect this event would have on his relationship with her, and on the tenuous marital bonds that bound her to a man who had not been a husband to her for many years. If that is so, then it is not surprising that he would offer a plea to Fate, or to whatever Supreme Being was closest to his heart, that this move might free her, and that she might be his at last.

"I can only live wholly with you or not at all."
"Can you change it that you are not completely mine, I not completely yours?"
"Were we wholly united..."

In three separate lines in the Beloved letter Beethoven used the words *wholly* and *completely*, words which naturally contrast with *partially*. The implication is that they may have once lived together some time in the past, albeit not wholly or completely, not legally, not as husband and wife. There is only one woman with whom the adult Beethoven had ever lived in a near-conjugal relationship, and continued to live close to whenever he was able to do so, and that woman was not Antonie Brentano, nor Josephine Brunswick, nor any other woman with the exception of Anna Marie Erdödy.

"I am resolved to wander far away until I can fly to your arms and say that I am really at home..."

If he had written this to Antonie, then it is an odd line. He certainly had not ever been very "far away" from Antonie, since both she and Franz were close to him throughout most of the summer. Had he left his Beloved behind in Vienna, then he certainly would have been "far away" from her in Czechoslovakia, and would remain so until she either joined him or invited him to "fly to [her] arms." Both Anna Marie and Josephine were "far away" that summer.

"You will compose your mind all the more since you know my faithfulness to you."

As we have seen in his letters, Beethoven once had pledged his eternal devotion to Josephine; however, she had not accepted it. On the other hand, Beethoven wrote two messages of reassurance to Anna Marie several years after the Beloved letter. In one he exhorted her:

> do not believe all the gossip you may have heard about why I have not written to you... I think between you, my dear Countess, and me, no go-between is needed.

A second time, when he was considering changing the dedication of a work he had promised to her, he told her that "this will not change you and me," again, assuring her of his devotion to her, reminding her that between them there was a special bond that could be neither altered nor destroyed. Why should he have felt the need in either of these situations to reassure her, if she had been nothing more than a friend to him?

Both Anna Marie and Josephine were the only women Beethoven had known long enough to prove his fidelity over many years. By contrast, how could Antonie *know* of his faithfulness, if he only had had only a short time—far less than a year—in which to convince her of it? By its very definition, "fidelty" implies that which is long-term: faithful devotion, loyalty, an adherence to vows, formal or implied.Unless Beethoven had a proven "track record" within the confines of a long-term relationship, as he had with Anna Marie and Josephine, how could he presume to assure his Beloved of his faithfulness with any hope that she would believe him?

"—at my age I would need some conformity, regularity of life—can this exist in our relationship?—"

In Part IV, an indepth look at Beethoven's relationship with Countess Erdödy will show that they had enjoyed very little "regularity" at all. The many years they had had together prior to the writing of the letter were filled with joys and sorrows, understanding and misunderstandings, intimacy and distance, separation and reunion. Might Beethoven therefore not wonder, given their long and erratic history, whether any of the stability he now required in a relationship might be achieved?

There was some fluctuation in his relationship with Josephine, though not nearly so much as with Anna Marie. Josephine had pushed him away, and then beckoned with friendship, only to distance herself from him once again. But while one might be able to apply Beethoven's statement to Josephine, in no way could it refer to Antonie Brentano. Not even Solomon could conjecture that their "affair" had lasted longer than eight months. Beethoven could not have encountered the same instability in his short-term relationship with Antonie, and with Antonie ill much of the time, we can see that their relationship had provided him with nothing but "regularity."

"Be calm, only through quiet consideration of our existence can we reach our goal to live together—be patient."

We have noted that there were some legal options open to Anna Marie, and perhaps even means by which she might circumvent familial pressures placed on her by the Erdödy family. These would have required calm consideration and patience if they were to come to fruition. Thus Beethoven had reason to be guardedly optimistic in relation to Countess Erdödy; somewhat less so in regard to Josephine Brunswick, although extricating herself from her marriage to Stackelberg would have had the same requirements of contemplation and patience, for the dissolution of a marriage was a slow process.

By contrast, there were no options open to Antonie Brentano at all, particularly since she was pregnant mother.[18]

Legal ramifications aside, who else would Beethoven have needed to ask to "be calm" except his fiery Hungarian countess, Anna Marie, whose temper easily matched his own?

"Never misjudge the most faithful heart of your beloved..."

After their quarrel in 1809 over a servant, Beethoven had believed that Anna Marie had misjudged him—and unjustly punished him— by thinking that he had hurt her intentionally. We believe there were other instances in which he had pressured

---

[18]Of course, it cannot be assumed that Beethoven was aware of Antonie's condition at this time, but he certainly did know that she was the mother of several small children.

her too much in his attempt to make her free herself from Peter Erdödy, and that she had misunderstood his frustration, taking it as anger against her personally. His intentions, he assured her, were always good and honorable, although she did not always see them as such. We know also that Josephine had once accused him of "pressing her;" there obviously had been misunderstanding there, as well.

This line is similar to earlier reassurance given in the Beloved letter, and also to a line in a letter he wrote to Anna Marie in which he said, "Do not believe all the gossip." He was fully aware that tales were sometimes told about him, that his being "perfectly natural"—at times, even "naughty," as he had confessed to his friends, the Bigots—caused him to be misunderstood. As do some biographers today who take too seriously his meaningless flirtations and his occasionally bawdy innuendos and thus proclaim he was "always in love," or, worse, always in lust, so did some of his contemporaries believe that he "always had a flame." (His contemporaries' views are notably far more innocent—almost as if they were speaking of an adolescent—than those of twentieth century writers). Yet, as Beethoven said, his heart was never unfaithful to his true Beloved. The question is, do we believe him, or do we brand him insincere—or worse, a liar?

Solomon claimed this line in the letter was a plea for forgiveness, that Beethoven was seeking absolution from his Beloved for his own weaknesses which kept him from accepting the responsibility of a conjugal relationship with her. This author cannot agree with that interpretation. Beethoven was far too straightforward for that. "Never misjudge my heart" was a plea for his Beloved's continued faith and trust in him, and his pledge of fidelity to her. It was not an admission of guilt, but a proclamation of devotion.

What of Antonie Brentano. Had she ever had the opportunity or inclination to "misjudge" him? Of course not. She thought of him as a holy being who walked god-like among mortals. There were only two women—Anna Marie and Josephine—to whom he would have offered his pledge of fidelity. They were the ones who saw him—and loved him—as the human being he was. And it was only Anna Mare, as we see by Beethoven's letters to her, to whom he did repeatedly give this reassurance.

❖ 12 ❖
Dissolution of the Brentano Marriage

"Can we help it that you are not completely mine, I not completely yours?" Beethoven asked in his letter. Solomon suggested—without any evidence—that Antonie Brentano had made it clear to Beethoven that she could indeed "help it" that she was not his, and would take steps to change her marital status, even risking condemnation by society, in order to be able to become Beethoven's wife.

If Antonie had made this declaration—which we are not convinced she had, at least, not in Prague—one must ask by what means did Frau Brentano think she could bring about this union with Beethoven? If Antonie did harbor that view, it was an unrealistic one, as was Beethoven's assertion that he would find a way for them reach their goal to live together. Unrealistic, that is, *if* he had been referring to Antonie Brentano. (It stands to reason, then, that if she *had* made such a declaration, it must have come at a time when she had been under emotional stress and not thinking clearly, such as in Franzensbrunn.)

First, the secular laws of divorce at the time were stringent. In 1803, new divorce laws replaced older codes which made divorces more difficult and more expensive to obtain. Grounds for the dissolution of a marriage were reduced from seven to three— and these were not increased again until 1840. The only three accusations which Antonie might have used against her husband in order to obtain a divorce from him were criminal convictions, adultery, or ill-treatment—which included desertion—none of which pertained to the man she called "her good Franz, the best of men." Although there were recorded instances of divorce by mutual consent, as a rule these did not take place when the couple had children. The needs of the children, of which the Brentanos had several at the time with another on the way, would have been a powerful deterrent to the granting of a divorce.

Second, one must consider the religious aspects of such a divorce since both Antonie and Beethoven were Catholic. Although Antonie's personality will be studied in greater depth later, we note briefly that upon her mother's death, when she was only eight years old, Antonie had been placed in the cloister of the Ursuline Order at Pressburg, were she received a stringent religious upbringing for seven years. Having been raised and married within the strict confines of the religion, its impact on her and her adherence to it cannot be ignored.

Although Beethoven's attachment to the church proper and its rituals was minimal at best, his friends thought of him as a religious man. Beethoven did not consider himself beyond the bounds of the church, and believed in adherence to its basic principals. Gottfried Fischer related that Brother Willibald in a local Franciscan monastery in Bonn had given young Ludwig van Beethoven instruction and training in Church ritual, as well as on the organ. These early lessons are evident in his concepts of morality, which remained strong his entire life.

In 1818 Beethoven employed a parson as a tutor for Karl, but was soon dissatisfied with him because

> On a Monday that reverend gentleman had not yet slept off his Sunday carousing and still behaved like a wild beast. Yes, I felt ashamed of our religion, that such a parson should be described as a preacher of the Gospel. That parson treated him [Karl] most brutally and roughly about the smallest thing. I absolutely forbade him to punish my nephew in this way, nor did I allow my nephew to go to church in the morning, for I had noticed the pupils' unseemly behavior and did not wish my nephew to associate with that gang. It can easily be imagined that that in itself was sufficient for people to accuse me of having no religion and of failing to give my nephew a religious education.[1]

---

[1] Anderson, p. 1406.

* * *

To the Magisträt der Stadt Wien, February 1, 1819: I
have found an excellent clergyman who gives him [Karl]
special instruction about his duties as a Christian and
a man. For only on such a foundation can genuine and
honorable people be reared and trained.[2]

* * *

Draft of a memorandum to the Court of Appeal, February 18, 1820: F[rau] B[eethoven] accused me ... of having written a letter to my nephew against confession.
But it will soon be realized that even so that defamatory
statement made by F[rau] B[eethoven] was not yet
withdrawn, although it was proved that on that very
day my nephew had gone from the boarding school to
her instead of to confession. For that very reason I
myself took him later on to confess to the worthy holy
Abbot of St. Michael.—. . .You need only summon my
nephew today and ask him whether I earnestly exhorted
him to fear God and to practice his religion.[3]

Beethoven was speaking the truth. There are numerous
notes and letters to Karl urging him to read the Gospels and follow the precepts of his religion. Later, just days bfore his own
death, Beethoven was attended by a priest and given the Last
Rites. From these examples it is clear to see that he was not alien-
ated from his Catholicism, and it is unimaginable that Beethoven
would have blatantly ignored both the Church's and his own
religious convictions in regard to the coveting of another man's
wife. As we shall see in the next chapter, Beethoven felt very
strongly about the Fourth Commandment which exhorts one to
honor one's father and mother. This author finds it difficult to
believe that he would have abided by one so strongly and ignored
another (the Ninth) which prohibited lusting after another man's
wife simply because it conflicted with his own desires.

---

[2]Anderson, p. 1393.
[3]Anderson, p. 1401.

THE SACRED AND THE SECULAR

Secular laws often ran counter to Catholic principles. We find that, under civil law, marriages could be terminated. By contrast, one of the foremost principles of the Catholic church was that marriages were virtually indissoluble. Although divorce was considered legal by the church, divorced Catholics were not permitted to remarry within the lifetime of their former spouses. And annulments—which would have left the previously married party in a position to remarry since the first marriage was considered as never having taken place—were rarely granted except in extreme cases of fraud or deception. There was even a negative attitude toward remarriage in the case of widows, who did not receive a nuptial blessing from priests. Remarriage of a widow was banned within a year of her husband's death, under threat of losing whatever inheritance rights she had gained from her late spouse. Having been raised within the confines of the Catholic church, it is unlikely that Beethoven would have been unaware of the church's view, and Antonie certainly would have known how binding her marriage vows were. Since Beethoven had not approached Josephine Brunswick von Deym with an eye toward marriage until she had been widowed nearly a year, this indicates that he, too, had at least some awareness of church-imposed restrictions upon marriage, divorce, widowhood, and remarriage, as well as his society's view of a proper mourning period.

Since Beethoven wanted a woman who would *completely* and *lawfully* be his—a wife, not just a woman to live with—he would not have thought it possible to achieve that end with Antonie, nor that they could somehow "reach their goal" to be so united. Within the existing confines of secular and church law, reaching such a goal would have been extremely difficult at best, and more likely, impossible. Why then such optimism in the Beloved letter when there was obviously no reason on earth for it? Only if the letter were not intended for Antonie Brentano does the optimism in it not seem ill-founded.

From both the optimism and other sentiments expressed in the letter—e.g.".…awaiting fate, if it will grant us a favorable hearing"—one might consider that Beethoven was addressing a woman who, although perhaps married, had a status not so firmly locked into matrimony as Antonie Brentano. Two such women were Anna Marie Erdödy and Josephine Brunswick Stackelberg,

Anna Marie having been separated from her husband for many years, and Josephine's marriage being on the verge of possible termination on grounds of cruelty and desertion on the part of Stackelberg.

IN THE CASE OF JOSEPHINE

We know from Therese Brunswick's diary that Josephine and her husband suffered marital problems almost from the time of their marriage in 1810. Evidence is inconclusive as to when their bitter separation occurred: some researchers claim as early as 1812, others as late as 1814. The latter date seems more likely, based on letters written at the time, even though Therese's diary has the break occurring earlier. It is possible that one of Josephine's siblings—Therese or Franz—could have told Beethoven of their mother's decision to support Josephine if she chose to divorce Stackelberg. This was a decision that Josephine ultimately did not make, partly because of her own moral and religious convictions, but mainly for her children's future welfare. She would have had to relinquish her title, and perhaps even her children, and she and Beethoven could not have married within the church. This probably would not have mattered to him; for him, a civil marriage probably would have sufficed. We do not know if this would have been true of Josephine's feelings in the matter, but cannot imagine that it would not have bothered her, given her reluctance to divorce an unsatisfactory husband in the first place.

IN THE CASE OF ANNA MARIE

In the 19th century—and certainly earlier—desertion sometimes was difficult to prove in that men often left their wives and families for many years in the course of making a living. In Anna Marie's case there was no doubt that Count Peter Erdödy completely—emotionally and by affinity—separated from his wife around 1801. Although he had no reason to "be on the road" in terms of his work, he never lived with her thereafter. Police reports written in later years described him as "disinterested in his family." While the Catholic church frowned on divorce, it did make provisions for annulment and legal separation in the cases of adultery, irreconcilable hostility, and willful desertion. The latter was considered grounds for the termination of a marriage, because the marriage was considered ended in social and sexual terms. Like the problem with Josephine, even if Anna Marie had divorced her husband, remarriage within the church would have been out of the question. We cannot know if this would have mattered to her, though she certainly was far more liberated in her views than Josephine.

It is not known for certain whether the Countess ever explored the possibility of receiving an annulment from Peter. There was the matter of his legal announcement which gave his wife control over his properties, but how this step was initiated, who had caused it to come about, and whether this could have been a move toward the dissolution of the Erdödy marriage, is unknown. Yet only an annulment would have negated Anna Marie's marriage to Peter, treating it as a contract that had never existed, and have permitted her to marry Beethoven within the confines of the church.

Here is a situation worthy of further exploration. Anna Marie had, by all appearances, uncontestable grounds for annulment, yet she chose not to take this step. Why not? What prevented her? Should we assume social snobbery, that the loss of her title was too great a sacrifice, even for the love of a Beethoven? We do not think so. We believe the consequences of such an action on the Erdödy's minor children had been the deciding factor. Prior to 1812, annulment would have brought into question the Erdödy children's legitimate claim to the inheritance of their father's estate. However, by 1812 Anna Marie had gained control of Peter's capital, and her children could have inherited directly from her. Thus inheritance could not have been the issue. As we shall see in Part IV, other pressures were put upon Anna Marie by the Erdödy family.

Given Peter's lack of concern for this children, we do not believe he would have taken the children away from Anna Marie, as Stackelberg had threatened to do—and actually did do—with Josephine. Peter's family, however, was another matter. We believe that Anna Marie's sister-in-law, Countess Sigismund Erdödy, whose role in Anna Marie's life and in her relationship with Beethoven will be explored later, would not have hesitated to challenge Anna Marie for guardianship of her children. Had Anna Marie married Beethoven and, as a result, become a commoner, the Erdödy family would have had grounds for taking from her the custody of her noble-born children, and Anna Marie no longer would have been able to appeal to the courts for assistance. (We note from Beethoven's custody suit over Karl, that two separate court systems existed: one for the nobility and one for the common people.) We shall see also that various relations—Peter, Anna Marie's father, her sister-in-law—repeatedly exhibited unusual animosity toward Anna Marie, and, knowing how much they hated her, they would have had no qualms about taking her children away from her.

Both the Erdödys and the Nizckys, Anna Marie's birth family, were part of the ruling class of Hungary. Their ancestry was old, wealthy, and powerful. The marriage of any two such people like Anna Marie and Peter—which united two families like the Erdödys and Nizckys—was considered too important a transaction to be left to the individuals themselves. Parents and other relatives felt they had a legitimate right and duty to influence and interfere with, if not outrightly control, both the marriage and any progeny issuing from it. There would have been strong opposition to *any* legal dissolution of Peter's and Anna Marie's marriage, but the dissolution of this union in particular would have been especially scandalous in light of Anna Marie's desire to replace her aristocratic husband with a commoner like Beethoven. When such a move was opposed by as powerful a family as the Erdödys, complete legal separation would have been very difficult—even if not totally impossible—to achieve.

Beethoven, with his egalitarian and somewhat naive outlook, probably did not consider how much power the Erdödy family wielded, and thus did not consider these obstacles too great to overcome. Surely he would have cared very little whether the Nizcky and Erdödy clan approved of his relationship with Anna Marie. While he may have acknowledged that problems existed in relation to Anna Marie's children—as it also did with Josephine—it must have hurt him to know that the women he loved were forced by circumstances and the virtual powerlessness of their sex in that century, to place their children's welfare and their own motherhood above their love for him.

We believe that Beethoven's views, and maybe his own naivete, kept alive for many years that glimmer of hope that he would someday be able to marry his Beloved. Thus the optimism in his letter was not false or misleading: he truly believed that their union was something which might be achieved, if the fates gave them a "favorable hearing." The same cannot be said in the case of Antonie Brentano.

❧ 13 ❧
Beethoven's Character:
Concepts of Morality and Marriage

Psychologically, emotionally, the implications of the Beloved letter for its principle players were many. To see them clearly, it will be important to have an understanding of the participants' characters and backgrounds which invariably influenced how they acted and reacted. Beethoven will be considered first, followed by the alleged Beloved, Antonie Brentano.

Would it have been possible for Beethoven to have coveted the wife of a friend? Certainly there is very little in the universe that is completely *im*possible. Yet *probability* is another matter. Certainly, love and desire are substantial forces which have been known to compel more than one person to abandon their principles, and the heart all too often has been known to dominate the head. However, in this instance we must consider the heart and head of not just any man, but of *this* man, Beethoven.

Beethoven was not the sort of man to act upon his feelings if he thought them morally improper. Even if one wishes to point to his behavior in the matter of his nephew as an example of his ability to be less than scrupulous,[1] his letters show that he *believed* he was doing the right thing. We know, too, that he loved Josephine Brunswick a great deal, and that his love for her was

---

[1]Some biographers have accused Beethoven of underhandedness, such as altering his brother's will, in an attempt to "appropriate" his nephew by any means possible. While the issue is too complex to explore here, one can be sure that Beethoven did not act outside what he considered morally right.

present while she was married to von Deym. Yet not even his apparent love for her made him abandon his ideals. Propriety and his sense of morality made him keep his feelings in check—hidden even from her—until circumstances no longer demanded that he do so.

> ...it is just you, your whole self with all your individual qualities—this has compelled my regard — this has bound all my feelings —all my emotional power to you — When I came to you — it was with the firm resolve not to let a single spark of love be kindled in me.[2]

Only when Josephine had been widowed a year, with a proper mourning period observed, did he declare his love to her. He admitted that he had suppressed his feelings for her. Josephine had never been happily married to von Deym. She might well have responded emotionally to Beethoven had he made overtures to her. Yet he did not tempt her, nor did he allow temptation to make him abandon his own values, no matter how dearly he cared for her. If he had not been swayed from his moral path by his passion for Josephine, then why would he have abandoned them so easily for Antonie? Had Beethoven loved Antonie, he would neither have declared his feelings for her, nor wittingly responded to her in any way that might have encouraged her to act improperly or immorally. One of his notes to himself said "The frailties of nature have been given to us by Nature herself, and Reason, the ruler should be able to guide and diminish them by applying her strength."[3] That strength of will, that moral conviction that he displayed in his relationship with Josephine, would not have permitted him to have acted on his feelings of love. Through Countess Brunswick he has proven himself to us.

Further, both Anna Marie and Josephine were married to men of poor character who treated their wives badly. While Beethoven surely could have defended any attempt to take either of them out of their unsatisfactory marriages, in effect saving them with his love, he could not have done the same with Antonie Brentano. He never could have rationalized coveting the wife of a man he esteemed as highly as Franz Brentano.

In seeking answers to the question of whether Beethoven could have coveted another man's wife, let us explore further, and

---

[2]Anderson, p. 132.
[3]Steichen, p. 337.

we turn to those who knew Beethoven best, among them, Ignaz von Seyfried. Seyfried was a fellow musician and conductor who knew the composer for many years. Thayer tells us that

> Their acquaintance during thirty years—which for at least half of the time, was really the 'friendly relationship' which Seyfried names it—was he says, "never weakened, never disrupted by even the smallest quarrel—not that we were always of a mind or could be, but we always spoke freely and frankly to each other, without reserve, according to our convictions. . . [4]

Seyfried[5] had known Beethoven for most of his adult life, and had this to say of his friend:

> Justice, personal decency, the moral code, a devout mind, and religious purity meant more to him than all else; these virtues were enthroned in him and he demanded that others cultivate them. He took pleasure in helping others out of pure love for his neighbors, only too often making considerable sacrifices greatly to his own disadvantage. Anyone who turned to him in free and full confidence always could count upon certain, actual aid. Only a few people were capable of estimating his lofty human values to their full extent. Why was this? Because the majority were rebuffed by the rough outward shell and never even guessed at its noble inner kernel. Yet is not the most costly well-nigh priceless diamond often concealed in a pallid, dull, colorless and unpolished wrapper?[6]

---

[4]Thayer/Forbes, p. 370.

[5]Seyfried lost favor among researchers because of a scam he had perpetrated after Beethoven's death. Seyfried authored a book published by Tobias Haslinger fraudulently called *Beethoven's Studies in Thoroughbass, Counterpoint, and Composition*. There was a deception on the author's part to sell this book using Beethoven's name, even though the contents had been developed by others such as Fux, Turk, Albrechsberger, and Schulzer. Seyfried had lost his post as music director in 1825, and his need for money probably prompted him to attempt this subterfuge. However, this one black mark against Seyfried, however substantial, should not detract from the man's personal reminiscences of the composer. Schindler claimed that Seyfried had no association with Beethoven, and that Beethoven disapproved of Seyfried because of the latter's relationship with a married woman who had deserted her husband. Yet warmly written letters to Seyfried by Beet-hoven over the years disprove Schindler's contention, and we consider Seyfried an acceptable authority on the composer's character.

[6]Scherman & Biancolli, p. 92, et. al.

In 1793, a young Beethoven wrote to a merchant by the name of Voche: "Even though wildly surging emotions may betray my heart, yet my heart is good. Precepts. To do good whenever one can, to love liberty above all else, never to deny the truth even though it be before the throne." From what those who knew him reveal, these were precepts he followed all his life.

Wilhelm Rust wrote in 1808 that "He is as original and singular as a man as are his compositions; usually serious, at times merry, but always satirical. On the other hand, he is also very childlike and certainly very sincere. He is a great lover of truth and in this goes too far very often; for he never flatters and therefore makes many enemies."

It is often amusing to read of people's encounters with Beethoven, for those who met him were invariably surprised to find him far different than "rumor" had portrayed him. Rather than the ill-tempered misanthrope they had expected, they had found a man of an interesting and inviting nature:[7]

• Carl Junker, who knew Beethoven in the 1790s, thought of him as an amiable, light-hearted man who was exceedingly modest and free from all pretension.

• John Cramer knew Beethoven in his late twenties. Although Cramer admitted that in unfamiliar company Beethoven often was reserved, stiff, and seemingly haughty, when he was with friends he would be comical, lively, and witty. Cramer found him sometimes to be sarcastic and indiscreet, especially in expressing his outspoken political and social views.

• Of a thirty-year-old Beethoven, Carl Czerny remembered that other than those times when he was in a melancholy mood because of physical illness, he always was "merry, mischievous, full of witticisms and jokes, and cared not a whit what people said of him." Czerny compared him, as did Baron de Trémont, to Jean-Jacques Rousseau in temperament, but added that Beethoven was "noble, great-hearted, and pure in character."

• Xaver Schnyder von Wartensee wrote to Nageli in December 1811 that he had been well received by Beethoven, but found him to be "very peculiar." Schnyder believed that Beethoven had no command of words and that his ideas could only be ex-

---

[7]The reminiscences of Junker and Cramer may be read in their entirety in Sonneck's *Beethoven: Impressions by His Contemporaries*, p. 13 and 31, respectively.

pressed through music. He added that Beethoven was "crude, however, honest and without falsehood."

• Phillip Cipirani Potter[8] in 1818, noted that many persons thought Beethoven to be a morose and ill-tempered man, but felt that this opinion was "perfectly erroneous." Potter called him irritable, passionate, and of a melancholy turn of mind, but blamed his shortcomings on his deafness. Potter added that despite "peculiarities in his temperament, he possessed a kind heart and most acute feelings."

• Friedrich Rochlitz found the Beethoven of later years rather eccentric and peculiar, but thought that he "radiated a truly childlike amiability, carelessness, and confidence in every one who approached him." Rochlitz called his bursts of temper "barking tirades" and felt they were only "explosions of his fanciful imagination and momentary excitement." Even in a rage, Beethoven, he said, was without haughtiness, without any feeling of bitterness and hatefulness—and his tirades were simply "blustered out lightly, good-humoredly, the off-springs of a mad, humorous mood." Rochlitz also noted that to the very person who had injured him, whom he had most violently denounced, he willingly gave his last dollar should that person need it.

• In 1823, Carl Maria von Weber recalled that Beethoven had received him with the most touching affection. The composer had embraced him at least six or seven times in the heartiest fashion and finally, full of enthusiasm, cried, "Yes, you are a devil of a fellow, a fine fellow!" Weber recalled that they had spent the noon-hour together, very merrily and happily, and that it had given him a special exaltation to see himself "overwhelmed with such affectionate attention by this great spirit."

• That same year, Edward Schultz noted that Beethoven was a great enemy to all *gêne*. Schultz did not believe that there was another individual in all of Vienna who spoke with so little restraint on all kinds of subjects, even political ones, as Beethoven. Unlike Schnyder, Schultz felt that Beethoven spoke remarkably well, and that his observations were as characteristic and original as his compositions.

---

[8]The reminiscences of Potter, Rochlitz, and Weber may be read in their entirety in Sonneck's *Beethoven: Impressions by His Contemporaries,* pp. 108-109, 127-128, and 160, respectively.

• Even late in life, the Beethoven of younger, happier days could, on occasion, still appear. In 1826, Dr. Samuel Spiker noted that in general, Beethoven was "exceptionally merry and laughed at every jest with the good-humored readiness of a man without guile who believed in all, something not to have been expected in view of the generally current rumor that Beethoven was very gloomy and shy."[The "current rumor" of which Spiker spoke actually was accurate. In the last years of his life, Beethoven occasionally appeared merry, as Spiker had observed, but in reality, he was exhibiting only a forced gaiety. See also page 389.]

It is regrettable that despite these many positive observations about Beethoven's demeanor from those who had known him, he still is generally characterized as a morose, ill-tempered and reclusive man. Worse, some modern biographers have attempted to portray Beethoven as a man who was deceptive about his morality and honesty, who was emotionally repressed, self-serving, hypocritical, and even deliberately cruel. However, this author has found *that* Beethoven only in the misinterpretation and distortion of fact.

ON WOMEN AND FIDELITY

From his research, Thayer concluded that:

> The practice, not uncommon in his time, of living with an unmarried woman as a wife, was always abhorrent to [Beethoven]—to a still greater degree an intrigue with the wife of another man. In his later years he so broke off his once familiar intercourse with a distinguished composer and conductor of Vienna, as hardly to return his greetings with common politeness. Schindler affirmed that the only reason for this was that the man in question had taken to his bed and board the wife of another.[9]

Thayer generally was wary of Schindler's observations, therefore for Thayer to include one of Schindler's remarks, he must have thought it to be the truth, even though we cannot be assured of it. Beethoven himself, however, gave a legitimate reason for not wanting another man's wife. To Herr Bigot he wrote:

---

[9]Thayer/Forbes, pp. 245.

> Never by such a relationship [with another man's wife]
> would I fill my heart with distrust against her who some
> day will perhaps share my fate.

From this letter, and his feelings toward Johanna, his sister-in-law, it is clear that Beethoven did not trust a woman who would cheat on her husband. But wasn't he right to be mistrustful of such a woman, even if she would leave her husband for *him*? How could he ever be certain that he himself would not end up the cuckolded husband if some other man caught his wife's fancy? Thayer continued

> Certain of his friends used to joke him about these ladies
> (two married women to whom he was "warmly attached")
> and it is certain that he rather enjoyed their jests even
> when the insinuations, that his affection was beyond
> the limit of the Platonic, were somewhat broad; but
> careful enquiry has failed to elicit any evidence that
> even in these cases he proved unfaithful to his principles.[10]

Beethoven had known Nicholas Simrock in Bonn and his friendship extended to Simrock's son, Peter, long after the composer had moved to Vienna. They knew each other many years. The elder Simrock noted that once during a journey to Mergentheim in their younger years, it happened at some place where members of the company[11] dined, that some of the young men prompted the waiting-girl to act seductively toward Beethoven. He received her advances and familiarities with repellent coldness; and as she, encouraged by the others, still persevered, he lost his patience and put an end to her unwelcome behavior by a smart box on the ear. This was hardly chivalrous on his part, given that he was man who was generally respectful of women. However, his conduct was not always decorous when dealing with servants, even female ones, and it was not unusual for him to harangue and throw things at a serving woman who displeased him. Yet toward refined women his behavior was quite different. It also is apparent from Simrock's anecdote that Beethoven did not appreciate the attentions of just any woman, but that he had high standards for the women with whom he chose to associate.

---

[10]Thayer/Forbes, p. 245.
[11]The "company" was the Court Orchestra, of which both men were a part in the mid-1790s.

Had he truly been the womanizer he has been made out to be, he would have taken advantage of the serving-girl's flirtatious attentions, and ignored the fact that she was from the lower classes.

A story related by Otto Jahn concerned

> the refusal of Beethoven to play before [Madame Hofdamel] because he held the general belief at the time that too great an intimacy had existed between her and Mozart. Jahn, it may be observed, had the great satisfaction of being able to prove the innocence of Mozart in this matter and of rescuing his memory from the only dark shadow which rested upon it.[12]

Again, we cannot know this story to be the absolute truth, yet it is interesting that it reflects the "lofty human values" which Beethoven's friend Seyfried ascribed to him.

Beethoven's strong dislike for both his sisters-in-law stemmed primarily from their rather loose morality. Johann's wife, Therese, had an illegitimate daughter prior to their marriage and likely took lovers afterwards. Johanna, Caspar Carl's wife, had been pregnant with Carl's son at the time of their marriage, and she took lovers later as well. One of them, a man named Hofbauer, either lived in or visited the Beethoven house during Carl's final illness. After Carl's death, Johanna, like her sister-in-law Therese, had an illegitimate daughter presumably fathered by Hofbauer.

Many biographers believe that Beethoven lived by a double standard, condemning Johanna and Therese for behavior in which he himself engaged, and that his anger with them actually was a form of self-reproach. Yet this author is not convinced that this psychological analysis is accurate. Accusing Beethoven of such hypocracy is merely a convenient means to "prove" that he was capable of coveting another man's wife, and condoning the wife's infidelity toward her husband. Convenient. . . but unfair. There is no proof that Beethoven ever betrayed his moral values. In fact, his private notes to himself, in which he could express his deepest fears, faults, and convictions without answering to any other man, show unequivocally his constant striving to be a good and decent man. In no way would he ever have encouraged Antonie to be unfaithful to Franz, even for his own benefit. He most

[12]Otto Jahn, *Gesammelte Aufsätz über Musik*, Leipzig 1866, p. 230.

likely would not have maintained a friendship with Antonie *at all*, rather than place either of them in a position where they might have been tempted to do something morally wrong.

On the issue of why he dismissed Bettina Brentano as the Immortal Beloved, Richard Specht wrote:

> In 1812, Bettina von Brentano had already become the wife of Achim von Arnim—a fact which cannot be ignored; for we know what was Beethoven's conception of marriage. We know it meant for him a divine sacrament against which it would be sacrilege to offend. We know he would have torn out his tongue rather than suffer to utter words of such glowing passion to another's wife. We may think him frivolous and fickle... this is the reverse of the truth.[13]

Specht does not tell us how he "knows" this to be true, but again, his impression reflects the opinions of Beethoven's contemporaries. Even if Beethoven had had no moral standards at all, surely a sense of self-preservation would have kept him from wanting a woman who was easily lured away from her husband.

Even Solomon reported in his footnotes that Max Unger, too, dismissed Antonie Brentano as the Immortal Beloved, without giving his reasons, although one could suppose that it was for the same reason that Specht dismissed her sister-in-law, Bettina. They both were married women. Likewise other biographers did not think Antonie was a possibility, either, notably, Romain Rolland, Jean and Brigitte Massin, and George R. Marek, for similar reasons. While it seems that many biographers in recent years would like to see Beethoven tossed in the gutter in order to deliver him from the Victorian morality of earlier writers, the fact is, no such evidence of his immorality exists. What *does* exist is a great deal of speculation gleaned from Beethoven's writings by biographers who simply are better at reading *between* the lines than what actually was written *on* them.

There is no alternative for those who choose to believe that Antonie was the Beloved, but to also believe that Beethoven—whom his friends called unpretentious, a lover of truth, a "man of his word"—was a liar. This author does *not* believe it, because of the vast number of *authoritarian quotes* and *enlightened interpretations* found which have proved to be nothing of the sort. We

---

[13]Specht, p. 472.

digress a moment to give an example of one of these amusing explanations of Beethoven's behavior: In April 1810, Beethoven broke his looking-glass and asked his friend, Zmeskall, to loan him his. From this simple request—and from Beethoven's purchase of some new clothes—biographers concluded that Beethoven was preening himself so that he might propose marriage to Therese Malfatti.[14] That Beethoven might have needed a mirror so that he could shave without cutting his throat escapes them as a plausible reason, though goodness knows he was awkward enough shaving *with* a mirror. Had Beethoven known how much importance would have been attached to a simple looking-glass, he might have been inclined to grow a beard. As for his new apparel, surely 1810 was not the only year he had bought clothes or he would have been shabby indeed!

Unfortunately the same writers who attach such deep significance to Beethoven's mirror are the ones who find "proof" of his immoral and deceptive behavior in his letters by *interpreting* what he wrote rather than simply *reading* it. For this author, doubting Beethoven's basic honesty is difficult to do, for he speaks with candor even about his own shortcomings:

Johann Streicher, who had known Beethoven since the 1790s, wrote to Carl Peters (March 5, 1825) about Beethoven that "What am I to say about Beethoven's behavior to you and how can I endeavor to excuse it? This I can only do by letting you have his own opinion of himself which he expressed in my home: 'Everything I do apart from music is badly done and is stupid.'"[15] Is this the comment of a man who does not know his own flawed character? Beethoven added,

> To do something like putting my papers in order, I need a *dreadful amount of patience* which, however, when it does make its appearance, anyone like myself *must hold on to*, because usually it is never there.

Beethoven wrote to Baroness Marie Augustine von Poser in 1814: "On account of my personality I shall sink considerably in your estimation of me."[16]

---

[14]In spring 1810 he moved back to the Pasqualati House, once again becoming Anna Marie Erdödy's neighbor. At the same time he requested the mirror, he was breaking off whatever minor relationship he had with Therese. If he was "preening" for anyone, it surely had been for Countess Erdödy.

[15]Anderson, p. 1154, n. 2.

[16]Anderson, p. 483.

Of course, Beethoven also was aware of his virtues, and expressed them as easily as he did his faults:

> To Carl Peters, September 1822: Treat my frankness with charity; and you must never fear that I shall do anything that might disgrace my character or injure another person. Beware of giving heed to false reports about me.[17]

(If only biographers would heed that last sentence.)

> To Archduke Rudolph, May 1819: She [Johanna] will not scruple to indulge in all kinds of calumnies about me. But I trust that these will be easily disproved by my moral character, which is publicly recognized.[18]

Beethoven also adhered stringently to the precepts of the Ten Commandments, even though the rituals of religion did not concern him. Despite his deep personal animosity toward Johanna, he insisted that his nephew Karl follow the Fourth Commandment and honor his mother. He protested having the boy testify against her in court, even though his attorney urged putting the boy on the stand, believing Karl's testimony would help Beethoven gain the boy's guardianship.

> Continuing to the Archduke Rudolph, May 1819: One of the chief considerations which have made the judges decide to remove her son as far as possible from her is a religious precept connected with the fourth commandment [i.e. Honor thy father and thy mother.] And certainly one must bear in mind the difficult position of the guardian and instructor who must not infringe this commandment; and the necessity that the son must never be induced to ignore or break this commandment.

Since Beethoven felt strongly about keeping the Fourth Commandment—as he even did when speaking of his abusive father, about whom he would not speak a harsh word, nor let anyone else do so—presumably he felt equally as strongly about keeping the Ninth. (Thou shalt not covet thy neighbor's wife.)

Beethoven wrote to his friend, Herr Bigot, in 1809 in the wake of a misunderstanding with Bigot's wife, the following:

---

[17]Anderson, p. 971.
[18]Anderson, pp. 810-811.

Only with the deepest regret am I forced to perceive that the purest, most innocent feelings can often be misconstrued. It is one of my first principles never to stand in other than friendly relationship with the wife of another man. Never by such a relationship would I fill my breast with distrust against her who may one day share my fate with me—and so taint for myself the most beautiful, the purest life. Occasionally I am very free in speech—but how can good Marie [Bigot] put such bad meaning on my actions—Mistrust on your part would be a real offense to me. Never, never will you find me ignoble. From childhood onward I have learned to love virtue—you have pained my heart.[19]

When Beethoven's words contradict a theory, some biographers simply claim that Beethoven was being untruthful. However, we cannot and will not assume that Beethoven was lying to Bigot simply to make amends. This was not an isolated sentiment, nor one expressed in the idealism of his youth. It was given as the pledge of a mature man.

We are not suggesting that Beethoven was always pure in thought and deed. All human beings slip from time to time, even those committed to high standards. But wanting a friend's wife, not simply in thought where covetousness has no consequences, but in deed, to the extent where he would write her a love letter and encourage her in her desire to leave her husband, where a number of innocent people would have suffered pain as a consequence, could hardly be considered a mere "slip" in one's moral makeup. Finding Beethoven guilty of this immoral and selfish behavior, when there is no evidence to support such a claim, does him—and all of those who wish to understand him—a grave disservice. Beethoven's love of virtue and truth is evident time and again in his letters and notes and in the remembrances of his friends. "A man of his word was his motto," Seyfried noted about Beethoven, "and nothing angered him more than an unkept promise."

Schnyder also claimed that Beethoven was "honest and without pretentions. He says straight out what is on his mind." If those who knew him believed in his sincere desire to be an honest and moral man, must it really be so difficult for us to take their word for it, and do the same?

---

[19]Anderson, pp. 163-165.

❖ *14* ❖
Antonie Brentano:
Character and Background

Antonie Birkenstock Brentano's mother died when she was eight years old. Subsequently, she was sent to the cloister of the Ursuline order at Pressburg where she received a vigorous Catholic upbringing for seven years.[1] She was an only child and Solomon described her existence as "sheltered." Antonie had an obsessive love for her father, perhaps brought about by the early loss of her mother. While she was at the convent, she wrote to Birkenstock, "Dearest Papa, please write to me soon. It is my happiness and consolation." Solomon wrote "She managed to present a controlled exterior to visitors... but the cool surface was readily shattered upon slight provocation," and noted the observations of others in 1805, seven years after her marriage and move from Vienna to Frankfurt. Sophie Brentano, wife of Clemens Brentano, Franz's half-brother, said that "Toni's appearance... astonishes me greatly." Antonie's sister-in-law, Bettina noted that "Toni is in a bizarre correspondence with me: she has rouged and painted herself like a stage set, as though impersonating a haughty ruin overlooking the Rhine toward which a variety of romantic scenes advance while she remains wholly sunk in loneliness and abstraction." Brother-in-law, Clemens, for unknown reasons, in later years grew to dislike her, and wrote to his wife, "Toni's character is ever more developing into that of a cold

---

[1]Additional information on Antonie Brentano can be found in Maynard Solomon's book, *Beethoven*, 1977, and *Beethoven Essays*, pp. 166-189.

and slanderous wife." In Antonie's defense, it must be noted that at the age of eighteen, she had been expected to handle the large Brentano household, and as the wife of the family's oldest son, had been cast into the role of mistress of the house, a role which undoubtedly sparked jealousy among the other women. Despite the uncomfortable situation into which she had been thrust, one would assume that, with time and maturity, she would have learned to deal with her environment. Certainly most people would have adjusted to a new environment after seven years! Yet she did not, not for many, many years.

Solomon said further that "Antonie's malaise soon manifested itself in physical symptoms, notably headaches and irritability, seizures, compulsive crying. She wrote to her brother-in-law, Clemens, in 1806 that 'A deathly silence reigns within my soul.'" Was this simply "malaise?" If ever a woman exhibited classic symptoms of severe depression it was Antonie Brentano. According to Solomon, her "malaise" stemmed from her life in Frankfurt, a city she hated. We do not know why she had such animosity toward Frankfurt, although it is not now, nor was it then, as beautiful a city as Vienna. As an industrial center, it did not have the artistic population of her native city. Apparently her only happy moments came from visits to her family's estate in Winkle, Germany, and she never stopped longing for Vienna, the place of her birth.

Although Solomon reported that there was no "great love" between Antonie and her husband, Franz, he noted that "[Franz's] surrender to her request that they leave his paternal home and business... certainly shows that he was prepared to go to great lengths to please her. For her part, Antonie regarded her husband as a good man—she called him 'my good Franz' and... 'the best of all men.'"[2]

In suggesting Antonie as the Beloved, we must also consider her small children, and how they fit into their mother's life and relationships. Antonie had lost her own mother at a young age. She knew too well the pain that losing a beloved parent caused a child. Would she have considered subjecting her own dear children to that same heartache by abandoning them, by leaving their father for another man? In her diary she had written: "Blessed is the house where the virtues of the parents

---

[2]Solomon, p. 179.

never depart... Happy is the daughter who does not live far from her mother..." This attitude hardly makes her a likely candidate to abandon her children. She wrote to her father that, "These dear children mean everything to me." A woman like Antonie Brentano, who, despite her emotional difficulties, was kind and generous, does not appear to be the sort to be so terribly selfish and self-serving as to leave the children who depended upon her for their emotional well-being.

The Brentano family moved back to Vienna in 1809, when Antonie's father became gravely ill. According to Solomon, following her father's death that same year, Antonie was "frequently ill for weeks at a time and went repeatedly to Karlsbad in search of a cure, but without success." On June 5, 1811, she wrote "My health is completely shattered, and that prevents me from having a pleasant life." Solomon said that "It is my assumption that she fled to Beethoven seeking salvation." Perhaps she did, however, if so, it is our belief that this was a flight she made only in her on mind and that she did not make Beethoven aware of her fantasy, at least, not until overwhelming stress might have forced her to do so.

But a woman who thinks of a man as her "savior" is hardly capable of loving him "as a man," as Solomon claimed. Even Solomon admitted in his *Beethoven Essays* that Antonie

> engaged in a great Romantic charade, a pretense that her grand passion for a supreme artist, for a composer who walks "godlike among mortals," would lead her to a heroic overthrow of convention. She was scarcely a liberated Romantic heroine. If anything she was more constrained by convention than her models.

Is this statement not a contradiction of Solomon's claim that Antonie was the only woman who ever "loved Beethoven as a man?" From her behavior, we see Antonie Brentano as a weak, ill, desperately unhappy woman who after two years still grieved for her father, and who was looking for a diversion which might rescue her from her bitter state of mind. It is no wonder, then, that she may have developed an obsessive and unrealistic love for Beethoven. But clearly, she was incapable of separating the real Beethoven from the glorified being she imagined him to be.

Had Franz not been tied to Frankfurt by his business, he might have consented to remain in Vienna and thus become the savior his wife required. Instead, Antonie may have attached herself emotionally to someone who *was* rooted in Vienna: Beethoven. It also is no wonder that Beethoven's music touched her deeply, and that she found it uplifting. Many people did, but without succumbing to any fantasies about a love affair between themselves and the music's composer. It would not be surprising, given her unstable mental state, for her to have secretly entertained the notion that she might be more to him than a friend, much as Fanny Giannatasio nurtured her adolescent fantasies. Yet with a background so firmly seated in religion, and being a mother of small children dependent upon her, it is unlikely that, under normal circumstances, she would have acted upon her hidden desires. Her diary entries show that she was resistant to change, as her inability to adjust to life in Frankfurt also indicates. She wrote "God grant that I will find joy in housewifely everyday life." She also expressed her fear of the dangers of "wanting to live as one would love to live" by "departing from the beaten track." This is not the sort of woman who easily would abandon her safe life to run off with another man.

As we learn more about her, we come to see that Antonie probably was obsessed with Beethoven. How can we resist entertaining some suspicion about a woman's hold on reality when she speaks of the "holy hands of Beethoven," and believes that he "walks godlike among the mortals." Solomon claimed that Antonie spoke of Beethoven "in terms which we can now interpret only as expressions of love." Can Antonie's worship of Beethoven actually fit Solomon's definition of true and mature love? In this author's opinion, it is most definitely *not* the love of a woman for a real man of flesh and blood. It is rather like the love a disciple might ascribe to a holy presence, filled with religious fervor and blind adoration. Her "love" was little different than that of the hysterical female fans who cling weeping to the gates of Graceland. The depth of her reverence for Beethoven would have prevented her from seeing him and loving him as a human being. And we know from Beethoven's letters that however much he wanted to be loved, he was not the sort who wanted to be worshipped, nor depended upon to be anyone's emotional savior.

Now let us turn to Beethoven and his feelings for Antonie. Certainly it is plain to see why Antonie, so pitifully unhappy, would have been drawn to Beethoven, but how on earth can we imagine that Beethoven could have been attracted to such a sorrowful woman when typically he had chosen as his friends and companions those lighthearted beings who lifted him out of his own darkness? Could she have hidden her profound sadness from him? Perhaps she attempted to veil it behind physical illness, and thus was able to "present a controlled exterior to visitors." Yet how could Beethoven be oblivious to her depression? When he went to visit her, most often he would find her shut up in her room. Naturally he would have felt sorry for her, for she and Franz were kindhearted people, and he empathized with those who suffered, but as a rule, Beethoven did not enjoy associating with people who were gloomy and withdrawn. Paul Nettl noted that "Beethoven preferred Nanni Giannatasio del Rio, whose refreshing temperament he enjoyed more than Fanny's [her sister's] silent reserve."[3] This observation is supported by Fanny's diary, which indicated that Beethoven enjoyed Nanni's company more than he did Fanny's. This same aversion to people of a somber nature, prompted Beethoven's note to Schindler:

> I would much rather try to repay frequently with a small gift the services you render me, than have you at my table. For I confess that your presence irritates me in so many ways. If you see me looking not very cheerful, you say 'Nasty day again, isn't it?' For owing to your vulgar outlook how could you appreciate anything that is not vulgar? It is impossible to have you beside me permanently because such an arrangement would upset my whole existence.[4]

Over and over one finds that his closest friendships were with those who were gay and cheerful, people who did not "upset his whole existence," as a closer association with Antonie surely would have done. Thus it is unimaginable that Beethoven had had more than sympathetic friendship for this poor woman. Solomon himself admitted that she had "desolate moments in Vienna" when during "long periods of illness she withdrew from company and remained 'in her room inaccessible to all visitors.'" Beethoven, however, did come to visit on occasion, improvising on the pianoforte in her anteroom—though apparently not often visiting her in person—and "bringing comfort." Beethoven's kindness toward her was not unusual, nor should it be misinterpreted

---

[3]Nettl, p. 195.
[4]Anderson, p. 1124.

as an "ardent passion," for this was simply his way with friends. He comforted Antonie in the same way he comforted Dorothea von Ertmann when she lost her child—with music, the way he expressed himself with all except those closest to him. As Ignaz von Seyfried said, "Friends could expect actual aid from him." Music was Beethoven's aid to an unhappy friend.

Fanny Giannatasio observed that the Distant Beloved— whom Solomon also thought was Antonie—a woman Beethoven admitted loving, "must be very similar to him." The only, remotest similarity Antonie shared with the composer was depression. Yet even there, there were sharp differences. Dark clouds frequently hung over Frau Brentano's emotions, darkening her entire life. In Beethoven's case, these same dark clouds only sporatically wafted over him in reaction to adverse situations in his life. Time and again, Beethoven lifted himself above these threatening clouds in a way that Antonie never could. She remained forever cast into the gloom from which she found no escape, in the end, not even in the fantasy love she had imagined between herself and Beethoven. In all other ways, Antonie Brentano's personality was not the least bit similar to that of the fiery, spirited, outspoken nonconformist that Beethoven was. They differed even in their opinion of Vienna—she, loving it completely; he, always finding fault with his adopted city.

While initially Beethoven may have found Antonie's reverence for him flattering, the composer would not have desired such a woman as a wife, a woman who would do nothing more than add yet another burden to his already heavy load. Would he have relished fulfilling the role of savior to a such a person, to playing the role of god to a worshipful disciple? No. Antonie Brentano could never have been the true companion, the true "other self" Beethoven was seeking. Despite his obvious pity for Antonie, Beethoven would not have sacrificed himself and his art to "save" her from her misery by casting his lot with hers. Never would he have been so foolishly altruistic, particularly when he already had in his life a woman who *was* his equal in mind and spirit, a true and intimate companion.

Solomon claimed that Antonie Brentano had been willing to risk the condemnation of society in order to be with Beethoven. Can one imagine that a such woman, one who could not so much as cope with living in a city she despised even after many years, would be able to find the strength in her character to cope with not only the condemnation of society but also the Catholic church, with the knowledge that she had abandoned her small children and left them motherless, with the thought that she had deeply wounded "her good Franz, the best of men" who loved her and tried so hard to please her? This author finds it *un*imaginable.

Whatever secret feelings she may have had for the composer, we believe that Antonie kept them to herself until circumstances may have forced her to make a sudden, unplanned, and desperate move. If she had ever openly declared her love to Beethoven, it had not been in Prague, but in Franzensbrunn. It was there that she would have had to face the fact that she soon would have to leave her beloved Vienna for Frankfurt, and perhaps never see her home again. In a panic, she could have abandoned her rational behavior, pushed all concerns for her husband and children out of her mind, ignored the fact that her pregnancy would have caused Beethoven to rebuff her, and impulsively threw herself on his heart. Had she been thinking clearly, she would have known that such a religiously fervent declaration of devotion would have done nothing more than shock him, and, as this would have made him uncomfortable in her presence, drive him away from her. If the "startling event" about which Beethoven wrote his publishers had been a personal encounter rather than the war raging in Europe in 1812, then we believe he had been referring to an unexpected outpouring of emotion from Antonie. As quickly as he was able, without arousing Franz's suspicions, he distanced himself from her, concerned that his presence might encourage her to act as rashly as she had spoken.

Despite this prudent decision on Beethoven's part, he may not have been entirely successful in discouraging Antonie's ardor, and his friendly overture to them in 1815 may have once again unwittingly fanned the flames of her devotion. If so, then it is not surprising that we find in his *Tagebuch* of 1816-1817, the following entry, which we will address more fully later, in Chapter 20:

> In the case of T., there is nothing to do but to leave it to
> God, never to go where one might do a wrong through
> weakness. But be as kind as possible to T., her attachment
> deserves never to be forgotten.

Solomon suggested that the *T* in this entry referred to Antonie "Toni" Brentano. Perhaps it did, for it reflects the same weariness Beethoven spoke of in his letter to his publishers.

However, this clearly was not written by a man speaking about his Beloved. Interestingly, this entry came close to the same time as a number of letters Beethoven wrote to Frankfurt which are now missing. If Antonie had written to him of her longing, her desires, her need for him, the missing letters could have been Beethoven's attempt to quash her feelings once and for all. If he had spoken frankly in them, flatly refusing to respond to her ardor, it certainly would explain why they had been destroyed, no doubt by Antonie herself.

.*15*.
The Psychological Impact of the Letter

If Antonie Brentano was the Beloved, then Beethoven was a liar, living by a double standard and deluding everyone, including himself, about his morality and values.

If Antonie Brentano was the Beloved, then Beethoven was a fool, lusting for a woman incapable of being faithful to her husband, and making himself vulnerable to heartbreak, something he said he would never do.

If Antonie Brentano was the Beloved, we must accept one more thing about him: that he was a complete dolt with no feelings for his friend, Franz Brentano, and as little concern for the Beloved herself. Why do we say this? Let us imagine the following scenario:

Beethoven knows that his Beloved and her husband, his close friend, are staying together at an inn in a nearby resort. Despite the fact that she is not alone, Beethoven decides to risk sending her a highly passionate love letter in which she is implicated as being unfaithful to her husband, and which says that the two of them have a "goal to live together." (Stupid, is it not?) In addition, Beethoven does not consider that his friend, her husband—who, remember, is there with her—probably would be the one to retrieve the mail, and certainly would see this letter addressed to his wife. And this was no easily hidden little note. This letter was thick, ten pages long. Beethoven does not consider that such a letter might upset Franz, or make him suspicious. He also is oblivious to the fact that Antonie would have an emotional reaction to receiving such a letter, and that Franz would notice such a response. The letter, in effect, betrays both of them, but that never occurs to Beethoven. (Is this stupid, or merely insensitive?)

Neither.

Beethoven was not a liar, he was not a fool, and he most definitely was not an unfeeling imbecile. Not only was he an intelligent man, he also was a cautious one, a suspicious one, a man who as a rule did not like committing his thoughts to paper, who feared letters being seen by those other than the intended recipients, a man fond of saying, "more about that by word of mouth."

Like his wife, Franz was ill. He would not be out and about, cavorting at the spa. And as he was at a resort, he also would not be conducting business. Likely he would be in his wife's company almost constantly. Beethoven knew that. Why then would Beethoven—a man whose friends thought honorable and good-hearted —have risked wounding his friend Franz Brentano in a cruel and heartless way by sending such a letter to Franz's wife? Worse, why would he put his Beloved in a terribly awkward and painful situation, where she must try to hide not only this long, passionate love letter, but also her own feelings? Sending such a letter would not just have been foolhearty, it would have been insensitive beyond measure

Could passion alone have made Beethoven forget not only his high moral convictions but his own common sense? Although lust often is stronger than both, in the Beloved letter, love was expressed spiritually, nor carnally. The letter was not motivated by immediate sexual desires, but by genuine love. Thus it was not dashed off in the heat of a sexually needy moment, but written over a two-day contemplative period, certainly enough time for Beethoven to fully realize what he was doing, and to consider the consequences of writing such a letter, consequences that would have been dire for a married woman. That Beethoven went ahead and wrote his letter—and, as we believe, also sent it—should show us that he saw it posed no immediate risks to his Beloved.

In the Beloved letter, Beethoven clearly stated: "...arrange it so that I can live with you" and "only through quiet contemplation of our existence can we reach our goal to live together." Even though no specific mention of marriage was made, from his note written in Baden which said "...let me finally find the one—who will make me happy in virtue—who will lawfully be mine"—we can be sure that he wanted his Beloved to be his wife, to form a true and legal union with him, and not simply be his mistress.

Solomon suggested that Beethoven decided that he would "love both of them—Antonie and Franz—as a single and inseparable unit." Yet anyone who has read the Beloved letter knows that it absolutely does not intimate that Beethoven had any sort of *ménage á trois* in mind, not even in a spiritual sense.

REUNION

Solomon wrote, "There is no point in speculating on the events which occurred during Beethoven's reunion with [the Brentanos]...during July to September 1812." But why not? Is this not exactly what *must* be considered? Why not test the theory against the actions and reactions of the people involved, to see whether it even makes sense? Solomon was eager enough to explore and speculate about the alleged symbolism in Beethoven's mention of the muddy road on which his carriage broke down, yet Solomon avoided completely something far more interesting and significant. Why? Could it be that he realized a close examination of the interactions of these three people—Beethoven, Antonie, and Franz Brentano—would show that his Antonie-as-the-Beloved theory made no sense?

If Antonie was *not* Beethoven's Beloved then, true, there would be little reason to speculate on their reunion, for in that case they were simply three good friends spending time together —at least as far as Franz Brentano and Beethoven saw the situation. But if one purports that she *was*, one must consider the ramifications of such a lengthy reunion. Under those circumstances it was not just three friends being together, but a highly emotionally charged love triangle which Beethoven stupidly initiated by going to Karlsbad when he could have and should have left well enough alone. (Are we to believe that he was so driven by love and lust that he simply could not stay away?)

Yet, is there any evidence of strain in the midst of this astonishing long-term personal drama? Any repercussions? Stress, arguments, anything that marred the "elation" Solomon noted that Beethoven exhibited while with the Brentanos? No. Now how could that be possible? Had the mere presence of the Brentanos' child managed to keep all emotions in check?

Let us take another look at Beethoven's impulsive journey to Karlsbad. Supposedly, after a month's separation, he suddenly decided he needed to be with his Beloved *and her husband*, and thus, ignoring the certain awkwardness of the situation, as well as the probability that his arrival would inflict emotional pain upon them, went to be with the Brentanos and remained with them over the course of nearly two months. Yet in a note to himself written some five years later, Beethoven asserted that he should "never...go where one might do a wrong through weakness." Are we to believe that it was not until Beethoven was 46 years old that he finally realized his mistake of 1812, that it had not been a good idea for him to expose himself and his Beloved to that kind of temptation?

As we said, Solomon wrote that "Beethoven was visibly elated during these months." He was elated to be with his Beloved *and her husband*? It was enough for him to merely see her, without touching her, without kissing her, without speaking intimately with her, without making love to her? He could feel elation even though he surely knew *her husband* was doing with her all the things—the touching, the kissing, the love-making—*he* wanted the right to do? Hercules at the crossroads indeed! How could he watch the days go by, knowing his beloved soon would be leaving his life forever, and feel elation? That certainly stretches the imagination! Would it not make more sense for his elation to come from anticipating a reunion with his true Beloved in Vienna?

Could a man whose friends called honest and straightforward be capable of maintaining a difficult pretense, hiding his true passionate feelings for Antonie behind a cloak of casual friendship, for two months? Could Beethoven and Antonie have kept their love and desires hidden from Franz. And what about Franz? Was he simply unaware that such feelings existed between the lovers, or did he just not care? Although Solomon believed that speculating about these issues was pointless, most people would find the situation so bizarre that it would be amazing if they did *not* wonder! Surely there is someone who believes Antonie was the Beloved who also wonders why Beethoven followed the Brentanos to the Bohemian spas, and lived as their next-door neighbor for two months, prolonging the agony of his inevitable separation from his Beloved, and of hers from him. Was he trying to punish himself and his emotionally frail Beloved for having immoral desires?

Rubbish.

There was no need for Beethoven to subject either himself or his Beloved to such anguish. Surely he would have realized (unless, of course, he really *was* a dolt) that the sooner he made a break with her the better. As the letter did not tell her goodbye, his presence in Karlsbad only would encouraged her further, dangled more cruel hope before her, and continued to mislead her with empty promises of a realized goal of living together. Now why would he have done that? It would not have been difficult for Beethoven to have distanced himself from the situation early on: he easily could have used the excuse that he simply was not feeling well enough to continue his trip. Thus he could have made the break cleanly, and spared himself and his Beloved unnecessary grief. In human psychological terms, unless the desired outcome was to suffer emotional pain, his behavior made no sense.

But of course it *did* make sense. Beethoven's decision to seek out the Brentanos was based only on his desire to be with friends. He was not aware of any romantic feelings Antonie might have harbored for him. His doctor had sent him to Karlsbad and Franzensbrunn, and as he knew his friends were there, he sought them out, not because he had a burning desire to be near his Beloved, but because he knew that their kindness and friendship which he enjoyed so much would be a pleasant distraction for him. He was disappointed that his doctor was keeping him at the spas so long[1] and the Brentanos would keep his loneliness at bay until he finally was able to return to Vienna and to the woman he loved.

PASSING THROUGH CRISIS

Solomon made the casual assertion that "in some way the trio managed to pass through the crisis into a new stage of their relationship" and saw no need to explore it further. Yet how can anyone help but wonder how they managed *that* incredible feat? In a mere two months. And without the assistance of a therapist, no less! Are we to believe that the passion inherent in the Beloved letter had been shrugged off by Beethoven so casually in so short a time? According to Fanny Giannatasio's diary, for Beethoven, even five years later his love was "still as it was on the first day."

[1] In December, Beethoven would write to Princess Kinsky that "My indisposition became worse at Teplitz, and I was obliged to stay there longer than I had originally intended." Anderson, p. 394.

Again, rather than ignoring the issue, we *must* examine the behaviors and interactions of these three people, for this should give us a clearer understanding of their relationship to one another. It would have made far better use of Solomon's analytical skills for him to explain Beethoven's and the Brentanos's behavior rather than wasting those skills in analyzing the muck and mire of an insignificant muddy road. Although time and again Solomon shows us how fond he is of psychological analysis, he dwells solely on the irrelevant and shrugs off with one short sentence that which is enormously important to the topic at hand. One wonders whether Solomon once again simply was avoiding dealing with an issue that would have destroyed his theory in terms of common sense.

Well, this author, for one, wants very much to know how the trio "managed to pass through this crisis." Assuming Antonie to have been Beethoven's Beloved, we also must look at Franz Brentano's behavior over the next decade. Brentano continued his friendship with Beethoven until 1823. He loaned him generous sums of money interest free, which in some cases became outright gifts. He did Beethoven business favors, serving as his intermediary with a music publisher in Bonn. He even allowed his wife and daughter to accept the composer's musical gifts. Is there not something wrong with this picture? Why would Brentano act this way toward the man who wanted to steal away his wife, the man for whom his wife would have abandoned him and their children? We could assume that Franz had remained unaware of this passionate affair, not only while it had been carried on in Vienna, but even after observing these two beloveds together day after day while they lived side-by-side at the spas. This alone is hard to imagine. Can a husband actually be so blind to rampaging lust? Or were Antonie and Beethoven simply so adept at concealing their desires? Actors worthy of any stage! On the other hand, it is an even greater strain on one's imagination to believe that he *had* been aware of the affair. Then we must assume that Brentano had not cared that his wife was passionately in love with another man, to the point where she was contemplating running off with him, and had liked Beethoven far too much to allow such a little thing as his wife's infidelity to come between them. Poor Franz. Beethoven's biographers ascribe as much idiocy to him as to the composer himself. No wonder Solomon preferred not to speculate on these bizarre events!

However, if Antonie was not the Beloved—and everything points to the fact that she was not—then and only then does Franz's continuing friendship with Beethoven, and his amenability to doing favors for him, make sense.

A MISGUIDED REACTION

Solomon suggested that the Beloved letter had been a reaction to Antonie's declaration that she would leave her husband and children in order to be with Beethoven. He further proposed that this declaration probably had come in Prague and that it had superceded Beethoven's plans with Varnhagen. If Solomon is right, then must we not believe that Beethoven had written this letter merely to placate a depressed and desperate woman, and that one of the most famous and passionate love letters in the world had been an insincere sham? This author is unwilling to make such a pronouncement.

Let us for the moment consider Solomon's premise that Antonie had declared her love and willingness to give herself to Beethoven while in Prague, prior to the writing of the letter. Our first difficulty with this supposition involves timing. Franz and Antonie did not arrive in Prague until July 3 and Beethoven left the morning of July 4. At most, the three of them could have had dinner together. When could Antonie have been alone with Beethoven without arousing Franz's suspicions? Surely this declaration would have prompted a discussion and not merely been a comment made in passing. Although this scenario is difficult to imagine, we will allow it to stand in light of greater problems with this supposition.

Solomon suggested that this declaration had surprised and shocked Beethoven. No doubt it would have. However, in Solomon's mind, Beethoven's shock was *not* the result of learning that Antonie had completely misunderstood his feelings of friendship for her. No, Solomon believed that the reason for Beethoven's shock stemmed from his own psychological inadequacies. Suddenly his fantasy love was on the verge of becoming reality, a prospect which, emotionally, he was unprepared to handle. All at once the romance that had existed only in the vaults of heaven was about to make him a married man. Faced with this responsibility, Solomon believed that Beethoven panicked, and used the letter as a means to gently extricate himself from the situation.

A scenario worthy of a soap opera...but also of closer examination.

In the first part of the letter, Beethoven asked "...can you change it that you are not completely mine, I am not completely yours?" If Antonie had made a declaration of intent in Prague, why would Beethoven have asked this? He would already have had the answer. According to Solomon, she had claimed that *yes*, she *could* change it, she *could* leave Franz, she *could* be completely his. Yet, clearly, at this point, Beethoven still had been wondering whether they could one day belong to one another.

In the second part of the letter, Beethoven told his Beloved, "I say to myself and to you, arrange so that I can live with you..." The man who could write this was not one who feared the responsbility of commitment. He *wanted* to be with her. He then closed his letter with "...only by calm contemplation of our existence can we reach our goal to live together." Again, if he had been attempting to gently reject her offer, he had done a poor job of it.

Clearly, the Beloved letter was not one of rejection. It was a letter of cautious hope, stressing continuance, not farewell. As Beethoven told her, "I have resolved to stray about in the distance until I can fly into your arms and can call myself entirely at home, can send my soul embraced by you into the realm of spirits." Here he promised her that, if Fate refused to grant their hearing favorably, someday they would at least be together in death. Until that time, he said, "you will compose yourself all the more since you know my faithfulness to you..." Although their wish to be together lawfully, as husband and wife, might not ever occur in their lifetime, still he pledged his eternal devotion to her, and asked the same of her: "oh love me on and on." Whatever happened, he assured her that their relationship would continue.

If written to Antonie, all Beethoven would have been doing would have been offering her false hope. Antonie was as legally, emotionally, religiously, and maternally bound to her marriage as anyone possibly could have been. Short of becoming a widow, she could never be free to marry Beethoven. Why then would he deliberately have misled her, when he knew firsthand from his experience with Magdalena how painful it was to be misled? As he told Josephine, "I certainly deserve that you be frank with me." Did his Beloved not deserve that same frankness? He knew he would never see Antonie and the Brentanos again once they went back to Frankfurt. Why pledge this woman his eternal devotion under such circumstances? Had this heartfelt letter been nothing more than Beethoven's awkward and misguided attempt to give some joy to an emotionally fragile individual? Nothing more than his desire to help Antonie through their parting, offering her false hope with the idea that she would eventually forget his promises to her? Had he he confused deception with compassion? We cannot believe that.

While Beethoven might have wounded his friends by lashing out at them in anger, deliberate, calculated cruelty was not part of Beethoven's nature. If Franz had seen the letter he would not have understood Beethoven's intention to merely soothe the desperation of an unhappy woman, and he would have been shocked and hurt by the betrayal of both his wife and his friend. Would any good purpose have been served by sending such an insincere letter? No, none at all.

As we have already noted, any declaration by Antonie must have come as a complete surprise to Beethoven, and could not have been made anywhere else but in Franzensbrunn. Nor could it have been a move that even Antonie had fully considered. She herself had called Beethoven a man of "pure intentions." How, under normal, rational circumstances, could she have imagined that such a man would agree to take a woman away from her family, or help her abandon them, particularly when she was carrying her husband's child? The only answer can be that the circumstances for her had *not* been normal—the emotional stress of her imminent and permanent departure from her beloved Vienna had prevented her from behaving rationally.

THE LETTER'S RETURN

Some biographers have suggested that Beethoven never posted his letter at all. Certainly it is possible that, had the letter been intended for Antonie, Beethoven had been struck with a sudden flash of good sense, considered the ramifications of sending the letter, and at the very last moment refrained from sending it to her. Possible... but improbable

As noted in the Karlsbad discussion, Beethoven had had two full days to consider sending this letter, and the last part closed abruptly so that he could post it. Under those circumstances, it is difficult to believe in any last-minute second thoughts. This author is inclined to believe that the letter had indeed been sent to Beethoven's Beloved, but, if so, how did the letter get back to Beethoven? We have explored possible scenarios involving Josephine Brunswick and Anna Marie Erdödy, but what if the letter had been sent to Antonie Brentano?

If Beethoven had sent the letter to Antonie, she, like Anna Marie and Josephine, would have had to return it to him or it would not have been in his possession. Now what would this scenario tell us about our third player in this odd love triangle: Franz Brentano? Here again we see the poor idiot husband stumbling about in the dark, oblivious to the highly emotional drama being played out before his very eyes as a heartbroken Antonie returns a love letter to her beloved, and bids Beethoven farewell for the last time. Or, perhaps there had been no great and mutual sorrow at their parting. Is not either one of those scenarios difficult to believe?

We do not believe that Franz would have been suspicious of his wife's emotional reaction to Beethoven's departure. He knew that she was a highly emotional and depressed woman and would not have given a second thought to any adverse reaction on her part to their friend's leaving. Only if Beethoven had exhibited similar emotions would Franz have begun to suspect their liaison. In this case, we must believe that Beethoven had not betrayed his own sorrow at leaving his beloved Antonie behind. Could he have done that? Perhaps. However, we believe the reason that Beethoven had been able to leave without rousing Franz's suspicions was because he *had* no broken heart, no deep sorrow to keep hidden. Though he may have been the object of Antonie's misplaced fantasies, he did not consider her his Beloved. He may have felt badly that Antonie had felt the need to make such a desperate play for his affections, but as it had not been his fault that she had taken his kindness for something more, he had no reason to feel guilt or to grieve. He likely felt only weariness and perhaps relief that he finally was able to separate himself from an awkward situation. Whatever sadness he may have felt over his loss of the Brentanos certainly dissipated as soon as he got to Hernals, replaced by the joy he expressed in the music he finished that momentous year.

❧ 16 ❧
The Psychoanalysis of the Beloved Letter

There is something unsettling about biographers, regardless of their qualifications, placing their long-dead subjects upon the analyst's couch, and then explaining to us what the subject's actions and words "really" meant. We might imagine ourselves visiting a psychologist, having him ask to see our letters, notes, and journals, and then making us sit mute upon his couch while he sifts through them. He would then procede to interpret our characters, our motives, our behaviors, our innermost selves, without any input, feedback, or explanation from us. How correct would we find his analysis of us under those circumstances? The deceased subject is no different than our silent selves, a person who obviously can offer no defense or explanations. What he said or did can be taken out of context and twisted to fit the biographers' intentions, and often readers are given interpretations and impressions which may not necessarily be correct. Most readers do not have the time, inclination, or in the case of primary materials being in a foreign language, the ability to conduct research on a topic for themselves, and naturally rely on what is reported to them. They are thus at the writer's mercy. It is important to remember that an impressive string of letters following a surname does not ensure infallibility, and that Truth is not always synonymous with what is Accepted. If we were able to rely totally on a credentialed professional knowing the Truth, we would not be advised to seek a second opinion when our physician, surely a skilled and knowledgable professional, renders a diagnosis. This is valid advice even in the area of scholarship, yet not even biographers always take it, preferring to "take for granted" that a sufficiently lettered predecessor's opinion is fact.

At times too many opinions also can muddy the waters of clear thinking. While we may not be able to read our medical records and draw our own conclusions, in most cases any literate person is capable of reading a biographical subject's letters for him- or herself and using common sense to decide what the writer meant without the aid of convoluted interpretation. Scholarly "insights" often can be more of a hindrance to knowing the truth than a help. Author Colleen McCullough made a pertinent observation in her recent book *A Creed for the Third Millennium.* She wrote:

> Common sense is never original! And what's so desirable about originality, anyway? Sometimes it's the oldest and hoariest commonplaces that people see least clearly, because everyone who ought to be guiding the people is trying so desperately hard to be original.[1]

Perhaps Beethoven's biographers are doing just what Ms. McCullough described: trying so hard to provide an interesting and original theory about the composer's love life and his Immortal Beloved that they have lost sight of plain common sense.

THE MASTER WRITES

Understanding Beethoven's letters is not very difficult. He was not Nostradamus. He did not attempt to disguise his true feelings or intentions in obscure verbage, although some biographers attempt to prove that he did so by *reading* more in his letters than Beethoven actually *wrote.* Beethoven did not write in riddles, or use language that would require his reader to guess his meaning, any more than any of us do in writing to friends. At times, a private joke written to a friend (in which he might be playfully naughty) may make us wonder what he meant. But as he was writing only for the benefit or amusement of his letter's recipient, there was no deliberate attempt on Beethoven's part to deceive or baffle future readers. No doubt he would be surprised, and perhaps even angered, to know that his letters have been

---

[1]McCullough, p. 127.

collected and studied so carefully, and, in many cases, searched for hidden meanings. But his writings were not meant to be cryptic. What he said and how he wrote was very much the same as the way he composed—straight from his heart to his pen. Unfortunately, at times, his strong opinions bypassed his magnificent brain. That he did not censor himself, neither in his speech, nor in his actions, nor in his letters, often caused him personal troubles: he offended people who did not know him well, and he hurt people who loved him. Yet the very letters that occasionally got Beethoven into trouble with others prove to us just how open, honest, straightforward, and unaffected his correspondence was. Michael Hamburger, in *Beethoven: Letters, Journals and Conversations*, noted that Beethoven's letters give the reader an almost embarrassing intimacy with him. How expressive is his creative punctuation—his multiple exclamation points, strong underlines, and emphatic dashes—coupled with stressed pen nibs, strikeouts, and ink blotches. Who possibly could be oblivious to the raw emotion in a sentence written thus:

> Was können sie noch mehr verlangen. Sie haben von mir den Bedienten *für den Herrn* erhalten—▬▬▬▬ sind sie noch nicht schadlos. Welcher Ersatz!!!!! Welch' herrlichter Tausch!!!![2]

Amusingly, Beethoven did not think he expressed himself well in letters, but one almost does not need to know German to see the explosive anger in *that* passage. Or the playful humor in this one:

> To His Well Well Highest and Bestborn, the Herr von Zmeskall—Imperial and Royal as also Royal and Imperial Court Secretary—Will His High and Wellborn, His Hernn von Zmeskall's Zmeskallity have the kindness to say where we can speak to him tomorrow?
>
> > We are your most damnably
> > devoted
> > Beethoven[3]

---

[2]"What more can they still want. They have received from me the servant instead *of the master*—(crossed out) Is the score not yet paid. What a substitute!!!!! What a magnificent exchange!!!!" Written in 1809 on the sketches of the "Emperor" Piano Concerto #5, at the height of Beethoven's quarrel with Countess Erdödy.
[3]Anderson, p. 31.

Beethoven also was not a poetic writer like Goethe. He did not sit and ponder, carefully constructing perfect phrases, putting great thought into the construction of each sentence, the choice of each word, testing his prose for subtle nuance. He simply picked up his pen—or, more likely, his sturdy pencil—and he wrote. Although he often lamented his lack of skill as a writer, it was precisely this liability that caused him to write openly, honestly, without pretension. That many of his emotional scribblings are on musical scores, scraps of paper, and even the shutters of his apartments shows us also that he wrote whenever, wherever, and however the mood struck him. Thus Beethoven's words may be taken on face value without applying deep psychological meanings to them. Amusing as these analyses may be, they do the composer a grave disservice.

It seems to this author that in addition to lacking common sense, many of Beethoven's biographers have no sense of humor. The naturalness and hilarious naughtiness Beethoven expressed in his letters (a tendency to which he freely admitted) have made some biographers brand him emotionally crippled, repressed, promiscuous, and even degenerate. What is so odd is that these are not Victorian writers whose sensitivities might have made them blush at some of the things Beethoven wrote,[4] but twentieth century writers for whom the shock value of the composer's letters should be small. It is true that Beethoven sometimes, though infrequently, used some "dirty humor." This has caused many of his modern day biographers to seek and find it "hidden" in many of his other letters where it simply does not exist, in order to prove that despite his sublime music his mind rarely left the gutter. Perhaps some biographers felt that such treatment would serve to humanize Beethoven. Yet the psychoanalyses of his letters often to go such extremes, and are so utterly unaware of the composer's mischievous humor, that one is left with the desire to give those writers a good shaking and a reminder that Beethoven was only joking. (Of course, all too often "kidding" also is assigned deep psychological meaning, so that the most innocent jest is made to seem indicative of severe and suppressed emotional problems.)

---

[4]We cite Beethoven's funny but indecent name for the "Obervormundschaft" which he called the "Ober-Arsch Hinterschaft." We trust it really needs no literal translation. See Anderson, p. 823, letter and note 4.

Despite the fact that in none of Beethoven's other 1569 surviving notes and letters did he attempt to disguise his feelings behind a psychological veil, Solomon went to great lengths to psychoanalyze the letter to the Immortal Beloved. Therefore, we should trouble ourselves as well, and consider some of the analyses to see whether they are valid.

SLIP OF THE PEN

What would any good psychoanalysis be without a traditional Freudian slip? It is hardly surprising then to find that Solomon uncovered a "revealing slip of the pen" in the Beloved letter. Beethoven wrote "If we were wholly united you would feel the pain of it as little as I."[5] Solomon apparently attributed this remark to a slip of the pen because he did not understand to what Beethoven was referring when he wrote the word "it." Thus he decided that Beethoven *meant* to say "Although we are not wholly united, you should feel the pain of our separation as little as I." Yet changing the word "would" to "should" and reversing Beethoven's positive statement "If we were wholly united..." to a negative one, "Although we are not wholly united..." alters the entire meaning of the sentence. Solomon's interpretation makes it sound as if Beethoven were telling his Beloved that he felt *no* pain at their separation, and that neither should she. His implication is that Beethoven *intended* to say "You *should* feel the pain...as little as I *do*," rather than "You *would* feel the pain as little as I *would*." This is not a true reflection of Beethoven's sentiment, for we see how strongly he wished for their togetherness, and how full of longing and the "pain of separation" his letter was. Beethoven *meant* just what he *wrote*: "If we were wholly united you would feel the pain of *it* [our separation] as little as I [*would*—implied by his use of the word "would" earlier in the sentence.]." That is, if he and his Beloved were legally married, neither one of them would ever again feel the pain of separation, for even if circumstances made it necessary for them to be physically apart for a short while, emotionally, spiritually, and legally they would not really be parted at all. Beethoven's pen did not "slip." He wrote exactly what he felt would be true, if he and his Beloved had a marital bond between them.

---

[5]A more literal translation is "were we wholly united, you would feel this painfulness just as little as I."

SUFFERING AND BETRAYAL

Beethoven's writing—and repeating—"You are suffering" Solomon took to mean that he was referring to his *own* inner conflict—that of both wanting and fearing love—and to the anguish which he himself felt as a result. Again, no deep meaning needs to be assigned to Beethoven's simple statement. His words may be taken as they were written: his Beloved was suffering—physically, perhaps emotionally—and he was empathizing with her, sharing her pain, as he had done numerous times before.

Solomon then claimed that "the suspicion of another possible betrayal surfaces: 'Much as you love me—I love you more—never hide from me anything that is you.'" This author finds it interesting that, to Solomon, the words "I love you" signal insincerity and mistrust—worse, an accusation! Beethoven had no reason to suspect betrayal from the woman he knew loved him. Yet perhaps we should not be surprised that Solomon interpreted the sentence as a suspicious demand rather than a loving invitation. After all, it was his contention that Beethoven had suffered repeated rejections and as a result was cynical, emasculated, and anxiety-ridden. One can almost envision fellow psychoanalysts gobbling up this juicy analysis, but again, no hidden meaning needs to be attached to Beethoven's affectionate plea. Is it so difficult to see that Beethoven simply was reminding his Beloved that she need not feel she must keep her problems, concerns, or needs a secret from him? (As we noted, he made a similar comment to Ries: "Why do you hide your need from me?") His statement invites his Beloved to share with him whatever life gave her—good or bad. His strength, his support, his understanding were hers for the asking. To attach anything mean-spirited or suspicious to Beethoven's loving offer is unfair to him, and to the love he had for, and trust he had in, this woman.

In the midst of his analysis of the letter, Solomon quoted the line from Beethoven's *Tagebuch* which he claimed showed Beethoven's severe doubts about his manhood and his lover's fidelity: "you may no longer be a man..." This already was dispensed with in Chapter 5 and will be touched on again in the discussion specifically devoted to the *Tagebuch* (Chapter 20). For the moment, we simply recall that this quote had been taken out of context, and that it had been written in early 1812 in regard to "the service business," rather than as a reaction to Beethoven's separation from his Beloved, or his vulnerability in relation to her.

Solomon further believed that Beethoven's union with his Beloved was barred by "unspecified terrors which overwhelmed the possibilities of a fruitful outcome." He then quoted another portion of a *Tagebuch* entry to prove his claim:

> To forego a great act which might have been and remains so—O fearful conditions which do not suppress my feelings for domesticity...

Solomon indicated that Beethoven's anxieties arose out of *imagined* inadequacies within himself, yet those things with which he had to contend were not "unspecified terrors" but real problems, many of which could never be overcome. His deafness certainly was not a product of his imagination! Nor was the fact that, under the rules of their society, his Beloved's marriage to him could strip her of her right to raise her own children. As such he was not anxious, since the term *anxiety* usually denotes a fear which is irrational and not based on any clear danger or threatening circumstance. There was nothing irrational about the frustration Beethoven felt as a result of the many substantial and possibly insurmountable barriers which stood him and his Beloved.

FOREVER...OR FAREWELL?

What Solomon—and other biographers, as well—also read into Beethoven's letter are explanations as to why his relationship with his Beloved tragically must be relinquished, even though spiritually their love would endure. They believe, in effect, that Beethoven was saying farewell to a love that could not be. What is interesting is that the biographers who see renunciation of love in the letter are all male. Now this author certainly would not be so brazenly sexist as to suggest that women read better than men. However, of the few female Beethoven biographers who exist, most do not read the Beloved letter the same way as the men. And as this was a love letter addressed to a woman, it perhaps needs a feminine perspective to counter the male view which burdens the letter with negativism.

It is true that Beethoven was cautious about believing in Fate's kindness:

> ...the gods must send us the rest, what for us must be and shall be...

and he knew that there was still doubt whether they would be allowed to be together as a legally married couple.

> ...waiting to learn whether Fate will hear us....

He also expressed doubts about the stability of their union:

> ...I require sameness... can this be under our relations?

Yet never does he say that their love cannot be, that their plans must be given up. While he and his Beloved inevitably must accept what Fate has in store for their relationship, he does not see it ending simply because they may be denied a legal union. Over and over he offers her his undying love:

> ...much as you love me I love you more...our love, firm as the firmament...I am yours...my eternally beloved...

and devotion:

> ...never misjudge the heart of your beloved...your faithful Ludwig

and requests hers in return:

> ...remain my true and only treasure... love me on and on...

And more than that, he shares with her the glimmers of hope still very much alive in his heart:

> I say to you and to myself, arrange it so I can live with you...

It is even with continued hope that he closes his letter:

> ...by calm consideration of our existence can we reach our goal to live together...

Simply because Beethoven expressed doubt that the gods would give him and his Beloved their "most blessed wish," this hardly meant he was renouncing his love for her. Where in Beethoven's pledges of eternal love did he indicate that their relationship must be abandoned? Where in "forever yours, forever mine, forever us" is the goodbye that is so evident to this author's esteemed male counterparts? There is none—not in the eyes of a woman.

A SYMBOLIC MUDDY ROAD

Solomon's last and most detailed attack upon the composer's psyche came in his analysis of the breakdown of Beethoven's carriage on the road to Teplitz. Solomon claimed he was not "seeking to burden Beethoven's letter with a heavier freight of interpretation than it may warrant," but reading his analysis makes this contention difficult to believe.

The situation simply had been this: the weather had been bad and the route to Teplitz poor. It had rained, the road had gotten muddy, and the carriage subsequently broke down. Possibly it had become stuck in the mud, but that is not actually what Beethoven said had happened, nor did he refer at all to a muddy road. Whatever the situation, such mishaps happen. Common sense tells us that none of these situations—the rain, the road conditions, the mud, and the carriage's breakdown—were Beethoven's fault. The composer was tired and sick and anxious to get to his destination. He did not want to spend the night at an uncomfortable way station. Yet Solomon still managed to place blame: Beethoven had been warned not to travel at night and he had not heeded that advice, thus, subconsciously he had caused his own misfortune. Likewise he should not have gotten involved with a married woman and was destined to pay the consequences for his indiscretion. Solomon would like us to believe that, when he finally arrived in Teplitz, Beethoven began musing about his trip and suddenly was struck by a profound insight which linked his love life to his carriage getting stuck on the muddy road. This flash of intuition immediately took on great psychosexual importance for him. He was compelled to share this symbolic connection with his Beloved, with the hope that she would be able to decipher his meaning—that he was not *really* speaking of a muddy road, but of his own emotional and sexual inadequacies—and offer him her understanding. Perhaps we should forego seeking the Beloved among countesses and Viennese aristocrats and focus our search on the 19th century equivalent of Dr. Ruth.

Although many readers—not to mention academicians—nod their heads in agreement with this scholastic poppycock, Beethoven's report of his terrible carriage trip was no more and no less than what Beethoven had said it was: a unfortunate inconvenience and an honest mistake. He had been in a hurry to get to his destination. Under the circumstances, that hardly can be considered odd. He had not heeded a warning, and had ended up being inconvenienced by his stubbornness.

To believe that a coach breaking down on a muddy road symbolized, as Solomon suggested, the "danger of [Beethoven's] own passage from a fearful isolation into manhood and fatherhood" is ludicrous. How can a happenstance of nature, an act of God, be symbolic of anything? Beethoven did not *cause* the muddy road; all he did was make a mistake in dealing with it. And how he chose to deal with it had nothing whatsoever to do with Antonie Brentano. Yet we are supposed to believe that Beethoven's error in judgment was a direct result of his subconscious fear of love: he had ventured where he had been warned not to go—that is, into a love affair with a married woman, symbolized by the muddy road (we are sure Antonie would have appreciated the analogy)— and consequently he had gotten stuck—presumably by both. That is, Beethoven had been so afraid of genuine love that he had deliberately driven his coach into the muck. We also must remember that Beethoven was not alone in his mishap. Obviously his coach driver had not heeded the warning either, and neither had Prince Esterhazy, nor *his* driver, nor any of their postillions! Could *all* these men have been involved with married women? Or been emasculated, anxiety-ridden, emotionally and sexually repressed individuals with the psychological need to thrash about in the mud? Is it not amazing how so many men with similar neuroses happened to be going to Teplitz from Prague at virtually the same time, and had ended up victims of that same psychologically symbolic muddy road? What an astonishing coincidence! If this amusing analysis is any indication, we certainly cannot accuse psychoanalysts of not having at least some sense of humor.

We might point out here that the "muddy road incident" of 1812 was not the only time when Beethoven failed to use good judgment when traveling. He repeated his error in 1820. In his letter to the Archduke Rudolph in Vienna, he wrote from Mödling:

> My indisposition is to be ascribed to my having taken a seat in an open post chaise as not to miss seeing Y.I.H. During the day it rained and when I drove out here it was almost cold. Nature seemed indeed to have taken umbrage at my foolishness or audacity and to have punished me for my stupidity.[6]

---

[6]Anderson, p. 901.

In 1820 there was no Antonie Brentano around for her to have caused Beethoven's error in judgment as a result of his psychological terror of her love. Once again, as in 1812, Beethoven was in a hurry to arrive at his destination, and did not heed his own common sense about traveling in inclement weather. Thus, despite Solomon's analysis that Beethoven's terror of the muddy road was actually his fear of Antonie Brentano's love, it remains, to Beethoven and to any sensible person, simply a muddy road, and a quite rational apprehension on Beethoven's part about traveling at night through a forest. How many of us have gotten on an airplane, even when bad weather had been forecast. If we believe the muddy road theory, then we must at all cost avoid telling loved ones that we had elected to get on an airplane in inclement weather for fear that our significant other would interpret this "obvious symbolism" to mean that our relationship was in serious trouble, or that subconsciously we had a wish to do ourselves bodily harm.

A STUDY IN CONFUSION

Solomon was not the only biographer to have found the Beloved letter "confused" as a result of great inner conflict. At this point, the reader might find an example of a *truly* confused Beethoven letter an amusing comparison to the Beloved letter:

> To Georg Treitschke, 1821: Let us begin with the primary original causes of all things, how something came about, wherefore and why it came about in that particular way, and became what it is, why something is what it is, why something cannot be exactly so!!! Here, dear friend, we have reached the ticklish point which my delicacy forbids me to reveal to you at once. All that we can say is: it cannot be! [7]

Now *this* is a letter that defies all clarity of thought and meaning! The Beloved letter hardly compares. One wonders if Treitschke had any earthly idea what Beethoven was saying to him. Yet this, again, was just typical Beethoven. It cannot be concluded that the composer wrote this muddled letter because of some deep psychological conflict with Treitschke!

It was not at all uncommon for Beethoven to move between exalted philosophy and a mundane description of various cures he

---

[7]Anderson, pp. 936-937.

was taking for ailments, to slide between a discussion of Goethe and the ordering of a piano, to soar to the vaults of heaven and end up on a muddy road. The Beloved letter was no more and no less "confused" than any of his other letters, and to this author, at least, its meaning is perfectly clear. To conclude that its "confusion" was the result of psychological conflict is not valid.

THE VALIDITY OF PSYCHOHISTORY

Since psychohistory has been a growing trend in the academic world, we would hope that those who read such biographies will keep in mind that analytic interpretation is not truth, it is merely speculation. Often presented with a tone of absolute authority, they frequently are deeply colored by the analyst's own experiences, prejudices, and unique personalities. In that light, the validity of such works must ever be questioned and examined. We have seen that innuendo, incomplete quotes, personal interpretation, and dubious authorities, can be presented under the guise of scholarly analysis so that what is written appears to be fact to the unsuspecting reader. We maintain that this practice— which attacks and degrades the character of another who not only is defenseless, but quite probably innocent of the charges leveled against him—is not simply inaccurate, it borders on unethical. Neither the dead nor their heirs can file libel suits, and without legal recourse, a biographer's subject, like the reader, is at the writer's mercy. What is unfortunate is that often the subject's honor must take quite a beating at the hands of those who wish to make him better "understood." We have no objection to opinions, as all historical writers must render them, but they cannot be presented as fact. Nor should readers gasp with amazement at some shocking insight, and assume that the writer's opinion is correct. If we would offer one piece of advice to a reader, it would be this: never devalue your own common sense. If something sounds too silly to be true, it probably is, regardless who wrote it. Conversely, if something *does* make sense, one should not be too quick to discount it simply because an "authority" has labeled it implausible or impossible.

In our opinion, psychohistory may provide interesting bedtime reading, or be suitable for a Movie of the Week, but it can taint more objective efforts, so that it becomes increasingly difficult for us as readers to accept the reliability of information presented to us for our enlightenment.

❖ 17 ❖
The Aftermath:
Fall and Winter, 1812

"Thereafter [i.e. after 1812] we know of not a single love relationship throughout the remainder of Beethoven's life." So did Solomon begin bringing his chapter on Beethoven's Immortal Beloved to a close. Apparently biographers are unable to recognize love without wildly raging passions afoot. Unless proclamations of love are shouted from the rooftops, they remain unheard. It was not that Beethoven's life suddenly became devoid of love after 1812. Far from it. But Beethoven's concept of it, what love for him was meant to be, was gradually evolving. When once the flames of passion brightly flared for all the world to see, now he drew the burning embers deep into his heart. With increasing maturity and understanding, his ideas of love and commitment, what could be and what could not, what reality deemed had to be relinguished and what could be retained, changed.

Beethoven's letter to his Immortal Beloved shows no ambivalence about marriage, no reluctance to accept responsibility, and no doubts about his lady's love for him or his own masculinity. Only the slightest germ of doubt is there, and it is there only because Beethoven had no clear assurance that things would resolve themselves so that he and his Beloved finally could be together. After so many years of waiting, hope was waning, but it never would disappear entirely until many years later.

Eventually, two things would become clear to him, although not in 1812. First, Beethoven would come to realize that his own personality had changed significantly because of his increasing deafness, and that it would be difficult if not impossible for a woman, a wife, to live with him. And Beethoven, now in his forties, might not have found it so easy to live with a wife, either. By 1815, he would admit to his friend, Karl Amenda, that although he still thought of and desired marriage, "...for my own good or possibly for that of other people Fate persists in refusing to fulfill my wishes in this respect."[1]

Second, he would come to realize that his Beloved's decision not to marry him would remain firm, although not because she did not love him. Over time, he began to recognize the wisdom of her decision, that the barriers which stood between them *were* insurmountable, and that it was indeed "for his own good and that of others" (hers and her children's) that she had to deny him this conjugal relationship. This posed a dilemma which required compromise, for while they could not live with one another, neither could they live happily without each other. In time, Beethoven would come to realize that true love could survive without becoming conjugal love.

A CHEERLESS OUTLOOK ON MARRIAGE

Solomon used a quote from the Giannatasio diary to show that after 1812, Beethoven had developed a "cheerless outlook on marriage." Following is the diary entry, written June 15, 1817, five years after the writing of the Beloved letter. It began:

> Every kind of fixed relation between human beings, he dislikes.[2]

Of course he disliked "fixed relations." This was not a "cheerless" reflection on the institution of marriage per se. It was the quite normal outlook of a man who found that it was precisely the nature of those "fixed relations"—i.e. the nearly unbreakable bonds of matrimony—that had kept him from being able to marry the woman he loved.

> I believe I understand him, if I say that he is against anyone's liberty being restricted....In the relation be-

---

[1]Anderson, p. 509.
[2]All quotations from Fanny Giannatasio del Rio's diary are translated from the complete text of Thayer's German edition of *The Life of Beethoven*, Vol. IV, pp. 513-541.

tween man and woman he believes perhaps the liberty
of the woman already limited.

This seems quite a liberal view for a nineteenth century
man, yet it is hardly so for Beethoven. He already had strong
ideals of equality, and the suffering and loss he had endured because of the restricted liberties of the women he loved would
naturally give him such an outlook. Of course he would feel bitterness about a woman's liberty being restricted. The woman he
loved most of all had had no say about her family's choice of
husband for her, and had been pushed into marriage with a man
she did not love. This was true to one degree or another for many
of the women he knew. Women in the upper classes were valuable
commodities, and were given to men like pieces of property in
exchange for certain concessions. If a woman dared to attempt
divorcing a man she did not love in order to find happiness with
one she did, she was unfairly punished, by losing her children, her
livelihood, her financial support, and her social status.

> Hence, it interests him much more, if a woman, without
> as he thinks being *tied* to him gives him her love and
> therewith the highest gift.

Here we see the first indication that Beethoven's concept
of love had changed. Once only married love would have satisfied
him. Now he shows a different view: it is receiving love *without*
benefit of marriage that is the greatest which can be realized.

"Can our love exist...except through not demanding everything?" he had asked his Beloved. At the time, he may have
still wanted to answer *No*, that it could exist only within a conjugal relationship. But, as time went on, he realized that the
answer had been *Yes* all along, that their love *could* and *would*
exist without demands and without legal ties. Five years after the
writing of the letter, he finally was able to accept the gift of her
love without asking for more, and to appreciate a woman who,
even though she would never be married to him, would never have
the privilege of taking his name as her own, nor have the joy of
calling herself his wife, loved him still, "remained always around
him," loved him without the wifely obligation to do so.

> Of a friend he told us, who said: one ought to marry en-
> tirely without love... We disagreed with the opinion of
> this friend even more than he [Beethoven], who repeated
> over and over again his uncertainty about it.

Despite repeated disappointment, it was still Beethoven's contention that one should marry primarily for love above all other considerations such as social and financial status. This certainly was not a "cheerless outlook," but a highly romantic notion. Although he had been continually frustrated in his desires to marry the woman he loved, nevertheless, true love still remained for him the only legitimate reason to marry. Loneliness, a desire for companionship, physical needs: none of these were sufficient reasons to form a legal union without love.

> Of his own experiences he said that he had never known a marriage which either one or the other party had not after some time regretted.

This portion seems to contradict the previous statement in which Beethoven shared his views about love in marriage—or does it? We note that he *disagreed* with the friend who said one should marry entirely without love. Since Beethoven saw love as *the* reason to marry, why then would he say that he "had never known a marriage which either one or the other party had not after some time regretted?" We believe he was speaking of those cases—and he knew of many—in which the man and woman had married for reasons *other* than love, primarily in deference to the wishes of the woman's parents, or for financial security. How easy it would have been for him to recall the circumstances under which Anna Marie, Josephine, and Guilietta Guicciardi were wed. Anna Marie's forced marriage to Peter had left her in a loveless marital limbo. And had not Josephine regretted her decision to marry Stackelberg, Guilietta to wed Gallenberg?

The diary continued:

> As for the few women whom in former times he would have considered it supreme happiness to call his own, he later had to tell himself how lucky he was that none of them became his wife and how fortunate that the wishes of mortals often are not fulfilled....

It is noteworthy that Beethoven himself considered that it was only a "few" women whom he had ever considered as potential wives and not the multitudes that biographers would have us believe he did. In this statement, we cannot assume that he was referring to his own Immortal Beloved, but more likely to Magdalena Willmann or Guilietta Guicciardi, or perhaps even to Therese

Malfatti, whom he might have considered for one fleeting moment. Any of these women would have been a poor choice as a wife.
Did he intend to include Josephine Brunswick in that statement?
We cannot know. But however much he once had loved her, he
might have considered himself fortunate that he had not married
a woman who placed other considerations, such as financial well-
being, above her love for him.[3]

> Nanni [Fanny's sister] remarked that he would always
> love his art more than his wife: that, he maintained,
> would only be right and he would not be able to love a
> woman who did not know how to appreciate his art.

We see that he did not agree with Nanni entirely, rather
he commented that it would be impossible for him to love a woman
for whom music was not as important as it was for him. That
should be no surprise to us, as his choice of friends and loved ones
is certainly evidence of that. Is it any wonder that Therese Malfatti had never won his heart?

THE PERSISTENT DREAM

As shown later in a more thorough discussion of Fanny Giannatasio's diary, Beethoven's "negative" comments about marriage had far more reason behind them than simply expressing
his own views on the subject. It cannot be assumed from these
diary entries that Beethoven had a dim view of marriage itself,
but rather of his own bachelor existence perpetuated by circumstances beyond his control. Two years before, on April 12, 1815 he
had written to his friend, "Dear good Amenda," the following:

> ...Count Keyserling paid me a visit and awoke the re-
> membrance of you in me, by saying that you are now
> living happily, that you have children, neither of which
> can I say of myself... I may say that I live almost entirely
> alone in this greatest city of Germany, and am forced to
> live apart from all the people whom I love, whom I could
> love—[4]

---

[3]Josephine was extravagant with money. She purchased a fine carriage with
four horses for the equivalent of $12,000 instead of making the payment on a
piece of property which was due at the time. We can imagine what a burden her
lifestyle would have been on Beethoven. Through her siblings, he surely had
been aware of her excesses, and that knowledge may have made him glad he had
never married her.
[4]Anderson, p. 509.

His assumption was then, as it always had been, that being married and having a family was what caused one to "live happily." In 1810, he had written a note to himself that said "Without the society of some loved person it would not be possible to live even in the country." And he wrote to Bettina Brentano von Arnim on the occasion of her own marriage in 1811 (in the only authenticated letter to her): "May all the happiness with which marriage blesses the married be with you and your husband." His attitudes about marriage per se, both prior to 1812 and after, were never substantially different. What had changed was his view of himself in relation to marriage.

His wistful tone in the 1815 letter to Amenda came from living "almost alone." He was Anna Marie's neighbor. Notes show she had once again made him a part of her life. He spent as much time with her and her children as he was able. But still they were not his lawful family. Although he was close to them physically and emotionally, legally he was not part of them. Thus he lived apart from the people he loved—not *once* loved but *still* loved—whom he could have loved as a husband and father, had circumstances been different. This cannot be considered a "cheerless outlook on marriage." Obviously he still longed for such a life, even though the harsh reality of a situation beyond his control already was apparent to him.

Despite the "fearful conditions," which made marriage prohibitive for him, and his acceptance of the fact that marriage to his Beloved never would be possible, his desire for a conjugal union persisted to the end of his life. As late as 1826, when his friend Karl Holz was engaged to be married, Beethoven jokingly addressed him as "Herr Lover." Yet his continuing sadness at not having someone to call his own is evident in two September 1826 letters to Holz in which Beethoven wrote

> One can see how much good can be done by better and purer air and also by the good influence of women... all hope has vanished of my having someone about me, someone similar to myself, at any rate, as regards my better qualities— enjoy yourself out there...[5]

> Mr. Enamoured, I bow my knee before the almighty power of love.[6]

[5]Anderson, pp. 1305-1306.
[6]Anderson, p. 1308.

Other than his comments in the Giannatasio diary, Beethoven's only remark regarding marriage that could be considered negative, was recorded in his 1823 conversation book and addressed to Schindler. Yet even there it was not the institution of marriage he was disparaging, it was marriage to a particular lady. In the book he wrote "And if I had wished to give up my vital energy with that life, what would have remained for the nobler, the better?" Here, Beethoven was referring not to marriage *itself,* but to a union with Guilietta Guicciardi Gallenberg, whom the two men had been discussing. When he said "that life," he did not mean life as a married man, but a life with *her.* Beethoven knew, and was expressing the view to Schindler, that the flirtatious, fickle Julie would have been a poor choice as a wife. Taken *out* of context, that remark does seem like a "cheerless outlook on marriage;" *in* context, its meaning becomes clear.

These are the sole bits of evidence for Beethoven's "cheerless outlook" on marriage. We contend that it was not *cheerless,* it was *realistic.* In addition to acknowledging his Beloved's hopeless situation, his comment to Amenda shows that he had begun to realize that, at this stage in his life, he no longer would have made a very good husband. He knew his deafness, growing worse every year, made him difficult and intensified his ill-temper, hypersensitivity, suspicion. By now, he also was used to his freedom, and living his life in daily concert with another person would have been a struggle, perhaps even detrimental to both his creativity and to his continuing relationship with his Beloved. She would have had to have been far more patient, understanding, and forgiving than most people are able to be. We believe that his Beloved had been perceptive to this reality, and wisely, lovingly, had refused his proposal with both their interests at heart.

AMALIE SEBALD

Solomon claimed that Beethoven sought out the "sisterly ministrations" of Amalie Sebald in order to "calm him during the aftermath of his turbulent affair" with Antonie. Where was this turbulence which would have required calming? Throughout the rest of 1812, Beethoven showed no emotional distress. According to Solomon however, he had supposedly just bid farewell forever to the greatest love of his life. It is not surprising, then, that Solomon would like us to believe that Beethoven had required "ministrations" in order to help him deal with his profound (and obviously deeply hidden) sorrow. Logically, if he had only just lost his Beloved, one *should* expect to find him deeply depressed, but neither his notes to Amalie nor his letter to his publishers show us anything of the sort. His subsequent trips to Hernals and Linz only weeks later, his involvement in dinner parties and other soirees, his ability to compose lively and lighthearted music, do not in any way show us a man in the midst of emotional turmoil. In fact, we do not see sadness strike him until May 1813 (*nine months* after separating from his alleged "eternally beloved"), beginning with his admonishment to himself "Learn to keep silent, O friend!" That is quite some delayed reaction!

Second, the truth is that Beethoven saw very little of Fraulein Sebald, and, as his notes suggest, he avoided most of her sisterly overtures by his own volition. In regard to Amalie, Thayer said

> The reader will be able to judge from the tone of the short letters written by Beethoven to the latter at this later time [1812] whether this was a growing friendship or the continuation of a deep love.[7]

Must we choose either? It would be more accurate to choose neither. All that shows in these notes from Beethoven is a rather tepid—not growing—friendship, and certainly not the "continuation of a deep love." Max Unger called them "charming billets." Sonneck, too, referred to the Sebald letters as "intimate," claiming that they used a tone not even a Don Juan would have dared use with a respectable lady. They *do*? Was Sonneck simply parroting Unger, or did he really believe this to be true? We are at a loss to find the intimate passion in these letters which appears so obvious to these two gentlemen. In nearly every one Beethoven professed to be ill, and therefore unable to see Amalie. Had she been a beloved, or at least a temporarily ardent passion, it is unlikely he would have kept her at such a distance, regardless of his health. And although he certainly must have had some opportunity to bestow on her one of those fiery kisses he had sent her the year before, he seems to have had no inclination to do so. The notes to Amalie, beginning September 16, 1812, read:[8]

---

[7]Thayer/Forbes, p. 516.
[8]All letters to Amalie Sebald are taken from Anderson, pp. 386-390.

Tyrant—I? Your tyrant? Only a misapprehension can lead you to say this even if your judgment of me indicated no agreement of thought with me!— But no blame to you on this account, it is rather a piece of good fortune for you—Yesterday I was not wholly well, and since this morning, I have grown worse...

* * *

I only wish to report that the tyrant is chained to his bed like a slave—So it is! I shall be glad if I get by with the loss of the present day only. Busy yourself meanwhile with Russians, Lapps, Samoyeds, etc...

* * *

I cannot yet say anything definite about myself; sometimes I feel better and next things appear to be in the old rut, or to be preparing a long sickness for me— Today too I must keep to my bed—

* * *

My illness does not appear to increase, but rather to crawl on, so no standstill yet! that is all I can tell you about it.—I must give up the idea of seeing you at your house; perhaps your Samoyeds will let you off your journey to polar regions, so come to

Beethoven

Beethoven would have seen nothing improper about asking a woman to visit him. One must remember that this was a man who thought nothing of getting out of his bathtub and standing in front of his open window on view to all passers-by,[9] or giving a piano lesson dressed only in the 19th century equivalent of his pajamas. At this point, instead of visiting him, Amalie sent him a chicken for some soup. That was the extent of her "sisterly ministrations." Beethoven's next note was one of simple appreciation:

Thanks for all that you find good for my body; what is most necessary has already been attended to—also the obstinacy of the malady seems to be giving way.— I

---

[9] Once when he saw people on the sidewalk under his window looking up at him in astonishment, he grumbled to a visitor (whose presence also did not deter his unconventional behavior), "What are *they* staring at?" He was mildly surprised when his friend pointed out his indecent (or more correctly, nonexistent) attire, and said, quite nonchalant, "Oh, quite right." And then, in deference to social propriety, he went and put on a robe.

deeply sympathize with you in the sorrow which the illness of your mother must have caused you. You know how much I should like to see you, only I cannot receive you otherwise than in bed—

Finally Beethoven felt a little better and asked her to come to visit him, although there was no urgency in his request. It was merely an invitation, and one which gave her the opportunity to decline had she thought it unseemly.

I am already better, dear A. If you think it proper to come to me alone, you could give me great pleasure; but if you think it improper you know how I honor the liberty of all people. And no matter how you act in this and all other cases, according to your principles or caprice, you will always find me kind and

Your friend, Beethoven

He then managed to visit with her one time, before suffering a relapse and becoming ill once again.

Dear good A!

After leaving you yesterday my condition grew worse, and from last night till now I have not left my bed. I wanted to send word to you today, but thought it would look as if I wanted to appear important in your eyes, so I refrained. What are you dreaming that you can be nothing to me?

No doubt a pouting Amalie had complained to him that he was neglecting her. Self-absorption must have made her forget that he was not a well man.

We will talk about that in person, dear A. I have always wished only that my presence might give you rest and peace and that you would confide in me—I hope to be better tomorrow and then some hours of your stay will still remain for us both to be uplifted and gladdened by Nature.

And that was the extent of the "ardent passion" which Beethoven supposedly harbored for Amalie Sebald. Beethoven may or may not have seen her one last time before she departed Teplitz. He did not maintain a correspondence with her after she returned to Berlin, and she married in 1815. During the short time they were in Teplitz together, Amalie did nothing more than provide him with a pleasant and innocent diversion while he awaited his doctor's permission to go home to his Beloved. Earlier, Beethoven had complained to Varnhagen that in Teplitz "there are few people...and no distinguished ones...Hence I am living— alone!—alone!—alone! alone! alone!" The friendly face of a person he had met the year before would have been a welcome sight, but not a prelude to a passionate encounter. If he had been "charmed" by her in 1811, he certainly had made no effort to keep in touch with her between then and the summer of 1812, nor afterwards. There is no reason to believe that Beethoven fell in love with the woman over a simple bowl of chicken soup, and loved her thereafter as his Distant Beloved, keeping his love for her alive in his heart for four years (the year when "To the Distant Beloved" was composed). She is and was a poor candidate for either role of Beloved, whether Immortal or Distant.

While there was nothing indecent in Beethoven's notes to Amalie Sebald, one might imagine how Unger and Sonneck drew their "Don Juan" conclusions. No doubt they saw his invitation for her to visit him *alone* as being improper, suggestive, even salacious. Yet even Beethoven called her attention to his invitations's possible impropriety, although that was surely not his intention. Perhaps they thought his line "I cannot see you other than in bed," was a proposal that she join him there! Had they, as apparently Amalie Sebald had herself, forgotten that the man was unwell? Does the mind turn to lacivious intentions when the body is in the throes of serious illness? Obviously Beethoven's biographers do not believe such things dampen sexual appetite.

Since he was already quite ill even before he left Vienna, it would be difficult to blame his poor health on any "emotional trauma" evolving from his separation from Antonie, which Solomon believed caused Beethoven's "dry spell" in 1813-1814. (Again, another incredibly long delayed reaction!) Rather, this period of inactivity, and later resurgence of creativity, coincided perfectly with Anna Marie's absence from and subsequent return to Vienna. A chronology of his productive periods (see Appendix B) matches closely to those times when she was in his life; his barren periods, likewise, occur mostly when they were separated. This happened too often to be mere coincidence.

BEETHOVEN IN LINZ

Solomon suggested that Beethoven's lengthy stay in Linz was to allow the Brentanos time to leave for Frankfurt, so as to avoid seeing them again. Once more, this points to Antonie's unsolicited declaration of love having occurred in Franzensbrunn. Otherwise, why should he want to avoid them at that late date when he already had spent weeks in their company? Without there having been the unforeseen catalyst of her desperate move, we would have to believe that *all of a sudden*, after two months, Beethoven finally realized that it had been a serious error in judgment for him to follow them all over Czechoslovakia.

While most biographies give the impression that Beethoven left Teplitz and went directly to his brother's in Linz, we now know that is untrue. His letter to Gleichenstein in September shows that Beethoven first returned to Vienna sometime at the end of that month, went on to Hernals, and then left for Linz from there the first week of October. Since he was in Hernals with Anna Marie, he surely did not give the Brentanos much more than a passing thought, if even that.

While it is understandable that he may have wanted to avoid the Brentanos, Beethoven had several other reasons—both musical and personal—for going to and remaining in Linz for as long as he did. There is hardly anything subversive about a man wanting to have a long visit with his brother whom he had not seen in quite a while. Yet it has long been assumed that Beethoven went to Linz solely to interfere in Johann's engagement to Therese Obermeyer and to prevent their marriage by whatever means possible. Was this true? Did Beethoven go to Linz and make of himself a pest *par excellence*? Thayer wrote "It seems hardly credible that Beethoven came to Linz for that purpose," but then he continued with "according to the evidence"—which he does not cite—and "unpleasant information from a perfectly competent authority"—whom he does not name—"apparently that was the case." As usual we are asked to believe people we do not know and to accept what is "known"—and what these dubious authorities tell us—without question. All Thayer offered as information on the matter was the following:

> a note confirms very unpleasant information obtained
> in Linz from perfectly competent authority, namely that

the principal object of the journey thither was to interfere in Johann's domestic affairs.[10]

This "authoritative" note told Thayer that Beethoven had taken
drastic steps to keep his brother from marrying the "unchaste
girl," and that a violent scene had ensued. These "drastic steps"
apparently included angry visits to the local church Bishop, the
civil authorities, and the police in an attempt to have the immoral
Fraulein Obermeyer sent away.[11] Thayer then preferred to "draw
a curtain" on what happened next.

It seems to us that all this worthy "evidence" bears some
closer examination.

What was the identity of Thayer's "good authority" that
Beethoven went to Linz with those mean-spirited intentions? We
do not know.

When did this authority give Thayer this information? If
one reads Thayer's account carefully, one finds that the testimony
was given in 1860, nearly a half-century after the event!

Does this authority offer any written confirmation of what
he (or she) claimed: police records, church documents, letters to
the civil authorities? No, he (or she) does not. The fact is, Thayer
conjectured all this on the basis of a report given him 48 years
after the fact, and from a simple note Beethoven wrote in his
journal which said, "In 1812, I was in Linz on account of B." All
we may suppose about this was that Beethoven mostly like went
to Linz for the primary reason of visiting his brother (although
one wonders why he referred to Johann as "B" and not "J" unless
he was abbreviating the word *Brüder*—brother). Yet even if Ludwig did go to Linz "on account of" Johann, we must say, So what?
How can one deduce such dreadful intentions from such a simple
statement and such paltry evidence?

Once again we must call on common sense and look at the
two brothers' behavior during this time and in later years in order
to decide whether our mysterious "authority" has any credibility.

It is difficult to imagine the two Beethoven brothers constantly being at each other's throats, while Ludwig remained in
Johann's house—in a very large, lovely room with a beautiful
view of the Danube, no less—for a *full five weeks*. Why would
Johann have been so kind and loving toward his brother, and

---

[10]Thayer/Forbes, p. 541-542.
[11]Under 19th Century Austrian law, a person could be expelled on grounds of
immoral conduct.

made Ludwig's stay so pleasant, if Ludwig were scurrying all over Linz stirring up trouble for him and his fiancee, and causing them both so much strife? If a "violent scene" had happened between the brothers, would Ludwig have continued to stay in Johann's house as his guest? Of course not. Either Ludwig would have left in a rage, or Johann would have tossed him out. Unless Johann was completely spineless, he never would have continued to host Ludwig in his own home if Ludwig had been treating him and Therese so terribly. Then too, would Therese's brother, Leopold Obermeyer, have put up with this treatment of his sister? Refrained from pummeling Ludwig into the ground? Or later agreed to rent Ludwig an apartment in his house? Surely he would have remembered such an ghastly incident! Again, the simple application of some common sense shows us that this scenario makes no sense at all.

When *did* Beethoven's conflicts with Therese begin? While his letters indicate that he did not care for the woman because of her loose morals, initially he had made an effort to accept her. In letters to Johann, Ludwig always closed with warm greetings to Therese and her daughter. (Stupendously insincere if the Linz incident had actually happened!) It was not until May 1822, when Ludwig first broached the idea of living closer to his brother, that true animosity began to surface. Apparently Therese had not been happy about the idea of having Ludwig close at hand. Ludwig wrote to Johann:

> I have nothing against your wife. I only hope that she will realize how much could be gained for you too by your living with me and that all life's wretched trivialities need not cause any disturbances between us. . . .I repeat that I have nothing against your wife, although her behavior to me on a few occasions has greatly shocked me.[12]

Would Johann have been stupid enough to believe this, that his brother had nothing against his wife, if Ludwig had once attempted to have Therese arrested? Could something like that be considered a "wretched triviality?" What an understatement! And if he had tried to have the woman arrested, why would Ludwig have been shocked by her less-than-loving behavior toward him? That is taking letting-bygones-be-bygones a bit far.

---

[12]Anderson, p. 946-947.

Apparently Johann *did* believe his brother because he rented Ludwig rooms in the house belonging to Therese's brother, Leopold, adjacent to the one where Leopold and his family lived. Ludwig, however, had not liked the dark, dreary apartment and Johann had taken offense, prompting Ludwig to write:

> Why this behavior? I have nothing against you. I don't consider that you are to blame for what happened about the rooms. Your intention was good, and indeed it was my own wish that we should be nearer one another. But in this house the evil is to be found on all sides. Yet you refuse to hear anything about all this, so what can one say?—What callous behavior after my being landed in such an embarrassing situation—[13]

Therese may have thought Ludwig ungrateful for the trouble her husband had gone through acquiring an apartment for Ludwig, despite the fact that it was everything Ludwig hated in living quarters: small, dark, dreary, with not even a pleasant view. No doubt there had been a quarrel and Therese surely had been involved. We cannot know to what "evil" Beethoven was referring, but as he said "you refuse to hear anything about this," this would seem to be the "embarrassing situation" Ludwig mentioned in his letter. Perhaps he had encountered Therese being unfaithful to her husband. The situation deteriorated from that point, and in his letters Ludwig showed nothing but contempt for his sister-in-law. In August 1823, Ludwig wrote Johann that "You will not be entirely neglected whatever those two *canailles,* that loutish fat woman and her bastard may do to you." The last part of that sentence had been crossed out by another hand. Schindler reported that several months earlier, Ludwig had wanted to report Therese to the police—for what reason, we do not know—and from then on repeatedly urged Johann to divorce her. If true, the story of Ludwig's interference with Johann's marriage occurred some *eleven years after* the summer of 1812, and *not* prior to the wedding, when Ludwig had not even been acquainted with Therese Obermeyer. We believe that Thayer's "competent authority" had, after nearly a half-century, either recalled the date of this episode incorrectly, transposed 1821 to read 1812, or perhaps Thayer himself had inadvertently misread the date on the note, substituting 1812 for 1822. This

---

[13] Anderson, p. 977.

would make sense in light of the fact that Ludwig continually made scathing remarks about Therese ("I refuse to have anything to do with his overfed whore and bastard.") in letters from that point in 1822 on.

We know from Beethoven's inscription on the autograph of the Eighth Symphony that the composer spent time in Linz finishing this piece, and working on a violin sonata which he had begun that February. He also visited Chapelmaster Franz Glöggl in whose collection of antique trombones Beethoven was interested. The composer went to Glöggl's house many times, sometimes staying all day and taking meals there. He also attended several soirees hosted by a wealthy gentleman named Count von Donhoff. Clearly, Beethoven had had more important and interesting things to do than to concern himself with Johann's love life. Can one truly imagine Ludwig spending his days wreaking havoc upon his future sister-in-law, and then attending parties at night? No, Thayer's "authority," or Thayer himself, must have been mistaken. After all, we already know he was not infallible.

After Johann and Therese's wedding on November 8, Beethoven did not "hasten away" in anger. According to Glöggl's journal, he stayed another two full days—still in Johann's house. (Now *that* must have been an interesting honeymoon if what Thayer's authority said was true!) We do not know exactly when Beethoven returned to Vienna but he was there in early December, preparing for a concert later that month. It is interesting that even Thayer thought the whole idea of Beethoven interfering in his brother's affairs to be incredulous. . .until some dubious authority convinced him otherwise, an authority who apparently had been grossly mistaken about the date of these events.

If Beethoven "hastened away" at all, it was likely to return to his Beloved. While Glöggl's journal stated that Beethoven left Linz on November 10, there is no indication where he was from then until early December. Gaps in his letters often indicated that he was in the country. Had he gone back to Hernals? There is unfortunately no evidence for such a lovely and romantic thought, but if that was where he was, then he and Anna Marie may have returned to Vienna together a week or so later. At that time the famous violinist, Pierre Rode, arrived in Vienna, and Beethoven completed the finale of the *G major Violin Sonata* for the occasion. Rode and the Archduke Rudolph gave this magnificent four-movement sonata its premier performance on December 29.

❧ PART III ❧

SECONDARY EVIDENCE
FOR THE IMMORTAL BELOVED

INTRODUCTION

In Part II, we saw that information presented as *prima facie* evidence[1] on Antonie Brentano's behalf falls woefully short in its intention. Surely, even among skeptics, some modicum of reasonable doubt has been established. Yet our task at hand is hardly over, for in addition, there also is much circumstantial evidence which has been presented in such a way that it appears to support Frau Brentano as the Immortal Beloved. This cannot be ignored, for our intent is to erase as much doubt from the readers' minds as possible. As in a court of law, we shall take each argument, examine it carefully, and show that in no way can it support Antonie as Beethoven's Beloved.

THE PROSECUTION'S SIDE

The prosecution, if you will, has entered the following evidence as proof of Beethoven's guilt in the matter of his coveting his friend's wife:

• an entry in a diary kept by a young woman named Fanny Giannatasio which seems to indicate that Beethoven had met or become acquainted with the Immortal Beloved in 1811, and the subsequent argument that this was "close to" the year in which Beethoven's relationship began with Frau Brentano.

---

[1]evidence which is adequate to establish a fact unless it is refuted by conflicting or contrary evidence.

• several *Tagebuch* (journal) entries which give as possible initials for the Beloved the letters *A* or *T* and, again, the argument that these referred to either Antonie or her nickname, Toni.

• a note written by Beethoven while he was in Baden which supposedly referred to the Beloved, this time, as *M.* The contention here was that the *M* had been Frau Brentano's daughter, Maximiliane who had "revived...the image of her mother."

• two musical allegations: one, that a song titled *To the Beloved* had been written for Antonie, and, two, that a composition, the *Diabelli Variations*, had been dedicated to her.

• letters written to Antonie Brentano by Beethoven said to show his deep and abiding love for her.

• the contention that Beethoven acted as an intermediary for Antonie in the selling of her deceased father's substantial art collection, possibly as an act of love.

• a portrait of a woman in Beethoven's possession, said to have been painted of Antonie Brentano in 1812.

THE DEFENSE'S STANCE

• the Giannatasio diary's entry must be considered invalid by the circumstances surrounding it, and by the nature of its author's relationship to its subject. In the event that the 1811 date is upheld by the reader, it cannot be connected to Antonie Brentano, as that was not the year in which he met her.

• the journal quotations also must be considered invalid on the grounds that they were sharply truncated and removed from their proper context, and therefore have been distorted to the point that they cannot be evidential.

• the Baden note cannot be shown to refer to Antonie Brentano because of the date that it was written.

- neither the *A* nor the *M* in Beethoven's journal refer in any way to Antonie or any member of her family, but correctly refer to other people or things entirely. Although it is possible that the *T* in the *Tagebuch* did refer to Antonie Brentano, the reference is such that it disproves Beethoven's romantic attachment to her.

- no song was ever written for Antonie, nor had Beethoven's wishes been carried out in the case of the composition which bears a dedication to her.

- no letter to Frau Brentano shows any depth of feeling beyond what Beethoven regularly expressed to friends.

- Beethoven did not serve as an intermediary in selling the art collection of Frau Brentano's father, and his importance in this role has been greatly exaggerated.

- the alleged 1812 portrait of Antonie Brentano was not painted in 1812, and is not conclusively that of Frau Brentano. Further, its importance in the case will be shown to be negligible.

❖ 18 ❖
The Brentano-Beethoven Relationship

Who was Fanny Giannatasio that her diary has gained such importance in the quest for the Immortal Beloved? We will meet her in a subsequent chapter when the reliability of the diary will be discussed. For now, it is enough to know that an entry made in her diary in 1816 has been used as evidence to further prove that Antonie Brentano had been Beethoven's Beloved. The entry read:

> Five years ago Beethoven had made the acquaintance of
> a person, a union with whom he would have considered
> the greatest happiness of his life.

As with the postal schedule, biographers were excited by this clue. They immediately subtracted five years from 1816 and came up with. . . 1811. They just as quickly jumped to the conclusion that if they could find a woman whom Beethoven had met in 1811, they could also identify the Immortal Beloved. A worthy, but too hasty idea. Following their lead, Solomon proposed that this entry referred to Antonie Brentano because he presumed that their love affair had blossomed in the fall of that year, even though Beethoven had not "made her acquaintance" in 1811.

While a later chapter will make it clear that the validity of that particular date is questionable, and that Beethoven had perfectly logical reasons for giving it to the Giannatasios, for the moment the statement will be addressed as it stands. Briefly, the reader should know that Fanny was the daughter of Cajetan Giannatasio del Rio, in whose institute for learning Beethoven had enrolled his nephew, Karl, in February 1816. Fanny's fiance had died less than a year before, and the heartbroken young woman had immediately transferred her affections onto the 45-year-old composer about whom she wrote so ardently in her diary.

THE FIRST TEST

If one is adamant about considering the 1811 date valid, it must be asked: did Antonie Brentano become acquainted with Beethoven in 1811? (One must recall that in the diary entry Beethoven had said, "made the acquaintance of..." *not* "fell in love with...") Solomon claimed that Beethoven had met the Brentanos through Bettina Brentano, Franz's half-sister, in May 1810.

Schindler claimed that Beethoven and Antonie's father, Johann Birkenstock, had met in 1792, however Solomon believed this date to be in error because Beethoven's letters do not mention him. However, Beethoven's correspondence from this time period is sketchy; we cannot be sure that letters are not missing. Yet even if the two *had* met between 1795 and 1798, they apparently made little impression upon one another: he was not yet a memorable celebrity, and she had four suitors vying for her attentions. Under the circumstances we probably should not count this time, if it did occur, as a genuine meeting.

Even so, why Solomon believed that Schindler had fabricated this story is not clear. Certainly Schindler had nothing to gain from doing so, and as Thayer also included it, he obviously did not consider it deliberately falsified. In fact, Thayer confirmed this early connection through the U.S. Consul to Frankfurt, W. P. Webster, in 1872. Webster told Thayer that "I understand that Hofrat Birkenstock was a friend of Beethoven's and that the acquaintanceship of the daughter with him began prior to her marriage to Herr Brentano." Yet again, Solomon attributed Webster's statement to a "misunderstanding" of a statement by an "unknown member of the Brentano family," a person both Thayer and Landon identified as Franz Brentano. The statement simply says that Beethoven had already known Birkenstock at the time when his daughter, Antonie, and her family came to Vienna in 1809. It does not imply, as Solomon suggests, that Beethoven had met Birkenstock on his deathbed. The statement reads:

The friendly relations of Beethoven with the Brentano family... had their origin in the friendly intercourse between Beethoven and Imperial Aulic Councillor Johann Melchoir von Birkenstock [Antonie's father], which had existed since the time when Frau Brentano visited her father in Vienna, whence she had moved with her older children in 1809. This relationship continued also after the death of 30 October 1809 of Birkenstock.[1]

If Birkenstock had been the initial connection between Beethoven and the Brentanos—and there is no reason to believe that Franz Brentano was mistaken—then they must have met shortly after the Brentanos arrived in Vienna in the summer of 1809. That places Antonie, at least in Beethoven's mind, *two years* away from the date in Fanny's diary. What is interesting is that Antonie and her husband, Franz, disagree as to the date. At an advanced age, Antonie recalled meeting Beethoven in 1810. Let us look at this discrepancy. In 1809, Antonie was completely distracted by her father's grave illness. This was, after all, a man she adored, and who was her sole link to her beloved Vienna. It is little wonder that Franz would recall meeting Beethoven upon their arrival whereas she would not. Her father died at the end of October. Six months later, when Antonie was somewhat recovered from her grief, Bettina prevailed upon her sister-in-law to go with her to visit Beethoven, and it was this meeting that Antonie recalled, even though in both Beethoven's and Brentano's minds they had already met the previous summer. What makes the 1810 date suspect is that in this version it was *Bettina* who was instrumental in bringing them together, whereas it is more likely that the reverse was true: the Brentanos introduced Bettina to Beethoven. Thayer reported that when Bettina arrived in Vienna, the Brentanos had told her that the composer was morose, unsociable, and disliked visitors—an opinion they could not have rendered if they did not know him—which must have made Bettina all the more determined to meet him. As Bettina enjoyed being known for "discovering" celebrities of her day, and of seeming to have a far more important role in their lives than she actually did, she certainly would have wanted everyone to think that she had been the one to bring Beethoven and the Brentano family

---

[1] H. C. Robbins Landon, *Beethoven: His Life, Work and World,* p. 164. The ellipsis replaces only the names and titles of family members.

together. Perhaps Antonie did not have the date of meeting so firmly in mind until Bettina "reminded" her of it, and Antonie, eager to find acceptance within the family, simply went along with Bettina's story and date as fact. The circumstances of the meeting were far more important to Bettina than to Antonie who did not mind giving her sister-in-law the credit. By the time she was in her eighties, Antonie was firmly convinced that the 1810 date was correct.

Thayer noted that "Birkenstock's house was one of those truly noble seats of learning, high culture and refinement, where Beethoven, to his manifest intellectual gain, was a welcome guest. Beethoven came and went in a friendly fashion."[2] What can be gleaned from this is that Beethoven became a friend of the Brentano family through Birkenstock, and that he visited them as he had Antonie's father. There is no evidence that an interest in the lady of the house was Beethoven's reason for his visits. In fact, it was not only at the Brentano house that he "came and went in friendly fashion." He had the same easy comings and goings at the homes of the Erdödys, the Ertmanns, and the Brunswicks. And even Louis Spohr, who only met Beethoven in January 1813, wrote about his relationship with the composer that it was not long after their meeting that

> after the opera he generally accompanied me to my house, and passed the rest of the evening with me. He could then be very friendly with Dorette (Frau Spohr) and the children.

Beethoven interacted with the Spohr family, whom he had known only a short period of time, much the same as he had with the Brentanos and his other friends. Apparently his "friendly comings and goings" were not as unusual in the homes and with the families of people he knew as we have been led to believe.

A BRIEF CHRONOLOGY OF 1811-1812

Solomon admitted that there was no evidence of any romantic attachment between Beethoven and Antonie Brentano up until the late fall of 1811. It was then, he conjectured, that the two of them suddenly fell in love, culminating in the passionate and intimate letter to the Immortal Beloved. In order to determine whether it was likely for such a close relationship to develop

---

[2]Thayer/Forbes, pp. 491-492.

during this time period, let us look at a chronology for both that year and the beginning of 1812:

- February to March, 1811, Beethoven gave three concerts necessitating time spent in rehearsals. Numerous letters during this time refer to Beethoven's involvement with them.

- Sometime before March 1811 Beethoven's close relationship with Anna Marie resumed. This in itself made a love affair with another woman highly unlikely. Had Beethoven become romantically involved with Antonie Brentano in 1809, it might have been understandable. As a broken-hearted man, he could have been vulnerable to another woman's adoration. But for him to have known Antonie for at least two years and then have suddenly fallen in love with her at precisely the time when his beloved Anna Marie had returned to his life makes no sense.

- From August to October 1811, Beethoven was in Teplitz, Prague, and Silesia at Prince Lichnowsky's estate. Consequently, Antonie and Beethoven did not see one another at all during this time.

- At the end of October, Beethoven suffered a serious illness as a result of a wounded foot and was incapacitated for several weeks. This means that, at most, he had three weeks in October to develop this "intimate relationship" with Antonie.

- Thayer noted that in two notes to the Archduke Rudolph and one to Zmeskall, all written in the fall (1811), Beethoven had referred to the rehearsing of symphonies and overtures which were in preparation for a concert for His Imperial Highness.

- On November 12, he gave another concert, which was preceded once again by rehearsals. However, his time was not entirely taken up by this activity, as a note to Zmeskall indicated that he was enjoying "Erdödyian feasts." During this period he also was completing his *Piano Concerto #5* begun two years earlier. Here we must eliminate all but perhaps two weeks in November to his alleged romance.

• From December 1811 to April 1812, he worked on finishing the Seventh Symphony. Nettl wrote "The *Symphony No. 7 in A major Op. 92* was completed during the summer of 1812 and was first performed at the University of Vienna in December of 1813." Actually, according to Beethoven's notation on the manuscript, the symphony was completed in the spring, specifically on May 13. He had worked on it diligently from the end of 1811, finishing it before his trip to Prague and Bohemia at the end of June 1812. During this time period, he also sketched the *Eighth Symphony* and added to his sketches for the *Ninth*, completed the *Piano Trio #8 in B flat*, and arrangements of Irish and Scottish songs, along with an overture concerto, the *Concerto in G*, an *Adagio in E flat*, and two overtures: *The Ruins of Athens* and *King Stephan*. Despite some problems with ill health, clearly his ability to indulge in Erdödyian feasts had put joy in his heart and sublime music on the page.

• On February 11, March 22, April 16 and 24, and May 5, he gave another series of concerts, with accompanying rehearsals.

• Around March, Beethoven was taken ill again although from then until May he still made attempts to work:

> Letter to Breitkopf & Härtel: "My health has again been frequently exposed to some very fierce attacks." (March, 1812)

> Letter to the Archduke Rudolph: "I have not felt well since yesterday and I have been forbidden to leave my room today." (March, 1812)

> Another letter to the Archduke Rudolph: "My condition has again become worse, and it will probably be a few days before I have recovered." (April 4, 1812)

Letter to poet Karl Theodor Körner: "For some time I have been constantly unwell and continually busy." (April 21, 1812)

Letter to the Archduke Rudolph: "No doubt I shall manage to shake off this condition (my illness, I mean) during the spring and the summer." (April 1812)

Letter to Joseph von Varena in Graz: "As I have been constantly unwell and extremely busy, I have found it impossible to reply to your letters—" (May 8, 1812)

Letter to the Archduke Rudolph: "I beg you to excuse me today because I have to make the arrangements about my opera which cannot be postponed." (June 1812)[3]

It is interesting that even though the poor man was too ill to write letters promptly, Solomon did not think that this indisposition precluded Beethoven from initiating and maintaining a passionate romance with Antonie Brentano. We also recall that the fact that he was almost constantly ill at this time did not deter another writer, Susan Lund, from accusing him of fathering Antonie's last child.

Even while in Teplitz in the summer of 1812, Beethoven referred to his illnesses of the past year which had necessitated his trips to the spas:

To Emilie H.: "My reply to your letter to me is late in arriving. My excuse must be a great amount of business and persistent illness." (July 17, 1812)

Postscript to Emilie's letter, addressed to Breitkopf & Härtel: "I have been owing this reply for at least five months" (i.e. since March 1812).

To Joseph von Varena: "As I was constantly unwell in Vienna I had finally to take refuge here [in Teplitz]." (July 19, 1812)

---

[3]This was a funny excuse since there is no indication that there were plans to present Beethoven's opera in 1812. As we know, Beethoven was tired of catering to the Archduke's demands for lessons, but probably wanted to avoid telling him so in precisely those words.

• In May 1812 Beethoven finished the Seventh Symphony and noted to his publishers that he was still working on new symphonies as well as something for the Hungarian theater.

• At the end of June, he left for Prague/Teplitz with General Willisen, a friend of Franz Oliva.

With so much activity in Beethoven's life during this time period—particularly the amount of musical composition on which he was working, periodic bouts with illness that incapacitated him, and his resumed relationship with Anna Marie—the question logically arises: when did Beethoven find the time (or, for that matter, the need) to develop an intensely intimate love affair with Antonie Brentano? The woman was not even living alone, but had her husband and children living with her at the time. She herself was frequently ill, as well. Solomon himself noted that Antonie spent much time in Karlsbad in search of health which continually eluded her. In 1811 she wrote that her health was "completely shattered." The woman was never a likely candidate for a genuine love affair, but particularly not at this time when depression and "shattered health" would have prevented an actual liaison with another man, even though her illness may have served to foster her fantasies about him.

It is true that Beethoven did visit the Brentano house on occasion, though it is unlikely that an unwell man would have made frequent trips to the remote Landstrasse suburb where the Brentanos lived. And, from his note to Zmeskall, Beethoven clearly was spending as much time or more with the Erdödy family who lived only three doors from him, and enjoying their "Erdödyian feasts." Thayer related that

> Madame Antonie Brentano was frequently ill for weeks at a time during her sojourn in Vienna, so that she had to remain in her room inaccessible to all visitors. At such times Beethoven used to come regularly, seat himself at a pianoforte in her anteroom (waiting room) without a word and improvise; after he had finished 'telling her everything and bringing comfort,' in his language, he would go as he had come without taking notice of another person.[5]

---

[5]Thayer/Forbes, p. 528.

This was identical to the behavior that Beethoven showed toward Baroness Dorothea Ertmann when her child died, and it is unfair to assume that "telling her everything" meant he was expressing his love for her. Antonie, like Dorothea, was a friend of his, and Beethoven endeavored to bring some comfort to her during a period of incapacitating illness. We can see that he felt sorry for her. Unfortunately, the most his kindnesses toward others has done for him is put a blot on his character: both Antonie and Dorothea have been proposed as Beethoven's ardent passions.

Solomon quoted Schindler, who was never personally acquainted with the Brentanos, as saying that the latter were Beethoven's "best friends in the world." If we want to take Schindler's word for it, as Solomon does, we must note that the rest of Schindler's opinion about Beethoven's "best friends" was omitted. He said, in fact, that "when he called the Brentano family in Frankfurt his best friends in the world, surely it was only because their distance would not allow closer contact."[6] With the amount of money the Brentanos generously loaned Beethoven, it really is little wonder that he might exclaim to Schindler that they were his "best friends."

We also do not know what Thayer meant when he said that Beethoven went "regularly" to the Brentano house, for he presented no evidence for the frequency or duration of Beethoven's visits. This ambiguous term could mean anything from once a week to once a month or once every two months. As pointed out, it is doubtful that Beethoven would have visited too frequently, not only because of his busy schedule, and both his illnesses and Antonie's, but also because the Brentano's house was quite a distance from the Pasqualati House where the composer was living at the time. Regardless of the frequency of Beethoven's visits to the Brentano-Birkenstock house, one notes from Thayer that most times Beethoven did not speak with nor see Antonie while he was there entertaining her with his music. During his visits he remained in her anteroom while she remained in bed, incapacitated "for weeks at a time...inaccessible to all visitors." How an intimate relationship and eternal love could have developed with very little if any conversation and personal interaction between them beyond Beethoven giving her offerings of his music, is inconceivable.

---

[6]Schindler, p. 381.

Let us quickly review: Solomon suggested that the love affair between Beethoven and Antonie Brentano had begun sometime between October 1811 and June 1812. A look at Beethoven's activities during this time shows that he was extremely busy, giving several concerts and writing music. Beethoven also was frequently ill, as was Frau Brentano herself. During this time, she occasionally left Vienna to seek treatment at Karlsbad. The timing was poor indeed for the blossoming of romance.

Also during this period, Beethoven had resumed his relationship with Anna Marie Erdödy, was her close neighbor, and obviously was enjoying her company. He did not live near the Brentanos. Antonie, who lived with her huband and her children, was not readily accessible to him, and since he sat in her anteroom "without a word" during most of his visits, he did not speak with her—at least, alone—very frequently. Given all this, how can one then presume that there had been the time, the inclination, and the opportunity for an intimate love affair to arise between Beethoven and Antonie Brentano? Note: not just an *infatuation*, not just a sudden passion, but an *intimate* relationship, one that would have prompted Beethoven to use the *Du*-form of address in the Beloved letter, which is one of the strongest pieces of evidence we have that the relationship of Beethoven to his Immortal Beloved had not been a "transient passion." We recall that this form of address was used *only* in cases where one had formed a close personal relationship, to the point of, and most often including, a physical union. It by itself reveals to us that the Beloved letter was written to a person on extremely intimate terms with Beethoven, terms which could *not* have been reached through sporadic visits over a period of a few months, visits spent primarily in silence, where music was the only language spoken.

Antonie might well have had the luxury to dwell upon the "holy hands of Beethoven" and muse about him "walking godlike among mortals" while languishing in her bed. Physically incapacitated and depressed, it is not difficult to imagine that her mind may have gone on flights of fancy, in which she fantasized a romantic intelude with the composer whose music to her was akin to a religious experience. But Beethoven, deeply involved with his music, joyfully feasting the table of his beloved Countess Erdödy, and combatting the chronic physical ailments which plagued him, had neither the same opportunity—nor the desire—to indulge in daydreams about the unhappy Antonie Brentano.

❖ *19* ❖
Fanny GiannaTasio's Diary

Is it valid to seriously consider entries in Fanny Gian-natasio's diary as "crucial evidence" for the identity of the Im-mortal Beloved? If so, which ones have validity? To make this determination, the reader must know far more about Fraulein Giannatasio and her diary than most of Beethoven's biographies relate. It would be a mistake to attach importance to it until the circumstances surrounding it were considered. On the surface, it would appear to be a sound and important first-hand document. It is, after all, a primary source. Yet we have already shown how misleading evidence can be—even primary source material—when it is presented outside the literary and historical context in which it was produced. A closer examination of the document—especially the diary's background and its author, Fanny herself—will show the reader that in its ability to provide crucial evidence in certain areas, the diary has flaws.

BEETHOVEN AND THE GIANNATASIO DEL RIOS

In February 1816, the Giannatasio del Rio family—who operated an institute for learning, actually a boarding school—was engaged by Beethoven to house and tutor his nephew, Karl. Beethoven did not know them well. In fact, he had only met them in January of that year, less than eight months before the diary entry cited as evidence for the Beloved's identity had been written. The Giannatasios and Beethoven were by no means close friends, although Beethoven respected them and was grateful to them for their kindness toward Karl. The Giannatasio's eldest daughter, Fanny, a young woman in her twenties, had lost her fiance the year before, and immediately developed an enormous infatuation for Beethoven. Her feelings for him are quite evident in many of her diary entries. A brief look at some of the notes Fanny recorded in her 1816-1817 diary will be enlightening.

THE DIARY[1]

For the moment, we will skip the September 16 entry—the one used as "crucial evidence" for the Beloved's identity—as well as the one written on June 15, 1817. The former needs more than a cursory look; the latter, used to prove Beethoven's "cheerless outlook on marriage" has already been discussed, and need not be repeated.

> February 22: I am very much afraid that with longer and closer association with this brave, excellent man my feeling for him will become more than friendship...
>
> March 2: The joking remark of my sister [Nanni]—not to fall in love with him—is very painful to me! That is the trouble with me! I let myself get excited! When I know him better, so he must become dear, yes very dear to me... How can I be so vain as to think that it is meant for me to chain such a spirit?
>
> March 12: I never thought him ugly, but now I even begin to like [his looks] especially his dear character. Beethoven... probably has no idea how dear he is to us, and to me sometimes very specially...
>
> April 11: I was completely alone with him and I was unpleasantly discouraged, as he seemed not to pay attention to what I told him.
>
> September 13: Yesterday I had a most interesting day at Beethoven's in Baden. I am so filled with it that it will take me a few days to regain my former quiet mood.

---

[1]Excerpts from Fanny Giannatasio's diary taken from the German edition of Thayer, Vol. IV, pp. 513-541.

November 10: If only it were given to me to take care of him... Sometimes I take the liberty to imagine such scenes... to make his life pleasanter through many domestic things!

November 17: I was hurt, because he likes Nanni better than me. My feelings are clear to me and it is endlessly difficult to resist them... it is a necessity to love... the feeling is too powerful to suppress sometimes. I ought to have checked my growing and all-absorbing interest in this noble being, but it is beyond me now... step by step I will have to give up the most precious wish of my heart's desire to be more to B. than just an ordinary friend... The strong wish to see this wonderful man in a carefree pleasant life brings me to such crazy thoughts... I would not be enough for this genius... now, now I dare not even hope! ... these exquisite feelings... must be hidden away out of sight, and suppressed!—

December 3: I would give half my life for the man!

Given Fanny's strong attachment to Beethoven, the composer hardly could have been oblivious to her affection for him. Despite Fanny's adoration, and the rather common practice at the time for older men to take much younger women as wives, Beethoven, at 45, would not have considered this girl, 20 years his junior, as a possible wife. His 1805 letter to Josephine Brunswick showed that his desire was for a true companion in terms of intellect and values. Unless Fanny had been extraordinarily sophisticated for her age—a trait she does not display in her diary —she would not have met with Beethoven's expectations. Her touching but adolescent infatuation will be important to remember later when we consider things that Beethoven said and did in regard to her and her family.

What follows is the text of the September 16 diary entry which Solomon and others believed provided critical evidence for identifying the Immortal Beloved.

THE CRUCIAL ENTRY

The high interest for Beethoven and everything that concerns him seduced us and our punishable curiosity had not limits... I made a painful discovery, that he is

often very very unhappy... A highly interesting conversation developed with Father remarking, that B. had
to live such a sad life among such people, and there is
nothing to do about it but if he would take a brave loving
wife, she would patiently put up with the thousand sad
circumstances caused by his hearing. My father asked
him if he knew anyone. I listened with the closest attention at some distance and heard, what has shaken
my soul to the very depths and proved my long suspicion,
he loves unhappily! Five years ago he met a person with
whom a closer union would hold for him the highest
happiness of his life. It was not to be thought of, almost
an impossibility, a chimera. But still it is now as on the
first day. I cannot get it out of my mind were the words
which struck me... It had never reached a confession,
but he could not get it out of his mind. Now were those
words [in his notebook that she had seen] explained to
me! This harmony—he said—he has not yet found! but
he did not explain, a stranger he stood before me and I
pressed my pain deep into myself.

The two most important factors to consider in examining
this entry in Fanny's diary are 1) the circumstances under which
Beethoven made the comment about meeting someone "five years
ago," and 2) the people to whom he made it. Of secondary importance is whether anyone actually might fit the 1811 criterion.

In the first part of the entry, we learn that Beethoven's answer was in response to a deeply personal question from Fanny's
father, who told Beethoven that he should "take a brave loving
wife" and then asked—and not very subtly—whether he knew of
anyone. We have, then, the following situation and cast of characters:

• The first is an infatuated young woman whose fiance had
   died the year before. She became attracted to Beethoven,
   both physically and emotionally, almost immediately. She
   is so in love with him, she goes into raptures about helping
   him move furniture.

• We also have the young woman's father, a man Beethoven
   did not know at all well, who was trying to play match-
   maker for his heartbroken daughter and secure an eminent composer as a son-in-law. It must have been evident
   to him that Beethoven had emotionally restored a grieving

Fanny, and he saw the match as a good thing for both his daughter's and Beethoven's well-being.

• Finally, we have Beethoven himself, an enormously private person who, despite engaging in harmless flirtations, nevertheless always was especially reticent about feelings of the heart, and kept silent about those women whom he loved and cherished most.

We must recall that Beethoven's close friend, Dolezalek, who knew him more than 20 years, claimed "he never showed that he was in love," and that another friend of 30 years, Seyfried, honestly believed the composer had never been in love at all! Logically, if Beethoven was so reluctant to express deeply felt emotions with long-term friends, why should he suddenly confide in near strangers, opening his heart to them, and giving them such intimate details about his love life? The fact is, he was not confiding anything.

Beethoven surely was aware that Fanny had very strong feelings for him. Only a man with the sensitivity of a lump of clay would have been oblivious to such open adoration. Thus when her father indelicately inquired about his love life, he knew that she was listening—perhaps hopefully—for his answer. Inadvertently then, Herr Giannatasio afforded Beethoven an opportunity to quash any hopes that either Fanny or her father might have entertained about being more than friends to him. Therefore, the "five years ago" simply had been a round number Beethoven used when he suddenly found himself in the awkward position of having to answer a deeply personal question posed by someone he barely knew. This was also a means to extricate himself from any plans the Giannatasio's might have had to make him a part of their family without offending them.

Why did Beethoven say *five* years? Why *not* five years? How many people would say "three years" or "seven years" when suddenly being forced to pull a number out of the air? And had he said *ten years*, Fanny might have believed his heart sufficiently healed to accept another woman in his life. Worse, what if he had told the absolute truth and said *fifteen* years? "Five years" allowed for the possibility that the pain which would prevent him from forming a new liaison might still be there. Beethoven also had told Herr Giannatasio that this love of his had been "unconfessed." This may have provided Fanny with a good reason why Beethoven was not with his Beloved, but we know that his love had very much been "confessed." He said as much in his letter to his Beloved: "*Your love* makes me the happiest and unhappiest of men at the same time....only by calm contemplation of *our* existence can we reach *our goal* to live together... remain *my all as I am yours*..." If we take Beethoven's "unconfessed" remark as the absolute truth, then it would also eliminate Antonie Brentano for, according to Solomon, their love *had* been confessed. Here again, we see that Beethoven probably was not being absolutely open and truthful with the Giannatasios.

A remark by Varnhagen von Ense also shows that the "five years ago" was not literal. Varnhagen noted that Beethoven's interest in Rahel Levin stemmed from the fact that her expression reminded the composer of a woman "close to his heart." If, in the summer of 1811, Rahel brought to Beethoven's mind someone he *already loved*, then Beethoven's statement that he had *only just made* his Beloved's acquaintance in 1811 was untrue.

That the Giannatasios had some ulterior motives—albeit ones they may have felt were in the composer's best interests—is evident in the schoolmaster's offer of his garden house to Beethoven, which the composer declined for "various reasons" he preferred not to enumerate. Fanny's adoration was surely one of them. Beethoven also exhibited some discomfort in having Karl there, for just six months after his nephew had enrolled (February to July 1816), Beethoven wrote to Giannatasio that "several circumstances induce me to have Karl with me." These "circumstances" could have related to Johanna, Karl's mother, although Giannatasio willingly complied with Beethoven's wishes that she not see the boy, because, in fact, the schoolmaster also did not like having Johanna visit her son at his school. Again, Fanny must have been part of the reason Beethoven suddenly decided to withdraw his nephew from the school for which he had nothing but praise. Illness and problems with servants did not allow Beethoven to carry out these plans until 1818. Instead, when the school moved to the Landstrasse suburb of Vienna in 1817, Beethoven took an apartment there as well, to be close to Karl, rather than having the boy live with him.

Under the circumstances, this "crucial" diary entry is tainted by the situation, and by Fanny's infatuation for Beethoven, and cannot be taken as irrefutable evidence for the Beloved's identity. However, for the benefit of those who still insist on taking the date 1811 literally, let us ask: to whom could this date possibly have referred?

1811 POSSIBILITIES

Could the date in the diary entry have referred to Antonie Brentano? We recall that the entry read "Five years ago he *met* someone..." Had Beethoven met Antonie in 1811? No, he had met her as an adult in 1809.

Could this date have referred to Amalie Sebald whom he *did* meet in 1811? No. After meeting her that year, he did not have any contact with her at all until 1812. When he saw her again, his letters to her were neither passionate nor intimate, and she had done nothing more for him than send him a chicken for some soup. That must have been some chicken if he was still in love with the woman who sent it five years later!

Beethoven also met Rahel Levin in 1811, but he barely knew her, and as we already know, she interested him only to the extent that her expression reminded him of a woman he already *did* love. Varnhagen's remark also places doubt on Antonie Brentano, for even Solomon admitted that "thus far [that is, prior to the *fall* of 1811] there was no sign of a romantic attachment between Beethoven and Antonie Brentano" and yet Beethoven had seen his Beloved in Rahel Levin's expression in the *summer* of that year.

Neither Therese Malfatti, nor Antonie Adamberger, nor Bettina Brentano qualify either, although Beethoven was associated with each of them *around* this time. With Therese, Beethoven had already broken off their tenuous relationship by mid-1810. He had had only the slightest interaction with Bettina whom he had known barely two months, and he did not see her again after she went back to Berlin that same year. In the case of Antonie Adamberger, she recalled that "Shortly thereafter [in the year 1810] he brought [the songs he had written for her], sang them for me and accompanied me on the piano. Apart from this, I had no further personal contact with him." None of these women fit the criteria noted in the diary.

The fact is, there is *no* woman whom Beethoven had met in or around 1811 who possibly could be the Beloved. With so much evidence pointing to the fact that the 1811 date was no more than Beethoven's gentle way of pushing Fanny away from him, it cannot be considered as "crucial" as has been proposed.

OTHER CONSIDERATIONS

Of the women Beethoven knew in 1811, only two women fit the criteria of a Beloved. One is Josephine Brunswick, discounted because there is no evidence whatsoever that Beethoven had any contact with her in that or any other year after 1807. The other woman, who is rarely if ever considered, is Anna Marie Erdödy. She certainly was someone Beethoven thought of as "close to his heart," and she had earned that special place far earlier than the summer of 1811. Yet it had been in early 1811 that she had been completely reconciled with Beethoven after their bitter separation in 1809. He had been elated by her return to him, and as their reconciliation had taken place before his 1811 Teplitz trip, it easily could have been her expression that Beethoven saw reflected in Rahel Levin's face. Could not his reunion with her have remained so sweet in his memory that it was easily brought to mind, so that when he said to Fanny "five years ago he had *met* someone," he was thinking of the time when he had "met someone *again*?" Perhaps by 1811, having endured a quarrel and separation, their love had matured in the light of better understanding of one another, and it was as if they had become acquainted all over again.

Beethoven also spoke of a union with this mysterious woman as being "almost an impossibility." A union with any of the other women he had known or met in 1811 was *clearly*—not *almost*—an impossibility, for they were all firmly married and tied to husbands and families. All of them, that is, with the exception of Josephine Brunswick. . .and Anna Marie Erdödy.

OTHER SIGNIFICANT ENTRIES

Despite the failure of the 1811 date to identify the Immortal Beloved, Fanny Giannatasio's diary contains other significant entries which usually are not alluded to in Beethoven's biographies.

The first of these is most significant because of its inherent truthfulness. It was not something Beethoven *said*, or Fanny *thought* he said, but rather something that Beethoven *wrote*, as he thought, only to himself. The entry comes from the time when Fanny, her sister, and their family were with Beethoven in Baden. As their lodgings were temporarily unavailable, they were given Beethoven's study as a bedroom. While housed there, the two sisters sneaked a peek at his journal, which they had found lying on a table. Even though they knew it was wrong to read his diary, they could not contain their curiosity. Fanny reported that in it Beethoven had written: "My heart runs over at the sight of lovely nature although she is not here." There is only one woman we can be certainly regularly enjoyed "lovely nature" with Beethoven, and that was not Antonie Brentano, who spent most of her days sick in bed, and who certainly did not wander about the environs of Vienna, communing with nature, and enjoying walks with Beethoven. Although one might believe Josephine to be a possibility, one of her own supporters, Mary-Elisabeth Tellenbach, inadvertently eliminated her by suggesting that Josephine was in Baden with Beethoven in 1816, the same time as the diary entry. Not only was Josephine seriously ill at the time and could not have been disposed to taking long walks for the purpose of enjoying nature, Beethoven's own statement, written *while in Baden*, said, "My heart runs over...though she is *not here*."

The only woman this could have referred to was the lady with whom the composer walked in the countryside as he composed his *Mass in C* for Prince Nicholas Esterhazy. She was the one about whom he had written, "I have made a really strong decision to come to the Countess... my nature can only get on well with beautiful Nature..." She was the one whose lovely estate had once been his refuge, and where in later years he always was welcomed. She was the one he referred to as having an "Isis temple"—Isis, the Egyptian goddess of nature. And she was the one with whom he had summered the year he wrote the music to the song in which are found the lines "...looking at the distant fields where I you Beloved found..." Who else could have been brought to his mind at the sight of lovely nature, but the mistress of Jedlersee: Countess Erdödy? We are reminded also that in the Beloved letter, Beethoven told his lady to "look at beautiful Nature and calm your mind about what must be—" Who else could have elicited that advice, but his Anna Marie?

The second diary entry to consider was written in December 1816 when Beethoven shared the newly published song *To the*

Distant Beloved [2] with Fanny and her family—again, using this as another opportunity to discourage the infatuated girl. Fanny recorded that her sister, Nanni, had asked Beethoven "whether he loved anyone except the Distant Beloved." Fanny did not record his answer, but wrote

> ...it stirred in me a sad feeling which is near jealousy... I am so small in comparison with a being which must possess great superiority if she could arouse such high interest in such a man.

Solomon painted such a pitiful picture of Antonie that it is difficult to imagine her as a "being of great superiority." And we have already seen in previous chapters that Antonie and Beethoven were vastly different in personality. This is interesting because Fanny added:

> How interesting must be this being. She must be very similar to him and therefore rightly be of a very high value.

Fanny's description of the Distant Beloved as someone very similar to Beethoven, is a noteworthy comparison to Richard Specht's brief portrait of Anna Marie in which he said of her:

> Though partly disabled... this noble lady overcame all physical ills by mental and moral strength and her indomitable will.

By changing the reference in this comment from the feminine to the masculine, Specht might have been writing about Beethoven himself. The composer, too, recognized and acknowledged how much Anna Marie was like him, as seen in the following letter he wrote to her in 1816 upon the death of her son:

> ...so I console myself, and also speak words of consolation to you. We mortals with immortal minds are only born for suffering and joys, and might almost say that only the most excellent receive joy through sufferings. [3]

---

[2] Beethoven began writing this song directly following Anna Marie's depature from Vienna in 1815, and he sent it to her upon its publication in 1816, unsolicited. More will be said about the Distant Beloved in Chapter 24.

[3] Steichen, p. 284; Anderson, p. 527.

It is interesting that Beethoven thought of himself and Anna Marie as two "... mortals with immortal minds...," both born to share in suffering and joy. She was very similar to Beethoven, indeed; as the Beloved letter said, Beethoven's "other self." It is also of note that Beethoven was able to "speak words of consolation" to her, whereas to all others, he was only able to express his deeply felt emotions through music.

We see here quite clearly that Beethoven's relationship with his Beloved was still very much alive, and most definitely not relegated to his past. He has recently written her this song; she has reciprocated with a ring, a token of her love for him. We also recall that Fanny's 1816 diary read:

> ...it interests him much more, if a woman, without as he thinks being tied to him, gives him her love...

This also is a statement tied to the present: she *gives* him her love. This was not Beethoven speaking of a love now gone, but about a woman still very much a part of his life, with whom he still was emotionally involved, and from whom he continued to receive the "highest gift" of her love, a love that was "still now as on the first day." His Beloved might have been "distant," but it was a physical separation only. And there was only one woman who had been involved with him in the past who was as yet very much a part of his life: Countess Erdödy. This is evident in one of his letters to Anna Marie that year, in which he wrote

> Let me know quite soon, very soon, how you are on the little misty spot of earth where you are now living. How long will you stay there, where will you live in the future?[4]

His concern about her and her future plans, his continuing desire to be with her, indicate Beethoven's ongoing relationship with her. Obviously he did not want his Distant Beloved to remain distant for very long.

CONCLUSION

From what we now know about Fanny Giannatasio and her diary, the comments that Beethoven made and that she recorded make sense.

---

[4]Anderson, p. 578.

The Giannatasios were good to Karl; Beethoven did not want to offend them. He also did not want to mislead a young woman who had such obvious deep affection for him, nor allow her father to entertain the notion that Fanny might be the wife that Herr Giannatasio felt Beethoven needed. Beethoven used every opportunity afforded him to gently discourage Fanny's romantic notions. When her father asked whether Beethoven knew of anyone he might marry, Beethoven responded that he already had found that someone—his "Distant Beloved"—a woman he was not able to marry, but whom he loved as much then as he had when they first fell in love. . .not only a further discouragement to Fanny, but also, sadly, the truth.

Beethoven used the round figure of five years as the time of his meeting this Beloved so that it would not seem unreasonable to Fanny that the love he felt for his Beloved might still be fresh enough to cause him sadness, and to keep Fanny at a distance from his heart which still very much belonged to another woman. When the subject of marriage arose, Beethoven maintained the importance of marrying for love. Those who did not marry for love, he said, regretted their actions. Here he again was speaking from his own observations, for few of the women he knew had been happily married, and just as few had married, or been able to marry, for love. Since Fanny was painfully aware that Beethoven did not return her love, his remark let her know quite clearly that the composer would never consider marrying her, for to do so would only cause one or both of them serious regrets.

Given these insights into the document in question, it is not prudent to use the September 16, 1816, entry alone as crucial evidence for the identity of Beethoven's Immortal Beloved, without viewing it in the context of the diary as a whole. Clearly there is more to be learned within its pages about Beethoven and his eternally beloved than simply a solitary and highly questionable date.

❖ *20* ❖
The *Tagebuch* Entries

Two pieces of information Solomon introduced to further his claim that Antonie Brentano was Beethoven's Beloved came from what has been called Beethoven's *Tagebuch*[1] Once again, it is important to be aware of the exact nature of this document, and the context in which its entries were written in order to judge its validity and importance.

A BRIEF BACKGROUND OF THE *TAGEBUCH*

First and most critically, the *Tagebuch,* Beethoven's journal, is not exactly what one typically thinks of as a diary, a chronologically dated record of one's day-to-day experiences. Rather, it is a collection of his notes, probably in chronological order, but which included everything from shopping reminders to philosophical musings. He included proverbs, poems, and pertinent quotes, but very little of his daily activities. Interspersed with his deepest personal feelings and expressions of emotion are mundane notes such as "Shoe brushes for polishing when somebody visits." The journal covered only about six years of his life, from 1812 to 1818, and, in all, there are approximately 171 entries. The pages of his journal were included within larger documents which added anecdotes and other material to the journal proper. Two of

---

[1]a journal or diary, literally a book (*Buch*) of days (*Tage*). A discussion of the *Tagebuch* and its surviving copies may be found in Solomon's *Beethoven Essays*, pp. 233-246.

these are the *Fischoff Manuscript*. and an older version, considered the more accurate of the two, the *Gräffer Manuscript*. Although many of the documents included—among them, his journal—had been written by Beethoven originally, the autographs have been lost, and both of these manuscripts are comprised of surviving copies of these documents. Thus, as neither of them is in Beethoven's handwriting their absolute reliability is shaky. The question arises, how accurately did the copyist read what Beethoven had written?

"THE SHOCKING SCRAWL..."

Because a primary caution in using the *Tagebuch* as evidence is that it is not written in Beethoven's own hand, but is a handwritten *copy* of his documents, a note about Beethoven's handwriting is in order.

Beethoven once had written a letter to Baron de Trémont in French, over which Trémont's friends expressed surprise. Trémont wrote: "Some musicians with whom I became acquainted were slow to believe [that he knew Beethoven]. 'Will you believe me,' I told them, 'if I show you a letter he has written me in French?' They exclaimed, 'In French? that's impossible! he hardly knows any and he doesn't even write German legibly!'"[2]

Beethoven himself often poked fun at his almost indecipherable handwriting, claiming that "Life is too short to paint letters or notes, and more beautiful notes would not help me out of my troubles."[3] Beethoven also noted the problem in an amusing note to his friend Zmeskall on October 8, 1813:

> Yesterday, I took a letter to the post and there I was asked to what address the letter was to be sent—So I see that my handwriting can be misunderstood, and perhaps as often as I am—[4]

Thayer remarked "In his early manhood he wrote a fair hand, so very different from the shocking scrawl of his later years... "[5] Further, the composition *Für Elise* likely had had the

---

[2]Shermann & Biancolli, pp. 527-529.
[3]Beethoven was punning, as usual, but his play on the words for musical notes (Noten) and troubles (Nöten) is lost in translation, the umlaut over the o making the difference. The German reads "Schönere Noten brachtren mich schwerlich auf den Nöten."
[4]Anderson, p. 426.
[5]Thayer/Forbes, p. 59.

original title of "Für Therese,"—based on the fact that the autograph was found among Therese Malfatti's personal papers and that she had requested from Beethoven a simple piece to play. Although it had not been written for anyone names "Elise," the copyist could not decipher Beethoven's "Therese" correctly and wrote the other name instead.

THE ENTRY: A PIECE OF THE WHOLE

Solomon asserted that "most Beethoven biographers believe that the following entry on the first page of Beethoven's *Tagebuch*, dated 1812, contains a reference to the Immortal Beloved." Obviously they came to this conclusion because they considered only a *portion* of the text rather than the *entire entry*, and disregarded the events in Beethoven's life during the time the note was written. In effect, they "lifted" this piece out of Beethoven's journal in what seems to be a desperate search for clues about the Immortal Beloved. It was misleading for them to do so, because in this case as in many others, both historical and literary context is crucial. The *Tagebuch* entry has been quoted as follows:

> In this way with A everything goes to ruin.

But this is far from being the entire entry which is necessary to consider before making the pronouncement that the *A* referred to Beethoven's Beloved. Interestingly, this is the same entry which was used previously to "prove" Beethoven's doubts about his manhood. Let us first see the line (italicized) within its context:

> Submission, absolutely submission to your fate! only this can give you the sacrifice—for the service business– Oh hard struggle! Do everything, that still is to do—in order to prepare for the distant journey—you must yourself find all that your most blessed wish can offer, you must force it to your will—keep always of the same mind. You may no longer be a man, not for yourself, only for others, for you there is no longer happiness except in yourself, in your art—O God, give me strength, to conquer myself, nothing must chain me to life.—*In this way with A everything goes to ruin.* The strict holding together of several parts impedes on the whole the progression from one to the other————.

Now, what does seeing this entry in its entirety tell us? It was written in 1812, prior to a "distant journey." Therefore, it must have been written between January and June, before Beethoven's trip to Teplitz. Does the entry have anything to do with his love life? No, as we noted in Chapter 5, he tells us that his concern was "the service business." Now why would Beethoven suddenly throw in a reference to his "eternally beloved" in the midst of ranting about his work? Already we must have our doubts that the *A* referred his Beloved or, more specifically, to Antonie Brentano. Rather, Beethoven was writing about something, or someone, relating to his work.

Some biographers have given attention to the last line, the one which immediately follows the *A* line:

> The strict holding together of several parts impedes on the whole the progression from one to the other———

Thayer, among others, thought this sentence was "curiously out of place," but is it? It *is*, only if one believes that the *A* in the preceding sentence referred to Antonie Brentano, or, at least, to Beethoven's Beloved. It *isn't*, if he was merely continuing his diatribe on the conditions under which he was being forced to work.

THE QUESTION OF "A"

Biographers who have questioned the *A* in the line remind us that the *Tagebuch* is only a copy, and that Beethoven's handwriting was often illegible. They pointed out that one could not discount an error on the part of the copyist in deciphering what Beethoven had written. Hugo Riemann noted in the German edition of Thayer's book that it is "a fair question... whether or not the initial which shows a flourish is really an *A*..." In the *Fischoff Manuscript*, the character in question indeed does have more unusual flourishes in the copy than a normal cursive *A* would warrant, although in the older, more accurate copy, the *Gräffer Manuscript*, the character does appear to be a genuine letter. The one thing that *is* unusual, however, is that in the manuscripts, we see that the letter *A* in two other words in the sentence—*Auf* and *Art*—are written strikingly different than the *A* by itself. The former adhere to proper cursive script while the *A* alone does not. It is no wonder, then, that some biographers have questioned whether the letter was actually a letter or not. In 1959, Dana Steichen, picking up on Riemann's comment, suggested that the *A* might well have been a musical symbol, perhaps standing for *mezzo forte* which does bear a resemblance to a cursive capital *A*. If this *was* a musical symbol, Mrs. Steichen argued, then the second part of that quotation, which sounded odd on its own, and which even Thayer labeled as being "curiously out of place," would make sense and it would not be "out of place" at all: Beethoven simply was attempting to work out a musical problem. Let us read the passage once again with *mezzo forte* substituted for the *A* and see if it fits:

> In this way with mezzo forte everything goes to ruin.
> The strict holding together of several parts impedes on
> the whole the progression from one to the other.

With this substitution, it is true that the "curious" second part of the entry no longer is quite so curious after all, although its "curiousness" was only there in the first place because biographers failed to take the *Tagebuch* entry as a whole, and therefore did not see that both lines, the one with the "funny A" and the last line, are connected to his work.

As the entry in the 1812 *Tagebuch* is very similar to the notes Beethoven wrote at the foot of each study in John Cramer's *Etudes*, a combination of sentences and phrases—for example: "Against the 16th bar is written— The melody in the third note of the triplet. Only thus will proper binding be achieved"—we suppose that Mrs. Steichen's hypothesis probably could have some credence. However, this author believes there is a far more plausible explanation.

A QUESTION OF LANGUAGE

In looking at this *Tagebuch* entry, we must keep some points in mind:

1. Beethoven wrote this in his journal, not in a letter. Thus there was no need for him to be clear to anyone as to what the *A* meant. The *A* was not ambiguous to him. In the case of a letter, Beethoven necessarily would have been forced to be clearer in his meaning to achieve understanding. He would not have written *A* without first indicating to his letter's recipient to what the *A* referred. For example, he could use the initial *K* to refer to *Karlsbad* when writting to his publishers because he had already

used the word "Karlsbad" twice in his sentence. Where he wrote this *A* is relevant because in a journal, meant only for himself, the *A* could stand for virtually anything: person, place, or thing.

2. If, despite its flourishes, the symbol is indeed a cursive capital letter *A*, and therefore it does refer to a *person*, why must that person necessarily be a *woman*? If we look at the German version—"Auf diese Art mit A geht alles zu Grunde"—we see that there is no indicative article (der, die, or das) preceding the *A* to indicate gender. Thus the *A* can as easily refer to a *man*, and only the desperate need for clues about the Beloved has made biographers assume a feminine reference for the letter *A*.

3. It cannot even be assumed that the *A* referred to a person. In German, inanimate objects (nouns) have "gender." English-speakers say "the bread and butter" without a thought to gender, but to German-speakers it is "das Bröt" (neuter) and "die Butter" (feminine). The assignment of gender to nouns is typical of many languages. In the case of *A*, we do not have the feminine *die* which would indicate either a woman or something of feminine gender.

4. In German, all nouns are capitalized, not simply proper names. Again, we see from our example above that *bread and butter* is not *bröt und butter* but *Bröt und Butter*. Thus we cannot assume that the *A* was referring to the initial of a person's name, but just as easily could refer to some *thing* or some *place*.

WHAT WE *DO* KNOW

With so many questions about the "case of A," is there anything we do know? A few things are clear:

1. It must be connected in some way with "the service business." The entire entry is devoted to Beethoven's complaint about the way he was being forced to work.

2. It was written in the first half of 1812.

3. It could refer to a person, place, or thing of unknown gender. That does not narrow down the possibilities much, but we do know that it was not a verb.

What do we also know about the historical context of the entry, the time period during which Beethoven wrote this statement? We can look at his letters for early 1812 for clues.

1. Beethoven was particularly bothered at this time with things connected to the "service business." His letters reveal that

the Archduke Rudolph was demanding lessons which interfered with what was truly important to him: composition. Numerous notes from Beethoven to the Archduke are filled with lame excuses about why Beethoven had to cancel a lesson. Regardless, he did sometimes acquiesce to the Archduke's demands; he could hardly do otherwise. This prompted notes to friends, usually Zmeskall, in which Beethoven complained,

> If, dear Z, it were only a matter of creating a *product* all would be well, but in addition to implant on a bad soil— Today I am again the slave of the A[rchduke]...[6]

This particular note was written at the end of 1811, around the same time as the *Tagebuch* entry. These ambivilent feelings Beethoven expressed to Zmeskall he wrote to others as well. To the sons of publisher Bernhard Schott he complained,

> I must now give His Imperial Highness the Archduke Rudolph a lesson of two hours every day. This is so tiring that it almost unfits me for any other work. Yet I cannot live on my income.[7]

The Archduke Rudolph was one of Beethoven's few pupils (Ries being the only other one he would acknowledge). Rudolph also was one of the composer's staunchest patrons and financial supporters. Beethoven could hardly refuse to give him lessons on the piano when he requested them. On the one hand, the Archduke was a good and loyal friend; on the other, Beethoven felt the Archduke's demands interfered with his work. The obligation annoyed Beethoven constantly. To Ries he wrote:

> The Cardinal's (Rudolph's) stay in Vienna for about four weeks during which period I had to give him every day a lesson lasting two and a half, sometimes three hours, has robbed me of a great deal of time. For after such lessons one is hardly able on the following day to think, and still less, to compose.[8]

Also late in 1811, Xaver Schnyder von Wartensee had come from Switzerland to see Beethoven with the hope that Beethoven might take him as a pupil. Schynder was adamant, despite Beethoven repeatedly refusing. Finally Beethoven raised his

---

[6]Anderson, p. 350.
[7]Anderson, p. 1151.
[8]Anderson, p. 1026.

voice and said, "No! no! I've only one pupil left, and I can't get rid of him, much as I should like to." When Schnyder asked him who this person was who gave him so much trouble, Beethoven answered "his voice grim with fury and violently stamping his feet, roared at me: 'Oh! He's Archduke Rudolph!'"[9]

We can see that giving piano lessons simply drove Beethoven crazy. Thayer wrote that in 1811-1812, Beethoven's

> duties to the Archduke had already become extremely irksome, and that the necessity of sacrificing his previous independence in some small degree to them grew daily more annoying and irksome.[10]

When we read Beethoven's letters to the Schotts, to Ries, and to Zmeskall, his remark to Schnyder, and Thayer's comment, it is not surprising that Beethoven had such strong negative feelings about "the service business" at this time.

2. Beethoven was having difficulty collecting money due him from Lobkowitz and Kinsky. The "service business" once again was the issue.

3. Beethoven was upset by the cool reception of his magnificent *Piano Concerto #5*, the "Emperor." As if the artistic disappointment was not enough, Beethoven knew that his survival depended upon his music being well-received by the public. He complained to Zmeskall in February (on the 2nd) how "cursed be life here in Austria's barbarous country," and (on the 19th) that "...I will not go on living here to be so insulted. Art, when it is persecuted, finds asylum everywhere." In May he continued his complaints to Zmekall, "...in the sewer where I am living in Vienna all that work is as good as lost." Beethoven believed that artists should not be restricted by the mundane necessities of life and the burden of acquiring such needs—that is, earning a living by selling ones talent in ways other than creating art. He did not like it, but he acknowledged it. It, too, was part of the "service business" he detested.

Knowing all this, is there any way to ascertain, without a doubt, to what *A* really referred? No, there is not. But it cannot be said that the *A* referred to Antonie Brentano or to Beethoven's Beloved. In fact, in its context, the line simply *could not* have referred to her. Even the substitution of a suitable noun, such as

---

[9]Hamburger, p. 103.
[10]Thayer/Forbes, p.

for "service business"—*Abfertigung* — or for "work"—*Arbeit*—
makes more sense in the sentence than anything else:

> In this way with work (or service) everything goes to
> ruin.

Interestingly, Solomon, who accepted without question that the
A referred to Antonie Brentano, did not come to that same hasty
conclusion in analyzing another entry with another unspecified
initial. In his discussion of the *Tagebuch* in his *Beethoven Essays*,
page 274, he noted the following about entry #89, which reads:

> In a thousand ways K. can be of help to you in daily life.

In his explanatory note, Solomon wrote

> "K" stands for "art" (*Kunst*) or Karl.

Thus we see that Solomon and other biographers probably would
have reached a conclusion similar to ours had they not been so
desperate to find something, anything, that might be a clue for the
mysterious Immortal Beloved.

"In the Case of 'T'..."

Solomon, and others, also attempted to use another *Tagebuch* entry as proof of the Beloved's identity, but before introducing the entry itself, he began by quoting Thayer, or more correctly,
*mis*quoting him, and claiming that this passage "precisely described Antonie and Franz Brentano." This author likewise will
present the *Tagebuch* entry in question later and give Thayer's
quote first:

> Now it happens that one of Beethoven's transient but
> intense passions for a married woman known to have
> occurred in this period of his life, has its precise date
> fixed by these passages in the so-called "Tagebuch,"
> from the years 1816-1817...

As always, readers must use caution when a biographer—
even one of Thayer's calibre—uses the word "known" unless he or
she relates specifically who it was who "knew" the information,
and whether that person has credibility, that is, truly was in a
position *to know*. When Thayer says "passions... *known* to have
occurred," one must immediately ask, "Known by *whom*?" To

state something as fact and not substantiate it relegates it to the level of gossip.

The first question regarding this entry must be: how could an entry made in 1816 or 1817 refer to Antonie Brentano if the woman in question was, according to Thayer, a "transient" passion? Beethoven had not seen Antonie Brentano in five years. "Transient" and "five-year's duration" is a contradiction in terms. The answer lies in the fact that Thayer's quote, like many others, has been taken out of its original context. In fact, this quote came in the midst of Thayer's discussion of Beethoven's 1817 relationship with *Marie Koschak-Pachler,* not Antonie Brentano.

> As the family name of this lady whose husband was a man of high position and distinction though not noble by birth, is known, it is certain that the T in the above citation is not Therese Malfatti, now Baroness Drosdick;

The husband to whom Thayer was referring with the high position and distinction was Dr. Karl Pachler, a lawyer in Graz, not the merchant Franz Brentano. Nowhere did Thayer say that the lady herself had been of noble birth, only that she had been married to a man who had not. Only Solomon wanted to "assume" that the lady had been an aristocrat in order to strengthen his case for Antonie Brentano. This is an assumption with which this author cannot agree. Thayer believed that Beethoven had had an "intense passion" for Marie Pachler in 1817 because she noted some years later that she and Beethoven had been "often in each other's company." It is not true, then, as Solomon asserted, that this "intense passion" noted by Thayer does "precisely describe Antonie and Franz Brentano."[11] It does, however, "precisely describe" the people Thayer had been discussing: Marie and Karl Pachler. The proof is in the rest of Thayer's statement:

> ...as her baptismal names have eluded search one can only hint at the possibility that the "T" and "M" may indicate the same person, and that this last cry of anguish was written a year or two afterwards when the sight of "M" again,for the moment, tore open a half-healed wound.[12]

---

[11]Solomon, p. 174.
[12]Thayer/Forbes, p. 686.

Thayer had hoped to find that Marie Pachler had been baptised with a name beginning with the letter *T* so that it could be shown that both the *Tagebuch* entry, and the note from Baden which mentioned an *M*, had referred to the same woman. Thayer's claim that the baptismal names of the lady in question had "eluded search" eliminates Antonie Brentano as the lady in question. Antonie's baptismal names most definitely *were* known, as Solomon himself noted in his *Beethoven Essays*: Johanna Antonie Josefa von Birkenstock. She had been a woman of noble birth, and her baptismal certificate would not have been any more difficult for a researcher of Thayer's calibre to find than it had been for Solomon. Thayer had traced Beethoven's ancestry back to the seventeenth century, and found the baptismal records of his entire immediate family, even though they were *not* members of the aristocracy.

Again, it must be reemphasized that Thayer gave no source for this story, stating only that it was "known." He wrote:

> There are few unmarried men of highly sensitive nature who have not had the bitter experience of a hopeless passion, who have not felt how doubly grateful at such times is intercourse [spoken, of course!] with a glorious creature like Madame Pachler, and how beneficial in preventing the thoughts from continually dwelling on the impossible, and thus aiding reason and conscience to gain victory over the heart and fancy.[13]

Thayer thought that Beethoven had sought out Marie Pachler as the result of unrequited love for someone else. But it is a leap of imagination to assume that being in someone's company necessitates having an intense passion for that person. Beethoven had been impressed with Frau Pachler's proficiency as a pianist. She, in turn, was a bride of just one year. He wrote her only two letters, one of which which was illegible and another which praised her extraordinary skill as a pianist. Nothing romantic between them need be assumed. In fact, later on, Pachler's own son completely quashed this notion. Thayer's "known" story about Beethoven's "intense passion for a married woman" thus falls into the realm of simply another bit of gossip which invariably is spread about men of distinction, particularly one like Beethoven who, as he himself admitted, was often "very free in

---

[13]Thayer/Forbes, p. 685.

speech" and who had often had his "purest, most innocent feelings... misconstrued." As we shall see later, it was at this same time that Beethoven had written to Anna Marie, asking her not to "believe all the gossip" about him. Would that all biographers heeded that advice!

THE ENTRY

What follows is the weary sounding entry in question, written in the 1816-1817 portion of the *Tagebuch*, thought by Thayer to have referred to Marie Pachler, and which Solomon used as further evidence to support Antonie Brentano as the Beloved:

> In the case of T., there is nothing to do but to leave it to God, never to go where one might do a wrong through weakness. But be as kind as possible to T. her attachment deserves never to be forgotten even if the results could never prove advantageous to you.

Josephine supporters attach this *T* to Josephine's sister, Therese, who they believe had been serving as an intermediary between Beethoven and Josephine. However, because the note speaks of *"her* attachment," this does not seem likely. Yet the supporters of Countess Brunswick need not have gone to such desperate measures to connect this passage to Josephine because there is no indication whatsoever that it referred to Beethoven's Immortal Beloved. To the contrary, this was a note written by a man who felt exasperated by, and not receptive to, the unwanted advances of a woman. How can anyone read this note and not see that? Beethoven wrote "Be as kind as possible to T—" *Kind*? This supposedly is the woman to whom he pledged eternal devotion, and he wants merely to remember to be *kind* to her? "In the case of T... leave it to God..." The *case* of T? Is this not a cool, detached way to speak about an "eternally beloved?"And if he were not weary of her attachment, why would he feel the need to leave the situation in God's hands? Beethoven also wrote "...her attachment deserves never to be forgotten..." We note that he said *her* attachment, not his, not theirs. In the Beloved letter, it was always "our goal" and "our love" and "forever us."

---

[14]Anderson, pp. 679.

This author is inclined to believe that this entry may well have referred to Antonie Brentano, as it has a tone similar to one Beethoven used in a letter he wrote in 1812 before leaving Franzensbrunn, in which he claimed to be weary of startling events. After three years of silence, Beethoven finally wrote to the Brentanos in November 1815. Perhaps he had hoped to renew his friendship with them, thinking that enough time had passed for Antonie to have come to see reality: that he did not and never would return her love. But reality seems still to have eluded her. It is possible that her unhappiness in Frankfurt had caused Antonie to be encouraged by Beethoven's letter, and she decided to pursue him once again, perhaps with the hope that he had changed his mind. By the time the *Tagebuch* entry was written a short time later, it is clear he had grown tired of her pursuit of the issue, even though he had no desire to hurt her. As there are several letters written by Beethoven to Frankfurt around this time which are missing, we believe he might have gently but firmly put an end to her fantasies about him once and for all. The last of the letters enclosed a song, which he may have sent to soothe whatever hurt his rejecting her might have caused, to let her know that he was not angry with her and still considered her a friend, even though he did not love her.

Consider also the line Beethoven wrote "never to go where one might do a wrong through weakness." Susan Lund suggested that the Brentanos had invited Beethoven to visit them. While he might have wanted to see his friends, particularly Franz, after the nightmare encounter with Antonie in 1812, Beethoven knew it would have been impossible to do so without encouraging Antonie's unrealistic and unreciprocated love for him. Beethoven suffered terrible loneliness at this time with Anna Marie out of the country, and his note indicates that under those circumstances he realized he might be tempted to accept Antonie's attentions, and take unfair advantage of her misguided feelings. If such an invitation had been extended to him (although there is no evidence of one) he made up his mind that he would not accept it. There is an indication that Beethoven had considered visiting some German spas that year, as he noted quite a few in his journal, and wrote of traveling. Lund believed that Beethoven had planned this trip to be near Frankfurt, but in most cases the spas are closer to Bonn. As Frankfurt was en route to his hometown, however, again, Beethoven must have reconsidered making such a trip.

ANOTHER POSSIBLE T

There was one other woman besides Antonie Brentano, who we know from her diary *had* had an infatuation for Beethoven in 1816-17: Fanny Giannatasio. Dana Steichen suggested another explanation for this *Tagebuch* entry: that the *T* had been a copyist's error, and that the person transcribing Beethoven's original notes wrote a *T* when the letter should have been an *F* for Fanny Giannatasio. Given the similarity between the two letters, the time of the *Tagebuch*'s entry (1816-1817)—the very years that Beethoven was associated with the Giannatasios—the weary tone of the entry itself, and the strength of Fanny's infatuation for Beethoven, Mrs. Steichen's theory is entirely plausible. Her explanation gains even greater strength when one notes the following:

First, in 1816, Beethoven asked Anna Marie "not to believe all the gossip about why I have not written to you." The gossip he referred to probably had involved Fanny because he did not meet Marie Pachler until 1817. Second, and most importantly, in 1817, Fanny's father invited Beethoven to live with them in their garden house. Beethoven politely declined with this noncommittal excuse:

> I beg you, my worthy friend, to inquire in the houses round about you, whether there is a small apartment to let. I should much have liked to make use of your kind offer to live with you in the garden-house, but for various reasons this cannot be. Kind regards to you and yours.[14]

If the *T was* actually an *F*, then both the *Tagebuch* entry and the note to Giannatasio, above, not only make sense, they fit together very well. Beethoven was following his advice as written in his *Tagebuch*, "never to go where one might do wrong through weakness." In this case, he was cautioning himself not to put himself in the position—such as a boarder in the Giannatasio's house—where, out of loneliness, he might have been tempted to

---

[14]Anderson, p. 679.

take advantage of or unwittingly mislead a young woman who he knew was very much in love with him.

THE REST OF THE STORY

Again, there was more to the *Tagebuch* entry than was quoted by Solomon. Directly after the passage "be as kind as possible to T., her attachment deserves never to be forgotten even if the results could never prove advantageous to you," Beethoven continued with an important piece of information:

> Work during the summer for the journey, only thus can you carry out the great task for your poor nephew, afterwards wander through Italy, Sicily with a few artists—make plans and be of good cheer for the sake of C.

Here, in 1816-17, we see that Beethoven was not only considering a visit to various spas, he also was interested in making a trip to Italy, which is where Anna Marie was. This is supported by his letter addressed to her that same year in which he asked how much a trip to her might cost him:

> As my nephew has vacation from the last of August up to the end of October, I could then, health permitting, come to you... Linke must write and tell me the cheapest way I could make the journey...[15]

In the *Tagebuch*, he also noted that he must "be of good cheer for the sake of C." We know that Beethoven was not referring to his nephew, as Solomon suggested, for he never spelled his name any way other than *Karl*, or otherwise referred to him as *K.*

Thayer did not want to admit that the letter might be a *C* as Jahn claimed and Nohl thought it was. He noted that some biographers have attempted to interpret Beethoven's letter *C* as an *L*, but that is hardly likely. The letter *C* looks nothing like an *L*, and anyone who has seen one of Beethoven's capital *L*s would know that it could not have been mistaken by a copyist for the letter *C* or vice versa. Also, there is no one Beethoven knew whose name began with the letter *L* for whom he would have had that sensitivity and care.

---

[15]Anderson, pp. 683-684. Although the destination of this letter was not noted, a letter sent a short time before to her was addressed "Padua, Italy."

Even Thayer did not ascribe to the letter *L*, mainly because he hoped to tie this portion of the *Tagebuch* entry to the earlier part by suggesting that the *C* actually was a *T*! The letters *F* and *T* may be mistaken by a copyist for one another, because only the tiniest of lines separates them in appearance... but a *T* and a *C*? As neither Jahn nor Nohl had ulterior motives for claiming the letter was a *C*—unlike Thayer in his *T* theory—this author is inclined to accept Jahn's and Nohl's assessment, but adds that the letter also might have been a *G*, which in some cases can look very similar. We put forth this idea because of supporting material which suggests that Beethoven may have been referring to Comtesse (*C*) or Gräfin (*G*): Erdödy. We know from his letters and dedications that he referred to her as both, using "Countess" as a kind of nickname. She was the only woman he consistently called by title, sometimes simply using an initial which stood for "Countess." If we accept the letter as either a *C* (Comtesse) or *G* (Gräfin), this would then tie in to her location, Italy, a place to where he considered traveling that year according to that same entry in his *Tagebuch*, and to his letter to her in which he inquired about the monetary feasibility of such a trip. A third tie-in would be his reference to being "of good cheer for the sake of *C* (*G*)," only logical when one recalls that she not long before had lost her only son. It would be natural for him to maintain a cheerful demeanor for her sake.

CONCLUSION

The preceding discussion can end with only one logical conclusion: the *Tagebuch* entries, examined in both their literary and historical contexts, cannot be used as evidence supporting Antonie Brentano as the Beloved. If anything, they once again point to the relentless and hopeless fantasy of a pitiable woman who could not, despite all of Beethoven's gentle discouragement, relinquish her unrealistic passion for him.

• 21 •

The Note from Baden

Only love—yes only love has the power to give you a happier life—O God—let me—let me finally find the one—who will make me happy in virtue—who will lawfully be mine—

> Baden on 27th July: as M. drove by and it
> seemed as if she glanced at me—

Solomon cited this note written by Beethoven as further proof of his longing for "Toni" Brentano. This is the notation from where the **M** referred to by Thayer in Chapter 20: *The Tagebuch Entries,* came. About this note Thayer wrote:

> ...one can only hint at the possibility that the "T" and "M" may indicate the same person, and that this last cry of anguish [in the Baden note] was written a year or two afterwards when the sight of "M" again, for the moment, tore open a half-healed wound.[1]

Solomon stated that "This hitherto mysterious passage in Thayer becomes crystal clear if we assume 'T' to be Toni and 'M' to be her daughter Maximiliane, the sight of whom in 1817 (thought Thayer) revived in Beethoven the image of her mother."[2] It is a wonder that Solomon found this passage so "mysterious,"

---

[1]Thayer/Forbes, p. 686.
[2]Solomon, p. 175.

for, as already noted, Thayer was attempting to connect the *M* in this note with the *T* in the *Tagebuch,* and both of those with Marie Koschak-Pachler. As Solomon noted, Thayer believed that the Baden note had been written around 1817, "a year or two" after the *Tagebuch* entry of 1816. But the Baden note could not have been written in any year even close to this date. Even without evidence provided by the Beethovenhaus in Bonn, a chronology of Beethoven's summer excursions as indicated by his letters would show that there were very few years when he had been, or could have been, in Baden on July 27.

In 1809, Beethoven did not arrive in Baden until September, and in 1810, not until August. In the summers of 1811 and 1812, we know he was in Teplitz and the Bohemian spas. In 1813 he was in Baden for a time, but already had returned to Vienna by July 24, *three days before* the date on the note. In July 1814 he also was in Vienna, dealing with a lawsuit involving Mälzel and the "Battle Symphony." He did not write the Baden note in either of the years of the *Tagebuch* entry, 1816 or 1817, either. In 1816, he did not leave Vienna for Baden until July 29, *two days after* the note was written, and, in fact, had had a visitor, Dr. Karl von Bursy, on that very day, July 27. On July 27, 1817, Beethoven was in Nussdorf writing to Frau Streicher who *was* in Baden, and another note to her dated July 30 from Vienna said, "About the housekeeper, I wish you were here, i.e. as if by chance, however much I rejoice at your enjoying the Baden air." In the summers of both 1818 and 1819 Beethoven was in Mödling with his nephew.

Already this shows that Thayer's date of 1817 was incorrect and that the *M* in the note and the *T*—or *F*—in the *Tagebuch* entry could not in any way have referred to the same person, and certainly not to Marie Pachler.

THREE YEARS

There were only three times in 25 years that Beethoven's letters tell that he was in Baden on July 27: 1804, 1807, and 1825. First, we certainly know that Beethoven would not have written this in 1825 when he was nearly 55 years old. By then he had given up on the idea of marriage and would not have written "let me find the one...who will lawfully be mine."

What of the other two years? Research conducted by the Beethovenhaus has suggested that, based on an examination of the paper's watermarks, the note had been written in 1807. Thus, it would seem that we can eliminate 1804 and concentrate solely on 1807.

In the autumn of that year Beethoven had made a last attempt to reconcile with Josephine. After no contact with her for over a year, what had prompted him to approach her again, or to respond to an overture on her part? She had, after all, rejected his romantic attentions in 1805, which must have hurt him greatly. This author believes that encountering "M" was somehow the catalyst for his action.

Beethoven's last letter to Josephine had been written in the spring of 1805. Another letter written after this one, was not addressed directly to her, but said "Tomorrow evening I shall see my dear, my beloved J—Tell her that to me she is far more dear and far more precious than anything else." After that, his next letter to her was not until May 1807, and although addressed to "Be-loved and only J," did nothing more than request his quartets be returned so that they might be copied. He spent June and July of that year in Baden, where apparently Josephine and her children were also, but there is no indication that they were particularly close at the time. Apparently, however, Josephine had made some effort to renew their friendship. By August 10 Beethoven was back in Vienna, and at the beginning of September he was briefly in Heiligenstadt, near Anna Marie's summer residence in Hernals. Did he seek advice from the woman he called his "father confessor?" Perhaps, for this short trip was followed by his letter of September 20 with a sudden appeal, asking Josephine for a chance to once again approach her with more than mere friendship in mind. Beethoven's brief encounter with "M" in Baden at the end of July—whoever she was—must have stirred his desires for marriage once again.

MORE IMMORTAL INITIALS

Although the note clearly referred to *M* and not to *T*, Solomon was ready with an explanation, as we have noted, suggesting that the *M* referred to Maximiliane, Antonie Brentano's young daughter, whose glance "revived in Beethoven the image of her mother." An imaginative explanation, however, Beethoven did not have any relationship at all with Antonie 1807, nor in 1804, the only other possible date if, for some unlikely reason, the reseachers at the Beethovenhaus were wrong.

To whom did the *M* refer? Some biographers have gone so far as to say *no one*, suggesting that the letter was not an *M* at all, but an *R,* and that it referred to Rahel Levin! As one can plainly see by looking at the facsimile, it would require quite a stretch of one's imagination to find anything even remotely resembling an *R* or any other letter other than what it is: an *M*.

Besides, Beethoven did not meet Rahel until 1811, and he knew no other women with *R* names. So we ask again: to whom did this *M* refer?

We know it was not Marie Koschak-Pachler. Schindler and Thayer both thought it was she, because they thought the note had been written in 1817, the year Beethoven met her. However, we already know that it was not Frau Pachler, because the note had been written ten years earlier.

Some have suggested Therese Malfatti, although there are problems with that assumption. There is no indication that he knew her in 1807. Further, as a rule, Beethoven did not refer to women by the initials of their last names. The only women Beethoven addressed by their last names were professional women, usually connected with the theater: actresses and singers. It is likely that they used their last names as "stage names," which is why Beethoven referred to them that way. Singer Anna Milder-Hauptmann, who had played the role of Fidelio/Leonore in the first version of Beethoven's opera, he called "Milder." Henrietta Sontag, the famous soprano who sang the solo part in his *Ninth Symphony* in the May 1824 concert, he addressed as "Sontag." He did the same with contralto Karoline Unger. Beethoven's friend, Karl Holz, spoke of these women in the same way. In the composer's conversation book dated May 22, 1826,

Holz wrote: "Today Schechner (Nanette Schechner) will sing in Schweitzer Familie. She sings almost as well as Milder, but with more flexibility in her throat..."[2] Anton Schindler also used their last names only when writing in Beethoven's conversation books. It is apparent that the use of a professional woman's last name as a proper way to address her was common practice, and not just confined to the way Beethoven addressed them. One should note that Beethoven did not address any other women of his acquaintance by their last name. In his letters to Therese Malfatti he never referred to her as *M* but only as *T* or "Therese." Beethoven used *M* only to refer to the entire Malfatti family. Why, then, should he suddenly use *M* to refer to her alone?

Josephine supporters would like to tie the *M* to her in some way and have suggested that Beethoven had seen her mother in Baden, and that seeing her had prompted him to think of Josephine. In this case, they argue, the *M* stands for *Mutter*, German for "mother." There is, however, no indicative article in the note. It is unlikely that Beethoven would have written "...as Mother drove by and it seemed as if she glanced at me" as he would only if he had been referring to his own mother. If he were referring to anyone else's mother, he would have said, "die Mutter"—the mother. Even then, this is a stretch of the imagination, for one cannot imagine Beethoven calling Josephine's mother anything other than Countess Brunswick.

Two Ms

There were only two *M* ladies who knew Beethoven in 1807: Marie Bigot and Marie Erdödy.[3]

Beethoven had no romantic attachment to Frau Bigot so the woman herself could not have caused him to write such an anguished note. Only if she merely had been a catalyst for strong emotions to surface can she be considered a possibility. The glance of a married woman of whom he was fond, but who clearly was bound to another, and who was part of a family, could have brought sharply to Beethoven's mind his own lonely singleness, and caused him to long for a Beloved, a wife, a family of his own.

---

[3]We know from the way she signed her one surviving letter to him that Beethoven must have called Countess Erdödy "Marie," at least in private moments.

As for Anna Marie Erdödy, we know that he did have a strong attachment to her, and that she could have stirred up thoughts of love as well as served as an impetus for Beethoven to once again pursue the idea of marriage. However, there are two problems with assigning the *M* to Marie Erdödy: *M*'s reaction to Beethoven, and Countess Erdödy's whereabouts that summer.

Anna Marie was extremely close to Beethoven. She would not have merely glanced at him without stopping her carriage, particularly in 1807. Only if Beethoven's perception had been wrong—he did say "*seemed* as if she glanced at me"—could this have been Anna Marie. She might not have seen him on the road, and that also could have been why she had seemed to ignore him. Plausible, but unlikely, for Beethoven, not only would have thought it strange for his dear friend to have seen him and not stopped, he would have been extremely hurt by her behavior. The other problem is that we have no evidence that she had been in Baden that year. It is not impossible for her to have been there, but Baden is south of Vienna, and both Jedlersee and Hernals are north and northwest of the city, respectively. Since she customarily spent summers at her estates, it is unlikely that she would have first traveled south to Baden. Of course, we know that Beethoven himself often went both south and north of the city in the same summer, so she certainly could have done the same, but we have no proof of that.

The most likely candidate for *M*, therefore, probably is Marie Bigot, not, as we have noted, because Beethoven loved her, but simply because she was a young and attractive wife and mother, a woman like one Beethoven wanted to be able to call his own. Her barest acknowledgement—real or imagined—or, at least, *his* glimpse of *her*, had once again stirred Beethoven's longing for marriage. What is interesting is that these desires did not send him at once to Josephine, who was there in Baden near him, but caused him instead to go to Heiligenstadt, very near to where Anna Marie was. His letter to Josephine indicates, in fact, that he was near Anna Marie twice, once at the beginning of September and again during the third week when he wrote his conciliatory letter to Josephine. As Anna Marie was one of the few people in whom he was able to confide, it would have been natural for him to express his feelings to her. If he had in any way indicated that he loved her, they both were aware that she was still married, even though in name only, and we cannot imagine him saying anything more to her other than something like "If only *you* were free..." As he had not declared his love for Josephine while she was still married to von Deym, he would not have done so as yet with Anna Marie, whose married state perhaps was still all too evident to him. Knowing that she was unable to give him what he wanted most, we believe Anna Marie had encouraged him to try once again to establish a romantic relationship with Josephine Brunswick, that she had been one of the "voices... whispering to me that you are...my only beloved" that he mentioned in his September letter. If Anna Marie *had* given this advice, and he had decided to take it, this would explain why, after so much time had passed, and after his first attempt to have more than a friendship with Josephine had failed, he was willing to approach her once again. It would also explain why Beethoven wrote to her from Heiligenstadt and not from Baden or Vienna, and why it had taken him almost two weeks to make this decision. It could not have been easy for him to ignore his wounded pride and take this risk. We do not believe he would have done so without someone giving him encouragement.

Unfortunately, Josephine was not to be swayed from her original decision, and it was not long before she made it clear to him that she would never give him more than her friendship. She did not allow him to visit her; in fact, he had been turned away from her door twice by the time he wrote the letter on the 20th. Her replies to him were cool: "My *friend* Beethoven," she pointedly called him. No doubt she had realized that her overture of friendship—likely given in Baden—had been misconstrued, and that he had been encouraged by her attention. She chose silence over being frank with him, which surely had hurt him more than the truth ever would have done. However she delivered her message to him, Beethoven certainly understood it all too well: "...it occurred to me again later on that—I was mistaken in you," he wrote to her. Shortly thereafter, Beethoven wrote his final letter to her. It was obviously one of farewell. We do not believe he would ever "mistake" her true feelings for him again.

While we do not mean to suggest that Beethoven's love for Josephine had not been genuine—his letters certainly reflect his sincere devotion to her—we are not entirely convinced that she had been his first choice. However much he may have loved Josephine, we believe that he had loved Anna Marie more, and that it had only been the respective marital situations of the two women—Anna Marie, separated but still married; Josephine, a marriageable widow—that had led him to pursue Josephine rather than the woman who was closer to him than almost any other person. Once he had decided to turn his attentions to Josephine, we believe he had been entirely faithful to her, until she herself turned him away.

The Baden note obviously is still frought with uncertainty. We have no way of knowing without a doubt to whom the *M* referred. But one thing is clear: in no way could it have referred to Antonie Brentano.

❖ 22 ❖
The Diabelli Variations

Another minor piece of evidence offered in favor of Antonie Brentano was the fact that Beethoven supposedly dedicated the *33 Diabelli Variations, Op. 120* to her. Although this dedication does exist, it is misleading. Beethoven's letters to his friend, Ferdinand Ries, disprove that Beethoven had intended to dedicate the *Variations* to Antonie. In fact, he never showed a strong inclination to dedicate anything at all to her.

On May 1, 1822, Beethoven wrote a letter to publisher Schlesinger that said: "As for the second sonata in A flat (Op. 110) I intend to dedicate it to someone and I will let you have the particulars about this in my next letter." To whom was he referring? The unsupported assumption is that he meant Antonie Brentano simply because one version did eventually end up dedicated to ber. However, at the time, he easily could have been considering someone else. The assumption was based solely on a brief note to Schindler that same year, in which Beethoven seemed to finally have made a decision:

> The two sonatas in A flat and C minor are to be dedicat-
> ed to Frau Brentano, nee Edle von Birkenstock. Nothing
> —to Ries—[1]

His mention of Ries indicates that his first inclination may have been a dedication of these works to him, but that he later

---

[1]Anderson, p. 982.

may have felt that he had a greater obligation to the Brentanos. But Beethoven was not firmly committed to this decision either, for later he changed his mind again, and when these two works, *Piano Sonatas Op. 110* and *Op. 111* were published by Moritz Schleinger in Paris, only *Op. 111* had a dedication, and that was to the Archduke Rudolph. A year later it was reissued by Clementi & Company and *did* have a dedication to Frau Brentano, most likely in gratitude for the 300 gulden the family had loaned him some time before.

The dedication of the *Diabelli Variations* was an entirely different matter, as Antonie had never been his first choice as the recipient of the dedication. Beethoven wrote to Ries on April 25, 1823:

> In a few weeks you will receive a new set of 33 variations on a theme, a work which I have dedicated to your wife.[2]

This was followed by another letter to Ries three months later on July 16, 1823, showing that his plans for the dedication had not changed.

My dear Ries!

> Presumably the variations will have reached London by now—I could not draft the dedication to your wife myself because I do not know her name. So write it out on behalf of your and your wife's friend [meaning himself]. Give your wife a surprise with this, for the fair sex likes to have surprises— Take whatever you can get for the variations for I shall be satisfied with anything. But I must stipulate that the only reward I shall accept for the dedication to your wife is a kiss which I am to receive from her in London.—[3]

There is no doubt that Beethoven had intended the *Diabelli Variations* to have been dedicated to Frau Ries. How then did Antonie become the recipient of the dedication? A letter written to Diabelli in May 1823 gives us a clue:

> For a whole three weeks I had in addition sore eyes (and by the doctor's orders I was forbidden to write or to read.)[4]

---

[2]Anderson, p. 1026.
[3]Anderson, p. 1064
[4]Anderson, p. 1039. .

Beethoven "sore eyes" were caused by conjunctivitis, a serious eye infection which lasted into 1824. Another letter, written to Ries on September 5, explains what happened to the dedication while Beethoven had been visually incapacitated:

My dear friend!

You say I ought to look about for someone to see to my affairs; well this was just what happened with the Variati[ons], namely, my brother and Schindler looked after them, but alas! how badly! The Variations were only to appear here after they had been published in London; but everything went wrong. The dedication to *Brentano* [i.e. Antonie] was only to be for Germany, *as I was under deep obligation to her and for the moment had nothing else to publish*. But everything was done through Schindler, a greater wretch on God's earth I have never known, an arch-scoundrel, whom I have sent about his business. In its place I can dedicate another work to your wife... I am sorry for both of us—and particularly about the Variations, seeing that I composed them more for London than for Vienna. It is not my fault.[5]

Thayer explained further: "The copy [of the Variations] made for London bore a dedication written in large letters by Beethoven to Madame Ries; but the printed copies were inscribed to Madame Brentano." Because of his eye troubles, Beethoven had entrusted the score to Schindler, and had not realized the mistake until it was too late to change the dedication back to what he had originally intended. Although the edition published by Cappi & Diabelli does contain a dedication to Frau Brentano, a manuscript copy made by Rampel and corrected by Beethoven, was dedicated to Frau Ries, the person to whom it rightfully belongs. This copy is now in the Beethovenhaus in Bonn, as part of the H.C. Bodmer collection.

Beethoven was quite angry with Schindler at this time, and the incident with *The Diabelli Variations* was at least one reason that a rift of several years' duration developed between them. Beethoven's fury is evident in two letters he wrote to Karl about Schindler around this time:

---

[5]Anderson, pp. 1086-1087.

> August 16, 1823: To Schindler, this contemptible object, I will send by you a few lines, for I do not want to have any direct communication with this wretched fellow.[6]

> August 23, 1823: ...he has a bad character, inclined to intrigue, and must be dealt with seriously.[7]

It has been suggested that these letters were induced by Beethoven's growing paranoia. However, it is clear that Schindler, while he may not have had the genuinely "bad character" Beethoven accused him of having, certainly took it upon himself —as he did in the case of other decisions—to make out the dedications without consulting Beethoven. The composer saw this incident as a broken promise to Ries, and such things angered him as nothing else.

COOL WORDS FOR A FORMER BELOVED

Looking again at Beethoven's September 5 letter to Ries, it is interesting how impersonally Beethoven referred to Antonie— as "Brentano." He shows a surprising lack of warmth toward her, someone he supposedly once called his "eternally beloved." Of course, his cool reference to her comes as no surprise to those who do not take seriously her candidacy as the Immortal Beloved, and to those who further consider the consternation she had caused him with her unwanted ardent attentions. We also see from this letter that Beethoven did not want her to have this dedication because he cared deeply for her, or because she was or had once been his Beloved, or even because he had loving memories of her. No, we see that he felt he was "under an obligation" to her, and that he had "for the moment nothing else to publish." As we shall see in the next chapter, Beethoven's letters to Antonie show that she may have assisted his dying brother, Caspar Carl, in selling an art object when Carl's illness had left him in financial difficulties. This was only one of the obligations he felt toward the Brentano family, which included several generous and interest-free loans of money to him, and Franz's willingness to serve as Beethoven's intermediary with the composer's Bonn publisher, Simrock. (See Chapter 23, *Letters to the Brentanos and Others*).

---

[6]Anderson, p. 1080
[7]Anderson, p. 1083.

In addition, the Brentanos apparently had offered Beethoven advice when he planned to send his nephew Karl to Father Sailer, a Catholic priest who was supposed to take over the boy's education. There are no existing letters to the Brentanos which mention Father Sailer, however he was discussed in Beethoven's conversation books. While one can concur that Beethoven had every reason to feel grateful to Antonie and Franz Brentano, gratitude, however deep, is hardly the same as an ardent passion.

The dedication of *The Diabelli Variations* was no different from Beethoven's inclination to dedicate other works of his, not only to the Brentano family, but to many other people, as his way of showing appreciation for the assistance given him by his friends. Although Solomon claimed that "the first and only full dedication to Antonie Brentano was in June 1823 [of *The Diabelli Variations*],"[8] we now know that is not true. The dedication was not Beethoven's doing, and at least one published version of the *Variations* has preserved the dedication as it was intended by Beethoven: to Frau Ries. Thus we may say with certainty that there were *no* full dedications of any work of Beethoven's to Antonie Brentano. Consequently, the *Variations* cannot be used even as a small piece of evidence to prove a romantic attachment by Beethoven to Frau Brentano.

---

[8] Solomon, *Essays,* p. 182.

❖ 23 ❖
LETTERS TO THE BRENTANOS
and Others

"As an example of the depth of Beethoven's feeling for Antonie in 1816," Solomon wrote, "we quote from his letter to her of February 6, 1816:"

> I am taking the opportunity afforded me by Herr Neate...
> to remind you and your kind husband Franz as well of
> my existence. At this same time I am sending you a
> copper engraving on which my face is stamped. Several
> people maintain that in this picture they can also dis-
> cern my soul quite clearly, but I offer no opinion on that
> point. In the meantime I have fought a battle for the
> purpose of wresting a poor unhappy child from the
> clutches of his unworthy mother and I have won the day.
> He is the source of many cares, but cares which are
> sweet to me. I wish you and Franz the deepest joys on
> earth, those which gladden our souls. I kiss and embrace
> all your dear children... But to you I send my best
> greetings and merely add that I gladly recall to mind the
> hours which I have spent in the company of both of you,
> hours which to me are the most unforgettable—
>
> With true and sincere regards,
> your admirer and friend
> (I know that you will be glad to welcome Herr Neate as
> a friend of mine.)[1]

---

[1]Anderson, pp. 557-558.

Pressed to provide at least one example of a letter which showed a modicum of "deep feeling" that Beethoven had for Antonie, it is not surprising that Solomon chose this particular letter. It is the *only* one that showed any "depth" at all—recalling unforgetable hours spent in the company of her *and her husband*—yet even that was hardly significant. None of Beethoven's surviving letters addressed to the Brentanos, or to Antonie herself, are in any way different—in depth of feeling—from those Beethoven wrote to other acquaintances, and are, in fact, much less intimate than those he wrote to many of his other friends. Time and again we have heard it argued that thus and such lady cannot have been the Immortal Beloved because Beethoven's letters to her do not contain the same passion inherent in the Beloved letter. Yet this argument is never leveled against Antonie Brentano, to whom Beethoven never wrote a single passionate word! Beethoven scholars have established an interesting double standard here, and one wonders why. Is it that they cannot bear to criticize the conclusions of one of their own?

During the precise time in which this sample letter was written, Beethoven was in regular communication with Sir Charles Neate, one of the founders of the London Philharmonic Society (June 1815 through 1816). Note that Beethoven mentioned that it was an "opportunity afforded by Herr Neate"—giving the latter an introduction to the Brentanos—that caused him to write this particular letter to the Brentanos in the first place. The three other letters were predominantly business-oriented, and they are presented here to give a clearer picture of Beethoven's relationship to the Brentanos, and to Antonie, than was afforded by Solomon:

Early November, 1815
Most Beloved Friend!

Having heard that you are in touch with Geymüller (a Viennese banker) I am therefore enclosing the testimonial—Indeed the receipts are rightly described as such — I am sorry that in spite of all your generosity to me you have to experience this as well —Truly our situation has again become very distressing owing to these wretched financial arrangements, the end of which is not yet in sight — There is another matter which I must tell you about. It's about a pipe bowl! A pipe-bowl!—Among the individuals (the number of which is infinite) who are now suffering, there is also my brother, [Caspar Carl, who died shortly thereafter] who on account of his poor health has had to retire on a pension. His position at the moment is very difficult. —He possesses a pipe-bowl which he believes he could dispose of most advantageously at Frankfurt. So on that account I am taking the liberty of asking you to let him send you this pipe-bowl. So many people are constantly calling at your house that perhaps you could manage to sell it— My brother thinks that you might possibly get ten louis d'or for it. He needs a lot of money... All good wishes my beloved friend. My heartfelt greetings to Franz and I wish him the happiest and most joyful life. My greetings also to your dear children.[2]

It should be noted that Antonie Brentano was not the only person to whom Beethoven applied for aid for Caspar Carl. Beethoven sent a similar request for assistance, on behalf of his brother, to Joseph von Varena in Graz. What is even more significant is that Carl himself appealed to another woman—Anna Marie Erdödy—and not to Antonie Brentano for help. He only would have done so had he been aware of a special relationship existing between the Countess and his brother, Ludwig. (Beethoven did not approve of Carl asking Anna Marie for help, and requested that she excuse him because of his illness.) To Frau Brentano Beethoven wrote again, on September 29, 1816:

All my difficult circumstances which, admittedly, are soon going to improve, have prevented me from hesitating to accept the cheque which you and F[ranz] have sent me. —I received it apparently from some stranger... I went to Pacher's (a bank) and... according to their statements, knew nothing of the person who had signed the cheque—Hence I thought it necessary to inform you at once; and I await your decisions in the matter—I understand nothing about business of this kind and therefore might easily have made some mistake—[3]

September 29, 1816 (a second letter written that same day)

I am introducing to you the son of Herr Simrock at Bonn. May I ask F[ranz] very politely to be so kind as

---

[2]Anderson, p. 531.
[3]Anderson, pp. 600-601.

to assist Herr Simrock in the event of his having to make payments to me here and to arrange for drafts to be forwarded to me in the least expensive way.— Otherwise I have no important news to send you from Vienna... I should like you to remember me for a moment with pleasure—[4]

Remember him for a *moment*? The woman with whom he supposedly shared such an ardent passion? That seems an odd thing to write to an "eternally beloved." The remainder of the second letter dealt with congratulating Franz on his new appointment as a senator in Frankfurt, and with the health of Beethoven's nephew, Karl. All the other survivng letters to the Brentanos are addressed *exclusively to Franz* with occasional "best regards" to Antonie and the children. This exclusivity, we think, may be significant if, indeed, the missing letters to Frankfurt, noted in Beethoven's *Tagebuch*, had been intended for Antonie Brentano.[5]

After three years of silence (1812-1815), we find Beethoven's first letter to her (noted here on pages 279-280). We suspect that his friendly overture may have inadvertently revived Antonie's romantic feelings for him. The missing letters may have been Beethoven's gentle but firm refusal, once again, to entertain any such ideas, and, if so, it is not surprising that their content had caused her to destroy them. These letters came at the precise time of the exasperated "T" notation in the *Tagebuch*, and thereafter —that is, after 1817—Beethoven never again wrote to Antonie directly. It must have become clear to him that a woman with her unstable emotional makeup was incapable of maintaining merely a friendship with him, which was all he had ever wanted.

To Franz Brentano, March 4, 1816

I am introducing to you, my dear friend, the chief connoisseur of wines in Europe, Herr Neberich. (The rest of the letter dealt primarily with Neberich's qualifications as a wine merchant.)[6]

---

[4]Anderson, pp. 601-602
[5]The *Tagebuch* does not give the name of the recipient(s), only that the letters had been sent to Frankfurt. As at this time Beethoven had been in correspondence with Ferdinand Kessler, who also lived in Frankfurt, we cannot know for certain for whom these letters had been intended.
[6]Anderson, p. 568.

To Franz Brentano, February 15, 1817

> Some time ago I sent you several musical works in order
> to recall myself to your friendly remembrance. All the
> members of the Brentano family have ever been dear to
> me; and you especially, my esteemed friend, I shall
> always remember you with sincere regard. I have prayed
> to Heaven for long preservation of your life so that for
> many years you may be usefully active for your family
> as its esteemed head— I very greatly miss your comp-
> any and that of your wife and your dear children.[7]

Beethoven was quite despondent and lonely in 1817, the
year this letter was written. Anna Marie had been gone over a
year and there was no indication when she might return to Vienna. He continued with his letter to Franz:

> For where can I find anything like it here in our Vi-
> enna... for I have never been able to get on with people
> unless there is some exchange of ideas. May you now
> and then call me to mind.— Best regards to my dear
> friend Toni.

There also were numerous letters addressed to publisher
Nikolaus Simrock in Bonn in which Franz Brentano was mentioned as Beethoven's intermediary. The letters to Simrock indicate that Beethoven sent Franz Brentano his musical scores
which the latter then forwarded on to the publisher, and Simrock
remitted payment to Beethoven through Brentano.

> Sir! Your good nature encourages me to hope that you
> will not refuse to have this enclosure forwarded to
> Simrock [in Bonn]. Nothing can be done now but to
> accept what he offers, namely, the 100 pistoles. As to
> what you as a business expert can obtain for me in
> addition by the valuation of the money, well, of course,
> I am convinced beforehand of your honorable intentions.[8]

Beethoven ended the letter with a casual: "My greetings to
all your family."

Beethoven explained why Franz was used as a go-between: "I received the fee very quickly through Herr Brentano,
and in future we shall keep to this method," Beethoven wrote to

---

[7]Anderson, pp.667-668.
[8]Anderson, p. 906.

Simrock. He sent a similar explanation to Adolf Schlesinger in
Berlin:

> The reason why I am asking you to send the fee to Herr
> von B[rentano] in particular, is that in any case I have
> sums to disburse and sometimes too to receive and Herr
> von B[rentano] is such a kind, lovable, and unselfish
> fellow who would do this in the least expensive way.[9]

Apparently, Franz was used as a go-between to get a better rate of exchange on the money due Beethoven, and facilitate
payment to him. Franz's son eventually moved to England, where
he, too, briefly served as an intermediary for Beethoven with London publishers. It is easy to see Beethoven's continuing obligation to the Brentanos, mentioned in his letter to Ries about the
Variations, in the following notes and letters:

> Journal note, 1814: I owe F.A.B. (Franz and Antonie
> Brentano) 2300 florins, that is 1100 f (florins) and 60#
> (ducats).

In order to reimburse the Brentanos, there was a notation
on Beethoven's calendar to sell a bank share. He later replaced
the share on Karl's behalf.

> To Franz Brentano, Sept. 13, 1822:
>
> Do please forgive me for delaying so long in discharging
> my debt to you. Once more I crave your forgiveness for
> this. I trust that if my health improves, as it appears to
> be improving here at Baden, I shall never again find
> myself in the position of making myself a nuisance to
> anyone. I shall always be grateful to you for your gen-
> erosity, and I can hardly wait for the moment when I
> shall no longer have to confess that I am deep in debt to
> you.[10]

Beethoven thought that as soon as he sold his Mass, he
would earn 1000 gulden, out of which he hoped to pay the Brentanos the money which had been owed them for several years:

> To Franz Brentano, March, 1823: You have heard noth-
> ing from me for a very long while. Meanwhile I trust

---

[9]Anderson, p. 933.
[10]Anderson, pp. 969-970.

that some time ago you received through Geymüller the
300 gulden which you lent me in such a noble way.[11]

To his attorney Johann Bach, August 1, 1824: If something comes of the negotiations with Mainz... the first
600 gulden should be paid to two of the most noble
persons who, when I was nearly destitute, lovingly
assisted me with this sum, lending it to me without
interest.[12]

This was apparently a second, or maybe even a third, loan
made to Beethoven by the Brentanos, since the first was referred
to as being 300 gulden, and his 1814 journal noted still a different
amount. It is not surprising that he felt such a deep obligation to
them, and why he had sometimes felt the need to dedicate pieces
of music to Antonie and her daughter.[13]

THE "INTERMEDIARY"

Solomon claimed "[Beethoven] acted as intermediary for
her [Antonie] in a proposed sale to his patron, Archduke Rudolph,
of rare manuscripts which [Antonie Brentano] owned."[14] This
statement makes it seem as if Beethoven had done his "Beloved"
an enormous favor by taking on a significant role in helping her
with her father's estate. This is an example of "elastic truth"—
truth which has been stretched to its limit until it is not nearly as
accurate as one would hope and expect. The actual extent to which
Beethoven served as an "intermediary" for Antonie Brentano was
very small indeed, as shown in the following letter.

To Joseph Anton Ignaz von Baumeister, July 3, 1811: I
am sending the titles of two old works which would be
suitable for the Archduke's library. Although the auction
of the Birkenstock library and collection of paintings
has not yet been held, Herr and Frau von Brentano (nee
Birkenstock) who live in the Erdbeergasse in the
Landstrasse, would certainly let the Archduke have
these works. In fact, I mentioned this to the Archduke

[11]Anderson, p. 1014.
[12]Anderson, p. 1135.
[13]As we know, it was not at all unusual for Beethoven to offer dedications of his
works to the family members of men to whom he was indebted, as in the case of
Ries.
[14]Solomon, p. 170.

when he was here. Hence, if you consider it advisable, you yourself may now discuss the matter with the owners for I do not know how old works of this kind should be sold—[15]

Johann von Birkenstock, Antonie's father, had been a famous art collector in Vienna. It is not accurate to suggest that Beethoven *assisted* Antonie with the selling of her father's collection. These are the only two works with which Beethoven dealt, and his involvement in their sale was a mere mention to the Archduke that they were available, if the latter were interested. His suggestion was far more for the benefit of the Archduke—who he thought would like to acquire the two manuscripts—than for the Brentanos, and Beethoven admitted he did not know anything about the selling of old works. He hardly could have served as Antonie's "intermediary" in this matter.

A LETTER OF DEDICATION

Beethoven dedicated his *Piano Sonata Op. 109*, to Maximiliane, the Brentano's daughter, a musically gifted girl. In his letter of dedication, addressed to her, he added a note to the Brentanos that it was given "as a token of my lasting devotion to you [Franz] and your whole family. But do not put any wrong construction on this dedication, by fancying that it is a hint to use your influence..."[16]

OTHER LETTERS: A COMPARISON

In regard to the importance of the February 6, 1816 letter Solomon quoted, it is unclear how a recollection of happy hours spent in the company of his two friends showed Beethoven's abiding love for Antonie. "Kisses and embraces" were something Beethoven sent regularly to nearly every one of his friends' family members, as the following few examples show:

To Wegeler 1810: "Embrace, kiss your worthy wife, your children, all that is dear to you."

---

[15]Anderson, p. 328.
[16]Anderson, pp. 933-934.

To Tiedge 1811 (a man he had only just met): "...to Amalie a right fiery kiss, when no one sees us, and we two embrace like men who love and dare to honor each other..."

To Count Lichnowsky 1814: "...I kiss the hands of the Princess [Christiane] a 1000 times for her thoughts and good wishes..."

To Anna Marie Erdödy 1816: "Dear dear dear dear dear Countess!...press kisses on your dear children..."

To Dr. Kanka [his attorney!] 1816: "My dear, beloved and affectionate Kanka... I kiss and press you to my heart..."

To Dr. Joseph Reger, another lawyer in Prague 1815 : "My beloved friend That is what I call you, and as my beloved friend, I shall one day embrace you— Kiss Gloschek [yet another lawyer!] for me.

People of the twentieth century often view this flowery language as being indicative of unusual depth of feeling. Yet it was perfectly natural, everyday speech with no special connotation for those living in the nineteenth century. Certainly most of us would not kiss and press our beloved attorney to our hearts! Yet sending hearty kisses and embraces in one's letters in Beethoven's time—to virtually anyone who was remotely a friend—was no different than our signing our personal letters "Love,...." or "Best regards." A combination of normal nineteenth century speech with Beethoven's natural exuberance in expressing himself in letters, gives an inordinate "depth of feeling" even when he wrote to male friends, such as "dear beloved Amenda" or

My good, dear Wegeler!

... That I could ever forget you, and especially all of you who were so kind and affectionate to me, no, do not believe it; thereare moments in which I myself long for you, yes, and wish to spend some time with you... Farewell, good, faithful Wegeler! Rest assured of the love and friendship of

Your Beethoven

The most important letters are those which are not simply filled with conventional "kisses and embraces," but rather are those lengthy epistles concerning mundane issues. True intimacy is not shown in "I kiss the hands of the Countess a thousand times" but rather in "[My physician] succeeded almost entirely in checking this violent diarrhea. He ordered tepid Danube baths, and I had to pour into it a little bottle of strengthening stuff..." and in "I had to rub myself three times with a volatile ointment... yesterday I received a new medicine, namely, a tincture of which I have to take twelve teaspoonfuls a day..." The former he wrote to his boyhood friend Wegeler, the latter to Anna Marie Erdödy. We do not write of our ills and ailments to mere acquaintances. We write them to those intimate friends who we know are truly interested in our well-being. It is to them that we impart our little joys and sorrows, our good health or ill, our small triumphs and tragedies, for they are the ones who care about us on a day-to-day basis. They also are sent the "kisses and embraces," but they receive so much more: our real selves, our unadorned selves, an openness of our spirits that is granted to only a very few. In this way the letter of 1812 was addressed not so much to an Immortal Beloved as it was to a Beloved Intimate.

Many biographers have felt that the Beloved letter is somewhat manic-depressive, confused in thought and expression, wildly jumping from subject to subject, with the confusion caused by raging and conflicting emotions: ardent desire at odds with fear of commitment. Yet by that standard, the letter to the Beloved is not much different than most of Beethoven's other letters. One example is an amusing letter Beethoven wrote to Sir Charles Neate in London. In it, Beethoven at first ranted and raved, and then, without so much as an intervening breath, closed quite calmly and cordially:

> I swear that *you have done nothing* for me and that you will do nothing again *nothing* for me, summa summarum, *nothing! nothing! nothing!!* I assure you of my most absolute regard and I hope at least for a last favor in the form of an early reply [about his sonatas].Your most devoted servant and friend.[17]

Jumping from subject to subject and displaying a wide range of emotions within the space of a few sentences was a com-

---

[17]Anderson, p. 681.

mon characteristic of the composer's correspondence. Letters normally reflected his fluctuating emotional energy. It was rare for him to write a letter which was not interspersed with bits of news, personal philosophy, and opinions, all expressed with a vividness that was typical Beethoven. Often, the more intimately he knew his addressee, the greater was the "confusion." But isn't that the nature of any letter we ourselves might send to our closest friends, those who understand us best? In business letters our language endeavors to be clear, concise, careful and deliberate. Our ideas flow with logic. We restrain our inclinations to include anything irrelevant. But in personal correspondence we need not be so rigid. We can move from the sublime, "My angel, my all, my self..." to the mundane mention of a pencil or a mishap on a journey, because we know that all those things are supremely important to the ones addressed. Our true intimates are those who are never bored by such trivialities, who accept our philosophies with enjoyment and understanding, our complaints with tolerance and sympathy, and our bits of pedestrian news with genuine interest. They are the ones who know us so well that the connecting thoughts, which might make for better, less "confused" letters in terms of flow and grammar, are unnecessary. The connections—the "sorting out" of our written thoughts—are made by the sheer understanding which is born of a long-term and intimate relationship.

It was no different for Beethoven than for us. Without having to ask, Beethoven knew that Franz Wegeler would be interested in the frustrations of his deafness and his annoying bouts of diarrhea, and that Anna Marie Erdödy would want to know the details of the treatments he was taking. We cannot imagine him expressing such personal things to people who were less than supremely intimate with him. Even if they had inquired about his health, he need not and would not have gone into such great detail. With these few intimates he could trust in their concern, in their desire to truly know, not simply receive assurance that all was "fine." And so it was with his Beloved. He was confident that she would be interested in hearing of the inconvenience of his carriage breaking down on the road, the time he had to waste waiting for a room, and that he was using a pencil she had given him. These things would mean nearly as much to her as hearing of his abiding love for her, because they allowed her to share his day-to-day life. With his Beloved he did not need to censor his thoughts, or compose them so that they flowed gracefully and coherently, or worry that his meaning might be misconstrued by a misplaced phrase. Beethoven did not write any of his letters with future biographers or psychoanalysts in mind, or with any concern that a stranger would misread or misinterpret what he wrote. The Beloved letter had been for *her* eyes, and hers alone. He knew she would understand what he wrote, and that was all that mattered to him. His devotion to the Beloved and the intimacy he shared with her is evident by what and how he wrote to her. Their love lived not only in the vaults of heaven, but also was firmly rooted in the earth.

It is easy to see the obvious endearments in Beethoven's letters to Antonie and Franz, the remembrances of good times past. But the small things, the commonplace things which he shared with his true intimates—and his supremely Beloved intimate—are obviously missing from them. Beethoven did not grant the Brentanos quite the same look into his heart, his life, and his soul as he did to those who truly were closest to him.

❖ *24* ❖
Songs to the Beloved

Most of Beethoven's creative periods centered around the presence of a beloved in his life. Not all scholars would agree with that. Some feel that Beethoven was able to separate what was happening in his life from his music, rather than his music being a reflection of his life. As this author believes the man's heart was too much a part of his music for this to be true, we must take the opposite stance: that love, and both the happiness and tragedy which accompanied it, was most often the inspiration for his finest works. There also is an interesting recurrence of musical themes in Beethoven's compositions relating to Anna Marie Erdödy, as well as an abundance of music composed whenever she was in his life.

Dana Steichen's 1959 study of Beethoven's beloved used his music as "the only mirror free of all distortion." She recognized two themes which occurred in nearly all of Beethoven's compositions whenever he was closely associated with Countess Erdödy. Mrs. Steichen named these two themes "The Beloved Theme" and "The Goddess Theme." Beethoven had an acute interest in Egyptian literature and philosophy. Framed and under glass on his desk, he kept several quotes written in his own hand —the originals of which were inscribed on an ancient temple of Isis, the goddess of nature, fertility, and resurrection:

I am that which is.
I am everything that is, that was, that will be.

No mortal man has lifted my veil.
He is himself alone and it is to this aloneness
that all things owe their being.

What makes these interesting is that Beethoven made
several references to Anna Marie in which she was portrayed as
a goddess herself. In an October 1815 letter to Anna Marie, he
wrote "God give you further strength to reach your *Isis temple*
where the refining fire will consume all your evil and you will
arise a new Phoenix." This referred to a monument she had erected on one of her Hungarian estates on which was inscribed a
loving dedication to Beethoven. It is not a surprising comparison.
As the Egyptian goddess of Nature had restored her beloved to
life, so had the Countess restored a despondent, almost suicidal
Beethoven in the early 1800s to his own life, and regularly shared
with him the beauties of nature. In that same letter to her, he
referred to her—and to himself—as "we mortals with immortal
minds."

Anna Marie was the goddess of his music, as well. In one
of his songs, *Lied aus der Ferne*, (Song from the Distance) written
in 1809, is the line *Die Gottin sei du*,[1] literally, "the goddess is
you," from where Mrs. Steichen took the name for one of
Beethoven's recurring musical themes. Dale S. Kugel from the
Julliard School of Music, in an afterword in Mrs. Steichen's book,
confirmed the latter's discovery:

> That both the above themes [the other being "the Beloved
> Theme"] appear exactly, or in slightly altered form in
> virtually every composition of Beethoven is undisputable.
> In her original manuscript, Mrs. Steichen gives many
> examples from Beethoven's scores to show the recurrence
> of the two "themes;" there are more than forty alone in
> which the first of the two musical ideas given above [the
> "beloved theme"] figures as part of the material used.
> The examples indicate the way in which Beethoven
> often used thematic, melodic material close to his heart
> as raw material for entirely "new" compositions."[2]

Mrs. Steichen wrote that "We had found Beethoven's beloved in his music, where she surely would be." In looking at a
chronology of his works and the people and events in his life at the
time of their development and completion, we find that Anna

---

[1]The title uses the familiar *Du*-form of address.
[2]Steichen, pp. 502-506.

Marie Erdödy was the spark that most often ignited Beethoven's creative genius. (See Appendix B.)

"TO THE BELOVED"

Had there been any significance in Beethoven giving Antonie Brentano the autograph scored for guitar for the song *An die Geliebte*? ("To the Beloved")? First, Ferdinand Ries tells us that

> Beethoven attached no importance to his autograph compositions. In most cases, once they had been engraved, they lay about... scattered over the floor. I could have carried off all those original autograph compositions... and had I asked him for them, I am sure he would have given them to me without a moment's hesitation.[3]

Although we cannot always be certain that Ries is a reliable source of information, Beethoven's own nephew, Karl, corroborated Ries's observation in a note he wrote to Beethoven in his conversation book:

> Don't give your original manuscripts away. They can always be sold for a good price. Some day they will be worth more. You can tell that by the autographs of famous men.[4]

Gerhard von Breuning also corroborated this in his book *Aus dem Schwarzspanierhause*:

> I have none of all the valuable manuscripts and autographs that got into other hands...because my father had strictly forbidden me to take even the smallest scrap of what Beethoven, when alive, would have given me by the armful if it had entered my mind to ask him for it.[5]

Schindler made a similar observation:

> Shortly before his death, Beethoven entrusted to me the score of the original Fidelio overture... with the specific injunction that I should keep the whole bundle in a safe

[3]Wegeler & Ries, pp. 100-101.
[4]Thayer/Forbes, pp. 488-489.
[5]Breuning, p. 114.

place. This request is significant, for he had not shown concern about the preservation of any of his other manuscripts.[6]

Thayer also confirmed this habit of Beethoven's by noting the small number of autographs listed in the auction catalog of the composer's posthumous papers. Apparently, Beethoven had given most of them away to friends who had wanted them.

When the song *An die Geliebte* was given to Antonie Brentano, she wrote upon it: "Den 2tn März, 1812 mir vom Author erbethen." ("Requested by me from the author on March 2, 1812.") It is interesting that Antonie had to *request* it from Beethoven; he did not give it to her unasked. Surely he would have done so, had he written it for her. Not only that, but the original version of the song had been published in December the preceding year, and it was not until *four months later* that she received her copy.

Solomon noted that

> The song—with an arpeggiated triplet accompaniment—was published as a "Lied... [song] with piano or guitar accompaniment," the only such designation in Beethoven's Lieder output. Since Antonie was an expert guitarist, this can be taken as additional evidence that the song was actually composed for her.[7]

This is another one of those "elastic truths." While it may have been the only *Lied* arrangement for a guitar that Beethoven had ever *published*, it was not the only *Lied* for guitar that he had ever *written or arranged*. In Beethoven's letter to Therese Malfatti, May 1810, he wrote:

> Kindly give your dear sister Nanette [Anna] the song [Lied] arranged for guitar. The song [Gesang] too would have been copied out, but I had too little time.[8]

Guitars and mandolins were extremely popular in Beethoven's time. Anton Diabelli was originally a guitarist, as was Gottfried Mylich, who came to Vienna in 1798 and belonged to the circle of Beethoven and Amenda. Beethoven's friend Wenzel Krumpholz was a virtuoso on the mandolin. Beethoven wrote

---

[6]Schindler, p. 129. It is unknown whether Schindler actually had received the manuscript or he had pilfered it, but this does not invalidate his observation.
[7]Solomon, p. 175.
[8]Anderson, p. 273.

several pieces for that instrument, of which two, a *Sonatina* and an *Adagio*, were published in the *Complete Works Series 25*. Nottebohm placed these works in the year 1805.[9] Beethoven was still friendly with the Malfattis up to 1817. Who is to say that it had not been Anna Malfatti who had requested the guitar arrangement of the piano score—which had been written for his instrument of choice—and then Antonie, also a guitarist, had seen it or heard it, and asked for a copy for herself? This was not unheard of, since the composer was known to transcribe arrangements for other friends. For example, for his new physician, Dr. Johann Schmidt, he arranged his *Septet Op. 20*, originally for four strings and three winds, making it suitable for family use. Beethoven converted much of his *Fidelio* score into pieces suitable for quartets and quintets for the Erdödy family. In fact, it had been through these arrangements that the Erdödys had come to love the opera so much that they named their family dog *Fidelio*. Therefore, it does not follow that Beethoven originally *wrote* the song for Antonie, when the most he had done was create the guitar arrangement at her request, as he had done with the song for Anna Malfatti the year before. This also would explain why a third of a year passed before Antonie received a copy.

The writing and publishing of *An die Geliebte* had taken place shortly after Beethoven's reconciliation with Anna Marie following their bitter separation. The poem's author, Johann Ludwig Stoll, had been a friend of Beethoven's for several years. Beethoven's friend, Grillparzer recalled that the two men met at coffeehouses, and sometimes talked of collaborating on an opera (which, of course, never materialized). When Stoll offered his poem[10] to Beethoven, the latter seized upon the opportunity to create yet another song which expressed his deep feelings for his Countess who had so recently returned to him.

Interestingly, Beethoven had this Beloved song reissued for publication in 1814, when once again he resumed his relations with Anna Marie after another brief separation, and following his receipt of her conciliatory gift as noted in his *Tagebuch*.

---

[9]Nettl, p. 130.
[10]Franz Schubert liked the poem as well, and wrote his own musical accompaniment for it in 1815.

"THE JOY OF FRIENDSHIP"

Songs similar to *An die Geliebte* were written at other times when the Countess was a prominent figure in Beethoven's life. For example, in 1802, after spending the summer with Anna Marie at her estate in Jedlersee, Beethoven wrote the song *The Joy of Friendship* (although we believe the word "friendship" can be considered a misnomer). The lyrics he chose to set to music read:

> He lives a life of rapture whose heart a heart wins.
> Shared joy doubles itself and shared grief melts away.
> He wanders down a flowered path with trusting escort on
> The arm of golden friendship given at this time.
> She awakens strength and spurs courage to beautiful deeds
> And nourishes in us the holy glow for truth and Nature
> Achieved has been luck's goal who has a friend found
> With whom love's tender feeling has him innerly bound
>
> Enraptured by her companionship the path of life
> Becomes a beauteous way. Through her alone blooms
> For him the world and everything smiles at him.
> He lives a life of rapture whose heart a heart wins.[11]

Beethoven used a variation on this same melody in his *Violoncello Sonata Opus 102 #2* which he composed for Anna Marie when they were happily together again in 1815. Since he had written the Op. 102 sonata for her, he had planned to dedicate it to Anna Marie as well, but for political and economic reasons, he briefly considered changing the dedication to Charles Neate of the London Philharmonic, a change he ultimately did not make. In light of this consideration, he wrote to Anna Marie, May 15, 1816: "There will be a change in the dedication, but this will not change you and me, Dear cherished Countess."

THE BELOVED SEPARATES

The year 1809, in which Beethoven first became friendly with the Brentanos, was the one in which he and Anna Marie quarrelled and separated. How deep is the anguish in the follow-

---

[11]Lyrics for all songs taken from the translated German text given in *Ludwig van Beethoven: Songs (Complete)*, Kalmus Vocal Series, New York: Edwin F. Kalmus Publisher n.d.

ing song he published shortly thereafter under the title: *Als die Geliebte sich trennen wollte* (translated literally from the German "As the Beloved Herself Wished to Separate"). The melody for this was originally composed in 1806 under the title *Empfindungen bei Lydiens Untreue*[12] (literally, "Feelings over Lydia's Disloyalty"), but its second publication was by Breitkopf & Härtel in 1809 under the Beloved title. It also is known by the title "At Parting from the Beloved." While it is true that Beethoven did not write the words to this song, he was quite selective about what text he chose to set to music. Nettl noted that:

> Whereas Haydn and Mozart used many inferior text [in their songs], Beethoven was very text conscious.[13] Beethoven struggled especially hard when setting words to music. Nottebohm shows in the *Beethoveniana* (II, 332) how Beethoven rewrote the beginning of the song *Sehnsucht* sixteen times. The same hard work is apparent from the sketches to the song *Adelaide* and the cycle *An die ferne Geliebte*.[14]

Out of all the poems he could have chosen, he selected this one. How appropriately its words reflect his quarrel with Anna Marie:

> So the last ray of hope hath now declin'd.
> Her vows are broken, fickle is her mind,
> And now I lose in infinite unrest,
> All consciousness that I was once so blessed!
> What said I? Still her charms enslave me
> No pow'r on earth, no force can ever save me;
> Yet when I reach the brink of wild despair
> Sweet memories stay with me there.
>
> Ah, gentle hope, to me once more returning
> Revive the fire within me burning
> Though love's sufferings indeed are great,
> Yet he who loves would never change his fate!
> And thou who all my love so true disdain,
> Thy image will within my heart remain.
> I could not hate thee, but love you more
> Forget thee? Not till this life of woe be o'er.

---

[12]An interesting title considering the sudden cessation of letters to Josephine around that time.
[13]Nettl, p. 122.
[14]Nettl, p. 234.

Mrs. Steichen noted that this same melody opened the Cavatina of the *B-flat major String Quartet #6, Op. 130*, the *Leibquartett* mentioned in his conversation books. The quartet was begun when Countess Erdödy was in Vienna in 1823, and was finished after she had left for the last time. It is no wonder, then, that it is a piece which moves between lighthearted joy and "La Melanconia" [Melancholy], a reflection of the emotions she alone was able to stir within him. When it was performed in 1826, Beethoven confided to Holz that the Cavatina had cost him many tears and

> ...that nothing that he had written had so moved him; in fact, that merely to revive it afterwards in his thoughts and feelings brought forth renewed tributes of tears.[15]

This music, filled with bittersweet memories of the year in which it had been sketched,was a perfect reflection of his despair at his final parting from his Beloved. Sullivan wrote the following about that Cavatina:

> That terrible yearning, a heartache which expresses itself both as a prayer and a sob, is surely the inspiration of one of Beethoven's last and most intimate confessions, the Cavatina of the B flat quartet. There is here sorrow without hope, sorrow for what is irrevocable, and a longing for what has not been and never could be...[16]

TO HIS BELOVED, AGAIN AND AGAIN

"Dry Not, Tears of Eternal Love," also was composed in 1810. Again, it was a song which closely followed both his separation from his Countess, and Josephine's marriage to Stackelberg that year, although his despondency is evident beginning early in 1809 and had no connection to her remarriage in 1810, as Josephine's supporters claim. Although Bettina Brentano said that Beethoven had written the song for her, given her unreliable nature, that is not likely. Besides, Beethoven had only just met her and hardly had any reason to shed tears of eternal love for her. The song was dedicated to Princess Kinsky, and a copy was inscribed to Antonie Brentano. We see little significance in this,

---

[15]Steichen, p. 466.
[16]Sullivan, pp 157-158.

however, for asking for a celebrity's autograph, and his com-
plying with the request, hardly is an indication that he is in love
with the requisitioner.

Another song which bore a similar title, *An den fernen
Geliebten* (To the Distantly Beloved), was composed in 1809—
again, that same tragic year in which Beethoven devoted time to
composing music for sad or wistful love songs—and was published by both Artaria and Breitkopf & Härtel in 1810. In 1809,
too, Beethoven set one of Goethe's poems "Herz, mein Herz, was
soll das geben" to music. The lyrics read, in part:

> Heart, my heart, what means this surging
> This oppressive wearying stress?
> Whither are these feelings urging
> Me? I know not, I confess.

"TO HOPE"

In 1800, Beethoven had composed *An die Hoffnung* ("To
Hope)" from Christoph Tiedge's poem *Urania*. Lichnowsky had
come across the score in 1805 while in Beethoven's apartment and
assumed—probably correctly—that it had been written for Josephine Brunswick. It was obviously a song for a beloved, or Lichnowsky would not have thought that she had been the inspiration. It is interesting that Beethoven recomposed *An die Hoffnung*
in 1813, on the heels of the Beloved letter—which was filled with
guarded hope—and following his second quarrel with Anna
Marie. It was one of the songs he asked be sent to Countess
Erdödy while she was away from Vienna between 1816 and 1818.

"TO THE DISTANT BELOVED"

Anna Marie and Beethoven had spent a great deal of time
together in 1815. It had been a happy year for them until his
brother's death. From late 1815 through 1818, Anna Marie
moved between Italy, Germany, and Croatia, to take care of
business with land she had acquired there, stopping in Vienna in
1816 during the course of her travels. It was at the time of her
leaving that Beethoven began work on *An die ferne Geliebte*, "To
the Distant Beloved," which used the poem by Alois Jeitteles. This
was the same song Beethoven played for the Giannatasio sisters
which prompted remarks about the Distant Beloved recorded in

Fanny Giannatasio's diary. Fanny's first impression was that "the new song brought tears to my eyes, the heart has written it."

Beethoven's 1815-1816 sketchbooks contain, among other works, 50 sketches for a sixth piano concerto (in D), a symphony in B minor (what would have been the Tenth), a Bacchus opera. Clearly he had many significant projects on which to work, yet he abandoned these in order to compose this song and the *Op. 101 Piano Sonata* on the score of which he wrote, "slowly and full of longing." The sixth piano concerto, the new opera, and the tenth symphony would never be finished; such was his consuming need to commune with his now-distant Beloved through music. "To the Distant Beloved" was finished in April 1816, published by Steiner in mid-December of that year, and immediately thereafter, Beethoven wrote to the publisher asking that copies of it and several other songs be sent to him quickly so that he could send them on to Anna Marie via Linke. Josephine supporters believe he had written the song for her, but why then had he sent one of the first copies to another woman? Besides the newly published "Distant Beloved," another song he requested for Anna Marie was entitled "A Man of His Word." The words to this song are revealing:

> You said, my friend, and said it clear:
> I shall come back and meet you here.
> You never came; then, pray, who can
> Put any faith in such a man?
> No greater man there is
> Than he who keeps his word...
> Who breaks it, e'en as women can,
> Does not deserve the name of man...

Had Anna Marie promised to return to him quickly but failed to keep that promise? His letters show she was in Vienna sometime in 1816. Had her trip there been in response to his reminder of her promise?

As we shall see, life for Beethoven from this time on began to deteriorate, and the year 1817 was one of the worst of the composer's life. He became more and more despondent, almost suicidal, and frequently thought of death. Why? Surely a main reason was his messy custody battle over Karl which drained him of his energy, his creativity, and very nearly his life force. We also believe his despair came from the fact that his Beloved stayed away from him too long, and his loneliness threatened to overwhelm him. We say this because although his problems with the custody suit remained through 1820, his depression lifted when Anna Marie returned to Vienna in 1819.

Through her children's tutor, Brauchle, Anna Marie had requested some music for them. Linke had brought the request, and his return to her employ was the "opportunity to send it off" Beethoven had mentioned in his letter to Steiner. The "Distant Beloved" song cycle says, in part:

> Take to your heart these songs that
> I sang to you, beloved...
> On the hilltop I sit gazing into the far-off blue
> Looking at the distant fields... where I you
> Beloved found. Far am I from thee separated,
> Divided by mountains and valleys that lie
> Between us and our peace, our happiness.
>
> Then through these songs
> What separated us so far melts away
> And a loving heart is reached by
> What a loving heart consecrated.

What emotion these unexpected gifts must have stirred within her. Fanny's diary shows that shortly thereafter, in January of 1817, the Giannatasio sisters noticed Beethoven wearing a gold ring he had not worn before. Nanny went so far as to tease him about it, wondering whether some other woman had captured his heart from the Distant Beloved. Fanny did not give Beethoven's precise response but wrote: "His meaningful answer to her childish question aroused in me a bitter sad feeling that bordered on jealousy." Fanny's jealous reaction to Beethoven's response about the ring indicates that it had been a gift from a woman close to his heart, and not from a patron or admirer. The love relationship most biographers cannot see clearly was very much alive, but if they could not recognize it prior to 1812, it is no wonder that they failed to see it afterwards when it became even less obvious. While it is possible that Josephine had sent the ring to Beethoven, as her supporters believe, we wonder if he would have accepted a valuable gift from a woman who was as destitute as Josephine was at the time. We believe it far more likely that, given the date when he began wearing it, and its connection to his Distant Beloved as noted by the Giannatasios, that it had come from the woman to whom he had only just sent his heartfelt songs, as a reciprocal token of her love.

To the Goddess

The choral finale of the Ninth Symphony, completed in 1823 when records show that Anna Marie was once again in Vienna, was not only Beethoven's tribute to brotherhood but also to a love far more personal and intimate. Beethoven used only half the words in Schiller's original poem, and rearranged them to suit himself and occasionally added his own. The usual English versions of the finale often drift from the meaning of the German words as Beethoven intended them. The literal German translation of the words Beethoven intended to be used are these:

> Joy, joy, transport of joy, joy!
> Beautiful divine spark of the gods
> Daughter out of Elysium (paradise)
> Intoxicated with thy fire, heavenly one,
> We enter thy sanctuary.
> Thy charms bind again.
> In the great gamble of life,
> He who has succeeded
> A friend's friend to be,
> Who a lovely woman has won,
> Mingles his jubilation with ours!
> Yes, if only one soul he can call his
> In the whole world!
> Kisses gave she us, and wine,
> A friend tried until death,
> Bliss has been given to the worm,
> And the Cherubim stand before God.

Once again we see the goddess present in his music, and it is obvious who had been the lovely woman won, the one soul he had been able to call his, whose fire ever intoxicated him, in whose sanctuary he had taken refuge, whose charms had ever bound him to her, and who had given him kisses and wine.

❖ 25 ❖
The Portraits

THE SIGNIFICANCE OF PORTRAITURE

"Beethoven sent a good many copies of the engraving [by Blasius Höfel after a drawing by Louis Letronne] to his friends," Landon noted. All manner of people associated with Beethoven, from close friends to barest acquaintances owned portraits of him. Some people asked for paintings of the composer to hang in their apartments while visiting Vienna, and Beethoven often obliged them. Beethoven wrote to painter Joseph Mähler: "I beg you to return my portrait to me— I have promised the portrait to a stranger, a lady who saw it here, that she may hang it in her room during her stay of several weeks."[1] Despite Solomon's assertion that "the gift of ... a miniature to a member of the opposite sex was often intended (and regarded) in Beethoven's time as something more than an expression of esteem,"[2] Beethoven's attitude shows that this observation does not apply to him. However

---

[1]Anderson, p. 125. Solomon used the last line of this letter, which read, "It is clearly understood, of course, that if all kinds of favors are going to be bestowed on me for this, your share will not be forgotten—" in an attempt to prove that Beethoven exchanged his portraits for sex. If so, would Beethoven had said to the artist that he would not forget his "share?" That would mean that Beethoven, in bed with this grateful woman with whom he had just had sex, turned to her and asked her to give herself also to the artist, as he deserved a fair share of her sexual favors. That is plainly ridiculous. Beethoven obviously was joking, but his humor was lost on his biographer.
[2]Solomon, p. 176.

others may have regarded the exchange of personal portraits, the sheer number of portraits and personally inscribed lithographs that Beethoven handed out shows that he regarded them much as we today look upon snapshots, or as a modern celebrity views the distribution of personal 8x10 "glossies:" as simple tokens of friendship, good will, or public relations.

One case in point was Joseph Stumpf, a musician and harp manufacturer, who met Beethoven in 1824. They had several dinners together, and Beethoven played for him on his Broadwood piano, the strings of which Stumpf had had repaired for him. He was not a close friend by any means, yet, at parting, Beethoven gave him one of his portraits as a remembrance. As another example, Beethoven gave a portrait to another casual acquaintance in 1814:

> Here, my dear Huber [identity not determined] you are receiving the promised copper engraving [by Letronne]. Since your yourself thought it worth while to ask me for it, surely I need not fear to be accused of vanity in letting you have it.[3]

Beethoven also collected portraits without attaching any great significance to them. To Joseph von Varena he wrote, July 4, 1813, "Thanks for your painting. What is the object of all this?" He also kept miniature portraist of some "unknowns," one of which may have either been Guilietta Guicciardi, or one of the Brunswick sisters—Therese or Charlotte—and another which we will speak more of later in this chapter. We know from letters that, at one time, he owned portraits of other friends: "I still have the silhouette of Lorchen..." he wrote to Wegeler in December of 1826, "so you see how precious to me even now are all the dear, beloved memories of my youth." And to Therese Brunswick, January 1811, Beethoven wrote "I still owe you most loving thanks for your beautiful picture." Anderson's footnotes indicate that this was an oil painting of Therese painted by J. B. Lampi which has a dedication to Beethoven on the back. It was in the composer's possession at the time of his death[4] even though she simply was a dear friend and not a beloved. Given his changes in lodgings and the complete disarray of his living quarters, the fact that many of them were lost over the years is not surprising.

---

[3]Anderson, p. 484.
[4]Anderson, p. 311.

THREE PORTRAITS...SAME WOMAN?

Solomon presented three portraits he claimed were all of the same woman—Antonie Brentano—remarking that the "resemblance between them is... especially striking." It is? A *striking* resemblance should be apparent at first glance, but there is nothing of the like among these portraits.

The first portrait Solomon presented was is an authenticated one of Antonie Brentano from 1798, taken from the Brentano estate in Winkle, Germany. The second was also Frau Brentano as painted by Stieler in 1808. The third was dated in Solomon's book as circa 1812.

Antonie Brentano, 1798

Unknown "1812"

Of these, it was the third one which had been owned by Beethoven and found among his personal effects. Naturally it would be that portrait which Solomon would call into question, since it long has been assumed to be that of Countess Anna Marie Erdödy. His challenge, while not surprising, is unconvincing.

No one, including Solomon, has been clear as to who made this identification, although he assumed it to have been A. C. Kalischer (a biographer circa 1890). How did this assumption come about? Following Beethoven's death, the portrait came into the possession of his friend, Stephen Breuning, who surely knew the Countess. If Breuning did not identify it to someone, how did Kalischer (if he was the one who identified it), with all the women that

Antonie Brentano, 1808

Beethoven knew, even venture a guess as to whose portrait it was? Breuning died less than three months after Beethoven, and whether Breuning had identified the portrait to his widow or anyone else before he died is not known. Interestingly, Schindler, who must have known Countess Erdödy since he had been in Beethoven's close association for four years before the Countess left Vienna, makes no mention of the portrait at all. Had he been reluctant to identify and thus compromise her?

COMPARISON

In comparing the portraits, Solomon said that "Frau Brentano's face became fuller with the passage of time, and her chin somewhat more prominent." Yet it is in the *earlier* portrait, the one done in 1798, that the face is fuller, rounder, not in the other one. In the latter, the cheekbones are clearly visible, and the woman's face is petite and delicate. We note that Reichardt described Anna Marie as being a "pretty, small, fine woman."

Points of resemblance that Solomon noted included:

• **the color and almond shape of the eyes.** Both sets of eyes are brown, true, but that hardly is an unusual color. In the 1798 portrait the eyes are far from "almond" shaped; they are decidedly round, heavy-lidded, and sad.

• **the curl and color of the hair.** In viewing color renditions of these two portraits,[5] the hair in the 1789 portrait is brown, frizzy, and has ashen tones, while in the "1812" portrait, the hair, although also brown, has golden tones and strong red highlights[6], and has visibly thicker and smoother texture. What has not been noted is the similarity of the hairstyles, as if women of any century tend to retain the same hairstyle for 14 years! This causes one to wonder: is the 1812 date of the second portrait accurate? A look at the woman's clothing says no. With the Napo-

---

[5]The 1812 portrait is found in color in Alan Pryce-Jones's *Beethoven*, 1957, and Antonie Brentano's color portrait is in H.C. Robbins Landon's 1954 *Beethoven*.
[6]Specht described Countess Erdödy as having reddish-brown hair. One might conclude he had written this description using the miniature, but he added that she had a sprinkling of freckles, not obvious in the portrait. His description must have come from another source.

leonic period (1789-1804) came the influence of the Empress Josephine on women's fashions. During this time, the Directoire style, a neoclassic trend, saw loose fitting skirts with high waistlines, usually in a white sheer fabric, worn with overdrapery in gay primary colors. The color reproduction of the "1812" portrait shows exactly this: the classic, high-waisted gown, low-necked bodice, and an overdrapery of green trimmed in red. This style, popular around 1796, went out of fashion about 1804, and most definitely would not have been in vogue as late as 1812, two years after Napoleon divorced Empress Josephine. We would have to believe that a wealthy woman like Antonie Brentano still was wearing the same dress she had bought twelve years earlier. As such, the 1812 date for this portrait is too late unless this aristocratic young woman was woefully unfashionable. More correctly, the date is around 1800. This would correspond with the lady's general appearance, for she seems younger than 32. If the portrait is Countess Erdödy and the date close to 1800, she would have posed for it around the age of 20, a more reasonable assessment. This would explain the similarity in hairstyle between this portrait and the one of Antonie Brentano dated 1798. If given to Beethoven at this time, following his tragic realization that he was facing deafness, it would have been a reminder to him that he always could find comfort with her.

  • **the idiosyncratic curvature of the lips**. We are unsure exactly how Solomon meant "idiosyncratic" since there is little unusual about the mouth of either lady. Most portraits of the time depict women having small, "rosebud" mouths, even if they did not. However, the gloomy 1798 portrait bears little resemblance to the "1812" portrait in this respect since in the latter the lady clearly is smiling. If the second portrait was completed in 1812, on the threshold of Antonie returning to Frankfurt, a city Solomon claimed she detested, and during a period of time when she was quite ill, one might also inquire not only why the bloom of health is on her cheeks, but also why on earth was she smiling? Was she merely putting on a brave front for the painter along with her makeup? If her health at this time had been "completely shattered" as she claimed, why would she engage an artist to do her portrait? Just to give it to Beethoven?

  Another important point is this: if portraits had the significance Solomon claimed—as being intimate gifts when given to a member of the opposite sex, would Franz not have wondered about her giving it to Beethoven? Would there not have been gossip among the servants about this married woman posing for a portrait intended for someone other than her husband? If she had lied to Franz and told him it was for him, would he not have wondered what had happened to it? Had Antonie kept it a secret from her husband, her children, her servants? Had the artist been sworn to silence? One cannot imagine so much intrigue!

Anna Marie Erdödy, circa 1796

• **the nose.** Solomon makes no mention of this feature, even though it is significant. An authenticated portrait of Frau Brentano from 1808 shows an extremely prominent aquiline nose, noticable in the 1798 portrait, but not evident in the "1812."

Further, if it *is* Antonie Brentano represented in both the 1798 and 1812 portraits, then like Dorian Gray, she never aged. In the first, she would have been 18, in the second 32. Yet, remarkably, despite her bouts with depression and what seems to be a generally gloomy outlook on life, she barely aged a bit in 14 years. Even more amazing the morose, frizzy-haired, round-faced teenager of 1798 and the woman with the Bedouin face and attire in 1808, became a pretty, slender petite woman by 1812!

Biographer Stephen Ley compared the "1812" portrait with an authenticated portrait of Anna Marie Erdödy owned by her great-granddaughter—which was destroyed in a fire in 1945 —and concluded that they were not the same person. Yet his credentials for being able to make a definitive comparison between the various portraits were not given, therefore it is difficult to lend credence to his opinion. Since his comparison was done in 1933 when forensic science was not nearly as capable of determining matches as it is now with computer enhancements, we cannot know whether Ley's determination is reliable or not. A look at the surviving reproduction of the authentic Erdödy portrait shows the same small mouth and shape of the brows as the unknown 1812, although the eyes themselves are larger. And since the hair is covered by a veil in the genuine Erdödy portrait (most likely it was a wedding portrait as she was pictured with her husband), it cannot be used for a point of comparison. But what can such comparisons tell us? Portraiture is a subjective art. Many portraits known to be of Beethoven do not look similar to one another, and a few are nearly unrecognizable as Beethoven, even though his face is probably one of the most easily recognized in the world. As one example, the shape of the composer's eyes and nose and style of his hair in a painting by Johann Heckel is surprisingly different than one done at nearly the same time by Ferdinand Schimon.

Solomon claimed that Stephan Breuning's son, Gerhard, did not recognize the woman in the "1812" portrait, but naturally the younger Breuning would not since he never knew Countess Erdödy. Gerhard was only a boy at the time of Beethoven's death, and by then the Countess already had been away from Vienna three years.

Josephine's supporters have suggested that the portrait was of her, but every one of her known portraits shows her with large dark eyes, a narrow-bridged nose, and dark, almost black hair, nothing like the reddish-gold in the "1812."

In the end, one must conclude that everything presented, both here, by Solomon, and by Ley, is purely subjective: in the eye of the beholder, so to speak. The arguments for the portrait in Beethoven's possession being Frau Brentano are not convincing. Therefore, one must compare the ladies' portraits and decide for oneself whether they bear any resemblance to one another. Yet, even if one decides that they do, what is the value in terms of evidence that the lady in the alleged 1812 portrait was the Immortal Beloved? Given Beethoven's casual view of the "meaning" behind the exchange of portraits, very little, if any. Perhaps those women he loved the most required no portraits—their images he carried in his heart. Thus, even this little scrap of proof falls by the wayside.

❖ PART IV ❖

THE ERDÖDY-BEETHOVEN
RELATIONSHIP

INTRODUCTION

Dana Steichen, in her 1959 book, *Beethoven's Beloved*, was the first biographer to give attention to Anna Marie Erdödy's relationship with the composer. Unfortunately, it does not seem as if "serious" scholars gave much serious attention to Mrs. Steichen, probably due to the fact that, by background, she was a musically-gifted stage actress. Admittedly she made some errors in her book—though not much worse than others. For one, she believed that the Beloved letter had been written in 1807 rather than in 1812. Yet in her defense, it must be noted that Mrs. Steichen died before she was able to complete her research. Important documents, such as Beethoven's letters to Josephine Brunswick, and Emily Anderson's full compilation of his other letters, did not surface until after her death. The 1300 pages of documentation she gathered in five years of research was formidable, yet she considered her work a mere "preliminary draft." Despite its unfinished nature, with so much effort having gone into her book, her husband, Edward, decided to have it published posthumously. It has been an invaluable source of information leading to additional research and evidence on which this present book is based. Not only had she collected a vast amount of documentation, she was also a woman with a great deal of common sense, and she presented Beethoven, not through the eyes of a worshipper, but with the warmth and understanding many other biographers lack.

ANNA MARIE[1] IN OVERVIEW

In his book, *Beethoven As He Lived*, Richard Specht gave a concise and accurate appraisal of the Countess:

> Maria Erdödy [was] his lady confessor, from whom he had no secrets. It was to her that he brought all good and all tragic tidings, all his joys, his sorrows and his failings. Beethoven confided everything to her, and obtained absolution from her for all the sins of his domineering anger, even when she herself had suffered from them. With Maria he forgot his obstinacy, his suspicious vigilance, and his perpetual attitude of defense against possible slights to his sensitive honor. With her he felt no constraint, and knew that he was understood, even on occasions when he had stayed away for a few days.[2]

Schindler did not write anything personal about Countess Erdödy prior to 1815. Thus when he does describe her, his observations must have been with some measure of firsthand experience. He wrote:

> What this lady had for many years been to Beethoven may be summed up in his name for her: he called her his "Father Confessor." To her nobility of birth she joined a nobility of spirit not always to be found to the same degree in her peers. Countess Erdödy never wavered in her friendly affection nor in the openly acknowledged reverence she felt for the master. The same cannot be said for many others of her class, almost all whom deserted Beethoven when a new constellation rose in the Italian sky.[3]

An examination of Beethoven's relationship with Anna Marie has led this author to believe that, despite the composer's strong desire for marriage and a family, he sacrificed that dream rather than separate forever from his only truly "immortal beloved." Anna Marie Erdödy was the only woman who, though plagued with some physical handicaps, was emotionally strong and independent, "movingly gay," and capable of providing Beet-

---

[1]Although Countess Erdödy referred to herself as "Marie," to distinguish her from other Maries in Beethoven's life, in the course of this book we will refer to her as "Anna Marie."
[2]Specht, pp. 190-191.
[3]Schindler, p. 212.

hoven with the strength, intellect, passion, and joyfulness of spirit he needed from a true companion.

Although Josephine Brunswick loved Beethoven on a spiritual level, we see through her acquiesence to her family's wishes that she did not have his indomitable strength by which she might have resisted them, had she been so inclined. Countess Erdödy had all the qualities which would have made a woman "eternally beloved" by Beethoven. Even though she had as much or more so at stake as Josephine—most importantly, her children—unlike Countess Brunswick, she was the one who, as he himself said, "despite this and that devilish human-thing" loved him enough to "have remained always with me."

It is odd that most often Anna Marie is dismissed as having being nothing more than simply Beethoven's patron and friend. In some cases, the Countess has been relegated to a few paltry sentences in Beethoven's biographies. Yet the evidence reveals that theirs was an intimate and long-term relationship, and that she was much more than a mere footnote in his life.

There was no passion between them, biographers conclude, summarily dismissing her. His letters to her have no fire. Yet even though his letters to Antonie Brentano are barely more than business correspondence, this has not stopped most scholars from agreeing with her candidacy as the Immortal Beloved. To this author, that is a strange double standard. Also discounted is the importance Beethoven placed on friendship. To him, it was friendship that formed the basis for a loving relationship. He could not have loved eternally a woman who was not first and foremost his best friend. What Beethoven's biographers fail to realize is that true passion for another person need not be obvious. Herriot observed that "the men who are the most active in love are those who say the least about it."[4]

Beethoven and Anna Marie had in common enormous pride and fiery temperaments, characteristics which sometimes caused conflicts and separations. Yet over the course of more than

---

[4]Herriot, p. 242. Herriot makes veiled, almost mysterious references to the Beethoven-Erdödy relationship, writing: "He dedicated several works to Countess Erdödy without compromising her by indiscreet disclosures. Anna Marie— one more shadow in the Master's secret life. We shall probably never know to whom the ring of gold bound him." Why did Herriot feel Beethoven needed to be discreet? We believe Herriot suspected more about Beethoven and Anna Marie than he was willing to admit.

20 years, they came back together time and again. Although Solomon claimed that Antonie Brentano had been the only woman who "loved [Beethoven] as a man," it is doubtful that she ever did, or could have. Even the "beloved J," Josephine Brunswick, did not love him that way. But Anna Marie certainly did, and Countess Erdödy alone had the strength and "staying power" to remain a part of Beethoven's life despite numerous obstacles.

ANNA MARIE AND ANTONIE

Comparing Anna Marie Erdödy to Antonie Brentano shows that these two women were vastly different in personality. Their only similarity lay in the fact that both had been given in marriage at a young age to a man older than herself. In that respect alone, Anna Marie's lot was similar to Antonie's. Yet while Antonie had the good fortunate to have a husband who cared for her, Anna Marie's indifferent spouse abandoned her when she was no more than 21, leaving her alone to manage her properties and her household, and to care for their three small children. Before she was out of her teens, she contracted an ill-ness which left her a partial invalid all her life. There is no clear diagnosis of her malady, although she was frequently in pain and her extremities were often swollen. Some have speculated that she suffered from a heart condition, resulting in periodic bouts with edema. This author is inclined to agree with others who have suggested that she had rheumatoid arthritis. This disease is painfully debilitating, frequently leads to deformity of the joints —one reason why her handwriting had been described as "aging" in 1823 police records even though Anna Marie was only in her early forties at the time—and becomes progressively worse over time.

Despite some physical limitations, Countess Erdödy was quite independent, able to manage her own household and the raising of her three children, as well as caring for estates she owned in Hungary, Italy, and Croatia. She received no assistance from either her own family or that of her husband. In the fall of 1822, a rumor reached Vienna from Croatia that the Countess Erdody had organized a force of 300 peasants to storm and take possession of her uncle's castle to which she felt she had proprietory rights. No Antonie Brentano, or Josephine Brunswick, or any other lady with whom Beethoven had been associated could have had the commanding presence or spirit undertake such a venture and to rally so many to her cause. We see in Anna Marie's life that same undaunted courage which was so much like her beloved Beethoven's. It is little wonder that he had cherished and adored this little noblewoman with the soul of a Magyar gypsy, a woman more likely to brandish a sword than to clutch a handkerchief. Yet at times the Countess's self-reliance and determination to make her own decisions caused Beethoven some chagrin. These qualities well might have caused him to write, with almost a sigh, "your love makes me the happiest and unhappiest of men at the same time."

The Countess had a respectable amount of wisdom and ability in business affairs. Although of noble birth, her wealth was not inherited. At one time she was left nearly destitute, but by her own business acumen and perserverance, she built an impressive estate. It is no wonder that Beethoven allowed her to negotiate contracts for him. To Count Gleichenstein he wrote in early 1809:

> Countess Erdödy thinks that you ought to sketch out a plan with her according to which she could negotiate, if she, as she certainly believes she will be, is approached.[5]

Anna Marie was well acquainted with the players involved in that negotiation. She had known Prince Kinsky, the Archduke Rudolph, and Prince Lobkowitz for many years. Thayer noted that

> It seems likely that the suggestion that formal stipulations for a contract [which guaranteed Beethoven an annual salary for 4000 florins] under which Beethoven would decline the offer from Cassel and remain in Vienna be drawn up came from Countess Erdödy...

Naturally Anna Marie would have taken whatever steps were necessary to keep Beethoven in Vienna, not simply because she felt a great talent would have been lost to the city if he had elected to accept the position in Westphalia, but because she wanted to be with the man she loved.

Unlike others such as Josephine, the Countess Erdödy did not allow her physical limitations to affect her ability to manage her affairs, to live life as she wished to live it, nor to cast her down into despair. To her credit, she maintained a light-

---

[5]Anderson, p. 216.

hearted, positive, and optimistic outlook. Reichardt described her in 1808 as

> a very handsome, small, fine, twenty-five-year-old wo-
> man [she was actually 28 at the time]. Only the enjoy-
> ment of music remained to her; she herself plays
> Beethoven's things extremely well and limps with still
> swollen feet from one pianoforte to another, nevertheless
> still so gay, so friendly and good...

Her effect on Beethoven was obvious, for Reichardt also noted that

> we brought the good-humored Beethoven to the piano-
> forte and he improvised for about an hour with such
> masterly power and skill, pouring out his whole soul,
> sounding the innermost depths and soaring to the
> loftiest heights...

Beethoven was not inclined to improvise when asked. In fact, he usually responded to such requests with an angry refusal. But he was not at all adverse to the idea at Anna Marie's. He was, in fact, "good humored" about it, showing none of his typical obstinacy. What force but the power of love could have trans- formed him so?

Solomon, in listing the women who had rejected Beethov- en, stated that "Countess Erdödy, although not the beloved, had wounded his feelings by preferring 'the servant to the master.'"[6] This is untrue. Beethoven's own letters show that his feelings had not been wounded by anything *she* had done, but by a misunder- standing on *his* part. Anna Marie Erdödy may, on occasion, have gotten angry with Beethoven, but she never rejected him. She was, in fact, the only woman who consistently overlooked his flaws; who saw him and loved him for the man he was; and, with time, was able to put his transgressions behind her. Occasionally they did quarrel. Their personalities were such that conflict was inevitable. A few times, their arguments led to painful separa- tions. But it is a reflection of their special relationship, and of the love that they had for one another, that nothing could keep them apart forever.

---

[6]Solomon, p. 183.

❀ 26 ❀
An Eternal Love
Begins

To Beethoven she was his *Beichtvater*, his "father confessor"—his supreme intimate, the one to whom he "brought all his joys, his sorrows." She was Anna Marie Nickzy Erdödy, and in letters written to her throughout the years, Beethoven called her his adored, cherished, and precious Countess. He had used those terms only with Anna Marie and with Josephine Brunswick; they occur in no other letters.

When the composer first realized that he was facing deafness, he initially confided what he called his "great secret" to only a very few people: to Franz Wegeler, a boyhood friend, and to Karl Amenda, who had arrived in Vienna in the late 1790s, and to whom Beethoven had formed a strong attachment. There is one other person to whom he also must have confided this great secret: his *Beichtvater*, Anna Marie. Why else would he have gone to her estate in this time of his greatest despair? And why would she have extended, and he accepted, an invitation for him to visit her Jedlersee estate, if not to give and gain solace there? It should be no surprise that these two kindred spirits would be drawn to each other, seek and find comfort with one another. While Beethoven was attempting to cope with his personal tragedy—the realization that he might be going deaf—Anna Marie was being forced to cope with her own personal dilemma: abandonment by Count Peter Erdödy, a man who had become indifferent to his wife and children. At such a time, it would have been natural for these two people to seek and find comfort with one another.

Although it is not known for certain when their association began, circumstances indicate that Anna Marie and Beethov-
en may have met as early as 1797. One year previously, the
Erdödys had married, and Anna Marie had moved from Hungary
to live with her new husband in Vienna. At the time, Beethoven
occupied an apartment in the residence of Prince Lichnowsky
who lived on the upper floors of the same house as Count and
Countess Erdödy.[1] Earlier, in 1793, Baron Gottfried van Swieten
had organized a musical society, among whose patrons were
included Princes Esterhazy, Lobkowitz, Lichnowsky, and Kinsky,
and Count Peter Erdödy. Three years later, the new Countess
Erdödy became part of this society. Most assuredly, Beethoven
and Countess Erdödy, moving within the same aristocratic and
musically-inclined social circles, began their acquaintance far
earlier than has been thought. Yet despite their living in the
same building and perhaps seeing one another occasionally, we
believe the true start of their friendship had been delayed by
serious illness on Beethoven's part.

If the dates in the *Heiligenstadt Testament*[2] are accurate,
and there is no reason to doubt them, it was some time in 1796
that Beethoven may have suffered an attack of typhus, the same
disease that in 1828 would kill composer Franz Schubert at the
age of 31. Beethoven did not survive unscathed. Some medical
experts have suggested that, based on autopsy reports filed in
1827, this infection had caused aural nerve damage resulting in
the gradual loss of his hearing[3] which would leave him profoundly
deaf some twenty years later. Regardless of its effects upon his
future health, if this time of Beethoven's illness is correct, he
probably became acquainted with Anna Marie upon his recovery
in 1797 or 1798, but surely no later or he would not have readily

---

[1] In that year, Swieten addressed a note to Beethoven "care of Prince Lichnowsky,
Alstergasse #45."

[2] In this testament, Beethoven noted that he had suffered with problems with his
hearing for six years. Since the *Heiligenstadt Testament* had been written at the
end of 1802, his hearing loss must have begun to be noticable by 1796 or early
1797. There is also an inordinate gap in his letters for that year—nearly nine
months—which could signal that he had been ill at that time, or recuperating.
In May 1797, Beethoven wrote Wegeler that "my health is steadily improving,"
again indicating that he had been seriously ill.

[3] More recently, medical experts have suggested other possible causes, although
results are still, and probably must remain, inconclusive.

accepted invitations to visit her estate shortly thereafter. Thus he would have been 26 and she 17 and still a bride, but one who had been married to her husband by the arrangement of their parents, not out of love. The marriage united two powerful factions of Hungarian nobility—the Erdödys and the Nickzys—whose histories went far into Hungary's dark and bloody past. These two families, along with the Esterhazys, the Palffys, and the Bathorys, had ruled their country for generations. Thus Anna Marie was politically bound to a man she did not love who obviously did not love her either.

Like Baron van Swieten, the Erdödys habitually hosted musical parties at their home—continuing the practice begun by Peter and van Swieten in 1793—and a rising star such as Beethoven, after recovering his health, certainly had been invited repeatedly. Beethoven and Anna Marie were in each other's company time and again. Her proficiency with the piano attracted him to her—at the time, platonically—for music was the magnet that drew him to most of those who became his closest friends.

NO RAVING BEAUTY

Anna Marie had brown eyes, reddish-brown hair, a sprinkling of freckles, and a delicate figure. She was considered handsome or pretty rather than beautiful. Some discount her as the Beloved on that basis alone. Surprisingly, lack of beauty has not dampened adherence to Antonie Brentano's candidacy as Beethoven's love interest, though it is obvious from her portraits that she also was far from being beautiful. Many have assumed that the Beloved must have been a woman of extraordinary physical beauty because of remarks Beethoven made about the issue. He had once joked that he could not love a woman who was not beautiful. He was also, like most men, fond of looking at exceptionally attractive women. But he was not so shallow as his flippant remark and innocent behavior has led some to believe. He was sensitive enough to recognize a kindred spirit, and find beauty that lay in the heart rather than merely on the face.

A PLACE OF REFUGE

The hundredth anniversary of Beethoven's death was observed in Vienna in 1927 with a special exhibit. Among the memorabilia displayed was a miniature portrait, Exhibit 608, noted in the catalog as that of Countess Marie Erdödy, taken from the collection of Dr. Stephan Breuning. The catalog noted her as "Beethoven's friend: with whom he sought solace in 1801 when in a despairing state of mind he spent several days at her estate in Jedlersee."[5]

Thayer believed that Beethoven had been in Hetzendorf, four to five miles southwest of the inner city of Vienna, in 1801. Yet another biographer following Thayer, O.G. Sonneck, wrote, "As to 1801, it seems to me that his sojourn at Hetzendorf during the first half of July is not as authenticated as one might wish."[6] Even if Beethoven *had* spent some time in Hetzendorf, it would not have precluded a trip to the north of Vienna that same year. For example, in 1802, he was for a short time in Baden, a spa approximately 16 miles south of Vienna, but also at Heiligenstadt, which is four miles north of the city, and near the Countess's estate, Jedlersee.

We do not know from where the 1801 date came. There is an inordinate gap in letters for that year, indicating that he probably was in the country. Perhaps the date came from Schindler who had written about Beethoven's alleged suicide attempt by starvation which Schindler claimed had occurred in that year while Beethoven had been visiting the Countess. Would Beethoven have done anything so drastic at the home of a dear friend? Doubtful. Schindler, writing many years after the fact with personal bias and no first-hand knowledge, is not a particularly reliable source, but it is odd that he mentioned Anna Marie here when he made so little note of her otherwise. When Schindler took to writing this tale, why did he choose Countess Erdödy's estate as the setting? There must have been some basis for his assumption that Beethoven had at least been with Anna Marie that summer, even if it is unlikely that a suicide attempt had taken place. Otherwise, why didn't Schindler place Beethoven in a more respectable setting, such as with his friends the Brunswicks? Who would have known the difference? If Schindler's tendency was to whitewash, or at least protect, Beethoven's reputation, why, if there was no truth to it, would he have placed him so intimately alone with a woman whose husband had deserted her,

---

[5]Solomon maintains the portrait to be of Antonie Brentano. For a discussion of this issue, refer to Chapter 25: *The Portraits.*
[6]Sonneck, *Riddle of the Immortal Beloved,* p. 62.

leaving Beethoven at the mercy of the very gossip mongers Schindler claimed to despise?

As for the suicide attempt, while both the date and actual attempt are questionable, Beethoven himself indicated that he had at least once considered such a drastic measure. Beethoven's first thoughts about it must have occurred between his illness in 1797 and 1802 because he spoke of suicide in his 1802 *Heligenstadt Testament:*

> Such experiences have brought me to the depths of despair—a little more and I would have put an end to my life... It was virtue that sustained me even in my affliction: to it, next to my art, I must give thanks that I did not end my life by suicide.[7]

Beethoven wrote of this issue again in an 1810 letter to his friend, Wegeler:

> If I had not read somewhere that a man should not voluntarily quit this life so long as he can still perform a good deed, I would have left this earth long ago — and, what is more, by my own hand. — Oh, this life is indeed beautiful, but for me it is poisoned for ever —[8]

From these letters we see that there had been times in his life when Beethoven had thought of taking such a step, but his commitment to his music prevented him from following through.

Beethoven's physician in the summer of 1802, Dr. Schmidt, had advised the composer to go to the country, thinking that the quiet of the countryside would spare his hearing and perhaps even cure his hearing loss. Beethoven had chosen to go north to Heiligenstadt which was only a few minute's walk from Jedlersee. It was during that summer that Beethoven worked on and completed the *Piano and Violin Sonata Op. 30*, the *Piano Sonatas Op. 31*, numbers 1 and 2, and the joyful *Second Symphony*. His choice of Heiligenstadt and his obvious happiness that productive summer leads one to believe that he had been there before—in 1801—

---

[7]Anderson, p. 1351-1354.

[8]Anderson, p. 270. This is the same letter to Wegeler in which Beethoven had requested his birth certificate in 1810, allegedly because he wanted to marry. It is a puzzle why Wegeler would believe in the "marriage project" when he had only just received a letter from the alleged "bridegroom" in which he spoke of suicide and the fact that his life was forever poisoned! It didn't surprise him? And they accuse Beethoven of having a cheerless outlook on marriage!

and, having enjoyed his stay there, had elected to return in 1802 in order to be near his loving friend, Anna Marie. Even Thayer admitted that "it is not at all improbable that the vicinity of the Erdödy estate at Jedlersee am Marchfeld was one reason for his frequent choice of summer lodgings in the villages on the Danube, north of the city." Over the years, his pattern of choosing summer residences shows that it was only when Anna Marie was not at Jedlersee or Hernals that Beethoven chose and remained in lodgings south of Vienna. For example, in 1803, Beethoven summered in Oberdöbling #4 near to both Heiligenstadt and the Canal part of the Danube—and Jedlersee. In July 1804, Beethoven initially had gone to Baden, but soon wrote to his friend, Ries, "I am tired of being here—it disgusts me. Urge him for heaven's sake to rent the lodgings at once because I want to get into them immediately." Beethoven's urgency apparently had been prompted by a quarrel with Stephan Breuning, and his desire was to move to Döbling. Yet, again, this was only a few minutes away, and just across the Danube, from Jedlersee.

THE "BELOVED J"

By 1805, while Beethoven's close friendship with Anna Marie continued, he had formed a romantic attachment to Josephine Brunswick, and during that summer he was her neighbor in Hetzendorf. Why did his affections turn to Josephine? As discussed in Chapter 20: *The Note from Baden*, Josephine had been widowed for a year, and was in a position to remarry, while Countess Erdödy, though separated, was still married to Peter, and it had only been a few years since her husband had deserted her. No doubt her marital status caused Beethoven to keep their relationship—at least initially—on a platonic level.

Beethoven happily proclaimed to Josephine in an 1805 love letter: "I have won your heart!" It is evident from distressed letters written among various members of the Brunswick family who were alarmed by the couple's growing relationship, that he had indeed caused her to love him, at least spiritually. Yet despite the existence of love between them, their relationship was not entirely happy. Beethoven was not always sure of her love for him: "I love you as dearly as you do not love me," he wrote to her. They quarreled, probably over his desire to become her lover and her reluctance to grant him that part of herself. He was easily wounded, and not adverse to retaliation. His sexual overtures to her probably had not been crudely overt. More likely he simply had become too amorous and she pushed him away, angering him, for we suddenly find Josephine writing to him, "If my life is dear to you—then treat me with more consideration. I cannot express how deeply wounding it is to be equated with low creatures." One can only guess what sort of scathing remark *he* must have made to elicit such a response from *her*! His annoyance with her also must have stemmed from frustration over her refusal to marry him. Beethoven saw love and friendship as *the* reasons to marry, and believed that he and Josephine had both: they loved one another and had much in common. Therefore, to him, becoming lovers and then marrying was the natural progression for their relationship. Josephine did not share Beethoven's view of love and marriage, and felt that other considerations, such as financial security and social status, took precedence in selecting a spouse. It is also quite probable that she was not physically attracted to him. Yet apparently Beethoven saw no good reason why she should not accept him as her husband. Even Prince Lichnowsky approved of their match. No one would have taken her children from her in the six years she was the Widow Deym. Her excuse to Beethoven was that a liaison with him, whether within or outside of marriage, would have violated her duty, as she called them, "holy bonds." She may have said this to avoid telling him that she did not love him "that way"—by putting a restriction of "holy bonds" upon herself. Perhaps he should have been able to expect a little more honesty on her part. He even told her, "I deserve that you should be frank with me." She never was, and it is little wonder that he begame angry.

Throughout this time period, Beethoven was living at the Pasqualati House—and close to his *Beichtvater*. Despite his vested romantic interest in Josephine, his comfort apparently rested in Anna Marie and in their friendship. Ries noted that "He moved out of this [the Pasqualati] house several times but always returned to it, so that, as I afterwards heard, Baron Pasqualati was good-natured enough to say, 'The lodgings will not be rented; Beethoven will come back.'"

In 1806, Prince Nicholas Esterhazy commissioned Beethoven to write a mass for his wife's name day, but illness prevented the composer from undertaking the project immediately. Instead, he took a short trip to the resort called Pistyan, part of the Erdödy estate. Pistyan, once a part of Hungary and now Slovakia, also was considered currative for ear troubles and had been used for that and other treatments since the early 18th century. It is of note that Beethoven had considered this place for a possible cure during the last weeks of his life. Perhaps he had wanted to surround himself one last time with memories of happier days with his beloved Countess.

In 1807, Beethoven spent the summer moving between Baden, Heiligenstadt, and Jedlersee, writing much of Esterhazy's requested mass—the *Mass in C*—at Anna Marie's estate. In the fall his home was—as usual—the Pasqualati House. That same fall Beethoven attempted to heal the breech in his relationship with Josephine Brunswick. Beethoven understandably had been hurt and angered by Josephine's rejection "for no good reason." The composer characteristically suffered great sorrow over such rifts in relationships, and it would have been natural for him to confide in his *Beichtvater*. We believe that he and Anna Marie had spoken of Josephine that summer, and that Anna Marie had encouraged him to give Countess Brunswick another chance. Josephine had been in Baden at the same time as Beethoven and had apparently made a friendly overture toward him, perhaps also feeling badly that their friendship had ended so bitterly. Yet, unless someone had given him encouragement, there is no explanation for his sudden impulse to ask for a chance to develop a more intense relationship with Josephine after a year's silence. From Beethoven's September 4, 1807, letter to her, it is clear that while Josephine had been amenable only to a friendship, her note to him kindled far more hope in him than she had meant it to do. Her expectations seem so insensitive: how could she think that the man who had offered her his heart could be nothing more than a friend to her? Did she really believe she could give him her friendship without him wanting or assuming more? Had she been shocked by his ardent response?

> Dear beloved and only J[osephine]!
> Again even a few lines, only a few lines from you— have given me great pleasure. How often have I wrestled with myself, beloved J, in order not to commit a breach of the prohibition which I have imposed upon myself —
> But it is all in vain. A thousand voices are constantly whispering to me that you are my only friend, my only beloved...

We believe Anna Marie had been one of those "thousand voices," giving him a feminine perspective, attempting to help her Beethoven find the happiness he felt only a wife and family could bring him. We know that he had been with her at her estate that summer, and that he had been living close to her in Heiligenstadt at the time he wrote this letter. Thus she had been in a position to influence his decision to respond to Josephine's request to renew their friendship, and perhaps affect a complete reconciliation. Anna Marie knew that, in all likelihood, she was destined to remain a married woman, and that she could not give Beethoven what he wanted most. She knew also that Josephine was a widow, and marriageable, and that Beethoven cared for her deeply. She certainly was that one voice to which he listened more closely than any other. Anna Marie also must have realized that his success with Josephine would have meant his marriage to her and perhaps a permanent separation from his *Beichtvater*. One cannot help but wonder how attached Anna Marie had been to Beethoven at this time, and whether it had cost her emotional anguish to unselfishly push him into the arms of another woman. His September 20 letter continued

> Oh dear J, let us wander unconstrainedly along that path where we have often been so happy—May heaven grant me one undisturbed hour to spend with you, so as to have just once that talk we have not had for a long time, when my heart and my soul may again be united with yours—[9]

His attempt to mend their relationship, to make amends for their bitter parting, to smoothe away the barriers he believed had been erected between them, and regain her love, failed. As his letters indicate, Beethoven had attempted to visit Josephine several times and had been turned away at the door by her servants. If she truly had hoped they simply could be friends, we again must marvel at her insensitivity. She wanted him in her life, but kept at a distance, which, given his love for her, was unfair of her to ask of him. Josephine remained unwilling or unable to follow her heart. Part of her may have wanted to marry Beethoven, but for reasons of her own she could not bring herself to do so, perhaps to her everlasting regret.

---

[9]Anderson, pp. 175-176.

Autumn, 1807
Dear J,

> Since I must almost fear that you no longer allow your-
> self to be found by me — and since I do not care to put
> up with the refusals of your servant any longer — well
> then, I cannot come to you any more — unless you let me
> know what you think about this — Is it really a fact —
> that you do not want to see me any more — if so —do be
> frank — I certainly deserve that you should be frank
> with me...[10]

Josephine's apology—if it can be called that—for having
had him turned away from her door was cool: "I cannot understand very well how there could be room for touchiness where true
mutual esteem exists." Apparently she did not think he had a
reason to be upset, for she even chastized him by adding, "a
malady [i.e. touchiness] which usually could be suspected only in
weaker souls." For Beethoven, the relationship ended with that
letter. Did she think it would make their inevitable parting easier
for him if he were led to believe that she had no love for him? Was
her own heart breaking? Perhaps her actions only seem cruel, and
her intentions had been good, but it is difficult to know and totally
forgive her behavior toward him.

    Late in 1807, Beethoven replied to Josephine's formal
letter inquiring as to the health of her "friend Beethoven." Why
did she write that letter? Did she think *once again* that she could
entice him into a "friends only" relationship? It seems a stupid assumption on her part. Yet if she truly believed such a relationship
could be achieved, she was disappointed. Beethoven would not
make himself vulnerable to her again. Following is the last known
letter from the composer to Josephine Brunswick.

> You want me to tell you how I am. A more difficult
> question could not be put to me — and I prefer to leave
> it unanswered rather than — to answer it too truth-
> fully—[11]

---

[10]Anderson, p. 177-178.

[11]Anderson, p. 179. Biographer Marie Elisabeth Tellenbach assigned this letter
to 1809. In this case, it would take on an entirely different meaning. It would
have come following Beethoven's quarrel with Anna Marie, when he had been
depressed. If written in 1809, it would indicate that he did not want to be too
"truthful" with Josephine about his intimate relationship with another woman,
and that his separation from this woman had been his fault.

If Beethoven truly had been dear to Josephine, he would never know. Her family had strongly urged her to tell him otherwise, and she had acquiesed to their wishes. By the fall of 1807, Josephine had left Vienna for Martonvasar and Budapest in Hungary. In the summer of 1808, Josephine and her two sons and her sister, Therese, travelled throughout Germany, Switzerland, and Italy for an extended period of time, during which time she was to meet the man who would become her second husband. In February 1810, Josephine married Baron Christoph von Stackelberg, and from that time on, she only occasionally revisited Vienna.

It may have been at this time that Beethoven began to acknowledge Anna Marie's faithful affection as something more than friendship. Had his heart been badly broken by Josephine's behavior toward him in 1807? Or had he not entirely believed they could be reconciled, and thus had steeled his heart for the inevitable? We cannot know for sure. We know only that Beethoven had the comfort of his *Beichtvater* still. Of course, Anna Marie's intervention in Beethoven's relationship with Josephine is pure speculation, but a logical assumption, nevertheless. Many a man with a close female friend has consulted her in matters of the heart, and sought advice from her when engaging in a romantic venture. And no one was closer to Beethoven than the Countess Erdödy.

A RESIDENTIAL DECISION

Beethoven spent the following summer of 1808 again in Heiligenstadt—near Jedlersee. During this time, Beethoven and Anna Marie must have admitted to themselves that Count Erdödy had no intentions of returning to his family. As Peter and Anna Marie had not lived together as husband and wife for at least seven years, they were not likely to do so ever again. Sometime that summer, with Josephine completely removed from Beethoven's life, he and Anna Marie either mutually decided, or she convinced him, that they need no longer deny their true feelings for one another. Their already deep friendship finally was allowed to "catch fire." As often happens when two close friends finally admit that there is more between them than the purely platonic, the relationship erupted into what would become a truly immortal love.

Count Peter Erdödy's desertion of his wife and family certainly would have given Anna Marie uncontestable grounds for annulment of their marriage. For reasons which were probably similar to, but far more difficult to resolve than Josephine's, she never settled the uncertainty of her marital status. The question of whether, under her circumstances, she would ever be free to remarry, easily would have been enough to keep the glimmer of hope that they would someday live together—so evident in the Beloved letter—alive in Beethoven's heart. Also, another event in the Erdödy marriage, to be discussed later, which happened the same year as the Beloved letter was written, would contribute to Beethoven's guarded optimism about their future.

A NEW HOUSE...

Speculation about Beethoven's relationship to Anna Marie the summer of 1808 is based on Beethoven's abrupt change of residence that fall. Upon returning to Vienna, Beethoven left the Pasqualati House where he had lived for four years, and moved three doors down into the Countess's home at Krugerstrasse No. 1074. His intention must have been to live with the Countess, rather than simply change apartments because of some restlessness in his nature. Despite occasional squabbles with the management, he had not been evicted from the Pasqualati House, and he had moved barely a block away. We cannot believe that in all of Vienna no other suitable apartment had been available.

Baron de Trémont, a contemporary who eventually wrote *Souvenirs of Beethoven*, related that the composer had "a strong inclination for Countess Erdödy, love reminiscent of Rousseau's love for Madame d'Houdetot," a love which had been consuming in its power. George Marek suggested that Trémont had used this particular analogy because the relationship between Beethoven and Anna Marie had never been physically consummated (as it had not been between Rousseau and d'Houdetot), but this author cannot agree. It is more likely that Trémont had been comparing the *intensity* of the feelings between Beethoven and Countess Erdödy with those that Rousseau had felt for d'Houdetot. When we later study the Beethoven-Erdödy quarrel, we will see that theirs could not have been a platonic relationship. Trémont repeatedly compared Beethoven with Rousseau, believing the two men to be similar in values and temperament. Perhaps that is why he compared Anna Marie with Elizabeth d'Houdetot, who was a gay spirit with a talent for music, not unlike Countess Erdödy. What gives Trémont's observation its potency is the fact that it was not firsthand knowledge. While we invariably seek "eyewitness" accounts, in this case, his ignorance is important. He obviously had heard of their relationship from other sources; it evidently was no secret among the music enthusiasts of Vienna. It might be tempting to relegate the relationship of Beethoven to Countess Erdödy to the realm of gossip were it not for so many other pieces of evidence connecting them to one another. On that basis, we cannot simply discount it.

When Rousseau met Elizabeth, he wrote "I was transported." Biographer Eduoard Herriot also was inclined to believe in a special and enduring love between Beethoven and the Countess, but perhaps had too much loyalty to the theories of his fellow biographers to stress his belief. Nevertheless, he admitted that, like Rousseau,

> Beethoven also was transported, but without saying so. He dedicated several works to Countess Erdödy without compromising her by indiscreet disclosures.[12]

Marek also pointed to Beethoven's openness at living at the Countess's home as a reason why she could not have been his Beloved. Marek felt, and rightly so, that a man as reticent about love as Beethoven would not openly proclaim that he was living with a woman without benefit of marriage. But did he? To the contrary, in letters he wrote at the time, Beethoven pointed to the fact that he simply had taken apartments in the same house as she was living, not that he was actually living "with" her, despite the fact that, in truth, he *did* live in her apartment. Perhaps they did maintain separate rooms within her apartment, but likely that had been done for appearances sake only, to give them some protection from gossip. We must recall that Beethoven had had no compunction about asking Josephine to become his lover, and had she agreed, Beethoven surely must have known that Viennese society would have caught wind of their liaison and found it an irresistably juicy bit of gossip. And since he had shown no reticence in pursuing Josephine, why then should he have done so when deciding to live with Anna Marie? Perhaps discretion

---

[12]Herriot, pp. 241-242.

became less of an issue for him when he felt he had a commitment to the woman, and secrecy was only important to him up to that point. Beethoven did, however, interject a note of propriety into the situation by making it a point to mention that Prince Lichnowsky lived upstairs. Since Lichnowsky most certainly was not living "with" Countess Erdödy, Beethoven was suggesting to his correspondents that their living arrangements were quite proper. Despite these precautions, evidently Viennese society saw their relationship in a more romantic—and perhaps, more correct—light. Otherwise, as we have noted, how could Baron de Trémont have come to the conclusion that Beethoven had a "strong inclination and love" for Countess Erdödy when he had not even arrived in Vienna until after the couple's quarrel and separation.

...A HOME

For a short time, Anna Marie's house became a true home to Beethoven, one he shared equally with her. It was here, with his Countess that he regularly entertained "good musical souls." Kapellmeister Johann Reichardt wrote that "Beethoven gave me the pleasure of inviting me to the Countess Erdödy's to let me hear something new of his work." Beethoven also invited friends to dinner on Anna Marie's behalf, and clearly was not her "boarder," otherwise he would not have taken such liberties. He acted very much the "man of the house," repeatedly opening the Erdödy home to visitors and guests at his own discretion. Reichardt alone was there three times by Beethoven's invitation, not hers.

It was in this home that Beethoven found warmth, laughter, the company of friends, and the companionship of a special loved one. As she was married in name only, it must have been at this time that Beethoven and Countess Erdödy had spoken of their commitment to one another, and the time when, having achieved a "true union of souls," the two of them had experienced the "exalted sensual relations" of which Beethoven would later write with such a poignant sense of loss. As we shall see later, only Beethoven's belief that he and Anna Marie had an exclusive commitment to one another—which included physical intimacy—could have spawned his jealous reaction to the servant he mistakenly believed had replaced him in the Countess's affections.

At Christmastime that year, Beethoven presented Anna Marie with the *Op. 70 Piano Trios*. On the autograph score is written, in Beethoven's hand:

> *2 Trios für die Gräfin Erdödy, geboren Niszky, für Sie geeignet und Ihr zugeeignet.*
> Two Trios for the Countess Erdödy, born Niczky, suitable for her, and dedicated to[13] her.

These pieces are significant in their rarity: not often did Beethoven compose music for specific people. In this case, it was not simply a trifle such as *Für Elise*, but two beautifully written trios. Reichardt remarked on their performance in his book, *Vertaute Brief*:

> Beethoven played wholly masterful, wholly inspired new trios, which he has recently composed, wherein there is such a heavenly cantabile movement such as I never heard from him and which is the loveliest and most graceful that I have ever heard, it lifts and melts my soul as often as I think of it... The lovely, ailing, and yet so movingly gay Countess... had such an inner enthusiastic enjoyment of every beautiful—daring passage, on each successful turn, that her look gave me just as much pleasure as Beethoven's masterly work and his playing. Fortunate artist who can be certain of such listeners.

Of these trios, other reviewers[13] have noted that

> This is music of healthy high spirits, showing the composer's most genial, sunny side. A most beautiful equiposed piece of music that shows us Beethoven at his felicitous lyrical best. A typical expression of the jocular, "unbuttoned" Beethoven, ending this delectable work with the most infectious and tonic of high spirits. (Harry Halbriech)

* * *

> It seems as if the Master thought that one could not speak of deeply hidden things in common words, but only in the sublime and noble language, even when the

---

[13]*Zugeeignet* can also have the more intimate meaning of "created for."
[13]Quotes by Halbrech and Hoffman taken from Schermann & Biancolli, p. 628.

spirit, closely penetrating into these things, feels itself exaulted with joy and happiness; the dance of the priests of Isis must take the form of an exultant hymn. (E.T.A. Hoffman, a contemporary of Beethoven's, 1776-1822)[13]

It is interesting that Hoffman believed Beethoven was expressing "deeply hidden things" in this music, for we believe this also. Had these pieces not been born out of Beethoven's joy at having achieved the home he most ardently desired? Had he not both written and performed these trios with love in his heart for his beloved? And had Anna Marie not received them with the same feeling for him? We do not deny that this is speculation on our part. However, there have been very few instances in which this composer had ever given such a gift of himself to anyone. And when else have we ever found him so utterly happy, in such an amenable and lighthearted mood, and so readily showing his "sunny side?"

Sadly, this would be the only time in Beethoven's life that he would live contentedly "at home" with the woman he loved for an extended period of time. Even Thayer pointed out that the years 1807-1809 were the happiest, most productive of Beethoven's adult life, and yet he never seemed to understand why. That Beethoven found happiness in sharing a home and his life with Anna Marie is reflected in the unprecedented output of glorious music that was born or completed at this time: in the exultant passion of the *Fifth Symphony*[14] and the sheer joyfulness of the *Sixth*, in the exuberance of the *Choral Fantasy*, the magnificence of the *Piano Concerto #5, the "Emperor,"* which was first sketched at this time, in the beauty of the *Harp Quartet,* and in the "loveliest and most graceful" of his trios, the Op. 70, that "lifted and melted" the souls of its listeners.

Beethoven's joy is evidenced, too, in his suddenly agreeable nature. Wegeler once noted that:

his aversion to playing for an audience had become so strong that every time he was urged to play, he would fly

---

[14]Hoffman wrote of the Fifth Symphony: "This reviewer never felt this romanticism so keenly as when listening to this symphony, which right up to the climactic finish develops Beethoven's sense of the romantic, expressing it more urgently than any of his other works, until the hearer is irresistibly compelled into the awesome spirit-realm of the eternal."

into a rage. He often came to me then, gloomy and out
of sorts, complaining...I could never cure him of his
obstinacy, which was often the source of bitter quarrels
with his closest friends and patrons.[15]

The Countess obviously provided the "cure" that Wegeler
sought and never found. For despite Beethoven's usual resistance
to performing upon request, he had no such reluctance there in
the house of Anna Marie Erdödy when driven by love "the good-
humored Beethoven improvised. . .pouring out his soul."

---

[15]Wegeler & Ries, pp. 24-25.

❧ 27 ❧
The Quarrel...
and Forgiveness

After the bliss of 1808 came the bitterness of 1809. Solomon wrote that "Countess Erdödy, although not [Beethoven's] beloved, had wounded his feelings by preferring 'the servant to the master.'" [1] *Not* his beloved? Beethoven had known her for years, he had confided to her his deepest secrets, opened his heart and soul to her, made every effort to live near her, and finally even lived *with* her. When she was with him, he was joyful; when she was not, he was despondent. He wrote music especially for her. How could he possibly not have loved her? The bond between them cannot be easily dismissed as mere friendship. It also is not true that she had ever "preferred the servant to the master." Never in her whole life did she prefer any man to Beethoven.

Though by turn kind, cheerful, and loving, Countess Erdödy also was fiercely independent, strong-willed, strong-minded, outspoken, and proud. Many of these qualities she shared with Beethoven. She was subservient to no peer, and held her own in male company. It was inevitable, perhaps, that two such kindred spirits should be drawn together and yet clash when placed day after day in the proximity of a shared household. Six months of near-conjugal bliss ended in a bitter quarrel born out of a misunderstanding. While Anna Marie's emotional interests lay with Beethoven alone, he mistakenly thought she had betrayed his affections with a male servant. What follows is what we believe

---

[1]Solomon, p. 183.

to be the most accurate account of the incident, supported by Beethoven's own letters. We include here the extensive research conducted by Steichen. The reader may find the cause of the dissention difficult to believe. Admittedly, the quarrel seems based on triviality and almost stupid; yet given Beethoven's sensitive and suspicious nature, not entirely surprising.

THE QUARREL

Anna Marie had given Beethoven's manservant a bonus, additional money to insure that he would not be tempted to leave the composer's employ. Living with him showed her that he was not an easy master to please, insisting on things being exactly to his specifications—such as demanding that there be precisely sixty beans ground to make his cup of coffee, and that his linens be spotlessly white. Although at this time he was not nearly as eccentric as he would become later on in life, he was, at times, demanding and irritable, and his conduct often resulted in driving off the very servants upon whom he depended to look after his household needs. Since she was aware that business affairs and domestic concerns were two of the greatest irritations in Beethoven's life, she hoped to avoid any disruptions the loss of Beethoven's servant would cause him. Anna Marie believed that sweetening his manservant's purse might persuade the man to overlook Beethoven's more trying behaviors. Anna Marie took this action out of concern for Beethoven, and certainly never considered that she might injure Beethoven's pride, nor that her motives would be so badly misconstrued.

Perhaps the servant's wife became jealous of her husband's good fortune or annoyed by what she believed to be Anna Marie's indecent interest in her spouse.[2] It also is possible that outside influences, which we will later find to have been at work undermining the Beethoven-Erdödy relationship, may have persuaded the woman to tell tales. Whatever the motive, she began spreading the rumor that the Countess Erdödy and the manservant were illicitly involved in a relationship. It was not long before the gossip reached Beethoven's ears; his letters indicate that the woman had told him herself. Why Beethoven had believed the

---

[2]If the woman's objections were of a monetary nature, she may have been justified in her feelings, for there is no indication how much *she* was required to put up with Beethoven's behavior without financial compensation.

story is not known, although he did sometimes believe strangers while discounting what was told him by his friends, and it may have been that the secrecy of Anna Marie's act had fueled his imagination. Naturally Anna Marie would not have told Beethoven of her intention to give his servant extra money on his behalf, as she was well aware of his aversion to accepting her help. If, before flying into a rage, Beethoven had given any thought to the situation and tried to understand why the Countess had kept the bonus money a secret from him, he might have avoided the consequences. But that was not Beethoven. His *modus operandi* was to become angry first, and save his contemplation for later. The very fact that all had been conducted without his knowledge only lent credence to the maidservant's story, and made him believe the worst of his Countess. Blinded by jealousy, by the thought that his beloved Countess would prefer any man, especially a servant, to him, Beethoven became enraged, far out of proportion to the "crime" if it had involved a monetary bonus only. The extent of his anger is evident in the note scrawled at the bottom of the sketches of his "Emperor" concerto and other works, complete with multiple underlinings and numerous exclamation points.

> What more can they still want. They have received from me the servant instead *of the master* [words crossed out]. Is the score not yet paid. What a substitute!!!!! What a magnificent exchange!!!!
>
> Beethoven is no servant— She wanted a servant— she has one now!

The depth of Beethoven's rage in these notes is not that of a man who merely is upset about a friend giving his servant some extra money. There is far more at issue here than that, and why no one has given this fact more than cursory treatment remains a puzzle. Even if Anna Marie *had* had sexual relations with Beethoven's servant (which she had not), why should Beethoven have cared? What she did in her own house was certainly of no one's concern but hers, was it not? The fact is, Beethoven cared very much, *too* much for her to simply have been his friend. If she had not given herself to Beethoven in every way, there would have been no reason for him to feel so possessive of her.

Hearing the gossip, he immediately accused the Countess of infidelity, and his March 7 letter to Zmeskall indicates he was not inclined to believe her explanation nor her claim to innocence. Whether Beethoven and the servant actually came to blows over the incident is unknown, although apparently the gossip around town was that it had. True or not, would a violent argument between the two men—rather than simply between Beethoven and Countess Erdödy—have erupted over what amounted to a rather small sum? Why had Beethoven become angry with the servant at all? He was, after all, just a servant, and why should he have refused money from someone who was his superior? This is the action of a man confronting another he believed to be his rival in love. As noted, whether Beethoven actually had come to blows with the servant is unknown, but since the story circulated that he had, this prompted his explanation (and denial) to Zmeskall:

> As to the blows, it is highly exaggerated—this story is at least three months old—the actual fact is far different—from what he now makes of it—the whole wretched story was cooked up by a huckster woman and a few other wretched creatures... I leave it entirely to you to arrange with my servant, only the Countess Erdödy must not exercise the influence over him; as *she says,* she had made him a present of 25 florins and given him five florins per month only in order that he may remain with me—I *must* now believe in this magnanimity—but I do not want things of that sort to continue...[3]

Beethoven's quarrel with Anna Marie had been so serious that he stopped speaking to her, making Zmeskall his intermediary, and without any forethought, moved out of her house. This was not done with calm consideration, for he took the only room available to him, a room that Baron de Trémont described as "the dirtiest, most disorderly place imaginable." More than simply changing residences, Beethoven also had considered leaving Vienna altogether, writing to Gleichenstein on March 14:

> Write to me soon as you can, and say whether you think that I could travel in the present warlike circumstances—and whether you are still firmly resolved to travel with me. Many dissuade me from it, but I will follow you entirely in this matter.... Now you can help me look out for a wife...[4]

---

[3]Anderson, p. 218.
[4]Anderson, p. 219.

Though he had made no mention of traveling before, suddenly Beethoven wanted to leave Vienna, even though "many"—maybe even the Countess herself—attempted to persuade him not to be so rash, particularly when the war would have made such an undertaking dangerous. It is apparent that his anger prevented him from thinking clearly. His asking Gleichenstein to help him find a wife has the tone of forced gaiety; wounded by Anna Marie, he would find someone else to be his wife. He'd show *her*! How touchingly childlike he was at times.

Somehow Beethoven was dissuaded from leaving town, but not from leaving the Countess's house. Of course, it is not known whether he moved out on his own, or she had demanded that he leave, for her own anger easily was a match for Beethoven's. Given their stubborn pride, it may have been a mutual decision, an "I'm leaving!" - "Good riddance!" situation. Under the circumstances, let us interject a question: the Erdödy apartment was quite large. If Beethoven and the Countess simply had occupied separate rooms there, and the real issue had actually been a disagreement over money, why had Beethoven felt such a strong need to move out so quickly? They easily could have avoided one another for a while until other, more suitable arrangements for Beethoven's lodgings could have been made. Had not Beethoven's irrational behavior, including the abrupt change in his living arrangements (clearly to his detriment), stemmed from the fact that he and the Countess had shared far more than a roof?[5] If Anna Marie was "just a friend" as so many claim, why this insanely jealous overreaction to a petty incident? As with the alleged fist fight with the servant, was not Beethoven acting every bit the part of the betrayed and wounded lover when he moved out in an angry huff? Logical, yet all that can be known for certain is that Beethoven moved out of the Countess's house so quickly that he could find only the most dreadful of rooms available. To his friend Gleichenstein, Beethoven wrote in early April 1809:

---

[5]Later, Beethoven would write that "sensual relations without a true union of souls leaves one not with an exalted feeling..." One assumes from this that Beethoven must have sometime experienced this "exalted feeling," and there were very few women with whom he would have had *both* a "union of souls" and the physical opportunity to enjoy sensual relations other than with Anna Marie Erdödy, here in Vienna, and at her residences in Hernals and Jedlersee.

> My rooms are in the Walfischgasse No. 1087, on the
> second floor. (It's a b[rothel], you will know it.)[6]

Thayer modestly declined to include Beethoven's parenthetical
note; nevertheless, it was to a house of ill repute that Beethoven
had been forced to relocate. This was a sad state indeed when one
considers what a shocking difference his new surroundings were
from Anna Marie's refined and luxurious house. Fortunately, he
did not have to be subjected to the indignity of such a residence for
long. Another letter to Zmeskall followed on April 17:

> Dear Z., a suitable apartment has just been found for
> me—but need someone to help me in the matter; I
> cannot ask my brother, because he is always in favor of
> what is cheapest—Tell me also when we could go to-
> gether to see this apartment today—[7]

The apartment he found was on the third floor in the
Klepperstalle on the Teinfaltstrasse, in a house belonging to a
lawyer named Gostischa. Shortly thereafter, his fury abating, he
began to discuss the matter with his friends. To Zmeskall he
wrote, again:

> I will tell you more by word of mouth, how abominably
> she [the servant] recently lied to *you*... I did not wish to
> take her husband back again, but partly circumstances
> necessitated it. I had to keep her because of my apart-
> ment; had I not taken him I should only have been the
> more swindled. Both are bad people.[8]

The intervention and calm rationale of longtime friends
like Zmeskall and Gleichenstein—who also had been a friend of
Anna Marie's—probably were instrumental in helping Beethoven's anger subside. When it did, he realized the dilemma his
unwarranted rage had caused: a hurt and angry Countess was no
longer part of his life. As usual when he had had a bout of bad
temper, and said hurtful things without thinking, he became
frantic to undo the terrible consequences of his anger. The "calm
consideration" he would later ask of his Beloved was not something in which he readily indulged, but when he did, it became
clear to him that he had misunderstood Anna Marie's actions

---

[6]Anderson, p. 227.

[7]Anderson, p. 228.

[8]Anderson, p. 252. Note Beethoven's reference to "bad people" and compare to
footnote #16.

entirely. Worse, he had wrongfully accused her of betraying him. One can only imagine the extent of his sorrow and remorse when he began to suspect that the servant had lied to him, that perhaps the Countess *had* been innocent of any wrong-doing. Unfortunately, Beethoven would find that angry words could not be always be recalled or be easily forgiven. He appealed to Gleichenstein for the truth:

> You are living on a calm peaceful sea, the distress of a friend who is in the storm you do not feel—or dare you not feel it—what will the inhabitants on the star of Venus Urania think of me, how will they judge me without my being seen—my pride is so humbled . . . — if only you would be frank, you are certainly hiding something from me, you wish to spare me, and with this uncertainty you cause me more pain than with certainty however fatal—Farewell, if you cannot come, let me know beforehand—think and act for me—it is not possible to entrust to paper more of what is going on with me.[9]

What Gleichenstein probably had been "hiding" was his belief that Anna Marie had been innocent of Beethoven's charges against her, that the money she had paid the servant genuinely had been on Beethoven's behalf, and that Beethoven alone had been culpable for the sorry state of his relationship with her. As Beethoven had asked Gleichenstein to "think and act for me," perhaps Gleichenstein had tried to smoothe things over with Anna Marie whose anger remained unquelled and whose heart was as immovable as stone. He must have relayed this to Beethoven, for the latter quickly wrote another note to Gleichenstein, which is obviously a reply:

> Your message hurled me from the regions of highest rapture to the lowest depths.—No, friendship, or feelings similar to it, has nothing but wounds for me—so be it then, for you poor B there is no happiness from outside.—I beg you to calm my mind, whether I myself was at fault, or if you cannot do that, tell me the truth;

---

[9]Anderson, p. 279. This undated note was originally placed in 1810 where it was thought to refer to Beethoven's relationship with Therese Malfatti. The internal tone of the letter does not support this placement, and several biographers (i.e. Steichen, Hamburger) agree. See related footnote #16.

I hear it as willingly as I speak it—now there is still
time, truth can still be useful to me—[10]

If Beethoven had hoped that Gleichenstein would provide
him with some justification for his anger, his hope was not realized. Rather than exonerating his behavior, Gleichenstein answered in the affirmative, that Beethoven *had* been at fault. How
Gleichenstein came by this information—from Anna Marie or the
manservant, or by other means— is not known, but he must have
given Beethoven the truth he had so desperately sought because
at this point, acknowledging his terrible mistake and believing
that there was "still time" to make amends, Beethoven immediately dashed off a letter of apology to Anna Marie, sending it to
her via Gleichenstein. His cover note to Gleichenstein reads:

> Dear friend so cursedly late—press all warmly to your
> heart—why cannot mine share in it?—the letter [an
> enclosure] is so written that all the world can read it—
> if you do not find the paper cover clean enough, put
> another round it; at night I cannot make out whether it
> is clean—farewell, dear friend, think and act also for
> your

> faithful friend Beethoven[11]

Most biographers have assumed that the enclosure had
been a marriage proposal to Therese Malfatti, but let us consider:
Beethoven wrote it in great haste, at night, in such a hurry in fact
that he could not be sure the paper cover was clean! If this *was* a
proposal, why did Beethoven not make every effort to present it
in such a way as to make a favorable impression on his intended
bride and her family? How well would they have received an offer
of marriage scrawled on dirty paper? Would he have written such
a document in a state of despair and panic? In the middle of the
night? And how on earth does this sad and desperate letter compare in any way with the dispassionate letter he did send to
Therese in 1810? Also, the letter which was enclosed with this one
Beethoven had "so written that all the world can read it." The
enclosure sounds far more like one of apology than proposal. We
also note that no letter of proposal to Therese Malfatti has ever
been found. She kept the other letter Beethoven had written her;

---

[10]Anderson, p. 269.
[11]Anderson, p. 218.

why then would she dispose of such an important one as this? We believe this proposal was never found simply because it had never existed. The enclosure given to Gleichenstein must have been this letter to Anna Marie:

> My dear Countess, I have erred, it is true, forgive me; it was certainly not intentional badness on my part, if I have hurt you—only since yesterday evening do I really know how everything is, and I am extremely sorry that I acted in this way—read your note in cold blood and judge yourself whether I have deserved it, and whether you have not paid me back everything sixfold, since I offended you without wanting to do so. Send me back my note today, and write to me with only one word that you are friendly again. I suffer endlessly through this, if you don't do this, I can do nothing, should it continue— I await your forgiveness.[12]

One can only imagine the scathing note that *she* must have sent *him* when originally he had refused to believe her explanation. If Beethoven felt that her letter had paid him back "sixfold" for the hurt he had caused her, her pen no doubt had been as sharp as her Beethoven's tongue. Although Beethoven realized he had been wrong to act as he did, and felt remorse for his rash behavior, he nevertheless felt her angry letter had been too harsh a punishment for his behavior. His letter of apology pouts, and his demeanor is touchingly childlike in the face of her justifiable anger. He was mortified to think that she believed he would hurt her intentionally, that he had some inner "badness." One almost can hear a child's wide-eyed profession of innocence: "But I didn't do it *on purpose!*"

In light of Anna Marie's "sixfold payback" which had convinced Beethoven that she had misjudged him, it is interesting that the Beloved letter contained the plea "Never misjudge the most faithful heart of your beloved." During the 1809 quarrel, he assured her that however rashly he might sometimes behave, he would never intentionally hurt her. His heart, his feelings for her, never wavered. He loved her still. For some reason, at the time of the Beloved letter, he felt the need to offer this reassurance once again. This author believes that this line in the Beloved letter harkens back to this time.

---

[12]Anderson, pp. 223-224.

FAILURE TO UNDERSTAND

We cannot find Anna Marie entirely blameless in this painful episode, even though she certainly had been the victim of Beethoven's unreasonable suspicion. He had been too hasty in misjudging her motives, too willing to listen to the lies of others, too quick to believe her capable of betraying him rather than trusting in her fidelity. Yet she also had misjudged *him*. For some reason, she never considered that he might react adversely to what she felt was an innocent gesture on her part, thinking that he would never doubt her motives and intentions. But this overly sensitive, easily wounded, and quickly angered man could not immediately accept her explanation. Knowing him as well as she did, she probably should have realized that he needed time to calm himself, to distance himself from the situation, before he could hear and believe the truth she gave him. That he questioned her honesty and fidelity no doubt had been very painful for her, or she would have realized that his volatile nature made him as deaf to the truth as his physical impairment made him to sound. As we will explore later, we believe Beethoven had "struck a nerve" in Anna Marie, accusing her of the one thing—infidelity —she found the most difficult to forgive. In a way, she had failed him. Yet circumstances were such that perhaps she could not have helped failing him.

Sadly, Beethoven was to find that the truth Gleichenstein told him was no longer of use to him, and that there was not "still time" to make amends with his heartfelt letter of apology: the damage had been done. Thayer assumed that "there is no reason to believe that a reconciliation had not been affected immediately." To the contrary, there is *every* reason to believe that no such reconciliation had come about. A quarrel between two such proud and stubborn souls that had escalated to one of this magnitude could not be easily forgotten or forgiven. For nearly a year, there was only silence between them, no letters, no notes, and Beethoven was decidedly depressed.

"I suffer endlessly through this," a penitent Beethoven had written, "and I await your forgiveness." But Anna Marie, too deeply hurt by her beloved Beethoven's lack of faith in her, would not give it. Beethoven had not expected her to be unforgiving, although an earlier rift with Breuning should have made him realize that serious transgressions could not be easily absolved, not even by those who loved him the most. Whatever had been her reply, his next letter indicates the depth of its sting. He immediately wrote to his publishers, Breitkopf & Härtel, and attempted to rescind his dedication of the *Op. 70 Piano Trios* to Anna Marie. We can see this as nothing but bitter retaliation for her refusal to forgive him—given that he had composed these pieces especially for her, and written such a heartfelt dedication to her.

> May 20, 1809: For the moment, only what still occurs to me about the [Op. 70] trios. First of all, if the title is not yet ready, I should like the dedication to be made at once to the Archduke Rudolph; if, however, it has been done, there is no help for it—...[13]

Fortunately, it *had* been done, and the lovely trios still bear his original dedication to her. In that same letter, he continued:

> The constant distraction amidst which I have been living for some time did not permit me to point this [error in one of the trios] out to you at once—however, I shall soon be myself again—and a thing of that sort will not occur any more—

His strong declaration notwithstanding, it would be a while before he was truly himself again. To his publishers he wrote, two months later, July 26, 1809,

> You make a great mistake in thinking that I have been so prosperous—we have passed through a great deal of misery.—The whole course of events has affected me body and soul.[14]

Some biographers have suggested that Beethoven's misery stemmed from Napoleon's invasion of Vienna, but while that surely troubled him, no foreign invasion could have devastated him nearly as much as the personal battle that he had lost through his own quick anger and obstinate pride. Thayer remarked that "Whoever makes himself even moderately conversant with the subject, soon perceives that a change in the man did take place too great and sudden to be attributed to the ordinary effect of advancing years." (Of course he had not been affected by "advancing years"—he was only 38 years old!) Thayer continued,

---

[13]Anderson, pp. 230-231
[14]Anderson, pp. 233-234

> The cessation of Beethoven's labors, although less absolute than in Handel's case, is even more remarkable, as it continued longer and was not produced by any natural and obvious cause.[15]

No obvious cause? Was he joking? Can there any doubt that Beethoven's bitter separation from his beloved Countess had been the reason for what Thayer called the "astonishing decrease in the composer's productiveness, an abrupt pause in his triumphant career?" Yet, unbelievably, Thayer could find no explanation for it! Josephine's supporters have tried to connect his misery to her marriage to Stackelberg which occurred in 1810, but we can see that sadness struck him much earlier than that.

Thayer noted that the year 1810 was devoid of music, at least music of a magnitude comparable to that which had been produced in previous years, and he believed that the failure of the "marriage project" had been the cause. He wrote, "Its disastrous effect upon Beethoven's professional energies is therefore for us the only measure of its severity." Yet, if there had been such a "project," it had failed in May 1810 and Beethoven's obvious sorrow was already present long before that, as evidenced by the song "As the Beloved Herself Wished to Separate" written in 1809. There is little doubt that the hurt and loneliness caused by his separation from Anna Marie was what had had the sudden "disastrous effect" upon Beethoven's musical career. Thayer also believed Beethoven's barren period stretched from 1810 to 1819, but had come to that conclusion only because he had not had the benefit of Beethoven's sketchbooks in order to form a different opinion. In fact, the composer's creativity surged in 1811 and 1812, and, as we shall shortly see, with good reason. Unger wrote that "the last 130 pages of the Petter sketchbook are to be dated from the middle of 1811 well into the following year." These sketchbooks contain sketches for various concertos, his Seventh and Eighth symphonies, two overtures, and many other pieces. These years hardly can be considered barren. However, both 1809-1810 and the year 1813—periods when Anna Marie was absent from his life—were not fruitful years. Clearly, Beethoven lived on a musical and emotional rollercoaster—"dry spells" followed by bursts of creative energy, and almost always coinciding with Anna Marie's return to Vienna . . . and to Beethoven.

---

[15]Thayer/Forbes, p. 483.

NEW FRIENDS

The summer following the quarrel, Beethoven began developing a friendship with the Brentano family, and with Antonie. Naturally he would have been drawn to their kindness at this lonely period of his life. He was deeply hurt and Antonie was "safe" for she was married, and therefore he would have no reason to worry about her having designs on his already badly wounded heart. She may even have known something about the situation (as, apparently, had Baron de Trémont) and been sympathetic to his plight.

Between 1809 and 1810, Beethoven also began spending time with the Malfatti family, writing to his friend, Gleichenstein, who had introduced them, "I am so happy in their company; it is as if the wounds, which bad people have inflicted on my soul, might through them be healed."[16]

In a February 8, 1810, letter to Professor von Loeb, Beethoven again requested lodging in the Pasqualati House, and it was in the spring that Beethoven was able to move there. His moving back to the Pasqualati House that year suggests his hope that by putting himself in proximity to Anna Marie, he might effect a reconciliation with her. Other biographers have noted that it was at this time that Beethoven took a sudden interest in his appearance, asking Zmeskall for a mirror and some boot polish, and investing in fine new shirts and suits. If such activity had any signficance at all, it surely was because he had become Anna Marie's neighbor once again and wished to revive her interest in him. His requests to Zmeskall (for the mirror in May and the polish in October) came *after* he ended his tepid friend-

---

[16]Steichen, p. 179. This reference to "bad people"—the identical sentiment Beethoven expressed to Zmeskall at the time of the quarrel—led Mrs. Steichen to believe that Gleichenstein had served as a go-between for Beethoven with Anna Marie. Based on this internal evidence, Mrs. Steichen reassigned the notes to Gleichenstein to 1809. [In 1951, biographer Michael Hamburger already had reassigned them to 1807-1808, again with no connection to Therese Malfatti.] Steichen wrote "the placid letter [to Therese Malfatti] bears no relation to the agitated notes to Gleichenstein. Although undated, these notes obviously belong to 1809 and to the quarrel with Countess Erdödy. The desperate one [to Gleichenstein] enclosing a letter 'so written that all the world can read it' cannot possibly have served to transmit a letter to Therese, a letter lacking in all sense of immediacy or strain." Because Mrs. Steichen's argument reflects both thoughtful analysis of the letters' contents and tone, and our own consideration of the matter, we likewise have placed the letters to Gleichenstein in 1809.

ship with Therese Malfatti (at the end of April or early May) and coincided with his move to the Pasqualati House. We also believe that, Anna Marie's anger having abated, she also began to have similar thoughts of a reunion with Beethoven.

Max Unger believed that the following note, formerly presumed to have been sent to Therese Malfatti, had been addressed to Anna Marie Erdödy instead. If Unger was right, Beethoven's move to the Pasqualati House must have had the hoped-for effect and precipitated his reconciliation with the Countess. Both of them had had time to evaluate what their pride had cost them in terms of their relationship, and were ready at last to offer each other forgiveness. Beethoven wrote, sometime around July 1810:

> It would be in vain for you to try to find yourself even remotely responsible for my present behavior—No, it is simply the way I am—

Whatever "behavior" he had been exhibiting may have been induced by lingering guilt over his mistreatment and mistrust of her the previous year, and doubts about whether they might be able to regain what he had caused them to lose.

> Already yesterday I wanted to come from Schönbrunn to you, but I would have had to go back again and when I am once with you I cannot go away without forcing myself, so it had to be given up—I do believe that perhaps you somehow care for me,

This last sentence sounds as if Beethoven was "testing the waters" to see whether she truly had forgiven him, still loved him, and was willing and able to forget past transgressions. He continued, risking her rejection by expressing his strong feelings for her and her family:

> therefore I take the opportunity to tell you also that you are all in the highest degree, dear and precious to me–
> – As soon as possible I will be with you again.
>   Hold dear your true friend
>   Beethoven[17]

Not long afterwards, only a few months later in fact, he was indeed very much "with" Anna Marie again.

---

[17]Anderson, p. 282. See also her note #3. Anna Marie was then in Hernals, within walking distance of Schönbrunn.

RECONCILIATION

Early in 1811, we find Anna Marie again firmly ensconced in Beethoven's life, having offered him at last the forgiveness he had so long awaited. In March 1811, Beethoven wrote to her:

> With much pleasure have I received your last lines... as regards the trio, you have only to let me know whether you wish to see to its being copied at your house or whether I shall undertake it? Both will be the same to me, and what is most suitable to you, will be dearest to me. Herr Linke who has something good for his concert tomorrow, is in a hurry, hence only everything dear and good to you and your children. I will seize the very next opportunity to be in the very midst of you all, till then farewell, dear esteemed Countess.

your true
friend
Beethoven[18]

Thayer thought Anna Marie and Beethoven had been immediately reconciled; other biographers thought they had had a long estrangement, lasting until 1815. Neither are correct. Linke's concert was held on March 24, 1811, thus this note was written on March 23. Also in March Beethoven wrote to the Archduke Rudolph regarding a new trio he was composing for the piano. The trio mentioned in both letters evidently was the *Piano Trio in B-flat Op. 97*, the "Archduke" a piece brimming with joy over the return of his beloved Countess and her love for him. Their reconciliation brought about a sudden surge in his creative energy, which had been dormant since their quarrel. So exuberant was he over her return that he completed the Op. 97 trio, which he had abandoned in 1809,[19] in an astonishing three weeks. In addition, the *Piano Sonata #26 in E flat major, Op. 81a,* entitled "Farewell, Absence, and Return," that he also had begun in

---

[18]Anderson, pp. 315-316. For some reason, a postscript had been cut, not torn, from the bottom of this letter's autograph. It is likely that other letters to her written around this time are missing, for this one begins too abruptly for there to have been none preceding it. Beethoven also mentions her "last lines," indicating other letters written prior to this one.

[19]Although Solomon claimed Beethoven had begun composing this piece in 1810, Nottebohm found sketches for it in the composer's 1809 sketchbook.

1809 (with a farewell to Anna Marie) was finished in 1811 (with her return to him). Beethoven was upset with his publishers who had changed the sonata's title from *Lebewohl, Abwesenheit, und Wiedersehen* to *Les Adieux*. In an October 9, 1811, letter, Beethoven claimed that, although technically both words meant *farewell*, "the first, [*Lebewohl*] one only says, heartfelt, to one alone, the other [*Adieux*] to a whole assembly." Clearly Beethoven had wanted this sonata to reflect a personal, heartfelt goodbye—and a subsequently joyful and equally personal welcome—to one beloved person, and it is difficult to imagine that he meant the Archduke!

Upon his doctor's orders ("...the physician is already grumbling at my remaining here [in Vienna] so long...") Beethoven went to Teplitz from the end of July until autumn, returning to Vienna in October via Prince Lichnowsky's estate in Silesia. Although Solomon suggested that Beethoven's love affair with Antonie began around this time in 1811, a note from Beethoven to Zmeskall in fall 1811 says that "we are ill again.—We wish that you likewise will soon get ill on a rich Erdödyian feast—" It is unlikely that he would have embarked upon a love affair with Antonie at the same time he was so happily indulging in these "Erdödyian feasts." The chronology of the years 1811-1812 presented earlier also showed that Beethoven had had very little time in which to develop an intimate relationship with Frau Brentano, even if he had been so inclined.

In a mid-1812 note to Anna Marie, Beethoven wrote:

> I said to you today, dear C, that I came for my own
> sake,—actually I wanted to say that I came on your
> account and on my account, Also, *when you do not see me
> I wish that you believe me always*, that without all other
> reasons and considerations without all other human
> mixing-in *I am with the greatest pleasure around you
> and your to me, loved children.*   B.[20]

Note how the line in the Beloved letter—"Ah where I am you are also with me."—seems to echo the italicized portions in the letter, above. We can only guess what Beethoven and Anna Marie discussed on that day in 1812. Given the events of the summer close at hand, the Beloved letter, the "heart full of many

---

[20]Anderson, p. 539, and Steichen, p. 207. This undated note was placed in 1815 by Anderson; in 1812 by Steichen.

things to say," the observations Beethoven made about his life during his journey, one can imagine the conversation that had transpired between them. Perhaps she had revealed to him her plan to persuade—or force—her estranged husband Peter to relinquish his property to her, a move she ultimately made, and which we feel precipitated Beethoven's guarded optimism in the Beloved letter. She also may have expressed her concern over family pressures which would still prevent her from breaking with Peter legally. The year of 1811 was a difficult one for her, and would mark the beginning of ten years of legal entanglements with her husband's family, most notably her sister-in-law, Countess Sigismund Erdödy.[21] We believe the problems that were to plague her were unrelenting attempts by the Erdödys to force her to give up her relationship with Beethoven.

In 1812, Anna Marie also may have expressed to Beethoven her uncertainty whether, given their similarly strong personalities, they might be able to form a harmonious union. Having once been deeply disappointed in her attempt to live with him, she may have indicated to Beethoven her reluctance to do so again, prompting his musings about "not demanding everything" in the Beloved letter. We do not, and cannot, know for certain what they did discuss. We only know, from the Beloved letter, that Beethoven still held tightly to his belief that somehow they might yet achieve the lasting union they both desperately wanted.

Although 1813 would deal Beethoven another crushing blow in terms of his relationship with Anna Marie, through much of 1811 and all of 1812, Beethoven's eternally beloved remained firmly in his life, and hope was still very much alive in his heart.

---

[21]A full accounting of Anna Marie's legal problems with her husband's family will be given in Chapter 29, *The Final Years*.

❖ 28 ❖
The Later Years: After 1812

Following his sojourn at the Bohemian spas, Beethoven had joined Anna Marie in Hernals, and from there, he traveled to Linz and visited with his brother. After leaving Linz, he returned to Vienna in December 1812, but, as noted, his whereabouts between his departure from Linz on November 10 and his presence in Vienna in early December, are unknown. Possibly he had returned to Hernals. Thus far, he showed no change in demeanor. Then several months into the new year, something occurred to alter Beethoven's disposition and level of creativity. His letters took on an air of sadness; his musical productivity dropped, he became slovenly and depressed. What was it that had happened? Solomon claimed a delayed reaction to his loss of Antonie had caused his despair, but as nearly a half year had passed since he had last seen her, that is hardly likely. No, it was another woman, far closer to him than Antonie ever had been, who had briefly departed from his life that year, and it was to her loss that Beethoven reacted.

We find that there were no letters to Anna Marie in 1813. One possibility is that the Countess had gone to Hungary in a continuing battle again several charges first brought against her by her sister-in-law, which were not completely resolved until 1821. But, if so, why had Beethoven not written her there? Another possibility is that their interaction during this time had been purely personal and not conducted through letters, or that the letters for this period had been lost or destroyed. However, there are several bits of evidence which point to the likelihood of another quarrel. First, it was at this time that Beethoven had written the note to himself which had said, in part, "Oh fearful conditions which do not suppress my feelings for domesticity... Learn to keep silent, friend! Speech is like silver, but to hold one's peace at the right time is pure gold." Second, there was a letter written by Beethoven to the Archduke Rudolph on May 27, 1813, from Baden in which the composer expressed his unhappy state of mind that year. Although much of that can be attributed to the Kinsky affair, Beethoven said in this letter that more than one issue troubled him:

> ...a number of unfortunate incidents occurring one after the other have really driven me into a state bordering on mental confusion. However, I am convinced that the glorious beauties of Nature and the lovely surroundings of Baden will restore my balance and that a twofold calm will take control of me.[1]

Third, in an 1815 letter to Anna Marie, Beethoven spoke of her "renewing your friendship for me." If their relationship had required renewal, what else could have happened but another quarrel? If so, what might this quarrel have been about? Because Beethoven lamented his inability to "hold his peace," this author believes he had once again urged Countess Erdödy to divorce Peter and marry him. Earlier, perhaps while at Hernals in September, Beethoven may have assured Anna Marie that he would no longer press the issue of marriage between them, and simply accept his relationship with her as it was. While he surely had been sincere at the time, her warm reception, coupled with her legal acquisition of Peter's property and Beethoven's assumption that she might soon be free to remarry, might have encouraged him to once again broach the idea of marriage with her. Her refusal, on the heels of their time together in Hernals, might well have thrown Beethoven into "mental confusion." If she had thought him insensitive to the consequences of such a move, the discussion could have ended in another quarrel between them. His anguished state of mind, similar to the time when she had repaid him "sixfold" in 1809 for his behavior, indicates that this may have been the time when she had returned the Beloved letter to him in a fit of anger. Unless their correspondence for this time

---

[1]Anderson, p. 420

period had been lost or destroyed, there is otherwise no explanation for the abrupt cessation of letters between them.

Despite their strong difference of opinion on the subject of marriage, nothing could destroy totally the feelings that they had for one another, and this separation would not last very long. It did, however, change some things between them. If up to that point Beethoven had operated under any delusions about them being able to live together as husband and wife, from then on he surely had no more self-deceptions. One must remember, however, that there is a great difference between realism and defeatism. Defeated, he would have given up on their relationship entirely. In achieving acceptance, he was able to hold onto a small portion of his long-cherished dream.

LOVE WITHOUT MARRIAGE

Anna Marie undoubtedly loved Beethoven very much, but for several reasons she could not agree to marry him. The first and most important surely was the jeopardy in which such a move would have placed her children. By marrying a commoner, Anna Marie, like Josephine, would have had to forfeit her title. That in itself probably meant very little to her, for she had enjoyed few benefits from her noble status. It had been her uncommon busines acumen, and not the fact that she was a countess, that had caused her to survive and prosper financially. However, if she had relinquished her title, the guardianship of her children would in all probability have been assumed by her husband's family. Perhaps Beethoven did not recognize, understand, or admit to this threat to her motherhood, just as he had not seen it in his relationship with Josephine. (We believe his relationship with Karl later would bring him this understanding.)

Second, but of lesser importance, she may have been reluctant to give up her hard-won financial and emotional independence which she would have been required to relinguish or sublimate were she to become another man's wife. Beethoven's pride hardly would have allowed her, as his wife, to contribute to the family finances. He had trouble enough accepting gifts from her as it was.

Third, avoiding a legal alliance with Beethoven may have been in part to protect him from the Erdödy family, who, as we shall see, already caused him professional problems. She must have felt that their marriage would have exacerbated an already bad situation.

Last, she knew first-hand how difficult it would be to once again share a home with him. We can well imagine her saying to him, "I love you, but I cannot live with you." So much alike, their personalities would have clashed time and again, just as they had in 1809, and eventually driven them apart. Somehow she knew as he did not (or at least, would not admit until later) that they both required some distance be kept between them in order to maintain the love and harmony that was theirs during the best of times. Although she must have made it clear to Beethoven that she could not and would not marry him, she never had another man in her life, not so long as she lived. From her twenty-first year of age to her death at fifty-six, there was only her "beloved Apollo." Beethoven and Beethoven alone.

UNDERSTANDING AND COMPROMISE

Knowing Anna Marie's will was equal to his, Beethoven at last realized that on the issue of marriage she was not to be swayed. Perhaps he also came to comprehend her reasons for refusing him. We believe that this understanding came about with his adoption of Karl. A person who is not a parent cannot fully understand the sacrifices parents often are willing to make for their children. Before this time, Beethoven may have demanded more from Anna Marie than she as a mother was able to give him: the sacrifice of her children out of love for him. He probably had become hurt and angry by her seemingly placing her love for her children above her love for him. However, once he became a father to Karl, he came to appreciate the extent of a parent's love and what it meant to a parent to lose a child. It was then, as he remarked to the Giannatasio sisters, that he was able to accept the gift of her love without the legal ties that would have destroyed her maternal bonds. His comment shows he had convinced himself that her love was superior to the affection a wife gives her husband out of obligation. Fantasy gave way to reality. His desire for marriage and a family notwithstanding, Beethoven made the decision to compromise: he would sacrifice marriage rather than separate forever from his only truly immortally beloved, the one, he said, who loved him enough to "have remained always with me." Although he could not live with Anna Marie "wholly and completely," he knew he could still be close to her. As much as he was able, he contented himself with living near her and having that same intimate place in her life and her heart as he had already enjoyed for more than a dozen years, without having or asking for more than that. Though legally she never became his wife, Beethoven's letters to her show that they took spousal comfort in one another, sharing the intimate and mundane details of their lives with one another, taking the flames of passion and creating a warm companionship. He was often at her estate. Her family became his, as much as his eccentric ways and her independent spirit would allow. It is unfortunate that this arrangement did not always bring Beethoven the happiness which he hoped and believed it would, yet there would be happy and harmonious times now and then for another eleven years.

In 1812 Beethoven was only 41, and his age would not have prevented him from taking a wife. Yet he chose not to pursue any other woman, deciding to accept and nurture the loving relationship he already had, imperfect as it was. That is why there is no obvious evidence of any romantic endeavors after 1812. Yet one who looks closely can plainly see that love and his Beloved were still there for him. As Beethoven himself said, it was "still now as on the first day." Was not his continued devotion to his Distant Beloved evidence of that? However, biographers preferred to give Beethoven a "cheerless outlook on marriage" rather than admit that Anna Marie was, then as always, far more to him than simply patron and friend.

IN THE HOUSE OF ILL REPUTE

Solomon suggested that in 1813, despondent, almost suicidal, and bitterly resigned to a solitary life, Beethoven began making it a habit to engage in sexual activities with prostitutes. Solomon's preoccupation with psychosexual matters and his tendency to give most of Beethoven's activities sexual connotations made it difficult at the outset for this author to take this claim seriously. Solomon's adherence to old Freudian interpretations made us wary of his conclusions and eager to review the primary source materials for ourselves. We were not surprised by the findings.

Solomon based his opinion that Beethoven frequently patronized prostitutes on five letters which the composer wrote to

Zmeskall between 1813 and 1816. It was Solomon's belief—with which a later writer, Susan Lund, agreed—that Beethoven had taken to visiting brothels in the company of his long-time friend, and that sexual activity had been caused at first by his despondency over losing Antonie Brentano and what was probably his last chance for a normal relationship, and later, by his problems with Karl and his mother, and by Beethoven's own anxieties about his masculinity induced by repeated rejection in love. While Beethoven was for the moment disheartened by his temporary separation from Anna Marie, letters do not support the contention that his mood had plummeted to the point where he contemplated suicide. Nor had the sad times he endured in both 1813 and later in 1816-1818—when his worsening deafness and bitter struggles over custody of his nephew deepened his despondency —caused him to habitually frequent houses of ill repute.

Beethoven regularly teased Zmeskall, who was an official in the Hungarian chancellary, about his work and there is reason to believe that his references to "fortresses of the empire" could have been connected to that. It was at this time that the Austrian government was indulging in a "rape" of Hungary by imposing its laws upon that country, and destroying its sovereignty. Although we might argue this point successfully, unless Solomon's contention is addressed outright, we feel we will have no impact against his accusation. Let us therefore assume that Solomon was right, that in his letters to Zmeskall Beethoven was using code words for sexual activity, and that the "fortresses" were, indeed, prostitutes. In actuality, this author need not defend Beethoven against these charges, for a reading of his own letters, rather than simply the summaries provided by Solomon and Lund, shows that in whatever activity Zmeskall was engaged, Beethoven was not a participant. The first four references[2] to the "fortresses" read as follows:

> February 1813: Let us postpone our meeting today, dear Z, for the only time I too could manage today is immediately after dinner—...But I hope that we shall soon be able to see and talk to one another. Be zealous in defending the fortresses of the Empire which, as you know, lost their virginity a long time ago and have already received several assaults.

---

[2]Letters taken from Anderson, p. 408, 527, 596, 619, and 639, respectively.

> October 1815: Enjoy life, but not voluptuously — Proprietor, Governor, Pasha of various rotten fortresses!!!!

> September 1816: I need not warn you any more to take care not to be wounded near certain fortresses.

> December 1816: Keep away from rotten fortresses, for an attack from them is more deadly than one from well preserved ones.

Assuming the "fortresses" to be prostitutes, it is clear that in each of these letters, Beethoven was issuing a warning to his friend to beware of engaging in sexual activity with them. Nowhere does the composer allude to joining Zmeskall in his escapades—if indeed Zmeskall had been a regular customer of brothels as Solomon contends—nor did Beethoven indicate that he had the slightest inclination to do so. Let us now see the final letter on the matter for the most conclusive remark:

> Month not given, 1816: In regard to the fortresses, I fancy that I have already given you to understand that I do not want to spend any time in marshy districts. I call you my friend also. Even though in many respects we both act and think differently.

This letter shows without a doubt that if Zmeskall had invited, and perhaps even urged Beethoven to accompany him in his visits to brothels, Beethoven had not taken part. His adamant note shows that Beethoven was quite firm in his refusal, and that there is no basis for accusing Beethoven of such habitual behavior. Of course, we will not claim that Beethoven had *never* availed himself of the services of a prostitute in times of abject loneliness and despair, such as he certainly suffered during 1813 and again in 1816-1818. Had he completely abstained, had he not experienced sex both within and outside of the confines of a loving relationship, we do not believe he could have written the following in his *Tagebuch:*

> Sensual relations without a spiritual union is and remains beastial, afterwards one has no trace of an exalted feeling, but rather remorse.

Simply because Beethoven did not remain sexually pure should not cause us to overlook the word "remorse." A sexual act exchanged for money obviously disgusted him, and his self-reproach for indulging in such behavior would have prevented him from making such an activity habitual. In 1813, he had sustained another quarrel with Anna Marie, his obstinacy had driven her away from him, and she had returned his heartfelt letter to him. In 1816-1818 she also was away from him, though not through any fault of his own. Beethoven's loss of his "spiritual union" with her, and his subsequent despondency—as evidenced by his sudden slovenliness and drop in his creativity during both periods—may well have impelled him to seek comfort in the "beastial" arms of a whore. But he quickly realized that there was no solace to be found there, only deep guilt and self-reproach. One cannot imagine him punishing himself in this way by repeatedly engaging in an activity he found abhorent. One also must not point at these few lapses in his morality as evidence that all his "lofty values" were nothing more than a myth he perpetuated about himself. Such infrequent mistakes are not enough to convict him of such deception. Since we can think of no better rebuttal to those who would ascribe such behavior to Beethoven and believe him capable of it, we shall quote the man himself, as he wrote in a note to Amalie Sebald in 1812:

> People say nothing, they are just ordinary folk, that is to say, as a rule they see in others only their own reflection.[3]

AGAIN, REUNION

In February 1814 Beethoven moved into the Bartenstein House which, like the Pasqualati House, was in the Molkerbastei district and very near Anna Marie's Vienna home. His creativity suddenly increased, and, as usual, we see that the impetus for this upswing in his musical output was the presence once again of Anna Marie. Sometime that year, a note in the *Tagebuch* indicates that the Countess had sent him a gift of 34 bottles, but of what, it does not say. It has been suggested that they were bottles of wine. Beethoven did fancy Hungarian wine and if Anna Marie had gone to her homeland on family business she might have sent him that. Given Beethoven's love for water, they also could have been bottles of spring, mineral, or spa water which he often drank for his health. He did ask her to send him a bottle of spa water in

---

[3]Anderson, p. 386.

1815—interestingly, the only thing other than the loan of her piano which he ever asked of her—which she apparently sent *gratis*. He complained, though not too vehemently, "You again make me a present, and that is not right, you thus deprive me of all pleasure in the small services which I could give you—"

Other than the 1814 note about receiving her gift of the 34 bottles, there is no other existing correspondence between them, though it is unlikely she would have sent a gift without an accompanying letter, and just as unlikely that he would not have acknowledged it. Obviously there *were* letters, perhaps important ones which might have given greater insight into their relationship, that are now missing. Exactly *why* they are missing—accidently lost or deliberately destroyed because of their content—is unknown, although we will find evidence of their destruction later on.

There was an interesting note to Zmeskall in April 1814 in which Beethoven said

> I am not going to travel. At any rate, I refuse to submit to any compulsion in this respect — the matter requires more mature consideration— I should very much like to discuss my rooms with you and what arrangements I ought to make—[4]

Beethoven's firm resolve not to leave Vienna indicates that the he and Countess Erdödy were on the verge of another reunion. On November 30, 1814, a note to the Archduke also leads one to believe that the loving relationship between Beethoven and his Countess was being rekindled:

> I am still exhausted by fatiguing affairs, vexations, pleasure and delight, all intermingled and inflicted or bestowed upon me at once.[5]

The "pleasure and delight" he referred to in his note must have come from some initial overtures on Anna Marie's part to reclaim what they had lost. She sent him a more definite invitation to renew their relationship shortly thereafter, for early the next year he sent her this joyful response:

February 29, 1815 [He probably meant March 1]

---

[4]Anderson, p. 453.
[5]Anderson, p. 476.

> I have read, my esteemed Countess, your letter with
> great pleasure, also the renewing of your friendship for
> me. It has long been my wish once again to see you and
> also your dear children, for although I have suffered
> much, I have not yet lost my earlier feelings—for
> childhood, for nature—and for friendship.[6]

He repeatedly used the term "friendship," yet his eager-
ness and the sudden change in his frame of mind suggests something far deeper. Though his true feelings were couched in an in-
nocuous word which would never compromise her, surely she
could and would read the word *love*. His letter continued:

> The trio, and everything which is as yet not published,
> stands, dear Countess, from the heart, at your service—
> Not without sympathy and solicitude have I often
> inquired after your state of health, but now, once again,
> I shall present myself personally to you and I will be
> glad to be able to take part in all that concerns you.—

We see here that Beethoven had kept track of Anna Marie
throughout their separation, and we suspect it had not simply
been her health, but also her feelings about him, about which he
had regularly inquired. Joseph Linke, the "Accursed Violoncello," who had known Beethoven for many years, and had likewise
been in the Countess's service a long time, might well have provided the "link" between these two stubborn people which eventually led to their renewed relationship.

Ludwig's brother, Carl, ill and financially troubled, had
written Anna Marie himself sometime early in 1815, asking for a
favor, probably in the form of a monetary gift or loan. He no doubt
had approached her for assistance because he knew of her relationship with his brother. Had he not been well acquainted with
her, or known how close she was to brother Ludwig, it would have
been odd for Carl to have requested help from her. How else could
he have known her, or felt comfortable enough to ask her for help?
Beethoven was not happy with his brother's appeal, and in his
February 29 [or March 1] letter, he asked Anna Marie to "make
allowances for him, because he is really an unhappy, suffering
man."

Three days after this letter to Anna Marie, Beethoven
wrote an inscription in Ludwig Spohr's album, a three-part canon

---

[6]Anderson, p. 499.

on a line from Schiller's *Don Carlos*, "Kurz ist der Schmerz und ewig wahrt die Freude"—from a song Beethoven had composed in 1813. This time Beethoven omitted the word *wahrt* so that the line translates as, "Brief is pain, eternal is joy."

Despite his desire to resume his relationship with the Countess, he knew by now that marriage for them was out of the question, and the memory of the heartbreak his relationship with her sometimes caused him must have been very much on his mind. After so much instability (something, as he had said in the Beloved letter, he did not want), it appears that Beethoven had, initially, some reluctance to become as deeply involved with Anna Marie as he had once been. We see this in a letter Beethoven wrote to her children's tutor, Brauchle, in March 1815:

> It has been difficult for me to shake off several misgivings in regard to this matter [to visit Anna Marie]; and yet I believe that I really had firmly resolved to go to the Countess—Hence I shall certainly make haste, the more so as at the present moment my spirit can only feel at ease in the presence of the beauties of nature, and so far I have made no arrangements anywhere else to give free play to this irresistible inclination of mine.[7]

These "misgivings," in conflict with his "irresistible inclinations," must have prompted this note to Breitkopf & Härtel, March 10, 1815:

> If I hesitate about the publication of my numerous more recent works, you must ascribe this hesitation to the uncertainty of all things pertaining to human relationships.[8]

Initial misgivings and uncertainties proved unfounded, and once again, as always, Beethoven and his Countess found their way back to one another. At last they had reached an easy compromise. He wrote her from Döbling at the end of July 1815:

> Let me add that I shall confidently take the road across the Danube [i.e. to Jedlersee] as I did before. Courage, provided it be justified, enables one to triumph everywhere. [9]

---

[7]Anderson, p. 500.
[8]Ibid.
[9]Anderson, p. 518

Throughout 1815 until his brother's final illness and death in November, Anna Marie and Beethoven spent many happy times together. In Anna Marie's sole surviving letter to him—an invitation she wrote in rhyme—she sent an "ardent entreaty" for her "beloved Apollo" to come and live for a time among his "Jedlersee Muses."[10] This was an invitation often given which he accepted whenever he was able, staying in rooms she kept ever ready for him, and with her own piano at his disposal. He accepted this loan with an odd reluctance. To Brauchle he wrote.

> I must fill up the measure of my bothersomeness by asking for her piano for a few days in my room... I do not deserve this, and my perplexity increases when I think of how I shall make it up to her—[11]

Although he was willing to accept gifts and assistance from others—such as large sums of money from the Brentanos—it was only with hesitation that he would accept small things from Anna Marie. We have already seen his strong reaction to her paying his servant a bonus, and even a simple bottle of spa water prompted him to tell her "that is not right." Perhaps he saw taking things from her as a sign of weakness on his part, something he could not show the woman he loved. In their relationship, as in no other, he wanted to be the provider, the giver of "small services," which seems very much like a husbandly role.

INTERFERENCES

Unfortunately, toward the end of 1815, the severity of his brother's illness and Ludwig's involvement with Caspar Carl's affairs, began to interfere with their happiness. To a member of Anna Marie's staff, probably Brauchle, he wrote:

> I am truly in despair that I have not yet been able to dine with you again. I have just begun a very urgent task today, or I should have been able to see our kind Countess— I am so sorry that I am unable to contribute to the recovery of her health as much as my heart desires.— But the Countess must take courage and then she will certainly overcome her illness to a great extent at least — [12]

---

[10]Text of the invitation in Chapter 11, pp. 145-146.
[11]Anderson, p. 511
[12]Anderson, p. 545.

The Countess also began suffering more frequent bouts of illness, for Beethoven's letters inquired about her health, and expressed the wish that she was improving. He wrote again to the Erdödy family's tutor, Brauchle:

> I do not come today — but for certain tomorrow evening, or at latest early the day after—it would be unfair—if you were to measure my affection for the Countess and for you all, according to the visits I pay you — There are causes for the conduct of people which are based on unsolvable necessity.[13]

Despite problems, Beethoven once again was inspired by his beloved Countess and his creativity. In this year of 1815, Beethoven wrote two sonatas, Op. 102, which he would later dedicate to Anna Marie, and about which Eduoard Herriot wrote:

> It is a joy to find the beloved poet again in the wonderful *Two Sonatas for Piano and Cello, Op. 102*, composed in July and August 1815 and dedicated to Countess Marie von Erdödy. We find our great Beethoven again in... these compositions...transported by this lyricism which mounts to the stars... this impassioned spirituality... Beethoven leads us back to the heights... there is the same insight, the same pure melody as in the *Archduke Trio*... Beethoven was transported, but without saying so. He dedicated several works to Countess Erdödy without compromising her by indiscreet disclosures.The men who are most active in love are those who say the least about it.[14]

In November, Carl died and his death brought new burdens into his brother's life, not the least of which was his legal battle for guardianship of his nephew, Karl.

INTO THE DARKNESS

Although Thayer believed the relationship between Anna Marie and Beethoven ended in 1815, this is not true. Late in that year, however, she inherited property in Croatia (Schloss[15] Paukovich) and Italy, and left Vienna for a time to oversee the management of her new estates. "God give you further strength to

---

[13]Anderson, p. 538.
[14]Herriot, pp. 224-225, 242.
[15]"Schloss" translates as "castle."

reach your Isis temple where the refining fire will consume all your evil, and you will arise a new Phoenix," Beethoven wrote to her on October 15, 1815, in a sorrowful letter of farewell.

The almost simultaneous loss of both Anna Marie and Caspar Carl dealt Beethoven a devastating blow. It is little wonder that he focused his attention so singlemindedly and completely on the custody battle with his sister-in-law, Johanna Reiss van Beethoven, over the boy, Karl. Although this complex issue cannot be adequately explored here, we will say here that it was not guilt, sexual ambiguity, an abnormal psyche, or an underlying streak of cruelty in his personality that were the motivating forces behind Beethoven's actions. He did not continue this nonproductive and even harmful lawsuit because of abnormal sexual inclinations, a need to be "maternal," or any other aberrant reas-on suggested by the Sterbas (et.al.). He was driven by pain, by the pain of loss and abandonment and loneliness, by the need to have someone in his life whom he could love and who, unlike Anna Marie who left and Carl who died, could not and would not leave him. Karl, a minor child, would be under his control, tied to him, thus be there always to receive the enormous amount of love that Beethoven had to give him, and to give back love in return. Of course, this scenario did not come to pass. Love cannot be elicited simply because one wills it so, not even by the indomitable will of a Beethoven. Sadly, not only was Beethoven to waste his creative energy in this endeavor, it would serve only to drive Karl away from him rather than give the composer the warm closeness he craved from his nephew. Cooperation rather than contention between Johanna and himself certainly would have been better for all concerned, especially for the nine-year-old boy caught in the middle. In this matter, Beethoven might have listened to Anna Marie's counsel, but she was not there to give it.

Beethoven has been accused of heartlessness, cruelty, and of aberrations one finds shocking simply because they are leveled at a basically decent man. How easy it seems to forget his pain. If at this time he was not entirely the Beethoven we know, the Beethoven of the high morals and lofty values, certainly he was not entirely to blame. Utterly alone, he is more to be pitied than condemned.

Throughout this sordid affair with the lawsuit, one is in inclined to believe that Anna Marie was less than sensitive to Beethoven's need for her. But Carl's death had come surprisingly quickly [16] and when she left Vienna, she had no idea that Beethoven would be facing his brother's loss so soon after her departure. She also had no reason to suspect a vicious custody battle would ensue in the wake of Carl's death. Her precarious health made traveling difficult for her, so repeated returns to Vienna, however much she may have wanted to be there, were out of the question. Yet she would never be far from Beethoven's thoughts, nor he from hers. One letter to her from him indicates that she did make at least one visit to Vienna in 1816, and likely in response to his need.

On May 8, 1816, Beethoven wrote to Ries: "Unfortunately I have no wife. I have found only one whom no doubt I shall never possess." Just five days later, on May 13, after some time had passed between his letters to her, he suddenly wrote to "dear precious" Anna Marie: "Perhaps you believe, and quite rightly, that I have completely forgotten all about you. But indeed that is only what appears to be the case." It is interesting that these two letters should come so close together, as if Beethoven's note to Ries had prompted his letter to Anna Marie. In this letter, Beethoven added that "for the last six weeks I have been in very poor health, so much so that frequently I have thought of death."

Before he could mail his May 13 letter, Beethoven learned through his old friend Linke that Anna Marie's teenaged son, August, had died or been killed under mysterious circumstances. He added the following to his already lengthy letter:

> ...what comfort can I give you? Nothing is more painful than the unforeseen departure of those who are near to us; but I feel the deepest sympathy for you in your irreparable loss.—Grief seizes me for you and also for me, for I loved your son— Heaven watches over you, and will not wish to increase your already great sufferings, even though your health may be uncertain. I weep here with you. [17]

With the recent loss of her son, perhaps she felt they were both in need of each other's consolation. Sometime that year, despite the fact that her own ill health made travel difficult for her, Anna Marie returned to Vienna. The salutation from one of Beethoven's letters to her shows how glad he was to see her:

[16] So quickly, in fact, that Beethoven had suspected Johanna of poisoning Carl and ordered an autopsy which showed that his suspicions had been unfounded.
[17] Anderson, p. 579.

> Dear, dear, dear, dear, dear Countess!
>
> I am taking baths and am not stopping them until tomorrow. Hence I was unable to see you and all your dear ones today. I trust that you are enjoying better health. It is no consolation for more noble-minded people to tell them that others are suffering too. Yet no doubt comparisons must always be drawn, and, if one does, one will certainly find that we all *suffer, that we all err, though each in a different way* . . . As soon as I am with you again I shall make a point of driving him [Linke] into a tight corner for a bit—[18]

But all too soon Anna Marie left Vienna once again. For various reasons, including her absence, Beethoven began to sink into dark despair. Beethoven's unprecedented attacks upon Johanna may have been caused by Anna Marie's failure to remain in or return promptly to Vienna. He dared not rail against her, for he had already seen that his anger did nothing more than drive her away from him. He thus took out his bitter disappointment and anger on the most logical and available person: Johanna.

Prince Lobkowitz had died in 1816, and his portion of the annuity due Beethoven was discontinued at that time. As in the Kinsky affair, this made it necessary for Beethoven to embark on another unpleasant lawsuit to claim the money owed him. Notes in his conversation books later on indicate that he was successful, but not until after another stressful legal battle. His desolation weeps from this 1816 journal entry:

> Help me, O God! Thou seest me deserted by all mankind...O harsh fate, O cruel destiny—no, no, my unhappy condition will never end..

At the end of 1816, Beethoven published *An die ferne Geliebte*, one of only two works he completed in that sad year. To the song's publisher, Steiner, he wrote in late December 1816 or early January 1817, as soon as the printed copies of the score for *An die ferne Geliebte* were available:

> Please send me some vocal duets, trios, and quartets from various operas, and also some arrangements of them as violin quartets or quintets; and please include the songs "Merkenstein," "Der Mann von Wort," (A Man

---

[18]Anderson, pp. 642-643.

of his Word),"An die Hoffnung" (To Hope), and "An die ferne Geliebte." (To the Distant Beloved). Please let me have the whole lot by this afternoon at latest, for I have found an opportunity of dispatching them... I have had a letter from the Countess Erdödy. All sorts of things are happening in that quarter too. Brauchle, the Magister, is in an advanced state of childbirth which means I must send him a midwife immediately.[19]

The "arrangements as violin quartets or quintets" were the form in which the Erdödy children had become ardent fans of *Fidelio*. Dana Steichen explained Beethoven's joking note about the children's tutor by recalling one of the composer's favorite puns: *Nöten* (need) and *Note* (musical note). In German, the word for "childbirth" is *Kindersnöten*. Broken down it becomes *Kinders* (children's) and *Nöten* (needs). Thus, Brauchle, the tutor, had "children in need" of music, and Beethoven's "midwife" was his gift of music to the Erdödy family. His opportunity to dispatch these pieces of music probably came through his usual "link," Joseph Linke, who frequently came to Vienna from the Countess's various estates.

Can there be there any doubt that there was a message for Anna Marie in the songs Beethoven chose to send her?

> On the hilltop I sit gazing, into the far-off blue
> Looking at the distant field where I you
> Beloved found. Far am I from thee separated
> Divided by mountains and valleys that lie
> Between us and our peace, our happiness.
> Take to your heart these songs that I sang
> to you, Beloved...
> For the sound of song transcends all space
> and time...
> Then through these songs
> What separated us so far melts away
> And a loving heart is reached
> By what a loving heart consecrated.

Had Anna Marie promised to once again return to Vienna, and soon? Was his sending her *Der Mann von Wort* a reminder to her to keep that promise? The words say much:

---

[19]Anderson, pp. 662-663.

> You said, my friend, and said it clear,
> I shall come back and meet you here
> You never came...

Is that why Beethoven also sent her the reissued song *To Hope*? In vain, perhaps, for it would be nearly two years before Anna Marie kept that promise and returned to her beloved Beethoven, although we believe she had been the one who had sent him the gold ring he began wearing only weeks after having sent the songs to her, and that it had been meant as a token of her continued fidelity. In the meantime, sorrow was ever on the composer's horizon.

Beethoven's letters for 1817 are heartbreaking to read. Often his despondency seemed close to overwhelming him. He was ill, financially poor, and emotionally strained by his lawsuit over Karl which he stubbornly was unwilling to relinguish. And, with his hearing all but gone and his *Beichtvater* far, far away, he also was socially isolated and exceedingly lonely. On June 19, 1817, while Beethoven was in Heiligenstadt, he wrote Anna Marie a lengthy letter which began:

> My beloved suffering friend! My dearest Countess! I have been all along tossed about, overloaded with too many worries... I caught a very severe cold which forced me to keep to my bed for a long time... I had then from the 15th April to the 4th of May to take every day six powders, six cups of tea; this lasted up to the 4th May; after that I received again some kind of powder which I had to take again 6 times a day, and I had to rub myself three times with a volatile ointment...[20]

Typically when writing to his Countess, his thoughts drifted to those mundane things which he knew instinctively would concern her. His letter is of a husband writing to a beloved wife of many years. One cannot imagine Beethoven telling any other woman that he had to "rub himself three times with an ointment." There was no other woman, then or ever, with whom he had the intimacy to tell of his illnesses and complaints, his remedial powders and treatments. He made a strong play for sympathy in this letter, perhaps once again hoping to induce her return:

---

[20]Anderson, 683-684.

It will be a long time before I am completely cured. My hearing has become worse; and as I have never been able to look after myself and my needs, I am even less able to do so now; and my cares have been increased still further by the responsibility for my brother's child— I have not yet found even decent lodgings.

Everywhere I am abominably treated and am the prey of detestable people—my own misery had made me feel depressed— my expenses are great... I can compose very little... my earnings are meagre... I am writing you very frankly, my dearest Countess, but precisely on that account you will not misunderstand me. Nevertheless I need nothing and would certainly accept nothing from you.

Once again, his fierce pride made him refuse her help. As before, he could accept assistance from others—with reluctance— but never from her. At this time, mid-1817, while Anna Marie probably was still in Padua,[21] Beethoven must have conceived the idea that if she could not or would not come to Vienna, he might go to her. Finally, he got to the point of his letter:

A thousand times have I thought of you, dear beloved friend, and also now, but my own misery has cast me down... I recently wrote him [Linke] to inquire how much a journey to you would cost? But I have received no answer. As my nephew has vacation from the last of August up to the end of October, I could then, health permitting, come to you; surely there it is likely we will not lack rooms for study and a comfortable existence. And if only for once I could come for a certain time among old friends who, despite this and the other devilish human thing, still have remained always around me, so would maybe my state of health and joy come back again.

His wish to visit his Countess was not to be realized. He was too proud to accept her financial assistance to make the trip,

---

[21]Alfred Schöne believed she might have been in Munich, but a letter written a short time before this unaddressed one bears the inscription: "Padua, Italy." Also, in this letter, Beethoven inquired about the cost of such a trip. Munich was approximately the same distance from Vienna as Teplitz. Padua, however, much farther away, and in a foreign country, more likely would have caused Beethoven to inquire.

and that, coupled with continuing illness and his problems with Karl, prevented the desired trip from occurring. Earlier he had written in his journal: "There is no salvation for you except to go away, only thus can you swing yourself up to the summits of your art again." But no departure, no sought-after salvation, was ever to come about. It is not surprising that shortly thereafter Beethoven wrote the music to the song *Resignation:*

> Gone out Gone out My light
> What thou hast wanted that is now gone.
> That place thou cans't not find again.
> Thou must now unbind thy self
> Once thou hast gaily flamed
> Now the air from thee has been withheld.
> When this keeps on the flame wanders,
> Seeks Seeks Findeth not. Gone out my light.
> Gone out Gone out My light.

Who else could have been the "air" that had been withheld from the flame of his being except his beloved Countess Erdödy? The letters[22] which follow show how desperately dim his light of life had become:

To Zmeskall, August 21: "...As for me, I often despair and would like to die. For I can see no end to my infirmities. God have mercy on me, I consider myself as good as lost."

* * *

To Nanette Streicher, August 25: "Today I am still far from well — How one feels when one is uncared for, without friends, without everything; left entirely to oneself, and even in suffering, all that can only be known from experience..."

* * *

To Zmeskall, September 9: "I now know what it feels like to move daily nearer to my grave—and without music."

* * *

---

[22]All excerpts taken from Anderson, pp. 701, 702, 709, 715, 736, and 741, respectively.

To Zmeskall, October 28: "In the predicament in which I am now placed I need indulgence in all directions. For I am a poor, unhappy man."

* * *

To Frau Streicher: "I was given hardly any supper last night. The housekeeper's departure terrified me so that I was already awake at three o'clock — My lonely condition demands the assistance of the police — What a dreadful existence?!"

* * *

To Frau Streicher: "All I can tell you is that I am better, though indeed last night I frequently thought of my death; but in any case such thoughts occur to me occasionally in the daytime as well."

* * *

To the Archduke Rudolph, 1818, speaking of 1817: "Despondency and several distressing circumstances and my very poor health at that time had made me lose courage to such an extent that it was only in a state of great nervousness and diffidence that I could even approach Y.I.H. from Mödling. By the end of my stay my health was better, it is true, but very many other sorrows assailed me.

The utter despair heartbreakingly evident in this correspondence would have destroyed a lesser man, but not a Beethoven. The same man who had been able to seize Fate by the throat in 1802 was able to do so again. Once more his indomitable spirit and his commitment to his music helped him to survive. Finally the bitterness of 1817 and 1818 melted away, when, in 1819, his Countess at last came home.

THE LIGHT RETURNS

In January of that year, Artaria published a new edition of the *Op. 102 Violoncello Sonata* which Beethoven had written in 1815 for Anna Marie. When it was initially published by Simrock two years later (1817), the work had had no dedication. Notably, however, the Artaria edition of 1819 *did* have a dedication: to Anna Marie Erdödy.

Once again there is an unexplained gap in letters between them. Lost, destroyed, or never written? We cannot know, but here we suspect lost or destroyed, because there is this sudden dedication of music to her and, after two years of utter despondency, Beethoven's letters of 1819 abruptly show a spiritedness that had been lacking since Anna Marie's departure. As so many times before when she reappared in his life, Beethoven took a renewed interest in his work, and for the first time, in the publication of an edition of his collected works, a dream that would never come to fruition in his lifetime.

In May 1819 Beethoven went to Mödling north of Vienna, and near Jedlersee and Hernals, where he stayed until October. Returning to the city, he moved into a house on the corner of Rauhensteingasse and Blumenstockgasse, but his interest soon would be focused on the Landstrasse, with good reason.

On December 19, 1819, Beethoven wrote Anna Marie a short note. Here there is no doubt that she was in Vienna—and probably had been for some time given his choice of summer residences—and that Beethoven was overjoyed by her presence. He wrote:

> To the Countess Marie Erdödy born Nizky — Everything good and beautiful to my dear adored cherished friend from her true and adoring friend. L v. Beethoven in haste
>
> 19 Dec 1819 soon I come myself.[23]

On this note was scribbled a bar of music. He would use it later to compose for her a three-part canon entitled *Happiness, Happiness in the New Year*, which he would present to her on New Year's Eve, December 31, 1819.

On the same day as he wrote this note to Anna Marie, he wrote another to the Archduke Rudolph. In it Beethoven apologized to the Archduke for being unable to see him.

> Y.I.H. must ascribe all this to the pressure of circumstances. This is not a suitable time to explain everything. But as soon as I consider that the right moment has arrived, I shall have to do so, lest Y.I.H. should pass an undeservedly hard sentence upon me.[24]

---

[23]Anderson, p. 860.
[24]Anderson, p. 859.

Although he said only that "circumstances" prevented his visit, it is easy to imagine what—and who—those "circumstances" involved. One hopes the Archduke was understanding, for Anna Marie had been away from Vienna for a very long time.

Despite his joy at once again having his Countess near him, memories of happier times, when there had still been hope of their one day being united, seemed to pain him. In his conversation book for March 1820 there is an interesting entry:

> Czerny: The last trio [i.e. the "Archduke" Op. 97, written in 1811] makes as much effect on the women also.
>
> Beethoven [implied from Czerny's next response]: Which movement had this effect?
>
> Czerny: the Andante. Can you remember exactly about the trio?

Apparently, Beethoven was unwilling to recall the trio, for he abruptly changed the subject. Czerny's next entry was a totally unrelated comment: "It was here about 7 o'clock." We believe the Op. 97 trio was a subject too painful for Beethoven to discuss, for this was the trio he had written out in an astonishing three weeks following the Countess's return to him in 1811, the one which he had offered to have copied at her house, the one he had chosen to perform in his last public concert. It was a piece of music so closely tied to memories of Anna Marie that he could not bear to remember those happier times, now gone. As we shall soon see, the Anna Marie who was now with him in Vienna was becoming less and less the Countess he had once known and loved.

MOVE TO THE LANDSTRASSE

In Beethoven's conversation book dated January 1820 there is a note that reads:

Countess Erdödy, Kärntnerstrasse 1138, 2nd floor

Thus Beethoven knew that the Countess had found an apartment in the Landstrasse, a remote suburb of Vienna, and this knowledge had prompted him to start seeking housing there as well. In October 1820 he was finally able to make the move to the Landstrasse, taking apartments in "Das grosse Haus der Ausliner #244." Except for customary excursions to Oberdöbling and Baden, he remained there until May 1822—as long as Anna

Marie was there. His change of residence, a financially unwise move to make at the time, surprised his friend Franz Oliva who wrote the following in Beethoven's conversation book, urging the composer to reconsider:

> You must by all means see that you live in the city. It is too unpleasant to be always alone and far away in the suburb. It would be better for you in the city. On the Landstrasse you are beyond all associations.

Oliva need not have been concerned for his friend. Beethoven knew that he would not be alone there, and that if he would be beyond most associations, he would not be beyond the one that meant the most to him.

The move close to his *Beichtvater* stimulated his life and creativity once again. Thayer noted that at this time "Beethoven's high spirits could at times dominate him in spite of his general misery." This "misery" of which Thayer spoke was physical only, for his emotions were soaring. Time and again we see these same "high spirits" whenever Anna Marie was in Vienna, so often, in fact, that their simultaneous occurrence throughout the years cannot be attributed to mere coincidence.

In the fall of 1820 he wrote to Adolf Schlesinger in Berlin:

> Everything will go more quickly in the case of the three sonatas. (Op. 109, 110, 111) — The first is quite ready save for correcting the copy, and I am working uninterruptedly at the other two. My health is completely restored and I will make every effort to fulfill my obligations to you as soon as possible.[25]

There was a flurry of letters to other publishers as well about works in progress. This creative activity continued for two years, with an interruption at the beginning of 1821 when an attack of jaundice made him too ill to work. In a June 1822 letter to Carl Peters, a publisher in Leipzig, Beethoven listed numerous pieces which he had completed during this time, among them his *Grand Mass*, the *Diabelli Variations,* various songs, a grand march, a grand trio, four military marches, various bagatelles, a sonata, and a quartet. He again expressed his willingness to take on the compilation of an edition of his collected works.

---

[25]Anderson, p. 902.

SHARING OTHERS' WIVES?

It was during 1820 that Solomon believed Beethoven had begun engaging in sexual relations with the wives of friends, and not only that, but by his friends' invitation! He drew this conclusion from a brief interchange in Beethoven's conversation book which took place between the composer and Carl Peters. At the time, Oliva, Bernard, and Neffe were also present. In German, the line reads:

> Peters: Wollen Sie bey (bei) meiner Frau schlafen? Es
> ist kalt hier.

Solomon translated this as "Do you want to sleep with my wife?" In this author's opinion, this is not an accurate translation, and, actually, in footnotes, Solomon admitted that other translators did not agree with him. To corroborate this, we gave this line, as well as the context in which it was written, to several native German speakers, and asked them to give us their translation.

Let us make a few important points. First, Peters began by telling Beethoven that "Ich muß mit meiner Frau um 5 nach Gumpendorf," which translates as "I must go with my wife about 5 [o'clock] to Gumpendorf," that is, to a town which is some distance south of Vienna, a place obviously warmer than Vienna, or at least, with a more comfortable climate than the Inner City. We note from the Conversation Book that this was written in January. Beethoven regularly complained about the winters in Vienna and their adverse effect on him in his letters. ("Since the winter here always nearly finish me off, my health demands that I at last should leave Vienna."—to Franz Brentano, 1822.)

Second, Peters' alleged offer of his wife's sexual favors comes in the presence of three other men, and in the midst of an ongoing conversation, that is, Peters' entry, and Oliva's and Bernard's all appear on the same page. What we must suppose from this is that Peters asked Beethoven, "Do you want to have sex with my wife?" to which Beethoven casually answered, "Sure," or "Yes, thanks," and then the conversation simply went on immediately from there without so much as the bat of an eye from anyone.

Solomon's contention also was based on the "fact" that Peters' wife was considered promiscuous. And who was his authority for this assessment? We find that it was a young woman with whom we already are well acquainted: Fanny Giannatasio. As we recall, Fanny was infatuated with Beethoven, and jealous of his attentions toward other women. She expressed this twice, once in connection with the Distant Beloved, and again with her own sister, Nanny, whom she knew Beethoven favored over her because of Nanny's more lighthearted temperament. *Any* woman who had friendly relations with Beethoven would fall under Fanny's jealous eye, thus we must take with a large dose of salt any "catty" remark she might make about Peters' poor wife. We do not believe that Peters' wife was promiscuous, but even if she were, would Peters advertise that fact? Would it not be a source of shame to him? According to Solomon's theory, Peters—who, as we recall was not alone with Beethoven at the time, but was in the company of several others—announced, "Hey, my wife is promiscuous!" and then made the magnanimous offer, "Anybody want to sleep with her? How about you, Ludwig?"

Now, let us return to the translation. Every one of the native speakers asked, who were not given the particulars as to who was speaking, translated the line as "Do you want to sleep *at my wife's house* [that is, in Gumpendorf]. It is cold here." When further questioned about the euphamism of "sleeping with," their response was that only the noun, *Beischlaf*, has a sexual connotation. Had Peters actually been soliciting sexual activity for his wife, he would have said, "Wollen Sie *mit* [with] meiner Frau schlafen?" not *"bei* [by] my wife..." They also expressed their doubts that any such offer made by one friend to another (which, in itself, seemed rather incredulous) would have been made in formal German, that is, using the *Sie*-form rather than *Du*. Surely the offer of one's wife should be made informally!

Solomon tried to further his already ludicrous argument by stating that several days later (eleven, actually) Beethoven was referred to as "Adonis," implying that he had had a successful sexual escapade with Peters' wife. This comment occurred in a conversation between Beethoven, Bach, Neberich, and Janschikh, none of whom were in on the original conversation regarding Peters' wife, and could not have known about his "offer" unless Peters' generosity was far greater than even Solomon imagined, and most of the men in Vienna were aware of her availability.

We see once again that Solomon's imaginative venture into the realm of psychosexual history has little basis either in fact or common sense.

❖ *29* ❖
The Final Years:
1820-1823

In 1811, Anna Marie was accused of crimes against the state. At the time, Austria was bankrupt, currency was devalued, and censorship was tight. One of the most powerful Austrian statesmen of the time was German-born Clemens von Metternich. His system of government depended upon political and religious censorship, espionage, and the suppression of revolutionary and nationalist movements. As such, it is little surprise that the outspoken Countess Erdödy should have come to the attention of the police. Official documents Nos. 1262Z2 and 1917 show that Anna Marie was questioned by the police for having criticized the Austrian Finance Law of 1811, claiming that the law had "maladroit application in Hungary," and for signing—and perhaps even writing—petitions to that effect. Like Beethoven, she was opinionated about political issues and not adverse to involving herself deeply in such affairs. The Countess was a strong Hungarian patriot, a courageous if somewhat foolhardy position to assume in the Austrian Dominion at the time. Her aristrocratic status brought her to the attention and concern of police far more often than the equally opinioned Beethoven, who often openly espoused inflamatory views himself. His role in Austria's political life was far less active than Anna Marie's, and no doubt the public's esteem, which came as a result of his artistic genius, for the most part protected him from police harrassment. However, that did not stop Metternich from occasionally having Beethoven spied upon by police for suspected "subversive activity."

Exactly what defense Anna Marie offered for those charges is unknown. Police records originally had been housed in the Palace of Justice, a building which had been stormed and set afire in the uprising of 1927. While some documents survived, many more were burned or charred to the point where they were rendered illegible. Since no punishment was ever exacted against Anna Marie, we must assume that the evidence against her had been insufficient to find her guilty.

Anna Marie's activities and the police interrogations which ensued, brought to light the fact that this was not the first time that she had been under official investigation. The exact year is unknown, but based on Anna Marie's testimony, her first brush with the legal system must have come sometime shortly after Peter had deserted her, possibly between 1802 and 1804. At that time, Anna Marie's sister-in-law, Countess Sigismund Erdödy, had charged Anna Marie with being a spendthrift and willfully wasting Erdödy property. In response to these charges, the Countess had made the following statement to the police. She began:

> Some time ago when both my husband and my father
> refused me any financial support,

Already we find an interesting situation: not only her husband but her own father displayed inexplicable coldness toward her. When Anna Marie separated from her husband, Peter, around 1801, her father denied his daughter assistance, even though she was ill, had little money, and had three children to support, and despite his net worth at the time of some 600,000 florins (in present terms, roughly $3,600,000). Obviously, her father could have afforded her some help, but chose not to give it. Her husband likewise was indifferent to her plight and that of his children, even though she had only just given birth to Peter's only son, August. Unlike most men of his day who were delighted to have a son, he showed no feelings toward his heir. In fact, he chose that precise time to leave Anna Marie, even though their two daughters also had been quite young: Mimi, about three years of age, and Fritzi, 18 months. One wonders whether Anna Marie's interest in the young composer from Bonn and his in her—albeit, at the time, strictly platonic—had had anything to do with the poor treatment she received from her father and husband. Her statement continued:

> I was capable of making things with my hands, selling them to a shop here, and bringing up my children decently. It is many years since I or my children have received the slightest financial support from the shaken fortune of my husband...

Here we see Anna Marie taking her first steps toward total independence, uncommon for a 19th century woman. Her early enjoyment of personal autonomy may have been one contributing factor—though perhaps small—which had deterred her from remarrying, even if the man was her beloved Beethoven. Earlier, when financially needy, she would not have placed the burden of herself and her children on Beet-hoven's shoulders. Later, she knew his pride would never have allowed her, as his wife, to contribute to the family finances. She avoided both problems by not marrying him.

Anna Marie's statement continued:

> I have been able not only to bring my father's possessions, once robbed of livestock and furnishings, by the provisions of his testament, into a flourishing state, but was successful even in paying off most of the debts which my father left, using that part of the Erdödy fortune which is my rightful due by marriage.[1]

Anna Marie was an uncommon businesswoman, unlike her father, who somehow had managed to bankrupt an estate worth several million dollars. In this respect, she would have made the perfect mate for Beethoven, who hated the business aspect of his art. The Countess had taken virtually nothing and made herself a wealthy woman. Under those circumstances, the court hardly could have found that she had been a "spendthrift" as Countess Sigismund had alleged, and the charges against Anna Marie had been dropped.

Unfortunately, Anna Marie's troubles with her family and the law did not end with these relatively minor accusations of squandering her husband's property, and speaking out against finance laws. Far more serious charges were leveled against her in 1820. A few letters among various members of the Erdödy

---

[1]Reported in Marek, p. 272. She may have been speaking of some sort of monetary settlement given her under the terms of their separation.

household, Anna Marie, her sister-in-law Countess Sigismund, Anna Marie's daughter Mimi, and her children's tutor Brauchle, survive. Researcher Gunter Haupt, who was able to study these letters, concluded from these and from Anna Marie's statements, that it had been Countess Sigismund once again who had brought charges against Anna Marie, and that police interference into the matter had been her doing. Countess Sigismund's reasons for hating Anna Marie so vehemently are unknown, but lend themselves to interesting speculation.Were her reasons similar to Peter's and Anna Marie's father?

FAMILY INTRIGUE

Many of the police records which could have shed additional light on this sordid family story also had been destroyed by the 1927 fire, although enough remain to piece together a likely scenario. In 1820, Countess Sigismund charged Anna Marie and the tutor Joseph Brauchle—who had been with the family more than twenty years—with mistreating Anna Marie's eldest daughter, Mimi. Countess Sigismund demanded that her niece "be freed" from their custody. Haupt's studies led him to believe that Countess Sigismund's motives included removing Anna Marie from the guardianship of her daughter so that Sigismund could secure Mimi as a wife for her son, and thus gain control over a substantial dowry provided by Anna Marie's estate. This may have been Countess Sigismund's way of reclaiming Erdödy money and property to which she felt Anna Marie had not been entitled. Perhaps she had believed Peter justified in leaving his wife, and that Anna Marie had deserved no monetary settlement. However, at the time, there were three small children involved. It seems odd that neither the Erdödys nor the Nickzys thought that they, at least, were entitlted to support from their father. Haupt felt there was also an indication that Countess Sigismund wanted Brauchle for herself, but in what capacity is unknown.

A statement written by Anna Marie to Count Sedlnitzky, the Prefect of Police, on July 29, 1820, recorded in police records Nos. 5722 and 5741, shows that Countess Sigismund had charged Brauchle with having had an affair with Mimi, and with having murdered young August (Gusti) Erdödy, Anna Marie's son, in 1816. The Countess claimed that this sexual harassment by her teacher, the harsh treatment she received from her mother, and her brother's unexpected death, had driven Mimi to attempt suicide on April 14, 1820.

The aunt's claim, connecting Mimi's suicide attempt with Gusti's death, makes little sense. With so much time having elapsed between the two events, the former could not have precipitated the later. Yet Countess Sigismund did not allow the illogic of the situation to deter her. She attempted to reopen the case against Anna Marie and Brauchle in the wrongful death of August, using her niece's attempt to take her life as an excuse to do so. Although there had been a police investigation at the time of Gusti's death, family concern for him was strangely lacking. Not only had his father chosen the time of his birth to abandon his family, but the boy's death caused little reaction from the Erdödy relations, except to focus on Anna Marie's involvement in the crime.

We have no doubt that August Erdödy had been Peter Erdödy's natural son. The question is, did Count Erdödy and his relations believe that? Peter was very fair in coloring. Had August perhaps been dark, a throwback to his mother's ancient Hungarian ancestry? He had been born in the midst of Anna Marie's budding emotional intimacy with Beethoven, and, coincidentally, his name, August, was the same as Beethoven's youngest brother, who had died as a toddler in 1783. Had an innocent remark on Beethoven's part, that the young count had his sibling's name, as well as the composer's friendly interest in the Count's musically inclined wife, have planted a germ of suspicion and jealousy in Peter Erdödy's heart? Had Peter refused to believe his wife's protestations of innocence, and was that why she reacted so strongly when, years later, Beethoven, too, accused her of infidelity? And was that why Peter had left so abruptly after his son's birth, refusing to scandalize his family with a divorce, and yet wanting nothing more to do with the wife he thought, unjustly, had betrayed him with another man?

Not only the Erdödy family, but her *own* family, the Nickzys, had ostracized her and bore her ill will. Why should they do so? Surely they thought they had just cause, and it is difficult to blame their treatment of her merely on her outspokenness. She was, after all, a Hungarian patriot, as both families also were, and even if she spoke rashly, nevertheless, it was in defense of their homeland. They could not have taken such a strong stance against her simply because of political motives. We recall the

Baron de Trémont had assumed a love relationship between Beethoven and Anna Marie, most probably because of Viennese gossip. We suspect that the Erdödy and Nickzy families also had heard the stories which may have circulated far earlier than 1808. Later, they saw Anna Marie and Beethoven take up residence together, and their worst suspicions had been confirmed: she was intimately involved with a commoner. This "scandal" was likely why, much later, she would have to fight for not only her uncle's Croatian property—which she simply should have inherited without resorting to force—but also for custody of her surviving child.

All this makes for interesting speculation. It is unfortunate that, at least for the time being, we have many questions for which there are no concrete answers. At this writing, this author had just located, through the help of an American graduate student of Croatian descent, a professor at the University of Zagreb in Croatia, whose great-grandfather had managed the Erdödy estate in Paukowitz. Perhaps further contact with this gentleman will reveal more about this intriguing family and its mysteries.

IN THE CASE OF THE SON

Let us take a closer look at both incidents with the Erdödy children, beginning with the son, August. In 1816, one of Beethoven's letters indicates that prior to August's death, Linke had told Beethoven of Anna Marie's concern with her baliff, a man named Sperl, and that she was considering releasing him from her service. However, Linke had not given (or perhaps could not give) Beethoven much detail, for in his letter to Anna Marie in May, Beethoven had requested more:

> As to *Vogel* [bird] Sperl, I hear you are not satisfied with him, but I do not know why. I hear you are looking for another steward, but do not rush the matter, and let me know your opinions and intentions, maybe I can give you some good advice. Perhaps you are not quite fair to the Sperl in the cage?[2]

---

[2]Anderson, p. 579. Beethoven was punning on Sperl's name which, in English, means *sparrow*. "Vogel" means *bird*.

Beethoven's next letter was one of condolence to Anna Marie upon learning of Gusti's death. We do not know if he had ever been given any details of the incident, although he surely had inquired of Linke, who had brought Beethoven the news, for the sudden death of one so young is always cause for shock and wonder.

The mystery surrounding the death of young Count Erdödy is an interesting one. The results of the investigation conducted by a police official named Siber are sketchy, and as there are few details available, the best we can do at this time is present what *is* known and pose some questions. Although August could have died from natural causes, the oddity of the situation points to foul play, and we shall assume, as the police had at the time, that this had occurred. According to official reports, the young count had collapsed at his sister Mimi's feet, clutching his head in agony. The implication had been that August had been severely beaten, badly enough to cause hemorrhage and death. The police's findings had been inconclusive. *Had* Gusti been murdered? If so, he would have been around the age of 15, at the beginning of his maturity. If Peter and the Erdödy family had long suspected August of not being of their bloodline, they may have wished him eliminated before he reached his maturity and inherited Erdödy property. Or perhaps his death had been a threat, a warning to Anna Marie that the Erdödy family would tolerate no more scandal at the hands of their very black sheep. Had Sperl been planted in Anna Marie's household to accomplish this task? We do not know how she came to hire him, only that she was displeased with him. Even though Sperl was the more likely suspect—far more than the tutor, Brauchle, who had a good reputation and had been with the family a long time—he was only cursorily questioned, with police interrogation being directed toward Brauchle and Anna Marie. In fact, Sperl barely was mentioned in Siber's report, while the teacher, Brauchle, who had known the boy since birth and had been employed by the family for twenty years without incident, was accused of unprecedented violence. Unless someone had directed the focus of the investigation, police accusation against the tutor and the Countess, rather than toward the more obvious perpetrator, Sperl, makes little sense. There are too few answers in this intriguing mystery.

IN THE CASE OF THE DAUGHTER

In April 1820, Anna Marie's eldest child, her daughter Mimi, attempted suicide. Doctor's reports indicated that Mimi had taken an overdose of opium, and she hardly had done so by accident, but what had prompted her drastic action is unknown. Unfortunately, the drug had been readily available to her since her mother had already become dependent upon it to alleviate her pain. In those days, suicide, even if only attempted, was considered a crime against God, punishable in the case of a woman by confinement in a convent.[3] Mimi was sent to St. Pölten for "instruction" while Brauchle once again was implicated, charged with having had illicit sexual relations with the young Countess,.

Countess Erdödy strongly denied the accusations levelled against herself and her children's tutor. Neither of them, she claimed, had contributed to her son's death, nor had Brauchle made—nor she allowed—sexual advances toward her daughter. Initially, her protestations of innocence were disregarded. Anna Marie was charged with having been unusually harsh with her daughter, and Brauchle was imprisoned pending further investigation. As we noted, this suicide attempt prompted another investigation into August's death, but apparently no new details surfaced. An Inspector Sicard was appointed to investigate Mimi's attempted suicide and related incidents. His report of April 14, 1820, stated that the young countess had been

> maltreated by employees of the mother and as a result had become extremely frightened and shy. Indeed it seems advisable that the young Countess...be freed from the clutches of the Secretary [Brauchle] and the so-called Fraulein Nina [a Croatian woman serving as governess]. The mother has tongue-lashed the daughter with such words that in a kind of despair she went into her room and decided to poison herself with opium.

Anna Marie again denied the charges, claiming that this was yet another one of the intrigues her sister-in-law had thought up against her. Far from being intimidated, she accused the police of having robbed her of "her holiest posession, her honor."

---

[3] Beethoven's nephew, Karl, received similar treatment after his suicide attempt, and even Beethoven was questioned about his conduct which officials felts might have contributed Karl's "immoral" act. Anna Marie was likewise held accountable for her daughter's action.

While confined at the convent, Mimi wrote to her mother and requested some of Beethoven's music to give her comfort and alleviate her loneliness and boredom. A letter to Anna Marie from Beethoven indicates that Mimi also had written him to thank him for sending her some music. "I have much pleasure in the letter of your dear daughter M.," he wrote, "and wish to see her soon as well as her dear mother..."

Letters exchanged among Anna Marie, Mimi, and Brauchle—which the Countess presented as evidence to the police—evidently convinced them that she was telling the truth: that nothing untoward had existed between the girl and her teacher, only the affection and respect a student would naturally have had for a teacher who had literally watched her grow up. Countess Sigismund could provide no evidence to prove her claim, and both Brauchle and Anna Marie eventually were exonerated. Mimi, however, remained at St. Pöltens under religious instruction for several years.

Although some biographers have reported that Anna Marie was banished forever from Austria in 1820 as a result of this incident, this is not so. No official records list the banishment of any member of the aristocratic Erdödy family from that country, as they surely would have had such a thing actually taken place. And if the Countess had been forced to leave the country, she would have been unable to apply for the renewal of her passport in Vienna three years later, as recorded in 1823 police records. Nor would her new address for a Landstrasse apartment have appeared in Beethoven's 1820 conversation book.

In 1821, the Hungarian Court formally exonerated Anna Marie of all charges, and if there had been any injunctions against her which had restricted her movements in Vienna, they were officially removed at that time.

We have only one surviving note (from 1819) written directly from Beethoven to Anna Marie during this time period, but his wretched despondency, so evident in 1817-1818 during which time he wrote repeatedly of his wish to die, was suddenly alleviated during the years that the Countess was in Vienna, and despite the fact that Josephine Brunswick died in 1821. His anxieties over Karl, housekeeping problems, and personal illness were unalleviated, yet his desire to quit life was no longer present, and there was a sudden surge in his creative energy. Schindler attributed this musical outburst to Beethoven's need to prove that the gossip that he had "written himself out," was unfounded. With his ability challenged, Schindler said the composer had produced three piano sonatas (Op. 109, 110, and 111) "in a single breath." Yet time and again we have seen this same burst of musical energy whenever Anna Marie was part of Beethoven's life.

Exactly how much Beethoven ever knew of Anna Marie's legal entanglements is unknown, but he would have had to have been a rock in the road not to have been aware of at least some of the details. No matter how sordid the gossip may have become, however, Beethoven remained loyal to her and never said a word against her. Thayer tried to suggest that Beethoven was oblivious to the charges brought against Countess Erdödy, even though Thayer knew that Anna Marie's situation—what Thayer referred to as her "sordid affair"—had been a topic of discussion in Beethoven's conversation books. It would have been unlikely for a man who read the newspaper as avidly as did Beethoven not to know something of what must have been a widely known story, unless the family had been successful in shielding themselves completely from adverse publicity. We know, too, that Beethoven had received a letter from Mimi, and he certainly had spoken about it with Anna Marie herself, who would have told him something about what was happening to her and her family, even if she had tried to keep the worst of it from him. If Beethoven had heard nothing else from any other source, he had known the following details, taken from his July-August 1820 conversation book in which Beethoven had discussed the incident with an unknown person:

> Since that time curious things have happened. Brauchle was locked up in the police station and the Countess Mimi has been in the St. Pölten for some days.
>
> Gusti. [i.e. the Countess's son, August]
>
> As far as the young Count is concerned, that he had so mistreated him, and he [Brauchle] is accused of having beaten him to death. Sperl [the countess's chief bailiff or steward] and the servant together with the chambermaid are very often questioned. Sperl was all the time present at the questioning of Brauchle.

In the Waag Gasse 274. on the ground floor but also in the old Wieden.

The police are informed about everything possible even her way of living, he [Brauchle] is indeed a few hours free but always under watch — Secret service man—

The best would be to put her estates under the administration, which will also happen. She is now looking for quarters on the Landstrasse.

The old man still lives with the family. The small Gustav (i.e. August aka Gusti) in the Italian city Padua. Now the police are also writing there.

After being cleared of all charges in 1821, Anna Marie apparently stayed in Vienna for the most part, but may have made a few trips to her other estates, despite Beethoven's need for her to remain in the city. We know she made at least one to Croatia the following year. What happened to her Jedlersee estate and her summer home in Hernals is unknown, but they most likely had been sold years before, or had been taken by the state, for she never returned to either. The good times she and Beethoven had known there were long gone. And already, another, far more sinister force than Countess Sigismund Erdödy was at work which would contribute to Anna Marie's increasingly erratic and seemingly uncaring behavior.

BATTLE FOR A CASTLE

It must have been with mixed emotions that Beethoven heard the rumor in 1822 that Countess Erdödy had rallied 300 peasants and taken possession by force of property once owned by her uncle. The "rumor" was not quite that, for it was recorded in Police Document No.7498, which noted that on July 26 and 27 of 1822, the manager of the Erdödy estate, on Anna Marie's behalf and probably by her order, rallied a force of peasants to reclaim the land and castle to which she felt she had proprietary rights. The manager stated that Anna Marie's uncle by marriage, Joseph Erdödy, had held joint ownership of the property with Anna Marie, and that just before he died "he promptly made arrangements to have his niece thrown out of the castle." If Anna Marie truly had spearheaded this action to reclaim what her uncle was determined to deny her, given her frail physical condition, this was an amazing feat.

On precisely the day that Anna Marie's forces were storming the Croatian castle, Beethoven was writing a letter to his brother, Johann. In it we learn that he had given up his Landstrasse apartment, and would soon move near his brother as a lodger in Johann's brother-in-law's house. This was the residence which Louis Schlösser would later describe as a "low, mean-looking house," uncomfortable, with dark stairs. Although Ludwig claimed not to blame Johann for obtaining such unsuitable lodgings for him, this is precisely the time when friction became evident between Ludwig, Johann, and Johann's wife, Therese. It was in 1822, and not 1812, that Beethoven began speaking out against Therese, calling her a "loutish fat woman" and worse.

This was also the year when Beethoven was mistakenly arrested for vagrancy. He was detained for a short while, making such a fuss and racket that no one else in the jail could sleep. Finally, the police commissioner was summoned, identified Beethoven, and with great embarrassment, made certain the composer had a change of clothing, pleasant accomodations for the night, and a carriage to drive him home. The incident would be comic if it did not make one so painfully aware of Beethoven's abject despair over his Countess's absence from and only sporatic appearances in Vienna, and her obvious physical and mental deterioration, as well.

One would like to believe that Anna Marie's presence in Vienna, if not constant, did help to alleviate some of Beethoven's loneliness, but of this we cannot be certain. The woman who now resided in Vienna was very different from the "movingly gay" Countess he had known and loved. Anna Marie Erdödy, victim of a painfully debilitating illness, had become an opium addict.

Remaining information about her comings and goings comes, sadly, not from any of Beethoven's letters, but from yet another police report. We begin to see the drug's toll; her judgment was becoming impaired. On October 28, 1823, Anna Marie was questioned by police on charges of having smuggled into the city a young actor named Walter whom she had engaged as a reader. Bedridden a great deal, having someone to read to her was apparently one small entertainment she allowed herself. It happened that Walter had no passport or papers, but she claimed that she had taken pity on him because he was "the sole support of his elderly parents," and had needed employment. What Beethoven had thought of her action on the part of the young man is unknown, for no letters between them survive to give us that insight. It was foolhardy on her part, yet we find not one critical word from him, not even in the Conversation Books.

The police inspector who reported the incident, as before, Inspector Sicard, made mention of the Countess's "two lovers," implying that Anna Marie had been carrying on an illicit love triangle with Brauchle and Walter, who was young enough to be her son. There was no evidence supporting the claim and, once again, she was exonerated, although the incident certainly had not done anything positive for her already tarnished reputation. Biographer George Marek noted that the Inspector's "inimical remarks" made it sound as if he held a personal grudge against the Countess. This would not be surprising for, as we know, she had never been adverse to speaking her mind, and for that reason she sometimes made enemies in high places.

Once again, poor old Brauchle was accused of having illicit relations with an Erdödy woman, this time the mother instead of the daughter. Yet had this been true, Brauchle's widow certainly would not have done Anna Marie the favor of accepting and preserving Beethoven's precious letters which Anna Marie bequeathed to her upon her death. Nor would the Widow Brauchle have guarded the family so carefully as evidenced by her reluctance to share those letters with Otto Jahn. In addition, Anna Marie's extremely poor physical condition at the time makes even the idea of such an *ménage á trois* ludicrous.

MOTHER AND DAUGHTER REUNION

As police considered Anna Marie a danger to her daughter, Mimi remained at the convent for quite some time. But in 1823 Anna Marie took action to get her daughter back. She submitted a petition to the police which claimed that her daughter had been "incited by the rest of the family" to speak against her, and that Mimi desperately wanted to be reunited with her mother. With her petition, Anna Marie enclosed letters from Mimi indicating that her continued confinement at St. Pöltens was making her suffer, that she wept a great deal, and worried about her mother's deteriorating health. Countess Erdödy in-

cluded testimonials from friends which repudiated the claim that
she had ever neglected or maltreated her children. One of Anna
Marie's friends, Countess Theresia Strasotvo, stated that

> she treated them with unique tenderness and self-
> sacrifice. She nursed them herself like a wetnurse in
> spite of the fact that for twenty years she has suffered a
> serious illness which is painful, strange, and rare. She
> has guided their education herself, though the children
> had decent and able governesses, etc. (November 8,
> 1820)[4]

In Police Document No.9053 dated 1823, Mimi stated that
her mother's severe illness confined her to her room for weeks at
a time, without the strength even to write her daughter. In fact,
Anna Marie's health was nothing short of catastrophic. Mimi
claimed that her mother suffered so badly from ulcers and
vomiting that she could not even retain opium for her pain.

Anna Marie's persistence paid off. Mother and daughter
were reunited. In late 1823 Anna Marie, in a handwriting described as "agitated and aging" even though she was only 43 years
old, applied for a passport to travel to Munich with Mimi. Her
trembling hand shows what a terrible price the alleviation of her
pain through drugs had extracted. Countess Erdödy left Vienna
for the last time in early 1824. It most likely had been a condition
of her daughter's release that the two of them leave Vienna.
Schindler made no note of her leaving, but unwittingly showed us
what a terrible effect her final departure had had on Beethoven.
Schindler remarked that

> Suddenly the humor which had made him so compliant
> and affable with everyone disappeared. He received no
> callers, and even wished to see me less frequently,
> though before this time I could not visit him often
> enough. He wrote to me: 'Don't bother to come here until
> perchance a hatti-sherif[5] appears. Farewell—and don't
> bring anyone—farewell.[6]

Once again we find Beethoven suffering emotional anguish. Schindler offered no satisfactory explanation for the composer's abrupt change in mood. Yet the departure of the Countess, and Beethoven's sudden despondency, hardly could have

[4]Marek, p. 273.
[5]A summons from a sultan, that is, from Beethoven himself.
[6]Schindler, pp. 297-298.

been coincidental. Obviously her leaving with no hope of return devastated him and broke his heart beyond repair.

Beethoven did not pull himself out of this dark mood until quite some time had passed. Somehow he was able to finish the *Ninth Symphony*, but still, his sorrow never completely left him. Schindler attributed this odd change in the composer's personality in part to Beethoven's nephew—unlikely since the boy had occupied him since 1815 and most of his worst problems with the boy and Johanna were already behind him. Schindler also thought that Beethoven was depressed because of limitations being placed upon his musical composition by people who requested pieces other than the instrumental works which Beethoven preferred. Again, these are poor explanations. Schindler wrote,

> After the ninth symphony... the spontaneity of its creator seemed to wane. Moreover, reflection occupied an ever-increasing area of the master's being; indeed, it became a governing characteristic of the artist... The turning point in his essential being became obvious in 1824, although indications of it had been apparent in the two previous years...The master's nature had undergone a metamorphosis that was absolutely astounding...[7]

We believe that Anna Marie, upon departing from Vienna, had told Beethoven that she could not return. Once Beethoven had realized the greatest triumphs of his musical career—the performances of his beloved *Missa Solemnis* and the *Ninth Symphony*—the light of joy that her presence had kept burning in his life simply faded away. William Kinderman in his 1995 book noted that these last few years of Beethoven's life were filled with irreverent humor, more so than any other time. Here we find him writing absurd canons, mocking men of the church, being mischievous but devilishly so. This seems to us a forced gaiety. We see a man who must cling to his humor in order to survive, a man who, if he cannot laugh in his darkest moment, must die.

Laugh he did, and survive he did.

Laughter and his music sustained him, even though Anna Marie never did come back, not to Vienna, and not to the man who loved her. It was in Munich that she was forced to remain, forever separated from her beloved Beethoven, until her death in 1837.

---

[7]Schindler, p. 304.

A LAST GOODBYE

Thus we believe that the banishment of Anna Marie Erdödy and her daughter, Mimi, had taken place not in 1820 as has been supposed but in 1823, when Mimi was finally released from St. Pöltens and Anna Marie was issued a passport so that she could leave the city. We do not believe it had been an official act. Somehow the family managed to avoid scandal by keeping it out of court records. Likely Anna Marie had been strongly urged to accept the terms of Mimi's release by those who knew how dearly she wanted her daughter back. Only a threat against her child's well-being could have forced Anna Marie to act as she did, leaving Vienna and Beethoven behind forever, fully aware that her loss would devastate him. By this time her health was exceedingly poor, and she was almost constantly bedridden. The loss of her only child would have been too much for her to bear. No doubt she also was weary of fighting an endless series of battles with the Erdödy family, a fight she had no hope of winning. We do not feel she had been insensitive to Beethoven's need for her, but that she had no choice to act otherwise.

In some ways, she may even have seen this final blow to their relationship as a kindness for both of them, sparing herself and Beethoven more pain. Although she surely knew Beethoven would be despondent over her move to Munich, perhaps she considered how much more he would have suffered by watching her condition continue to deteriorate. It may already have become too much for her to bear seeing the anguish in his eyes when he saw her becoming ever more degenerate, drifting further and further away, both emotionally and physically, from the woman she had once been and he had once loved? Perhaps she even felt that her death was imminent. Always before, she had fought against unjust treatment, but this time she may have simply accepted her unofficial banishment, hoping that in doing so she might spare Beethoven the bitterness of watching her die.

Were there any letters exchanged between them? None survive, so we cannot say for certain. We know that by the time she left Vienna her handwriting had deteriorated into an illegible scrawl. Of course, someone else could have written letters for her, or served as a verbal messenger between them. Beethoven was still in touch with their mutual friend and sometimes link, Joseph

Linke, the Accursed Violoncello, as late as August 1826. A note made in Beethoven's conversation book at the time reads

> Linke knows of a quite newly discovered remedy for
> deafness. It did wonders for one of his friends.

Linke also served among the ranks of the honorary escorts that accompanied Beethoven's coffin to the church on March 29, 1827. Obviously the two men had never lost touch, and if Beethoven had "frequently inquired" after Anna Marie as he had once before, Linke would have been the logical person to keep the bond between them alive.

It would not be surprising if Anna Marie had chosen not to write to Beethoven directly—of what could she have written? She surely would have preferred to write nothing rather than subject Beethoven to a painful glimpse at her pathetic condition. Would she have sent him reassurances of her health, of her possible return, when both of them would have known her words were lies? We do not believe Anna Marie ever would have been less than frank with Beethoven.

There is also the possibility that her mind, under the influence of opiates and other drugs, could no longer think clearly enough to put pen to paper and convey coherent thoughts to Beethoven. We know that drug addicts—even unwilling ones such as the Countess—become insensitive to their surroundings and even to loved ones. Perhaps this had been Anna Marie's fate, as well.

Did Anna Marie's irrevocable departure from Beethoven's life spare him grief, or cause him even greater suffering? We do not know for certain. Yet Schindler's commentaries give us a sad insight: no matter whether he had seen her leave or watched her deteriorate further, the painful effect on Beethoven probably would have been the same.

Only Beethoven's own indomitable will—the strength which never seemed to fail him, even in the darkest days—sustained him through this time. This alone allowed him to continue setting his music on the page for another two years, despite terrible illness, financial woes, the cares that his stormy relationship with his nephew continually placed upon him, and the crushing personal loss of the one person who meant the most to him in all the world: his eternally beloved.

❖ *30* ❖
Beethoven and the Erdödy Family: Count Palffy

What, if anything, had Anna Marie's legal and political troubles to do with Beethoven? Maybe nothing at all. Yet the timing of these attacks upon her—and also upon Beethoven himself by other members of the Erdödy family—occurred every time when the relationship between the Countess and the composer was most intense. Coincidence? Perhaps. But when such coincidences keep occurring, it is difficult to keep relying on an accident of timing to explain simultaneous events.

Some biographers hold the opinion that the animosity between Beethoven and Count Ferdinand Palffy was the result of the composer's paranoia,and that no such hostility actually existed. However, Palffy's actions show that a real and long-term antagonism did exist between the two men. Why should this Count Palffy harbor such a dislike for Beethoven? The reason becomes less mysterious when one learns that Palffy's full name was Count Palffy *von Erdöd*—a relation of Anna Marie's husband. He was, in fact, a contemporary of Peter Erdödy's: Erdödy had been born in 1771 and Palffy in 1774. Could Palffy's feelings for Beethoven have stemmed from the composer's intimate relationship with Anna Marie which the powerful family opposed? This is entirely possible, for Palffy's animosity toward Beethoven is particularly evident at those times when Anna Marie was most closely involved with the composer. Let us review briefly a

chronology of those times[1] when Palffy figured most predominantly in Beethoven's life and caused him the greatest professional problems:

> 1801-1804: *Anna Marie's friendship develops with Beet-
> hoven; Peter abandons her after August'sbirth. Her
> father refuses her aid. Countess Sigismund charges her
> with squandering Erdödy property.*

> 1804: Beethoven's first conflict with Palffy: Beethoven
> takes lodgings as Anna Marie's neighbor and has been
> close to her for several years.

> 1807-1809: Beethoven has repeated problems with
> Palffy: his relationship with Anna Marie has intensified
> to the point where they begin living together.

> Late 1809-1810: no indication that problems with Palf-
> fy occurred after Beethoven's quarrel with and during
> his separation from Anna Marie.

> 1811: resurgence of problems for Beethoven with Palffy:
> Beethoven becomes reconciled with Anna Marie; i.e. is
> enjoying "Erdödyian feasts." Beethoven is spied upon
> and *Anna Marie is brought under investigation for sub-
> versive political activity.*

> 1813: no problems with Palffy are evident: probability
> of another quarrel between Anna Marie and Beethoven,
> followed bya brief separation.

> 1814-1815: another resurgence of problems for Beet-
> hoven with both Palffy and the theater he owned and
> managed; Beethoven reconciles with Anna Marie,
> beginning in 1814 with her gift to him.

> 1816-1817: Beethoven has continual problems with
> Palffy; *Anna Marie's son is murdered. Although Anna
> Marie has left Vienna, she visits periodically, and their
> connection is evident:* Beethoven corresponds with her,
> sends her music; she perhaps reciprocates with a ring.

---

[1] Interspersed in this listing are Anna Marie's problems with the Erdödys, as
indicated in italics.

> 1820: Beethoven and Anna Marie live as neighbors in
> the Landstrasse. *Anna Marie faces charges relating to
> daughter's suicide attempt and son's murder.*

Are all these dates simply coincidental? Perhaps, but again, repeated coincidences such as those shown here are difficult to explain. Time and again, we see the Erdödys attacking these two people for no apparent reason.

Palffy became one of the eight directors of the Royal Imperial Court Theater at the end of December 1806. The other directors included three members of the Esterhazy family, Princes Lobkowitz and Schwartzenberg, and Counts Lodron and Zilchy. Lobkowitz encouraged Beethoven to petition the new directors to engage him permanently with an annual salary. In his petition, Beethoven said that if this arrangement was not acceptable to the directors, then he would substitute this request with one for a benefit concert, to be held either on Annunciation Day or Christmas. Such a concert had been promised to him the previous year but had never occurred. Neither of these requests—the latter of which was certainly modest enough—were granted. In fact, no formal written reply was ever sent to Beethoven, even as a courtesy.

The animosity between Beethoven and Palffy seems to have dated back to 1803 or 1804—at the time when Beethoven first became Anna Marie's neighbor in the city several years after her separation from Peter. One evening, Beethoven and Ries were giving a small concert and were interrupted several times by the loud voice of a man Ries referred to in his notes as "Count P" who was speaking to a lady in an adjoining room. After Beethoven had several times tried to bring about quiet without success, Ries said he "sprang up, pulled my hands from the piano, and said in a loud voice, 'Für solche Schweine spiele ich nicht!' ('For such swine, I will not play!')" It has been assumed, though not proven, that the "Count P" was Ferdinand Palffy.

From Beethoven's letters, it is clear that he had a perpetual problem with the Theater Management:

> To Franz Brunswick, May 11, 1806: "I shall never come
> to an arrangement with this tribe of princes connected
> with the theatres."[2]

---

[2]Anderson, p. 168.

To Prince Nicholas Esterhazy, July 26, 1807: "I had the misfortune to fail to obtain a benefit day in the theatre..."[3]

To Heinrich Collin, February, 1808: "As it is, I have already become accustomed to the basest and vilest treatment in Vienna— ...I have three documents about a day in the theatre last year; and if I include the police documents, I have altogether five written statements about a day which has never been allotted to me. Why, if only on account of the trouble to which I have been put for nothing, the people really ought to give me a day, which in any case they owe me. I repeat, a day which they owe me, for if I choose to do so, I can by virtue of my right compel the T[heatrical] D[irectors] to give me that day. And indeed I have discussed this point with a lawyer— And why should I not do so? For have they not driven me to adopt such extreme measures?—Away with all consideration or respect for those vandals of art."[4]

To Heinrich Collin, Summer, 1808: "In any case I think that we shall probably have to wait a bit; for that is what those worshipful and high and mighty theatrical directors have decreed — I have so little reason to expect anything favorable from them that the thought that I shall certainly have to leave Vienna and become a wanderer haunts me persistently —"[5]

To Breitkopf & Härtel, January 8, 1809: "Conditions are worst of all, of course, at the Theatre auf der Wieden — I had to give my concert there and on that occasion obstacles were placed in my way by all the circles connected with music — The promoters of the concert... out of hatred for me... played me a horrible trick. They threatened to expel any musician belonging to their company who would play for my benefit.[6]

On June 11, 1811, Beethoven wrote the following directly to Palffy:

---

[3]Anderson, p. 174.
[4]Anderson, p 185-186.
[5]Anderson, p. 194.
[6]Anderson, p. 212.

> Your Excellency! I hear that the actor Scholz will give,
> in a short time, for his benefit at the Theater-An-der-
> Wien, the melodrama *Les Ruines de Babylon*, which I
> wished to write as an opera and which I have already
> announced to you. I am not able to fathom this entang-
> lement! I presume you know nothing about it? ... I hope
> from your better judgment that you will prevent the
> actor Scholz from giving this melodrama, since I, al-
> ready earlier, communicated to you my intention of
> treating it as an opera; I was so glad to have found this
> subject, that I myself communicated the fact to the
> Archduke and also to many other men of intellect, and
> everyone thought it excellent. I have even written to
> foreign newspapers to have it inserted, to prevent the
> subject being used for an opera elsewhere, and must I
> now recall it? and for such wretched reasons?[7]

His protests were to no avail; Palffy ignored Beethoven's
letter and nothing more was ever heard of the proposed opera.
Thayer felt that the bad feelings between Palffy and Beethoven
were "mere conjecture" but it seems to have been real enough to
Beethoven. He had told Palffy of his intention of using the play
as the basis of an opera, and he had been ignored. After Lobkowitz
went bankrupt, Count Palffy bought the Theater an der Wien in
1813, and he continued to manage it until 1825. Beethoven's
problems with the theater continued, and Palffy was in an excellent position to make certain that they did.

In 1814, the theater management again ignored Beet-
hoven's request for a performance of *Fidelio* for his benefit. Beethoven complained to the Archduke Rudolph on July 14, 1814:

> The t[heatrical] directors are so honest that notwith-
> standing all their promises they have already allowed
> my opera *Fidelio* to be produced on one occasion without
> arranging that it should be for my benefit. Moreover
> they would have perpetrated for a second time this de-
> lightfully honorable action if I had not lain in waiting
> like a former French customs official.—Finally after
> many troublesome appeals, it was arranged that I
> should have my benefit on the 18th July.—This take-in
> is more in the shape of a take-out at this time of year
> [i.e.when it is hot and theater attendance is usually
> low].[8]

---

[7]Anderson, pp. 324-325.
[8]Anderson, p. 458.

Fortunately for Beethoven, despite the uncomfortable season in which the concert was given, the performance was well attended, and he realized a worthy profit for his efforts.

At this point, Beethoven became aware of a pirated copy of his opera in Mainz and, interestingly, the perpetrators appear to have had a connection to the theater management. To Georg Treitschke, Summer 1814, Beethoven wrote:

> Well, the mystery how the opera Fidelio found its way to Mainz has now been solved — it was probably through the Hoftheater-Verlag [a small publishing firm connected with the Court Theaters]. I am waiting to hear from you what measures I should adopt to deal with those wicked people. Am I to inform Count Palffy, or what else could be done?[9]

Fidelio was performed once again in September 1814, this time for the monarchy of Europe which had assembled in Vienna. Beethoven was to have had a concert for his own benefit on November 20, but it was repeatedly postponed. One might have been able to shrug off Beethoven's problems with Palffy as simply a manifestation of his suspicious mind were it not for a letter written by Ignaz von Mosel, the composer and music critic, to Count Palffy. Mosel's letter indicates that Palffy, supposedly on behalf of the theater, had originally asked for one-third of the receipts in return for the use of the hall. After the third postponement he demanded half the receipts. It is important to note that the postponements had not been Beethoven's doing, but had been requested by the Grand Duchess of Russia who had been delayed in her trip to Vienna. Thus it was hardly fair for Palffy to insist that Beethoven bear the financial burden of the postponements, regardless of their effect on the theater. Mosel thought Palffy's demand for the higher percentage was unreasonable, and wrote:

> Although I have no influence in this matter, I believe that there not only has to be considered the support of an excellent artist, whom Vienna should be proud to possess, but also certain higher considerations, since the postponement of the concert was demanded by Her Royal Highness and was also wished by Her majesty the Empress herself. Therefore, it should remain as at the

---

[9]Anderson, p. 464-465.

first agreement since this is burdensome enough for the
concert-giver. Such great sums have never been demanded on similar occasions.[10]

Mosel's surprise at Palffy's unprecedented actions indicates that Palffy's hostility toward Beethoven was not simply a
product of the composer's suspicious mind. Palffy backed down,
but not without complaining that the postponements—which had
not been Beethoven's fault—had tied up the theater and prevented the rehearsal of any other operas. Subsequently, a concert
that Beethoven was promised in December for his benefit once
again was abandoned, and it is difficult to view this as anything
but retaliation by the theater management. From a conversation
book note written in 1824 or 1825 by Karl, Beethoven's nephew,
it appears that a violent argument between the composer and
Palffy had taken place in 1814. Karl wrote "Bernard told me
today, that you, on the occasion of Palffy asking one-third of the
receipts, said, 'You are a paltry Excellenz...'"[11] Ludwig Spohr, who
had become acquainted with Beethoven in 1813, noted that "His
favorite topic of conversation at the time was severe criticism of
Prince Lobkowitz and Count Palffy. He was sometimes overloud
in his abuse of the latter when we were still in the theatre, so that
not only the public but also the Count in his office might have
heard him."

Beethoven's problems with his opera and with the theater management dragged on continuously, even to the point
where they would not honor his smallest request, such as sending
concert tickets to his friend Zmeskall:

> To Zmeskall, Spring 1814: Palffy said yesterday that he
> was sending them to you— So nothing has been done.
> Well, the best thing for you to do would be to send in my
> name for the fourteen tickets—[12]

Two years later, things still had not changed significantly:

> To Frau Anna Milder-Hauptman, Berlin, January 6,
> 1816: ...I shall never contrive to come to an arrange-
> ment with these niggardly Directors in Vienna for a new
> opera.[13]

---

[10]Steichen, pp. 259-260.
[11]Frimmel, pp. 50-51.
[12]Anderson, p. 450.
[13]Anderson, p. 549.

Palffy came into the picture one last time in 1824 when another concert was to be arranged—the performance of the *Ninth Symphony*. Beethoven said to Schindler, "Very well, Schindler! Engage the Theater an der Wien. See Count von Palffy, the Honorable Director! Umlauf and Schuppanzigh shall conduct!" However, Palffy made it a condition of the concert that the permanent conductor lead the orchestra, knowing that Beethoven would insist on Schuppanzigh conducting. Palffy wrote to Beethoven that he could "command the men to play under Schuppanzigh, but he did not want to be answerable for the mischief which would result." Fortunately, Schuppanzigh, whom Seyfried called an energetic and natural leader, did conduct, there was no "mischief" on the part of the orchestra, and the performance was both well-attended and enthusiastically received.

From the numerous incidents cited, it is clear that Count Palffy's antagonism toward Beethoven was definitely not "all in his mind." Further, if Palffy's seeming persecution of Beethoven is purely coincidental to the composer's relationship with Anna Marie, then it is an odd set of coincidences indeed.

❖ 31 ❖
The Countess's Letters

This author has found the issue of Anna Marie's letters to Beethoven and his to her worth exploring. Our interest in this topic is not simply because many of his and all but one of hers are missing. We know that there must be many letters involving other people, written to and by Beethoven, that no longer exist. However, the Beethoven-Erdödy letters present us with a unique situation. In other cases, biographers have proposed that letters *may* have been destroyed because of their delicate nature, such as in the case of those Beethoven wrote to Frankfurt in 1817. But in those situations, the letters' destruction is only speculation. What is different about the Beethoven-Erdödy correspondence is that it is the only case where we have evidence—in the form of a confession—that some it had been *deliberately* destroyed.

It is not surprising that Anna Marie's letters to Beethoven, with the exception of the *Du*-form invitation, are missing. Most letters by a variety of writers which had been sent to Beethoven usually were not preserved by him. He was not by nature a "saver." Some exist only because their writers, such as Josephine Brunswick, kept drafts of the letters that were sent. As to the letters that were written to Beethoven by the Countess Erdödy, their fate is unknown. He may have lost them, destroyed them, or thrown them away. Whether there was any reason behind his action, such as their having been of a delicate nature, we also cannot know, nor even guess. In the case of those letters which

Beethoven wrote to Anna Marie, however, we have a few more clues about what may have happened to them.

Anna Marie faithfully preserved the letters that Beethoven wrote to her, from lengthy epistles to short notes. They were so precious to her that upon her death, she bequeathed them to Frau Brauchle, the widow of her children's long-time tutor, Joseph Xaver Brauchle. As carefully as the Countess kept these letters, there are without a doubt some that are missing. We cited the instance of her gift of the thirty-four mystery bottles in 1814. Beethoven surely had sent her an acknowledgement, yet it was not in her collection. We can assume the existence of such a letter because in 1815, in response to some other gift she had sent him, he wrote, "You are *again* bestowing gifts on me, and so soon too; and that is not right." In other cases, his letters seem to start in mid-conversation, indicating that prior notes had passed between them. In at least one instance, a postscript had been deliberately removed: not accidentally torn off, but cut. This was not done because someone was seeking to obtain Beethoven's valuable signature. It remained with the letter. These situations pique one's curiosity: what was in those missing letters and postscripts which either the recipient or someone else had not wanted any one else to see?

The second interesting issue in regard to the Beethoven-Erdödy letters is Frau Brauchle's fierce desire to keep them from public view. In this instance, there was no deception involved such as in the case of Bettina Brentano's fabricated Beethoven letters. The letters to Anna Marie were genuine, and the surviving letters do not seem in the least incriminating, either personally or politically. Why then the vehement reluctance for them to be made public? In 1852, long after both Beethoven and Countess Erdödy were dead, Otto Jahn had asked Frau Brauchle to let him see Beethoven's letters to Anna Marie. At first, the widow had flatly refused. Eventually, Jahn, who must have been quite a persuasive fellow given the interviews he was granted, coaxed her into letting him see them. We do not know whether she showed him the entire collection, but we suspect not. Jahn indicated that he had run off with them to his hotel before she could protest and copied them, an odd scenario. Did Jahn simply sneak out of her apartment without her knowing, perhaps after sending her off to the kitchen on the pretense of making him some tea? Did he take them by force, snatching the precious papers from the clutches of an elderly widow? We think not. The Widow Brauchle had been adamant about not showing Jahn the letters. If he had been able to abscond with them, she must have allowed him to do so, knowing that the collection no longer contained anything incriminating. In fact, later, when early Beethoven scholar Ludwig Nohl had asked Frau Brauchle about the letters, she insisted that she had burned them. Sonneck had heard otherwise, believing that a Dr. Ebert had found them still in the possession of an "old governess" who absolutely refused to let him publish them. We know from this only that she had not destroyed *all* of them. Perhaps she burned some and not others, others which she allowed Jahn to copy not only because they were not incriminating, but also so that he would be content enough with his "find" to drop the issue. We do not know. But her claim is odd. Why should she even consider such a drastic move as destroying these valuable letters which her own mistress had cherished? Again, what had been in them, and who did Frau Brauchle think she was protecting by her action?

As for the unnamed "old governess of the Erdödy family" who had refused to allow Ebert to publish the letters, we believe that this "old governess" must have been Frau Brauchle. Lest someone suspect that the missing letters simply were in someone else's possession, we must state that it would not have made sense for Anna Marie to have divided her collection between two persons in her household. Also, at the time of her death, Brauchle and his wife were the only ones still in her employ.

As we noted, by the time Jahn conducted his research, Beethoven had been dead 25 years and Anna Marie 15. Why should anyone care so deeply what had been in Beethoven's letters to her? The only person left to be protected from any potential scandal was Anna Marie's surviving daughter, Mimi[1], who, interestingly, was not bequeathed any of her mother's letters from Beethoven. Had this been done to protect her, and if so, from what or whom? And who knows whether any pressure had been placed on Frau Brauchle by the Erdödy family to keep the letters from the public eye in order to avoid further scandal. The Erdödys repeatedly had persecuted her husband, and she would hardly have taken lightly any threat they might have issued.

---

[1]There is no indication what had happened to Anna Marie's younger daughter, Friederike a.k.a. Fritzi.

One is compelled to address George Marek's observation that Beethoven's surviving letters to Anna Marie, although intimately friendly, lacked the passion inherent in the Beloved letter. Interestingly, this argument is not levelled against Antonie Brentano, nor even Marek's choice for the Beloved, Dorothea Ertmann, even though neither of these women, nor any other candidates other than Josephine Brunswick, had ever received such a letter as far as we know. Further, it is absurd to assume that because Beethoven had written passionately in the Beloved letter he would have written all or even most of his other letters to his Beloved with that same degree of passion. His outpouring of love might well have been confined to that single document, or to only a few letters or postscripts which were ultimately destroyed because of their content. If a man writes a woman he loves only one love letter in his entire life, does that mean he does not truly love her? How many wives have husbands who are genuinely in love with them and yet have *never* written them a love letter? More than most biographers would guess, we are sure.

One must also consider Beethoven's general suspicion of the written word. As already noted, he preferred discussing some issues "by word of mouth," rather than commiting them to paper. In some instances, he added postscripts in bad French so that his letter-bearers could not read them. It is unlikely, therefore, that he would have written anything of a delicate or compromising nature to Anna Marie very frequently. If he did do so on occasion, these may have been the very letters that Frau Brauchle destroyed.

Beethoven had not been reluctant to write of his passion openly to Josephine, but Anna Marie presented an entirely different case. While Beethoven's interest in Josephine made the Brunswick family nervous, they liked him, and would not have retaliated against him. On the other hand, Anna Marie was part of, and technically still married into, a politically and financially powerful family whose maliciousness knew few bounds. We know that they repeatedly attacked her through the courts, and that at least one member of the family, Ferdinand Palffy, in his position as theater manager, gave Beethoven professional headaches. The indiscretion of Beethoven living openly with Anna Marie in 1808 had caused him to suffer particularly nasty treatment at Palffy's hands; as Beethoven put it, during that time he had received "the basest, vilest treatment in Vienna." After this experience,

Beethoven would not often have risked giving anyone concrete evidence of their relationship, should his letters fall into hands or be seen by eyes other than hers. Of a generally mistrustful nature, by 1812 Beethoven would have become even more careful about what he sent and preserved.

There are two final points, one of which we have already explored: that the invitation which Anna Marie sent to Beethoven in 1815 had been written in informal and intimate German: the *Du*-form. If her other letters they exchanged had been written similarly, it is no wonder that neither Beethoven nor Frau Brauchle had kept them around, as they would have been far too incriminating, too compromising, too damaging to both of them. The second is that the Beloved letter contained no concrete reference to the lady at all, not even an initial, nothing which might have identified her. He obviously had taken great care to keep her identity a secret should the letter be seen. One might say that he naturally would have done so in a letter sent to Antonie Brentano, or any other married woman. Yet if he had sent it to Antonie while she was in the company of her husband, Franz would have known it was intended for her, and there would have been little doubt as to whom its writer had been. Keeping her identity hidden within the letter would have been pointless. The very act of sending it would have incriminated her. The same can be said for Josephine. In the case of either lady, the consequences of others learning of Beethoven's passion for the woman would have been minimal. Certainly Franz would have been deeply hurt and Beethoven's close relationship with him would have been severed. (Or maybe not. We already know that some biographers suspect him of immense stupidity.) Stackelberg would have been angry, but would have had little recourse, with the exception of taking Josephine's children away from her, something he did anyway. But the repercussions with Anna Marie's identity being revealed as Beethoven's Beloved would have been far worse. Only in her case would family members surrounding her have exacted dire retribution against both Beethoven and Anna Marie.

It is of note that Anna Marie's invitation, accidently left behind at her estate by Beethoven (and perhaps overlooked by Frau Brauchle), and Beethoven's letter to his Beloved, most likely returned to him rather than never sent, owe their preservation to the fact that both of these pieces of correspondence had been returned to their writers, and had not remained with their recipients.

❖ *Epilogue* ❖

In 1828, a year after Beethoven's death, Countess Erdödy attached to an application for the renewal of her passport a

> certificate from her physician, Dr. Feghlem. This practitioner testified that she was suffering from asthmatic pains, accompanied by blood-spitting and a sort of delirium, her nervous system was completely out of order, and nothing but opium or some other drug could soothe her.[1]

After the composer's death, Anna Marie's mental and physical health shattered completely. The grief she suffered over the irrevocable loss of her beloved Beethoven seems to have exacerbated her deterioration. If Dr. Feghlem's statement is any indication, she spent the remaining years of her life in torment.

Did she read in his obituary that "Beethoven never married" and regret never having been his wife? Did she ever wonder whether she could have done something more, something differently, so that they could have been together as he had wanted? What anguish did Anna Marie suffer, knowing that Beethoven had died alone, without the wife and family he had always wanted, with even the person dearest to him far away? One can well imagine that if the drugs she was given allowed her to be cognizant of these things, she suffered greatly.

---

[1]Steichen, p. 495.

There are two interesting coincidences remaining: The first involves Beethoven and Anna Marie. The composer died in March 1827 at age 56; she died in 1837 at age 56 near the tenth anniversary of his death. This author has not done any indepth research into this phenomenon, nor can present any hard, conclusive scientific data that loved ones' deaths are typically intertwined in some way. Yet even a cursory review of obituaries shows that in the cases of spouses who have spent many years together, their death dates show an interesting pattern not easily attributable to coincidence: in the case of exceedingly intimate relationships, the surviving spouse dies on or near the anniversary of their loved one's parting.

* * *

There is one other interesting, though admittedly unscholarly coincidence connected to this immortal romance.

Parade, a magazine supplement which appears in numerous Sunday newspapers nationwide, has a regular column, *Walter Scott's Personality Parade*. In late summer 1994, there appeared an article on Bernard Rose's film, *Immortal Beloved*. It reported that two of the film's principals, Gary Oldman who portrayed Ludwig van Beethoven, and Isabella Rossellini, who was Anna Marie Erdödy, had announced their engagement and intention to marry in romantic Prague a few months later—December 1994. They had met in Czechoslovakia on the set of the film, in costume and in character. Unfortunately, many of their tender scenes together had ended up on the cutting room floor (as evidenced by still photos of scenes never shown), and therefore movie-goers were deprived of seeing much of their interaction. Yet the fact is they had fallen immediately and passionately in love with one another. From where did this almost chemical reaction come? No such spark flamed between Oldman and the actresses who portrayed Guilietta Guicciardi or Rose's choice for the Beloved, Johanna van Beethoven, even though both of the latter were certainly attractive, appealing women.

Shortly thereafter, when the couple was no longer in their 19th century costumes, no longer surrounded by the opulently romantic city of Prague, no longer Ludwig and Anna Marie, but simply Gary and Isabella, they announced that the wedding had been postponed indefinitely. "I still love Gary..." Isabella said in a rather cautious statement about her grand love. "...but..." How eloquent is that simple preposition.

As of this writing, Gary and Isabella are still together and living with one another in New York City. Somehow they have managed to move beyond their characters and love one another simply as who they really are. But in an interview, Gary Oldman expressed wonder that Beethoven possibly could have loved anyone but Anna Marie Erdödy. He is more intuitive than he knows.

What is interesting is that, initially, these two people seem to have been swept away by the magnetic attraction of the two people that they had been portraying. It is almost as if, after nearly two hundred years, somehow, some way, the magic of Ludwig and Anna Marie's love for one another had survived.

❖ *Conclusion* ❖

Was Antonie Brentano Beethoven's Immortal Beloved? We realize that some may still say, *yes, she was.* Perhaps no amount of evidence to the contrary, however abundant or convincing, no amount of logic or common sense, will shake the beliefs and loyalties of some adherents to this theory. Yet given the questions and discrepancies which still cloud this issue, as well as the evidence which clearly refutes it, we must state without doubt: *no, she was not.* At the very least we hope that the reader, after carefully considering the documentation we have presented, will see that there is reasonable doubt remaining in this issue. We believe it was presumptuous to claim that the riddle of the Immortal Beloved had been solved. Highly presumptuous. But, as Beethoven himself wrote, "We all err, only in a different way."

But what about Antonie Brentano then? Was she special to Beethoven? Of course she was. She was a friend, someone Beethoven cared for platonically, and friends were always important to him. As for Antonie, she revered him. She even may have entertained notions about having a romantic relationship with him. But never did he forget that she was a married woman. Never did he go against his "first principle" and betray his honor by attempting to lure her away from her husband. We are not arguing that he *could not* have fallen in love with a married woman, it is simply that he *did not.* And if he had ever fallen in love with a married woman—a *truly* married woman—no one, probably not even the woman herself, would have known.

Whatever stresses may have caused Antonie to briefly consider abandoning her family, it was not Beethoven who ever placed temptation before her. If she ever entertained fantasies about being more than a friend to him, they were not reciprocated. The evidence presented on her behalf, claiming that she was Beethoven's Immortal Beloved, has no validity, no substance, and much was based on erroneous assumptions. Beethoven was never Frau Brentano's lover, having had neither the opportunity nor the inclination to be so. She worshipped him, and in her eyes he was too far above mere mortal to be loved as a man. To her he was without fault, a god-like being, a savior, whose music rescued her from the miseries in her life. Yet as a man and a woman they were as far apart as two continents separated by an ocean. Although her emotional strength seems to have grown as she aged, when Beethoven knew her, she was weak, sad, dependent, frail in spirit. He felt compassion for her as he felt for all beings who suffered, but his sympathies never translated into romantic love.

What of Josephine Brunswick and her claim to be the immortally beloved of Beethoven? Certainly her supporters make many valid points: the similarities of the letters, his obvious love for her. However, while his letters to her were flowery and romantic, they conveyed little of the comfortable and loving intimacy interent in the Beloved letter. We also have shown that there are problems with her claim: she had repeatedly hurt him. There is no proof of a continuing relationship with her, not even gossip. If they ever were together, they kept their relationship an amazingly tight secret. Not impossible, but not likely. Further, she was not inclined to give him more than her friendship. If her answer to his ardor had been *no* in 1805 and *no* again in 1807, there is no reason why she would have said *yes* in 1812. There are too many unknowns in her life to prove anything with any certainty, and until more concrete evidence can be presented in her behalf, we must say, no, she was not the Beloved either.

Was Anna Marie Erdödy the Immortal Beloved? Much evidence and common sense suggests she was: she had the long-term relationship to him inherent in the letter, she was in the right place in 1812 to have received it, she was deeply intimate with Beethoven, emotionally and probably physically as well. While his surviving letters to her are not passionate, there is evidence of other letters which may have been destroyed because of their content. The persecution both Anna Marie and Beethoven suffered at the hands of the Erdödys must have related to their relationship; it is otherwise inexplicable. Over and over, minute points have been made which, by their sheer number, make them difficult to relegate to simple coincidence. Of course, who knows what other information might yet come to light which may lend credence to Josephine's or still another woman's claim? While we will not presume that we have provided *irrefutable* proof, without new documentation, this author cannot and will not concede that anyone but Anna Marie Erdödy had been Beethoven's eternally beloved. She was everything he once told Josephine Brunswick that he sought in a true companion: a woman who shared his deepest values, his interests, his passions. They were soulmates in every sense of the word. Although Anna Marie adored him, he was neither god nor savior to her. With her, there was no need for pretense; it was to her that he could bare his soul. She did not require him to be a "Hercules at the crossroads," or an Atlas who bore the world uncomplaining upon his shoulders, but only to be himself, which was surely enough, a man of flesh, with all the strengths and weaknesses that flesh imparted to him. She loved him despite his hypersensitivities, his jealousies, his suspicions, his bad temper. Although these faults sometimes threatened to drive her away, her devotion to him was such that she always was able to find it in her heart to forgive him. Underneath the flaws she knew there lived his humor, his tenderness, his unshakable goodness of spirit. Thus to one woman he was a god; to another a dear friend. But to his beloved Magyar gypsy, he was a man first and always.

Although physically handicapped, it would be misleading to call Anna Marie fragile, as was Antonie and Josephine. She had a strong, independent spirit that never allowed her to languish in the pain she suffered. She was one woman who had never been intimidated by Beethoven, never been afraid to be angry with him. She met him on his own terms. She was so much like Beethoven that he referred to the two of them as "mortals with immortal minds." She had raised her family alone, built her own fortune, managed her own household and property. Yet she also had a light heart that softened Beethoven's darkness, a brightness that gave him his own "sunny side." For more than twenty years she shared with him his sorrows and joys, his tragedies and triumphs—and her own, as well. It is her reflection which is so often in the "mirror without distortion"—his music.

If composers like Beethoven were made of fire, then Antonie surely was water: calm on the surface, dark and turbulent below, a serene surface shattered by the smallest stone, a woman who would have dampened his spirit with her inability to cope with life and extinguished the blaze of his creativity. Josephine likewise was water, changeable as the tide, beckoning to him with her friendship one minute, pushing away his heart the next. Most likely he would have drowned financially from her extravagances and monetary needs, and by her family's tight hold on her. By contrast, Anna Marie was air: sometimes a gentle, life-sustaining breath, at others an unrelenting windstorm. She was the only one who remained always around him without confining him; always the one who, for two decades, fanned the flames of his genius.

A mystery presumptuously claimed to have been solved is so no longer. We believe that reasonable doubt has been cast upon it by the evidence presented here. It is a sad commentary on our society that so many were so quick to seize upon a solution which placed circumstantial evidence—such as alleged proximity within a time period or geographic location—above the content of a man's heart. It was perhaps fitting that it was Beethoven's innate goodness, the kindness he showed in answering a letter from a child who admired him—his 1812 letter to little Emilie—which had been the first piece of evidence found to exonerate him, and which formed the basis for his defense.

Beethoven had sworn that he would never be more than a friend to another man's wife. As there is little if anything left to suggest that Antonie Brentano possibly could have been his Immortal Beloved, we feel that we may once again trust in his oath. Whatever flaws the man may have had, in this issue he has been vindicated, his honor restored, his sense of honesty, morality, and virtue no longer in question.

Was Beethoven a man of his word? Without a doubt, he was. Beethoven trustingly wrote, "God knows my innermost soul; and however much appearances may perhaps be against me, everything will be cleared up in my favor." As we noted in the beginning pages of this book, it had been his dying wish for the truth to be told.

We can do no more than hope that this wish now has been fulfilled.

❖ Appendix A ❖
Summary of Arguments and Criteria
Regarding the Immortal Beloved

Following is a summary of the evidence which has been presented on the Immortal Beloved, both in this book and in other biographies, against which the leading contenders for the title are tested:

•Item #1: The Immortal Beloved was intimately associated with Beethoven, probably in Vienna, during the period preceding the letter.

A logical presumption. The Beloved letter is exceedingly intimate, not only in terms of content, but also format, i.e. its use of the familiar *Du*-form of address. Beethoven became acquainted with the Brentano family in 1809 and occasionally visited their house. However, they did not live near him, for their home was in the Landstrasse, a remote suburb of Vienna. Also, on those occasions when Beethoven went to give comfort to Antonie during her illness, there is no indication that he often saw or spoke to her. Thayer stated that she had no visitors and Beethoven was not an exception. In fact, he remained in her anteroom while he played.

Beethoven had maintained relations with Josephine Brunswick's siblings, Therese and Franz, and Josephine herself had been in Vienna that year. However, there is no evidence that Beethoven had had any contact with her directly.

As for Anna Marie, Beethoven had been Countess Erdödy's neighbor, and in fact, lived only three doors down from her. In 1811, he enjoyed what he called "Erdödyian feasts." Even more importantly, he had been close to her for many years, and referred to her as his *Beichtvater*, his confidante.

•Item #2: The Immortal Beloved was in Prague between July 1 and 4, 1812.

There is no reason to believe that Beethoven had to have seen his Beloved in Prague during the time preceding the letter.

1. In his letter he did not refer to any events which they had shared during that time period. Beethoven's letter makes no mention of having seen his Beloved in Prague at all, not even that he had been glad to see her. The observations he made, did not require her presence for him to have made them.

2. There is no evidence that Antonie Brentano made any declaration of love to Beethoven while there, nor that she had the opportunity to do so. In fact, she and her husband were in Prague with Beethoven only the evening of July 3.

3. Solomon said, "He has her pencil." There is no reason to believe this had been Antonie's pencil, nor that Beethoven had acquired it in Prague.

•Item #3: The Immortal Beloved was in Karlsbad during the week of July 6, 1812.

Evidence places doubt on Karlsbad as the "K" mentioned in Beethoven's letter. Briefly, the evidence which negates this long-assumed destination is as follows:

1. Beethoven's letters to Emilie M, the Archduke Rudolph, and Joseph von Varena show that Beethoven's initial intention was not to travel to Karlsbad at all. At the time he wrote the Beloved letter, his plan had been to stay in Teplitz until mid-August and then return to Vienna. It would have made no sense for Beethoven to have told his Beloved that he would see her "soon" if she was in Karlsbad, and he *knew* she was there, but he was not planning to go there himself. The fact is, he *did* see his Beloved "soon," but in Hernals, not in Karlsbad.

2. Twice Beethoven requested that his publishers send scores of music to him at Teplitz. The latest of these requests had been dated July 24, just days before Beethoven was instructed by Dr. Staudenheim to leave Teplitz and go on to Karlsbad. He would not have asked for music to be sent to him in one place (Teplitz) had he planned to be somewhere else (Karlsbad) when it arrived. He would have *asked that the music be sent to him in Karlsbad.*

3. It had been assumed that Beethoven misread the mail schedule when he began writing his letter, but Beethoven never read the postal schedule himself. He was *told*, first given the wrong information, and then given the correct information later. From the place where he was when he received the correct schedule (in bed, early in the morning) the information must have been brought to him by someone who worked at the inn. A Teplitz worker could not have made a mistake unless the postal schedule was extremely erratic during those turbulent years of the Napoleonic invasion of Europe. The 1815 mail schedule Unger found, which listed Karlsbad on a morning run, was not necessarily or likely in effect in 1812. In 1815, the mail also went to Vienna on Mondays and Thursdays, just like Karlsbad, except in the afternoon. There is reason to believe that this minor change—the addition of an afternoon mail run—occurred in 1815, after the war, and other conditions improved.

4. There is a considerable time-distance problem with Karlsbad as the destination. Karlsbad was too close to Teplitz (50 miles), to warrant a two-and-half-day delivery time. Vienna (or rather, its suburb, Klosterneuberg) *was* at such a distance, as shown by Beethoven's trip in early July from Vienna to Prague to Teplitz. Prague-Teplitz, also 50 miles, was only about a 10-hour trip. Even Prague-Karlsbad, a distance 20 miles longer than Teplitz-Karlsbad, took less time to travel. Mathematically, Karlsbad as the destination is an illogical deduction.

Thus, we have the following situation:

Was the letter's destination Karlbad?

Various factors, noted above, say *no*.

Had Beethoven planned to meet his Beloved there?

No, because *he* was not planning to be there.

Was the Immortal Beloved in Karlsbad during the week of July 6, 1812?

No, she was not.

Was Antonie Brentano in Karlsbad at that time?

Yes, she was.

Was Antonie Brentano the Immortal Beloved?

No, she could not be, because the Immortal Beloved was not *in* Karlsbad. She was in or around Vienna. We know that Josephine was there, but again, there is no evidence of contact between her and Beethoven. On the other hand, there is evidence of a meeting with another woman, a woman who was in Hernals where Beethoven must have *planned* to go, because that is where he *did* go. After leaving Teplitz in September, Beethoven's letter to his friend, Gleichenstein, shows that he then went on to Hernals where Anna Marie Erdödy was spending the summer.

• **Item #4: Beethoven was with the Brentanos in Karlsbad and Franzensbrunn by prearrangement.**

This is untrue. Letters to the Archduke Rudolph, Joseph von Varena, and his publishers show that it had been Beethoven's new physician, Dr. Staudenheim, who had sent him on to the two resorts. He had not prearranged any trip with the Brentanos. It had been his intention to go to Teplitz, recuperate, and then return to Vienna, just has he had the previous year, 1811.

• **Item #5: The letter to the Immortal Beloved used *Du*, a highly intimate and personal form of address which Beethoven did not use with any other woman.**

Did he use this form with Antonie Brentano? Not in his letters, which were little more than business correspondence. Beethoven had not known her long enough to suggest using that form, even verbally. He did not use *Du* in letters he wrote to Josephine Brunswick whom he had known and loved several years, although he could have done so verbally. The only evidence of his use of *Du* with a woman is in the form of an invitation written by Anna Marie Erdödy. It shows that she used this form with him, and as it was always used mutually, he must have used it with her.

• **Item #6: The Immortal Beloved was probably a woman whom Beethoven had met or become closely acquainted with approximately five years prior to 1816—that is, in 1811.**

The Giannatasio diary from where this date came is questionable in its validity on this issue, and thus in its ability to provide "crucial evidence" for the Beloved's identity. Beethoven did not know the Giannatasios very well; he would not have discussed a highly personal issue such as his love life with them. His statement that he had "met someone five years ago" was simply a round number used to discourage the author, Fanny, from her amorous intentions toward him, and her father from having notions of the composer as a son-in-law. Even taking this item at face value, it does not apply to any woman who could be the Immortal Beloved. Beethoven met Antonie Brentano in 1809, not 1811. He met both Anna Marie Erdödy and Josephine Brunswick many years before that. Of the few women he had met in 1811, not one even remotely qualifies as the Immortal Beloved. However, he did reconcile with Anna Marie in 1811 after their quarrel and separation in 1809.

- **Item #7: The first initial of the Beloved's name may have been an *A*.**
There is no clea indication to what or who the "A" referred. There is no feminine indicative article to suggest that Beethoven had been writing about a woman. And as all nouns, not just proper names, are capitalized in German, the *A* could have easily referred to "work/*Arbeit*" as anything or anyone else.

- **Item #8: The first initial of the Beloved's name may have been *T*.**
Again, this is from the *Tagebuch*. Possibly this was a copyist's error, who had misread an *F* as a *T*. The timing and weary tone of the entry suggests that the person in question may have been Fanny Giannatasiowho was infatuated with Beethoven. Even if Beethoven had been referring to Antonie "Toni" Brentano in this entry, it was not in the context of being his Beloved. The note speaks only of "her" attachment, not his or theirs. Antonie may have made overtures to Beethoven following his first letter to them (in 1815) after three years of silence. It would have made no sense for Beethoven to warn himself about avoiding temptation in 1816 by being too close to his Beloved, when Antonie had been gone from Vienna since 1812. He *would* have warned himself to be cautious of accepting the Giannatasio's invitation to live in their garden house, close to Fanny.

- **Item #9: The dedication of the *Diabelli Variations* was to Antonie Brentano.**
This had been Schindler's doing. The composer had intended the dedication for Frau Ries, Ferdinand's wife. One edition—to be published in Germany only —was to have a dedication to Antonie (Beethoven referred to her as "Brentano") because he felt obligated to her. This feeling came from some business assistance the Brentanos gave Beethoven, including a geneous loan of money. By contrast, Countess Erdödy had the *Opus 70 Piano Sonatas,* and a three-part canon (a New Year's gift), written especially for her and she had the *Opus 102 Cello Sonata* dedicated to her.

- **Item #10: The song "To the Beloved" had been written for Antonie Brentano.**
This is untrue.
1. Antonie had to *request* a copy of the song from Beethoven, he did not present it to her unasked, nor did he dedicate it to her.
2. Antonie had only received an *arrangement* of the song for her guitar, and she did not receive this until *four months* after the song had been written.
3. This was not the only song Beethoven had ever arranged for guitar, but had done one a short time prior for Anna Malfatti. He was in the habit of arranging pieces of music to suit other friends. Further, he placed little value on his autograph scores.
In contrast, other "Beloved" songs centered around Anna Marie:
1. "The Joy of Friendship" was written after his sojourn at her estate, Jedlersee.
2. "As the Beloved Herself Wished to Separate" was published in 1809, following their quarrel and separation. The writing of the sonata titled "Farewell, Absence, and Return" coincided with her departure (1809) and return (1811).

3. "To the Beloved" was written in 1811, when she had resumed her relationship with him and they were enjoying a closeness they had not had since 1809.

4. Beethoven began writing "To the Distant Beloved" immediately after her departure from Vienna in 1815. He sent it to her directly after its publication in 1816 without her solicitation, and there is reason to believe that she had sent him a ring as a reciprocal token of her love.

• **Item #11: The note written in Baden indicates that the initial of the Immortal Beloved may have been *M*.**

The Beethovenhaus's research indicates that the year this note probably had been written in 1807 when Beethoven had no relationship at all with Antonie Brentano. The *M* more appropriately referred to Marie Bigot, who served as a catalyst for the renewing of his desires for marriage and a family, and caused him to attempt reestablishing his relationship with Josephine.

• **Item #12: Beethoven may have owned a portrait of Antonie Brentano.**

This is irrelevant since he attached little significance to giving and receiving portraits, other than as tokens of friendship. He gave numerous ones of himself to friends. The portrait in question does not follow the 1812 style, and more appropriately belongs to 1800. This author still maintains the portrait to be that of Anna Marie Erdödy, but evidence is inconclusive.

• **Item #13: Beethoven had had a transient but ardent passion for a married woman. Further, this passion was directed toward Antonie Brentano who was "precisely described" by Thayer.**

This statement made by Thayer was in reference to Marie Koschak-Pachler and her husband, pertained to the years 1816-1817, and therefore had no connection to Antonie Brentano. Pachler's son denied that his mother ever had any involvement whatsoever with Beethoven.

Further, Beethoven did not indulge in "transient passions." Only Guilietta Guicciardi could qualify as a brief but hardly ardent interest, and Beethoven never entertained any notion of marrying her. The alleged "marriage project" involving Therese Malfatti is a fabrication: he did not pursue her and, in fact, had been forced to extricate himself from *her* notion of marrying *him*. His romantic involvements had included four years with Magdalena Willmann, and eight years (on and off) with Josephine Brunswick. By contrast, his relationship with his Beloved, Anna Marie Erdödy, spanned more than 20 years.

✥ Appendix B ✥
A Musical Chronology

This chronology is not meant as an exhaustive list of Beethoven's works. Rather, it shows that his most creative periods centered around having a "beloved," most notably Anna Marie Erdödy, in his life, and that she seems to have been the influence for his greatest works, the spark that ignited his creative genius.

1801, Finds solace with Anna Marie at Jedlersee whom he may have known as long as three or four years: *String Quintet in C major*, Op. 29; *Piano Sonatas* Op. 22, 26, 27; *Third Piano Concerto in C minor*.

1802, Beethoven at Heilingenstadt, near Jedlersee with Anna Marie: *Romance in G* Op. 40, and *in F* Op. 50; *Second Symphony in D*, *Three Sonatas for Violin and Piano* Op. 30; *Three Piano Sonatas*, Op. 31; song *"Joy of Friendship;"* sketches *Eroica Symphony*.

1803, Beethoven summers in Oberdöbling , near Jedlersee: *Violin Sonata* Op. 47; *Third Symphony* (Eroica); begins work on *Fidelio* and sketches the *Triple Concerto*.

1804, Summer in Baden and Döbling, near Jedlersee; autumn, becomes Anna Marie's neighbor in Pasqualati House: continues work on *Triple Concerto* Op.56, finishes *Piano Sonatas*, 53, 54, 57 (Appassionata); *Andante Favori in F*.

1805, Anna Marie is away from Vienna; Beethoven goes *south* of Vienna to Hetzendorf, near the widowed Josephine Brunswick with whom he begins persuing a romantic interest: works on *Fidelio*, and sketches of *Fifth Symphony*, finishes *Triple Concerto*.

1806, Anna Marie returns to Vienna; Beethoven moves to Pasqualati House in fall: *Thirty-two Variations in C minor*; *Fourth Piano Concerto* Op.58; *Violin Concerto*, three *Rasoumovsky String Quartets* Op. 59, *Fourth Symphony*.

1807, Beethoven once again briefly pursues, but then sadly ends his relationship with Josephine; his relationship with Anna Marie intensifies: Finishes *Mass in C*, Op. 86 for Prince Esterhazy at Anna Marie's estate in Jedlersee. Finishes *Fifth Symphony*; *Coriolan Overture*.

1808, Summer at Heilingenstadt: *Sixth (Pastoral) Symphony*; autumn, moves in with Anna Marie, *Piano Sonatas* Op. 70 written for her; *Choral Fantasy*, Op. 80 (Fantasia for Piano, Orchestra & Chorus), "Gloria" and "Sanctus" from Mass in C; *Fourth Piano Concerto*; four settings of Goethe's "Nur we die Sehnsucht kennt;" *Violoncello Sonata in A*, Op. 69.Began work on *Emperor Concerto*. Gave Grand Concert on December 22. Probably the most productive year of his life.

1809, Beginning of year, living with Anna Marie: *Fantasia*, Op. 77; Quarrels with and separates from Anna Marie, writes the "Adieux" (Lebewohl) portion of the *Piano Sonata in E flat*. Meets the Brentanos. Finshes *Emperor Concerto*, *Three Piano Sonatas in F sharp*, Op. 78, *in G*, Op. 79, *in E flat* Op. 81a. Productive period ends as he "awaits... forgiveness." Writes "As the Beloved Herself Wished to Separate."

1810, Summer south of Vienna (Baden and Schonbrunn) writes only few songs, including "Dry Not, Tears of Eternal Love" and simple piano piece "Für Elise" for Therese Malfatti..

1811, Countess Erdödy offers forgiveness,returns to Vienna and relationship with Beethoven resumes. Beethoven enjoys "Erdodyian feasts:" *Trio in B flat* Op 97 "Archduke" written in 3 weeks; completes "Absence and Return" portions of the *Piano Sonata in E flat*; writes*The Ruins of Athens* and *King Stephen* overtures; works on *Seventh and Eighth symphonies*.

1812, Anna Marie in Vienna: finishes the exuberant *Seventh Symphony* and *Violon Sonata in G,* Op. 96; Beethoven in the Bohemian spas, writes letter to his "Immortal Beloved,"by September he is with Anna Marie in Hernals: finishes joyful *Eighth Symphony* in Linz.

1813, Beethoven ill, poor, the countess is gone (probability of another quarrel) Only "Battle" Symphony, Op. 91 produced.

1814, Anna Marie sends gift indicating a willingness to resume their relationship: *Polonaise in C*, Op.89, *Piano Sonata in E minor* Op. 90; "Fidelio" Overture in E, "Namesfeier" Overture in C, Cantata "The Glorious Moment"; *Elegiac Song*, Op. 118.

1815, Second reconciliation with Anna Marie, and summer at Jedlersee. *Cello Sonatas* Op.102 (dedicated to her in 1819). Late in year, Anna Marie leaves Vienna and Beethoven begins work on song cycle "To the Distant Beloved" (In doing so, abandons work on 50 new sketches in his books devoted to a Piano Concerto in D, a second opera "Bacchus", a tenth symphony in B minor, and several fugues—one of which would later form the Scherzo of the *Ninth Symphony.*)

1816, Countess in Padua; finishes "For the Distant Beloved," Op. 98 and sends it to Anna Marie, writes *Piano Sonata in A*, Op. 101.

1817, Beethoven eager to visit Anna Marie in Padua, prevented by illness, finances, Mälzel lawsuit. Writes "Resignation" (Gone Out My Light), and *Quintet in C minor*, Op. 104. Emotional plummet.

1818, Anna Marie out of the country; Beethoven involved in legal problems with Karl's guardianship. Suffers severe depression. Writes *Sonata in B flat*, Op. 106 "Hammerklavier."

1819, Countess returns to Vienna late in year. Beethoven writes "Gluck, Gluck zum Neuen Jahr" for her. Op. 102 reissued for publication and formally dedicated to her.

1820, Anna Marie and Bethoven become neighbors again in the Landstrasse. He writes *Mass in D*, finishes *Piano Sonata* Op. 109, sketches *Piano Sonatas* 110, 111 and *Quartet* Op. 127.

1821, Both still in the Landstrasse, but Anna Marie periodically absent because of family problems. Beethoven finishes *Piano Sonata in A flat*, op. 110. Beethoven ill with jaundice. Death of Josephine Brunswick.

1822, Anna Marie back in Croatia. Overture "Consecration of the House," op. 124. *Piano Sonata* Op. 111, bagatelles. Arrested as vagrant.

1823, Anna Marie returns to Vienna in preparation for journey to Munich. Beethoven finishes the *Ninth Symphony, Missa Solemnis*, and *Diabelli Variations*.

1824, Anna Marie leaves Vienna for the last time. Beethoven writes only *String Quartet in E flat*, Op. 127.

1825, Beethoven "inexplicably" despondent and withdrawn. When asked to improvise, Beethoven chooses the theme from "The Distant Beloved." Finishes *String Quartets in A minor* Op. 132 and in B flat, Op. 130, the quartet that moved him more than any other and brought him to tears.

1826, Karl attempts suicide. Beethoven seriously ill. *String Quartets in C sharp minor*, op. 131 and in F, op. 135.

1827, Beethoven dies in Vienna, March 26, at the age of 56.

1837, Anna Marie dies in Munich, at the age of 56.

❖ Bibliography ❖

Anderson, Emily, editor and translator, *The Letters of Beethoven*, 3 volumes, New York: St. Martin's Press, 1961

Beahrs, Virginia, "My Angel, My All, My Self: A Literal Translation of Beethoven's Letter to the Immortal Beloved," *Journal of the American Beethoven Society*, San Jose State University, Vol. 5, No. 2, Summer 1990.

_____"The Immortal Beloved Revisited," *Journal of the American Beethoven Society,* San Jose State University, Vol. 1, No. 2, Summer 1986.

Breuning, Gerhard von, *Memories of Beethoven: From the House of the Black-Robed Spaniards*, translated by Maynard Solomon and Henry Mims, Cambridge University Press, 1992.

Comini, Alessandra, *The Changing Image of Beethoven: a Study in Mythmaking*, New York: Rizzoli International Publications, Inc., 1987.

Gates-Coon, Rebecca, *The Landed Estates of the Esterhazy Princes*, Baltimore: Johns Hopkins University Press, 1995.

Hamburger, Michael, editor, *Beethoven: Letters, Journals, and Conversations*, New York: Thames and Hudson, 1984.

Herriot, Edouard, *The Life and Times of Beethoven*, translated by Adelheid Mitchell and William Mitchell, New York: MacMillan, 1935.

Hevesy, Andre de, *Beethoven the Man*, translated by Frank S. Flint, New York: Brentanos, 1927.

Kinderman, William, *Beethoven*, Berkeley/Los Angeles: University of California Press: 1995.

Kohler, Karl-Heinz and Grita Herre, *Ludwig van Beethoven's Kon-versationhefte*, Vols. 1-6, Leipzig: VEB Deutscher Verlag fur Musik, 1972.

Landon, H.C. Robbins, *Beethoven: A Documentary Study*, New York: Collier Books, 1970.

_____, *Beethoven: A Documentary Study*, London: Thames and Hudson, 1992.

Lund, Susan, "A Fleshly Father," *Journal of the American Beethoven Society*, San Jose State University, 1988.

Marek, George, *Beethoven: Biography of a Genius*, New York: Funk & Wagnalls, 1969.

Nettl, Paul, *Beethoven Encyclopedia*, New York: Citadel Press, 1956, 1994.

Phillips, Roderick, *Putting Assunder: a History of Divorce in Western Society*, New York: Cambridge University Press, 1988.

Reichardt, Johann Friedrich, *Vertraute Briefe geschrieben auf einer Reise nach Wien und den Oesterreichisehen Staaten zu des Jahres 1808 und zu Anfang 1809*, Amsterdam: 1810.

Rolland, Romain, *Beethoven the Creator*, translated by Ernest Newman, New York: 1929.

Scherman, Thomas and Louis Biancolli, *Beethoven Companion,* Garden City, New York: Doubleday, 1972.

Schindler, Anton Felix, *Beethoven As I Knew Him*, translated by Constance S. Jolly, New York: 1970.

Schone, Alfred, *Briefe von Beethoven an Marie Gräfin Erdödy geb. Gräfin Niszky und Mag. Brauchle*, Leipzig: Breitkopf & Härtel, 1867.

Solomon, Maynard, *Beethoven*, Harvard University Press, Cambridge: 1977.

_____ *Beethoven Essays*, Cambridge: Harvard University Press, 1988

Sonneck, O.G., *Beethoven: Impressions by His Contemporaries*, New York: 1926 and 1967.

Specht, Richard, *Beethoven As He Lived*, translated by Alfred Kalisch, New York, Smith & Haas, 1933.

Steichen, Dana, *Beethoven's Beloved*, Garden City, New York: Doubleday & Company, Inc., 1959.

Sullivan, John W. N., *Beethoven: His Spiritual Development*, New York: Vintage Books: 1960.

Tellenbach, Marie-Elisabeth, "Beethoven and the Countess Josephine Brunswick, 1799-1821," *Journal of the American Beethoven Society*, San Jose State University, Volume 2, Number 3, Winter 1987.

Thayer-Forbes, *Thayer's Life of Beethoven* by Alexander W. Thayer, editor Elliot Forbes, Princeton: 1970.

Wegeler, Dr. Franz and Ries, Ferdinand, *Beethoven Remembered*, Virginia: Great Ocean Press Publishers, 1967.

❖ Index ❖